P9-CQM-337

BEYOND BROADWAY JOE

BEYOND BROADWAY JOE

JOE

THE SUPER BOWL *TEAM* THAT CHANGED FOOTBALL

BOB LEDERER

DEY ST.
An Imprint of WILLIAM MORROW

BEYOND BROADWAY JOE. Copyright © 2018 by Bob Lederer. All rights reserved. Printed in the United States of America. No part of this book may be used or reproduced in any manner whatsoever without written permission except in the case of brief quotations embodied in critical articles and reviews. For information, address HarperCollins Publishers, 195 Broadway, New York, NY 10007.

HarperCollins books may be purchased for educational, business, or sales promotional use. For information, please email the Special Markets Department at SPsales@harpercollins.com.

FIRST EDITION

Designed by Suet Chong

Library of Congress Cataloging-in-Publication Data has been applied for.

ISBN 978-0-06-279804-6

18 19 20 21 22   RS/LSC   10 9 8 7 6 5 4 3 2 1

*Dedicated to all 56 players, coaches,
and owners of the 1968–69 Super Bowl
New York Jets*

*"We didn't have team chemistry because we
were winning . . . We won because of the
intangibles that come from team chemistry."*
Jim Richards
Special Teams
Super Bowl Jets

To my wife, Linda,
who supported and encouraged me to
realize my dream of writing this book about
my favorite boyhood team,

My children,
who gave me the inspiration for this book,

My associate and friend, Chris Clow,
who helped me find my heroes,

Jay Pomerantz,
whose graciousness helped me tell
a more complete story,

and

Jo Anne Nathan,
who caught every spelling and
grammatical mistake

CONTENTS

PART THREE

FOREWORD BY MATT SNELL

(FOR THE OFFENSIVE SQUAD)

To be honest with you, even though most of the players from the Super Bowl team were with the Jets in 1967, I don't think we believed we deserved to be champions that year.

We put it all together as a team in 1968. We understood what it took to win, and we had to be lucky with injuries. Also key was developing personal connections, not only on the field but off the field as well. Tuesday was always an offensive day at practice, Wednesday was defensive day, and up until 1968 after practice everyone would go their own way. But in 1968, we got to know each other and started to come together as a family. Guys started to care about other guys— what they thought, how they practiced. We didn't look at criticism from other guys as an attack. I think we each realized that if we didn't get it done on the field, it didn't matter what the coaches told us in meeting rooms.

As I recall, the driving forces behind this unity on the offensive side were Winston Hill, Pete Lammons, Dave Herman, Curley Johnson, and myself. Twenty-five to thirty of us—the defensive guys, too—headed to a local meeting place away from Shea Stadium, like a pizza joint, particularly one called the Captain's Cabin. The owners set us up with all the pizzas we needed for a couple of hours. It was there that we put the pieces together.

Of course, the big offensive guy was Joe Namath. Sonny Werblin made him a superstar before his stats backed it up. Coach Weeb Ewbank had tried to get across to Joe to stop the partying and drinking while the rest of us were trying to build something. Then he was elected offensive captain before the 1968 season, and after two five-interception games Walt Michaels told him to let the defense and our running game win games for us. Joe agreed that he had to settle down and he focused himself on what was necessary for us to win. At that point, he became the polished quarterback we all knew he could become.

Babe Parilli was probably the best possible backup for Namath. He had experience and maturity. Even at thirty-eight, he could still throw the ball, and he had a strong mental approach.

Emerson Boozer (we called him "Booz" or "Boozer") was a great running talent when he came out of college, and I was glad to make the case for him to join us. Bill Mathis was one of the nicest guys in the world and a teammate who worked great alongside me or Boozer. Billy Joe was a heck of a running back who ran with a high-knee-action running style, like Boozer. Billy and I became friends and worked together, and he took some of the fullback load off me. I never got to know Lee White, our other backup fullback, very well. He was a big, quiet guy, our first draft pick in 1968, and it's too bad he got hurt in our first game. Smo (Mark Smolinski) and Curley Johnson got to the Jets a few years before me and were key leaders on special teams.

Pete Lammons was a fun guy who always had a smile—the tight end we needed to block, catch the ball, and run. George Sauer Jr. didn't say much, but he brought an unbelievable work ethic; he worked on his hands and his routes. Don Maynard, immensely talented and our only deep threat, followed George's lead and became a polished receiver and great route runner. Bake Turner didn't have a whole lot of talent or speed, but he made use of what he had and was a great third receiving option.

Clive Rush was a great teacher, had the right kind of demeanor and Joe's ear. He was a helluva offensive coordinator and play caller. We didn't have a radio in our helmets, so Namath had to learn the game plan each week and make the play calls. Sometimes Clive would shuttle in plays. I think he was a little more pass oriented—who wouldn't have been with a talent like Joe Namath? But emphasizing the passing game was true of the whole American Football League.

Joe Spencer, our offensive line coach, was a huge but docile guy. The linemen liked him a lot. He was responsible for one of the biggest acquisitions, Bob Talamini, who put our offense over the top. He was "my man": tough, ornery, and, boy, he had a winning attitude.

Our offensive line was special. Dave Herman didn't have the most ability in the world, but he worked his butt off and would fight you to the death. Randy Rasmussen, a soft-spoken guy, had calves as big as my thighs; he was one of the strongest guys ever from the waist down. Winston Hill, our best offensive lineman, was a big, fun-loving guy, a teddy bear, who dominated the line of scrimmage. He called me "Nate," though I never figured out why. John Schmitt was one of the few players from a small school (Hofstra) who made it in the pros. Mild-mannered Jeff Richardson was ready to step in anywhere if any of our linemen got hurt.

Jim Turner, if you got to know him, had a sense of humor. When it came to kicking, no moment was too big for Jim. We knew in the crunch that he would put it through the uprights.

Shea Stadium had its critics because of the wind and field conditions, including having to run from grass to dirt and back, but it was our home and those much-talked-about problems gave us a psychological home-field advantage.

What a season it was!

Matt Snell
Jersey City, NJ
February 2018

FOREWORD BY GERRY PHILBIN

(FOR THE DEFENSIVE SQUAD)

I n the 1967–68 season, we had gotten so close to the playoffs. Missed it by a half game! It was incredibly disappointing when we heard in San Diego before our final game against the Chargers that Houston had clinched the Eastern Division with their win the night before.

So, all summer long we looked at the coming season as the year we would get into the playoffs. Entering the season, I felt we had the nucleus of a great team. We had a great offense and a great defense. The Super Bowl? I don't think we thought about it until toward the end of the season. Truthfully, for us, beating the Oakland Raiders for the AFL Championship was almost as momentous as beating the Baltimore Colts in the Super Bowl.

The two best teams in the AFL had been Kansas City and Oakland, and they presented important but different obstacles that year. Our first game of the regular season, beating the Chiefs in Kansas City, was our way of showing that we belonged in the upper echelon of the AFL. It was a big win that catapulted us with some confidence going forward, and that made a difference when we had some dramatic losses that year that *weren't* supposed to happen.

The Raiders were our big rival, a good team, but they also had a reputation as a dirty team. On offense, they held more than any other team in the league, and their players chop-blocked, crack-back-blocked, and leg-whipped. These moves were legal, but ended the careers of many players. We ended up facing the Raiders twice that year, first in the so-called *Heidi* Game, so named because NBC preempted our game in Oakland before it was over because the game ran long. At 7 P.M. eastern time, NBC switched to a scheduled made-for-TV movie, *Heidi*. When our regular season schedule ended, Kansas City and Oakland played each other for the right to play us for the league title.

Heading into the playoffs, Joe Namath and I appeared on a Jets highlight show hosted by Kyle Rote on which we were awarded Jets offensive and defensive Player of the Year Awards by the Metropolitan Football Writers Association. On the show, we both agreed that we wanted to play Oakland again; it would be in New York this time. We hated the Raiders and distrusted their part owner, Al Davis. Weeb instilled that into us year after year, but in 1968 we had such a good team that we couldn't blame Davis anymore if we lost to them. We all felt as if we had beaten ourselves in the *Heidi* Game in November. That loss just amped up how much we hated them and the great satisfaction we'd get from beating them.

When we beat them in a hard-fought, seesaw game, 27–23, at Shea Stadium, it was sweet revenge. Any good coach tells his team never to look past the team you have to beat to get to the championship game. So many teams fall into a trap like that. If we hadn't beaten Oakland in the AFL Championship Game, we wouldn't have gotten to the Super Bowl. We put so much pressure on ourselves to beat the Raiders, and there was unbelievable relief when we finally did.

When I think back at playing the Baltimore Colts in the Super Bowl, it seems so ironic that a good number of our important players—our great left tackle Winston Hill; our free safety Bill Baird, our special teams captain, Mark Smolinski; our offensive right tackle in the early nineteen sixties, Sherman Plunkett; and our star wide receiver and special teamer, Bake Turner; and some others—had joined Weeb from the Colts after he came to us in 1963. And it was smart of Weeb to bring in Artie Donovan, the great former Colts defensive tackle, to teach me and the other linemen the ins and outs of playing like an aggressive, disciplined professional during training camp my first two years with the Jets.

Everyone remembers we were giant underdogs against the Colts. After playing and standing up against the great offenses of Kansas City, Oakland, and San Diego that year, there was no way we were going to get beat by 18 points. At worst, it would be a close game. I remember the Colts were so mad at Joe for his guarantee that we'd win. They tried to bury us from the start, but they didn't know how confident we were.

Watching the Colts on film, it would have been easy to become overconfident. Our defense saw their offense had no imagination whatsoever; they'd run the ball twice and pass on third down. They ran their traps and sweeps, which were easy to defend. Our defensive coaches, Walt Michaels and Buddy Ryan, were licking their chops. AFL offenses were so much more diverse than the NFL; teams in the AFL did things that the NFL caught up to ten years later.

There were other important factors that motivated us. We loved playing the game, but the $15,000 winner's check doubled the salaries of many of our players. If the Colts had beaten us the way Green Bay had won the first two Super Bowls, some AFL teams that weren't doing well could have folded instead of becoming part of the NFL. After our win, AFL owners insisted that the American Football League teams remain intact as a group—and they did, but with a new name, the American Football Conference, and three added NFL teams (Baltimore, Cleveland, and Pittsburgh). I thought that Bob Talamini had the best comment after the game: "Now the AFL and NFL can be mentioned in the same sentence."

I have to salute a number of our players. Talamini, our offensive left guard, and Larry Grantham, our right side linebacker, both deserve to be in the Pro Football Hall of Fame. Bob was voted an all-AFL guard by its players six times. Larry was an AFL All-Pro five times. I think you can make the case that Babe Parilli should also be in Canton.

It's important to realize that no one player was responsible for us winning the Super Bowl. Our defensive unit led the league in defense that year, but we didn't get the same amount of credit as the offense, which was also the AFL's best. My teammates on the defensive line did a great job that year, although we were probably the smallest defensive line in pro football. John Elliott put on a terrific pass rush, never gave up on a play, and chased ball carriers down the field using his great speed. Rocky Rochester had a nasty streak and was very smart. Verlon Biggs was a great athlete, the best at his position when he wanted to be. Carl McAdams played with a limp from smashing up his ankle at the Chicago Charities' College All-Star Game, but even with that handicap he was about as good as any tackle in the league. Steve Thompson also filled in very well for us that year.

In our defensive backfield, Johnny Sample was very misunderstood. He intimidated players and got into their heads. Randy Beverly was a great athlete and didn't get enough credit for his two interceptions in the Super Bowl. Cornell Gordon could play any position. Bill Baird was small for a free safety, but he was so smart and he'd wrap people up and make sure they were stopped, and strong safety Jim Hudson was, big, smart, and a great athlete. And our linebackers, Larry Grantham, Al Atkinson, and Ralph Baker, were as good as any linebacker group in the AFL. Paul Crane was a great backup to Larry, and a valuable long snapper on punts and special teams. Ralph and Rocky and I had a bond; we played for a long time on the left side of the Jets' defense.

Our game against the Giants in the 1969 preseason after Super Bowl III was the most rewarding I ever played. Were we looked down upon? One hundred percent by the press, which treated us like we were second-rate. At banquets, Jets players would get fifty dollars, and Giants players a hundred and fifty. If we had lost to the Giants, it could have flushed everything down the toilet that we had accomplished in the Super Bowl. Beating the Giants—and the way we did it, beating them badly, put the nail in the coffin as far as the AFL not being as good as the NFL.

Gerry Philbin
Palm Beach Gardens, FL
February 2018

1968 WORLD CHAMPION NEW YORK JETS ROSTER

NO.	PLAYER	AGE	POS	HT	WT	COLLEGE	BIRTHDATE
62	Al Atkinson	25	MLB	6'2"	230	Villanova	7/28/1943
46	Bill Baird	29	WS	5'10"	180	SF State	3/01/1939
51	Ralph Baker	26	LLB	6'3"	228	Penn State	8/25/1942
42	Randy Beverly	24	RCB	5'11"	190	Colorado St	4/03/1944
86	Verlon Biggs	25	RDE	6'4"	275	Jackson St	3/16/1943
32	Emerson Boozer	25	HB	5'11"	195	MD - E. Shore	7/04/1943
45	Earl Christy	25	KR	5'11"	195	MD - E. Shore	3/19/1943
56	Paul Crane	24	LS	6'3"	212	Alabama	1/29/1944
47	Mike D'Amato	25	ST	6'2"	205	Hofstra	3/03/1943
43	John Dockery	24	ST	6'0"	185	Harvard	9/06/1944
80	John Elliott	24	RDT	6'4"	244	Texas	10/26/1944
48	Cornell Gordon	27	DB	6'0"	187	NC A&T	1/06/1941
60	Larry Grantham	30	RLB	6'0"	210	Mississippi	9/16/1938
73	Ray Hayes	22	ST	6'5"	248	Toledo	9/05/1946
70	Karl Henke	23	ST	6'4"	245	Tulsa	3/08/1945
67	Dave Herman	27	G/T	6'1"	255	Michigan St	9/03/1941
75	Winston Hill	27	LT	6'4"	270	TX Southern	10/23/1941
22	Jim Hudson	25	SS	6'2"	210	Texas	3/31/1943
35	Billy Joe	28	ST	6'2"	235	Villanova	10/14/1940
33	Curley Johnson	33	P	6'0"	215	Houston	7/02/1935
87	Pete Lammons	25	TE	6'3"	230	Texas	10/20/1943
31	Bill Mathis	30	RB	6'1"	220	Clemson	12/10/1938
13	Don Maynard	33	FL	6'0"	180	TX - El Paso	1/25/1935
50	Carl McAdams	24	DT	6'3"	228	Oklahoma	4/26/1944

NO.	PLAYER	AGE	POS	HT	WT	COLLEGE	BIRTHDATE
12	Joe Namath	25	QB	6'2"	200	Alabama	5/31/1943
63	John Neidert	22	ST	6'2"	230	Louisville	6/18/1946
15	Babe Parilli	38	QB	6'1"	196	Kentucky	5/07/1930
81	Gerry Philbin	27	LDE	6'2"	245	Buffalo	7/31/1942
23	Bill Rademacher	26	ST	6'1"	190	N. Michigan	5/13/1942
66	Randy Rasmussen	23	G	6'2"	255	Neb-Kearney	5/10/1945
26	Jim Richards	22	ST	6'1"	180	Virginia Tech	10/28/1946
74	Jeff Richardson	24	ST	6'3"	250	Michigan St	9/01/1944
72	Paul Rochester	30	LDT	6'2"	255	Michigan St	7/15/1938
24	Johnny Sample	32	LCB	6'1"	203	MD - E Shore	6/15/1936
83	George Sauer, Jr.	25	SE	6'2"	195	Texas	11/10/1943
52	John Schmitt	26	C	6'4"	250	Hofstra	11/12/1942
30	Mark Smolinski	29	ST	6'1"	215	Wyoming	5/09/1939
41	Matt Snell	27	FB	6'2"	219	Ohio State	8/18/1941
68	Mike Stromberg	23	LB	6'2"	235	Temple	5/25/1945
61	Bob Talamini	29	LG	6'1"	255	Kentucky	1/08/1939
85	Steve Thompson	23	ST	6'5"	245	Washington	2/12/1945
29	Bake Turner	28	WR	6'1"	179	Texas Tech	7/22/1940
11	Jim Turner	27	K	6'2"	205	Utah State	3/28/1941
71	Sam Walton	25	RT	6'5"	270	TX A&M EC	1/03/1943
34	Lee White	22	ST	6'2"	232	Weber State	5/09/1946

Source: Pro-Football-Reference.com.

PART ONE

1

BEFORE THERE WAS A SUPER BOWL

The best way to begin a book about how the 1968 New York Jets shocked the football world is to trace how the league they played in came about. Oddly, the attitude and behavior of the owners of National Football League teams led to the founding of the American Football League, of which the New York Titans (later the New York Jets) were a founding member.

In 1958 the Baltimore Colts had helped thrust professional football into the public's consciousness with their sudden-death NFL Championship win over the New York Giants on December 28. After that game, the NFL became an avid interest of more American sports fans than ever before, and, as had happened many times dating back to the 1920s, it ignited a passion for wealthy businessmen to seek ownership of an NFL franchise.

Founded in the 1920s, the NFL took four decades to build a following for pro football that came anywhere close to baseball. The NFL as a league always enticed wealthy individuals to become team owners, but even owners in the 1950s were frightfully shortsighted in their marketing and expectations for success. Buying and running a professional NFL football team was attractive, but more often than not, the challenges of local marketing and selling enough tickets to survive quickly put new, frequently undercapitalized owners in a financial hole from which they couldn't escape.

Between 1921 and 1939, the number of NFL teams shot up and down, from a low of 8 to a high of 12. Over and over again, many owners had their wallets emptied as their plans and hopes fell through the floor. Even founding NFL franchises in large markets endured decades of growing pains. The New York Football Giants, in the country's largest, most prosperous market, had only a smattering of season ticket holders in the late 1940s. If they drew 15,000 to a home game at the Polo Grounds, they would break even.

By the mid-1930s, the NFL had become more discerning in its franchise applications, insisting on major-league baseball cities. Yet even successful NFL owners couldn't come close to matching the wealth of executives who came together to form a new league, the All-America Football Conference (AAFC), in 1944. The goal of these entrepreneurs was to become a partner of the NFL; instead, they and the NFL went to war.

After four expensive and hard-fought years, three of the AAFC teams (Cleveland Browns, San Francisco 49ers, and Baltimore Colts) joined the NFL, and the AAFC disbanded. The NFL decided it would teach the former upstart members of the AAFC a lesson by scheduling a 1950 opening game that pitted the four-time AAFC Champion Cleveland Browns against the NFL Champion Philadelphia Eagles. To the embarrassment and shock of the more established league, Cleveland romped. It was no fluke. The Browns went on to play in every NFL Championship Game between 1950 and 1955, winning three of them.

Throughout the 1950s, the NFL enjoyed peaceful, steady growth at the gate. By 1959, the NFL was in better financial and marketing position than at any time in its history, and yet it had not learned the lessons from its expensive war with the AAFC. In 1945, NFL owners had turned up their noses at multimillionaire businessmen who formed the AAFC. In the late 1950s, NFL owners did it again to even more prosperous businessmen who wanted an NFL franchise.

Two such individuals were oilmen Lamar Hunt and Bud Adams. Independent of and unknown to each other, Hunt and Adams each attempted to buy the Chicago Cardinals' NFL franchise. Each planned to move the team out of Chicago—Hunt to Dallas and Adams to Houston. Baseball executive Bob Howsam had the same idea; he would relocate the Cardinals to Denver. The owners of the Chicago Cardinals refused to strike a deal with any of the three, but Hunt learned of Adams' interest in owning a football team, and they met and agreed to build the new American Football League.

Hunt and Adams needed partners in six other cities for their new league. Another wealthy scion, Barron Hilton, heir to the Hilton hotel chain, claimed the AFL Los Angeles franchise, but heading up Hunt's list of franchises that needed an owner was the indispensable New York market.

How the New York Titans were conceived, established, and run into the ground is beautifully detailed in *Crash of the Titans* by William J. Ryczek. Lamar Hunt's effort to launch a New York franchise began with attorney William Shea, who had no time to get involved with the AFL because he was seeking a Major League Baseball team for New York. Shea weakly suggested Harry Wismer, a nationally known football broadcaster, as a potential part owner of the charter New York team.

Wismer had some financial means (reportedly, he was worth $2 million, most of it from a 25 percent stake in the Washington Redskins) and was enthused about plans for a multisport stadium in

Flushing Meadows, Queens, that could house his team. He loved the idea of other local coinvestors but struck out in attempts to recruit partners in the team he dubbed the Titans.

Wismer was instrumental in landing a five-year, national TV deal for the AFL with ABC. He was also widely credited with introducing the idea of the eight AFL teams equally sharing the TV revenue. In 1960, $200,000 was split between the eight AFL owners for the rights to televise an AFL *Game of the Week*. The ABC payment would increase slightly each of the five years, provided the network, each year, opted to continue its AFL coverage.

Regrettably for the AFL and New York, although Wismer came up with his initiation fee, he never traveled in the same financial circles as Hunt, Adams, or Hilton, which was vital. New York was the biggest market in the United States, and the Titans had to take on the entrenched, wildly popular, perennial NFL championship-contending New York Football Giants. Allowing Wismer to control the New York AFL franchise was an ill-fated decision. The league suffered three years of public humiliation at his hands before Commissioner Joe Foss rid the AFL of him and took steps to bring needed stability in the market.

In addition to Wismer's inadequate funding, the Titans were impaired by their home field, the dilapidated, fan- and player-unfriendly, oblong-shaped Polo Grounds. It was an 1890 structure that had last been fully renovated in 1911. Describing the Polo Grounds' playing surface, the Titans' first signee, Don Maynard, said, "[The Polo Grounds] was like playing in a vacant lot." It also had a poor field drainage system. Fans ignored Wismer's personal histrionics designed to bring attention to the team and had little interest in attending Titans games.

Wismer lost $500,000 in the Titans' first year, 1960, and his economic fate was tied to a fifteen-year contract with New York City to move the Titans into the new baseball/football stadium in Flushing, Queens, in 1961. His dreams of success at the gate were stalled and ultimately evaporated due to construction and weather delays in building the stadium.

None of the AFL clubs, even those with rich owners, paid their existing players very much. Hunt in Dallas, Adams in Houston, and Hilton in San Diego openly competed with the NFL for talent and did spend considerably on top-rated offensive college players. The league as a whole began dipping into small, predominantly black colleges in the Southeast (for example, Grambling State, Jackson State, Southern University) for talent. It was similar to the AAFC's pursuit of black football players, which had helped break football's color line less than twenty years before. Of course, the NFL caught on and started drafting the same black talent.

For the most part, AFL franchises in Buffalo, Boston, Denver, and Oakland, as well as the Titans, got by with creaky former NFL and Canadian Football League players, supplemented by late-round, low-cost draft choices ignored by NFL teams. Free agents, still looking for a job after the draft, drifted to the AFL as well. AFL teams that spent on talent won.

Won-lost records document the relationship between AFL spenders and teams incapable or unwilling to compete financially with the NFL for college talent. The aggregate record between 1960 and 1962 of the Titans, Buffalo, Boston, Denver, and Oakland was 81–121. Relying on their owners' personal wealth, Dallas, Houston, and San Diego were a combined 82–43–1 in that same three-year span.

A look at the Titans' drafts during the team's three-year existence catalogs formidable football talent that almost always opted for the NFL. The list of players drafted by the Titans is flooded with names that pro football fans in the 1960s instantly recognize: Hall of Famers John Mackey and Herb Adderley; running backs Don Perkins, Tom Matte, and Bill Brown; receivers Bernie Casey and Willie Richardson; offensive linemen Joe Scibelli, Tony Liscio, and Mike Pyle; kicker Fred Cox; defensive lineman Roger Brown; and defensive back Jerry Stovall. All made their mark in the established league as opposed to the Titans.

Indicative of their middling talent, the Titans broke even, 7–7, in 1960 and 1961. Their lack of college signings after each of those campaigns left the Titans in a state of mediocrity. By 1962, as the AFL as a whole pulled even with the NFL in signing draftees (76 by the NFL and 73 by the AFL, according to Buffalo owner Ralph Wilson), the Titans' chronic financial hardship seriously hindered the team's ability not only to be competitive with other AFL teams but its ability to exist.

The Titans' final campaign in 1962 was forgettable on numerous levels. At one point, Wismer did not issue payroll checks, prompting the players to refuse to practice with their coaches. Then Wismer bounced checks and even refused AFL game officials' requests to turn on Polo Grounds' lights one afternoon to save money. He was tapped out. The AFL stepped in and doled out $255,000 to cover the Titans' payroll and other invoices to get the team through the season. At the end of 1962, the Titans declared bankruptcy, with team losses, according to that filing, of $2 million.

Wismer's fiscal shortcomings doomed his ownership, but to those around him day-to-day, recollections of his charisma, show-business personality, and dynamism were more meaningful than his glaring, ruinous financial drawbacks. Over many years on his football radio broadcasts, Wismer had weaved fictitious details about what was happening on the field to cover his lack of attention. Unknowing fans hung on his every word as reality. That trick didn't work with the Titans' few ticket buyers and even less with the media, which had no trouble seeing past his bombast and "don't look here, look over there" diversions.

The AFL revoked Wismer's ownership of the New York AFL franchise on February 27, 1963, and on March 28 David A. "Sonny" Werblin and his four copartners acquired the team for $1 million. In April, the Titans were renamed the New York Jets.

Aside from a mostly underwhelming roster and George Sauer Sr., the one member of management under contract, the only other individual of note who would bring his skills and expertise from the Titans to the Jets was team surgeon Dr. James Nicholas, Harry Wismer's personal physician. Dr. Nicholas had joined the Titans' staff after the excruciating death of Titans' offensive lineman Howard Glenn during a 1960 game in Houston. His brother, Dr. Calvin Nicholas, would become the Jets' team physician.

Money ceased to be an obstacle for the New York AFL franchise, but the cupboard was almost bare in terms of talent. However, there was no shortage of young talent to be plucked from the college ranks. The Jets' money and Werblin would both be lures to bring graduating college seniors to New York, but the highest caliber of coaching was needed to mold these athletes who would become Jets.

THE FIVE-YEAR PLAN

The morning of January 8, 1963, Baltimore Colts' head coach, Wilbur Charles "Weeb" Ewbank, called his bosses about rumors of his imminent dismissal. He had led the Colts to 1958 and 1959 NFL Championships and was the toast of the town, but the three years that followed produced an unsatisfying 21–19 record. President and owner Carroll Rosenbloom had been listening to some of his top players plead with management for a coaching change. When Ewbank headed back north following the Senior Bowl in Mobile, Alabama, he was told at a train station that he had been dismissed and replaced by Detroit Lions assistant coach and longtime Ewbank player favorite Don Shula.

Meanwhile, two hundred miles north of Baltimore, David A. "Sonny" Werblin, head of the five-person ownership group that had purchased the AFL's New York franchise, needed to hire a coach for the newly minted New York Jets. The selection had to be top-flight, and, following his core belief in a star system, Sonny's head coach had to have a record and reputation that would capture the attention of the New York media and local football fans. Ewbank oozed all that, especially since the Colts had victimized the New York Giants in both of their 1958 and 1959 NFL Championship Game victories. Weeb even came with a recommendation from the Colts' owner.

At the April 16, 1963, press conference announcing the renaming of the franchise and Ewbank's hiring as general manager and coach, Weeb noted his five-year plan that Rosenbloom had outlined to Baltimore fans in 1953. It had set the Colts on a path to contention, although it took six years for Baltimore to win its first NFL Championship, the 1958 overtime contest that got the moniker "The Greatest Game Ever Played." Ewbank said he believed the same "plan" would put the Jets on a direct course to accomplish the same goal as in Baltimore.

The five-year plan established the offensive and defensive styles that Ewbank's team would follow on both sides of the line and set in stone the type of players who would fit those platoons. Athleticism and loving to hit were two obvious requirements of Jets' players (as they are for all pro football teams), but there was a third element—intelligence—that set the Jets apart from many other pro football organizations. Height and weight were secondary to smarts; Jets players had to handle intricate offensive and defensive maneuvers.

Adroit scouting would identify college football seniors who fit the Jets' mold. In the early 1960s, each member of a pro team's four-person assistant coaching staff doubled as a college scout with a delineated geographic territory. They bird-dogged players, cajoled, schmoozed, recruited, and entered into contracts with preferred college players. The five-year plan called to augment the Jets' roster with these young studs, free agent signings (unproven college and young, unseasoned professional players), and, to a much lesser extent, trade acquisitions. Youth would be served because by design most of the talent was supposed to peak by year five.

The Jets' coaching staff congregated at Peekskill Academy in Peekskill, New York, for the first training camp in the summer of 1963.

The New York Titans had never posted a winning record, so Titans returnees who reported to Peekskill were a weak talent foundation.

In training camp, Ewbank found some value in a few Titans: linebacker Larry Grantham, fullback Bill Mathis, receiver Don Maynard, punter Curley Johnson, and center Mike Hudock. Other Titans tried out and some earned a spot on the first Jets thirty-three-man squad, but were gone within a year or less. Weeb acquired a couple of ex-Baltimore taxi squad players to upgrade the squad: offensive tackle Sherman Plunkett and quarterback Dick Wood.

Not only was Weeb saddled with questionable professional talent, but he faced a highly unusual problem. The Titans had drafted extraordinarily well a few months before Ewbank's arrival, but the penniless New York AFL franchise had been powerless to sign anyone. With no fresh college talent, Weeb spent the 1963 season shuttling players on and off the roster. "In 1963, we had three teams," offensive assistant Clive Rush would recount, "one going, one coming, and one playing."

Fortunately for Weeb, in 1963, he still had "friends" looking out for him. That summer, the Baltimore Colts were injecting youth into the team's aging core and improving its backups. Don Shula and defensive coordinator Charlie Winner (Ewbank's son-in-law) cut players and they encouraged departing Colts to seek a job in New York. A number took the advice and were welcomed by Weeb.

On the 1963 Jets' opening day in Boston, four players who had been Colts only weeks before—FB Mark Smolinski, WR Bake Turner, OL Winston Hill, and DB Bill Baird—suited up in kelly-green-and-white Jets uniforms. Shula would discover six years later how big a favor he had done Weeb. Hill, Baird, Turner, and Smolinski were on the Jets' roster in 1968—and all four played instrumental roles in beating the Colts in Super Bowl III.

The Jets' investment in its drafts between 1964 and 1967 was a glittering display of Sonny Werblin's commitment to spend lavishly on whomever the Jets identified as star football talent. Jets signings were not difficult, although in the high-risk, high-reward nature of the professional draft, players tended to be spectacular contributors or embarrassing flops. Early drafts produced starters on both sides of the ball. As young, athletic football players joined the Jets, solid coaching and game experience remodeled the team from a league-wide joke, overrun with also-rans, into the future Super Bowl squad.

In 1964, 1965, and 1966, the Jets drafted and signed the nucleus of their future Super Bowl team. The 1965 draft was the best in Jets history, reaping five future AFL all-stars, including Alabama QB Joe Namath. Fruitful Jets drafts were far less commonplace after the NFL and AFL agreed to a merger in 1966 and an immediate "common draft" where NFL and AFL teams no longer competed for the services of college seniors. The Jets' first five 1967 common draft selections were forgettable, however rounds six, seven, and twelve landed several quality players. The 1968 Jets draft didn't produce stars; however, it generated several rookies who filled essential special teams' roles on the 1968 Super Bowl squad.

As in Baltimore, it actually took six years for Ewbank's five-year plan to generate its desired results, but on top of the 1968–69 Super Bowl victory, the Jets' offense and defense each finished number one that season in the AFL. That was a tribute to playing ability and equally (if not more so) to superb coaching, systems, and scheming by Weeb and his four assistants.

Forty-five players appeared in a Jets uniform in 1968–69, including three Titans. Of the 45, 26 had been Titans/Jets draft choices, 13 were free agent signees (highlighted by Don Maynard, Curley Johnson, Jim Turner, Bill Baird, Bake Turner, Winston Hill, John Schmitt, Mark Smolinski, Johnny Sample, Randy Beverly, Jim Hudson, Billy Joe, and John Dockery), 4 had been acquired in trades (Bill Mathis in 1960, Paul Rochester in 1963, and Bob Talamini and Babe Parilli in 1968), and 2 had been acquired on waivers (Al Atkinson and John Neidert).

WINNING THE AFL CHAMPIONSHIP GAME

The Jets' 11-3 record blew away the rest of the AFL East in 1968. Because pro football rotated the location of its league championship games each year, Shea Stadium hosted the AFL Championship Game on December 29, 1968. The visiting Oakland Raiders were made a seven-point favorite to beat the Jets, who had lost to Oakland in the *Heidi* Game just over a month earlier in Oakland.

Oakland had been forced to beat Kansas City in an AFL West playoff game after both teams finished 12-2. Almost to a man, Jets players preferred the Raiders to be their opponent and were energized when the Raiders blew away the Chiefs, 41–6. To the Jets, the AFL title game was more than winner-take-all. Instead, it was a chance to prove themselves and a shot at personal redemption.

The official game temperature was 37 degrees but dipped into the 20s as the game progressed. Twenty-four-year-old Pete Banaszak, a second-year Raiders' halfback, was one of Oakland's youngest players. In 2017, he was seventy-two but possessed more vivid memories than anyone else who wore an Oakland silver-and-black uniform that day. "It was a nasty afternoon," Banaszak recounted, "kind of like a football game should be in the wintertime. I can still see those wind swirls develop on Shea's infield and race like little tornadoes coming at us. You had to cover your eyes so they didn't get full of dirt. It was colder than hell."

The Jets' offensive game plan, created by Clive Rush and approved by Ewbank, noted: "[Oakland's] line is big & strong, but can and must be handled. Make a stand near their line and stay in the middle of them. . . ." Defensive tackle Dan Birdwell is the Raiders' "most active lineman, may line up anywhere [on the defensive line]. . . . Both Birdwell and [Ben] Davidson are cheap shot artists . . . sustain [blocks] on them [Birdwell and Davidson], beat them on the scoreboard. . . . We must pick up and burn their first blitz. If they succeed, they may continue."

Jets coaches fully expected a high-scoring matchup. *"We must score as much as it takes to win,"* concluded the Jets' plan. "Above all, keep your poise at all times."

Banaszak says the Raiders expected to wear down the shorter, lighter Jets in the second half. "If you were standing in our offensive huddle and looked across at the Jets' defense, the only mammoth guy was Verlon Biggs," he said. "[Gerry] Philbin and [John] Elliott were not massive guys, but we knew they made up for it in savvy and smarts. . . . They proved us wrong . . . the sons of bitches could play and didn't back down. We knew they were good, but we had confidence in our defense. But our 'Eleven Angry Men' defense were not very angry that day. Ben [Davidson] usually had big games against the Jets. We thought he would dominate on that side [Winston Hill's] of the line."

The Jets' wide receivers would aggressively attack Oakland's defensive backfield as they always had. The chippy Oakland defense had never intimidated or blunted the Jets or Namath. "All receivers— Be clever fighting through their crowding," said the Jets' game plan.

"We have been very successful versus their crowding [bump-and-run]. Don't stop fighting through and complain to officials when holding is not called."

In horrid winter conditions, both teams chewed up yardage and put points on the board. The punters, Curley Johnson and Oakland's Mike Eischeid, punted beautifully with the wind at their back—and an unaccustomed thirty yards against it.

The Jets throttled Oakland's running game, the Jets' swift front-seven limiting the Raiders' backs to 50 yards on 19 attempts, so Raiders' QB Daryle Lamonica threw often. He had sporadic effectiveness: 20 completions in 47 attempts, for 401 yards, but only 1 TD and a quarterback rating of 80.2. The Jets defense forced three George Blanda field goals; a fourth Blanda field goal—against the wind—struck the crossbar.

On one third-quarter goal-line stand backed up to their own six-yard line, the Jets made a stunning defensive statement to the Raiders. Strong safety Jim Hudson almost single-handedly stuffed three Oakland rushing attempts by fullback Hewritt Dixon to barrel into the end zone. The Raiders moved the football five of the six needed yards and were forced to try a Blanda field goal. Banaszak observed: "[The Jets] made a statement with that series of downs. We underestimated their talents and we tried to ram it down their throats—and they rammed it down ours."

The Jets rushed 34 times for 144 yards (Matt Snell, 19 for 71, and Emerson Boozer, 11 for 51). Namath completed 19 out of 49, for 266 yards, 3 touchdowns, and 1 interception. Joe's quarterback rating: 68.9. Don Maynard caught two of the TDs, Pete Lammons the third. Jim Turner kicked two field goals; a third attempt fell short.

Pregame expectations were that the last team with possession of the ball would win. It didn't work out that way. The Jets led for most of the game; Oakland tied it at 13 in the third quarter and then took the lead for the first and only time midway through the fourth quarter on a Banaszak run. Two plays after Oakland took the lead,

Namath connected on a 52-yard, fourth-quarter bomb to Maynard, who ran it to the Raiders' six-yard line. *New York Times* beat writer Dave Anderson calculated Namath's heave carried 75 to 80 yards against the wind. On the next play, Maynard corralled Namath's winning TD pass on his knees, a foot above the turf.

Another fourth-quarter individual defensive highlight came from Verlon Biggs, who sacked Daryle Lamonica on fourth down from the Jets 26 with New York clinging to a 27–23 lead. In the last two minutes, linebacker Ralph Baker correctly diagnosed Lamonica's casual incomplete toss to halfback Charlie Smith in the right flat as a lateral, and, therefore, a free ball. Baker's recovery stymied another Raiders drive.

Banaszak commented, "Everything went wrong [for us] that day. To top it off, as I was walking to the locker room, some a--hole dropped a beer on me." Two weeks later Banaszak watched Super Bowl III in the Orange Bowl and remembers feeling that "Baltimore also learned that the Jets were more physical than they thought."

As the joyous Jets team left the field at Shea Stadium, four of the players decided to pick up Weeb Ewbank and carry him to the locker room. He almost fell off their shoulders, a fan grabbed and injured his hip, and Weeb had to lean on a cane through two weeks of Super Bowl practices.

4

REACTIONS TO JOE'S "GUARANTEE"

T here were two weeks between the AFL Championship Game and Super Bowl III. Print and electronic media compared the teams and declared that Super Bowl III might be a bigger mismatch than the first two NFL-AFL Championship Games in which the NFL's Green Bay Packers had dominated their AFL counterparts. The Jets' players read it, heard it, and kept quiet, except for the key player in the game.

On the Thursday night prior to the big game (January 9, 1969), Joe Namath was driven to the Miami Touchdown Club banquet to be awarded a plaque as the "Outstanding Professional Football Player of 1968." The American Football League's hierarchy loved the ceremony because Namath was the league's first player to be so honored.

As chronicled in Dave Anderson's epic book that detailed the two weeks that preceded Super Bowl III, *Countdown to Super Bowl*, Namath delivered a few remarks to the packed audience. He thanked his parents and family, his high school coach Larry Bruno, Alabama coach Paul "Bear" Bryant, former Jets owner Sonny Werblin, Jets coach Weeb Ewbank, the Jets' owners, and his teammates for his past and current football success.

Then came the spontaneous words that would cement the legend of Broadway Joe Namath in the annals of NFL history: "You can be the greatest athlete in the world," he said, "but if you don't win those football games, it doesn't mean anything. And we are going to win Sunday. I guarantee you."

The *New York Times'* Anderson, the only New York media reporter there that evening, didn't think Joe's words were particularly noteworthy. It was just one more matter-of-fact utterance from the quarterback who had said several times over that he expected to win Super Bowl III, so Anderson didn't even send a dispatch about the dinner remarks to his editors.

Anderson didn't even report Joe's first public salute to the Jets' defense. ("I read where one [reporter] wrote that our defense can't compare with the Colts," Joe had remarked. "Anybody who knows anything about football knows that we have five guys on defense alone better than them [the Colts].")

The following morning, the lone article about Namath's remarks appeared in a *Miami Herald* sports section story under the banner headline "Namath Guarantees Jet Victory."

Well, even Namath almost immediately recognized that he had gone further out on a limb than in any of his earlier public pronouncements. "When he got back to the hotel that night, Joe called me," explained defensive captain Johnny Sample to NFL Films. "Joe said, 'I said something and I think it is going to be in all the news, the papers, TV, radio, everything.' What the heck did you say? Joe responded, 'I just told them I guaranteed we were going to win.' I said, 'You didn't do that, did ya?' Namath said, 'Yes, I did. We're going to win, aren't we?' I said, 'You're right. We're gonna win, but you shouldn't have said that.'"

In the first days of Super Bowl preparation, Weeb Ewbank, after studying films of the Colts, had told his assistants: "If we can't pass on these guys, we ought to get out of the business. . . . We can beat these guys. We're going to win this game." That set the tone for the team. However, according to defensive lineman Carl McAdams, Ewbank had admonished the Jets players the day before the awards dinner "not to say anything to make these [Colts] players mad."

Linebacker Ralph Baker was having breakfast when he saw the *Miami Herald* sports section. "Winning was tough enough without giving them extra incentive," he said. "I figured we'd be in for a lecture from Weeb, but it never happened." Ewbank read his newspaper and saw it as the worst kind of bulletin board material for the Baltimore locker room.

Center John Schmitt remembered, "Weeb was so pissed off. Weeb came down from his room and Joe was at the table next to me. Joe was kind of hungover to be honest. Weeb rarely lost his temper with Joe and he was never angry with Joe. Weeb held the newspaper. 'Joseph, did you say this? I asked you not to do this,' he scolded Joe."

Jeff Richardson was caught off guard by Namath's remarks. "We were upset and surprised," he admitted. "[The Colts] were saying so many negative things about us, and we were saying nothing but nice things about them," recounted Richardson. "I told the media that Bubba Smith [the Colts' giant defensive end] was a superstar and, tongue-in-cheek, I said I didn't know if we have anyone who could handle him. Bubba called me when he read it in the papers the next day and thanked me. We wanted them to think they were going to play a bunch of kids and that they were going to just slaughter us."

Joe's roommate, Jim Hudson, was absolutely convinced the Jets would win, but said to Joe, "Oh s--t. Why did you say that?" according to his second wife, Lise. Don Maynard had a muted reaction: "I didn't react because we were confident—and that's the big word that didn't come out in the press much before the game." Maynard's longtime teammate, Larry Grantham, agreed with Weeb. "You don't walk into a house and kick the dog and see if he will bite you," Larry explained. "We knew it was Joe [who said it], we never said too much about it, and we never have."

Another AFL original, Paul Rochester, wasn't entirely sure what Namath was up to. "I figured he must have had a few drinks. I didn't care—he got our attention and we had to back him up. If anything, it brought us together." Bob Talamini, also an AFLer since 1960, thought "Joe was stating a lot of confidence in the team. He was supposed to have confidence, but he did excite [the Colts] more than they would have been."

Halfback Emerson Boozer thought nothing of Joe opening his mouth. "Joe didn't say anything we didn't feel as a unit," he remarked. "Pete Lammons was also saying it." Matt Snell went further: "The Colts looked at us as this young, start-up league, with a young punk making a guarantee. They were determined to hand us our heads. I wasn't worried."

Jets special teams captain Mark Smolinski woke up to discover that "the guarantee" had embroiled him in a family controversy. "They called me from Michigan, asked about Joe's prediction and said, 'What's Joe doing?' They pointed to a *Detroit Free Press* Super Bowl prediction by popular columnist Joe Falls: Colts 270, Jets 0. They wanted to know how would I show my face at home if the Jets got humiliated? I told them I'd come home with my head held high; I even told some of them to bet the ranch that we would win."

Ralph Baker suggested to equipment manager Bill Hampton: "I think Joe's trying to add to the pressure on himself on purpose. He's at his best when the pressure is on. Like in the [AFL] Championship Game when we were behind in the last quarter, and in Houston when we needed to go 80 yards and get a touchdown late in the fourth quarter."

Namath was inspiring and rocketing the spirits of young teammates. Earl Christy grabbed Jets' broadcaster Merle Harmon in the Jets' hotel. "Merle, did you hear what Joe said?" Christy asked excitedly. "Joe said we're going to beat the Colts! We're going to win the

Super Bowl!" Harmon observed afterward, "I think that Joe's pre-diction helped the Jets win the game because it got his teammates hyped."

Bill Rademacher told newspaper columnist Jerry Izenberg, "Joe has been trying to shake us up. That's why he started all the talking. Well, now, we are properly shook, and I'll tell you something else. It's more than just pregame behavior. Joe is telling the truth. We're going to win."

To some, "the guarantee" was a master psychological ploy. "Joe said he didn't plan the guarantee, he just did it," remarked John Dockery, one of Namath's close friends on the team. "He had the guts to say it in a simple declarative sentence. You say to yourself, 'Our QB said it. Maybe it [a win] is a possibility. It drifts through your brain, drifts through your psyche and you think maybe he's right, maybe there is a chance. A lot of us were saying this is going to be one tough game and the likelihood of winning it is slim and none. So when Joe said it, it took the pressure off us. It all went in Joe's direction."

Defensive tackle Carl McAdams observed, "I kinda enjoyed reading it in the newspaper. Even some of the New York newspapers gave us such little chance of winning and questioned why we were bothering to go to Miami. What Joe said made me feel better. I think it really helped us more than it disturbed the Colts. With Joe coming out and saying this, we thought we're really going to see something [from Joe] this week."

Remembered Randy Rasmussen, "All I could think was, 'Oh God. What did you do?' I was a little disturbed, but it almost had to be done, and he was the guy who had to do it. We'll probably never know for sure if it psyched us up or psyched them down, but something happened." Rookie Jim Richards said, "We didn't need to rile them up any more. After thinking about it, it gave me confidence that Joe felt that highly of our team. It gave me a pick-me-up."

Another rookie, Steve Thompson, had seen enough of Namath in the locker room and on the field to feel "the guarantee wasn't out of place or over-the-top. This game was no David versus Goliath," Thompson commented. "In college, you were told not to poke the bear because it would rile the other guys. I didn't think professionals were motivated that way. He was our leader—and he said we can beat these guys."

Gerry Philbin saw only the guarantee's positive ramifications. "I'm beginning to think it's good," he told George Sauer Sr. "One of the troubles with the other two AFL teams in the Super Bowl was that they kept saying how great the Packers were, so as not to get the Packers mad. But . . . the AFL players began to believe it themselves. When he guaranteed, he was speaking for the defense and the offense. We had a quarterback who was this tough, who could back it up."

Rookie defensive lineman Ray Hayes would watch Super Bowl III from the sideline but recognized the impact of Namath's guarantee. "At our twenty-five-year Super Bowl reunion, I told everyone that I thought the turning point of the game happened prior to the game: Joe's guarantee. Other guys came over and said they thought so, too."

SUPER BOWL III
JETS 16, COLTS 7

I f you were alive in the United States on January 12, 1969, chances are that you watched the New York Jets upset the NFL champion Baltimore Colts in Super Bowl III at the Orange Bowl.

Propelled by Joe Namath's celebrity and his self-created controversy with a guaranteed Jets victory, the game drew a 36.8 rating (nearly double Super Bowl I and 62 percent better than Super Bowl II). It garnered a 68 share of TV sets on during the 3–6 P.M. EST time period (89 percent better than Super Bowl I and 58 percent above Super Bowl II). An estimated 60 to 70 million fans worldwide viewed it. The $2.5 million revenue from TV and radio rights created a pot that would reward the winning team $15,000 a player, with $7,500 going to the losers.

GAME SUMMARY

At the Jets' team breakfast, Joe Namath paraphrased punter Curley Johnson's two-week-long pre–Super Bowl III witticism, standing up and declaring, "Chicken ain't nothin' but a bird, and this ain't nothin' but another football game. Let's go out and win." In the locker room before the game, Coach Weeb Ewbank repeated his usual pregame pep talk about the Jets showing the world how "great a team we really are." He stressed poise and execution. Weeb reminded a few of the guys (Hill, Baird, Bake Turner, and Smolinski) that the Colts had gotten rid of them and that they now had a chance to get even. Johnny Sample recalled that after Paul Crane recited the Lord's Prayer, Weeb added, "One more thing: When we win, don't pick me up and ruin my other hip. I'll walk."

The Jets received the opening kickoff, but after gaining one first down they punted. Baltimore, the first team to enter the Super Bowl with 15 wins, stormed down the field until the Jets' unit asserted itself with single-man stops by John Elliott and, two plays later, by Gerry Philbin. They forced a 27-yard Lou Michaels field goal attempt, but he missed the gimme, the first of his two misses that day. Later in the half, he would miss a 46-yarder.

The Jets committed their only turnover of the game when George Sauer Jr. caught a pass, then fumbled deep in Jets territory. The Colts covered the loose ball on the Jets' 14-yard line. However, Baltimore QB Earl Morrall, after advancing the Colts to the Jets' 6-yard line, had his end zone flip tipped at the line of scrimmage. The partially deflected pass bounced off of the shoulder pads of the intended target, TE Tom Mitchell, and Randy Beverly intercepted to halt Baltimore's scoring threat.

From there, the Jets methodically drove 80 yards using a combination of Matt Snell power runs through the Jets' left side and pinpoint short passing by Namath. Capping the drive, Snell sprinted around the left end for a four-yard second-quarter TD, bouncing off Colts middle linebacker Dennis Gaubatz in the end zone. That and Jim Turner's extra point put the Jets up 7–0, the first time an AFL team had led in any of the first three Super Bowl games.

Baltimore halfback Tom Matte ripped off a couple of long runs in the first half, and the Colts sniffed the Jets' end zone a few times but didn't score. In the second quarter, the Colts penetrated deep into Jets' territory for a third time in the first half, but Johnny Sample stepped in front of Baltimore WR Willie Richardson and intercepted Morrall inside the Jets' 10-yard line.

As the first half was winding down, the Jets punted to the Colts, who had the ball at midfield. On the last play of the half, the Colts ran a flea-flicker. Tom Matte took Morrall's handoff, began a sweep around the right side with blockers in front of him, but he suddenly stopped, turned, and flung the ball back to Morrall. Instead of throwing to split end Jimmy Orr near the Jets' end zone (as designed for the play), the Colts' QB pitched a pass down the middle of the field to fullback Jerry Hill inside the Jets' 20-yard line. Jets safety Jim Hudson stepped in front of Hill and made the Jets' third interception of the first half. The Jets led 7–0 as both teams headed to the locker room.

Baltimore took the third quarter kickoff, but on the first offensive play from scrimmage, Matte fumbled when hit by Verlon Biggs, and Jets' strong side linebacker Ralph Baker recovered on the Colts' 33. Namath conservatively attacked the Colts' defense to make sure the Jets came away with points, and Jim Turner delivered a three-pointer from 32 yards out. The Jets led 10–0.

Morrall and the Colts went three-and-out on their next possession. Namath dinked and dunked the Jets all the way to the Baltimore 23, where Turner booted a 30-yard field goal. The Jets' lead expanded to 13–0. Namath's ball control offense ate up so much clock that Baltimore's offense had the ball for only seven plays in that third quarter.

The Colts yanked Morrall and inserted Johnny Unitas on Baltimore's ensuing possession, but they went three-and-out again. The Jets drove down to the Colts' two-yard line, highlighted by a 39-yard Namath-to-Sauer completion, and Jim Turner padded the Jets' lead to 16–0 early in the fourth quarter.

After the Jets' kickoff, Unitas took the Colts down field, but Baltimore was denied again—a 25-yard pass to Orr was intercepted by Randy Beverly (his second of the game) in the end zone. Namath played it cool, opting to eat up the clock, and did not throw a single pass in the fourth quarter.

It took the Colts and Unitas until the fifty-sixth minute to finally score—and even that was not easy. With a first-and-goal from the Jets' five-yard line, Baltimore twice ran into the middle of the Jets' defensive line; both runs were stacked up short of the end zone. That Jets' impressive goal-line stand consumed precious seconds the Colts needed for a comeback. On third down, Jerry Hill punched in from one yard out. The Jets led 16–7.

The Colts recovered a predictable onside kick on the Jets' 44 with barely three minutes remaining in the game. Three completions took Baltimore to the New York 19, but Unitas' floating fourth-down pass to Orr near the end zone was tipped away by Larry Grantham. One of two original New York Titans, Larry tossed his helmet straight up into the air and leisurely headed to the Jets' bench.

Only 2:21 remained. The Jets tried to run out the clock, but after gaining one first down Curley Johnson had to punt. Baltimore got the ball one last time. With eight seconds left, Unitas completed a sideline pass, and followed by lobbing another one that was complete to Richardson as the final gun sounded. In the game, the Jets controlled the ball for over 36 minutes, the Colts just under 24. Jets players hugged all over the field as Namath trotted toward the locker room and famously waved his index finger in a number-one salute.

WHY THE UPSET HAPPENED

Why the Jets achieved the greatest upset in Super Bowl history is an historic, multifaceted story. Prior to the game, Weeb Ewbank told AFL president Milt Woodard, "I guarantee we won't embarrass our league. We're going to go out there and sock it to 'em."

With the possible exception of Turner's multiple three-pointers, nearly everything else that happened was a surprise to the throng of Super Bowl reporters. NFL boosters said the Jets hadn't won the game, that the Colts had shot themselves in the foot. The reality was that the end result was as much about the Jets' execution and poise as it was the Colts' mistakes.

Invited to a Colts' practice the week prior to the contest, NBC lead announcer Curt Gowdy was told by Don Shula that he was having trouble focusing his superconfident Colts. Shula said to Gowdy: "I'm really worried. Football is all mental. Any time one team's more ready to play than the other, they can beat you." Shula heard players discussing how they would spend the $15,000 winner's share. Tight end John Mackey said, "We cut up our [winning Super Bowl] shares at the pregame meal."

Two NFL games that Weeb accessed were instructional about how to handle the Colts.

The Los Angeles Rams had upset Baltimore, 34–10, in the final game of the previous (1967) season. Weeb saw the need to blunt Baltimore's blitz and control the Colts' pass rush so that Namath could attack weaknesses in the Colts' secondary. Rams' coach George Allen's game plan had sent QB Roman Gabriel to the line to read Baltimore's defense and audible plays based on his reading of the defense. Joe Namath would do exactly that thirteen months later.

Weeb knew that a short passing game that didn't force the ball into tight coverage and a strong running attack were essential to upending Baltimore. That was how the Cleveland Browns had handed the Colts their only 1968 loss, 30–20. Browns quarterback Bill Nelson picked on Baltimore cornerback Lenny Lyles, as Namath would. Halfback LeRoy Kelly had the same success running the ball that Matt Snell would.

Joe Namath was pro football's number-one long-ball threat, but that was Baltimore's strength based on a supposedly impregnable deep zone defense. The pundits thought Namath's deep-ball artistry had no chance for success. *New York Post* football writer Gene Roswell wrote that Joe needed to "throw bombs . . . to keep the AFL champions in the game." But no one foresaw that wasn't going to be the Jets' game plan. Weeb, Clive Rush, and Namath received no credit for adaptability. Minnesota Vikings All-Pro offensive tackle Grady Alderman noted the Colts' single defensive vulnerability: "You have to throw everything five or six yards—and where do you get with that?"

As it turned out for the Jets, quite a lot. "Every time Namath read our weak-safety blitz, George Sauer would read as well, run an inside slant, and Joe would hit him with a quick pass," diagnosed Colts left cornerback Bobby Boyd after the game. The top receiver in AFL history, Lance Alworth, one of several stars of the league in attendance at Super Bowl III, thought "the Jets had a helluva lot of speed offensively. . . . Too much speed and too much youth."

Namath's excellence in Super Bowl III flaunted his physical and cerebral skills that, in some cases, had been underplayed or gone unnoticed. Namath had never quarterbacked in his four-year career as he did in Super Bowl III: part heady field general Bart Starr, part gunslinger Sonny Jurgenson, two heralded NFL quarterbacks in the late 1960s.

Execution of the Jets' game plan won Namath the respect of football executives. Complimented *Los Angeles Times* writer Bob Oates: "Almost certainly, no other quarterback could have wrecked the superb network of Baltimore zone defenses." To this day, no one thinks of the Joe Namath who performed in Super Bowl III as classic Joe Namath, but the complete package, including his sterling passing skills (notably his quick release) and reading of the Colts' defense, that day created an aura about him that hasn't diminished over a half century. "He beat our blitz more than we beat him," stated Colts coach Don Shula postgame. "One time, I came at him," said star linebacker Mike Curtis, "and knew I had him with the ball. I was going to get him good, but dammit if he didn't get it away."

The Colts' defense had surprising trouble controlling the Jets' running game from the first series. Entering the game, the Jets' offensive line as a group was acknowledged as the best pass blockers in pro football, yet received minimal credit for run blocking. That proved to be an oversight in Super Bowl III as fullback Matt Snell rolled up (to that point in time) a record 121 yards on the ground. The Jets' bread-and-butter play, 19 Straight (a run to the left side of the offensive line), had been normally unstoppable in 1968. In Super Bowl III, left tackle Winston Hill thrashed Colts' right defensive end Ordell Braase and got the bulk of the blocking credit for Snell's huge game. However, the other four linemen (Bob Talamini, John Schmitt, Randy Rasmussen, and Dave Herman) were superlative, and halfbacks Emerson Boozer and Bill Mathis took turns throwing lead blocks on Baltimore linebackers that sent Snell racing into the secondary. Matt ran like an untamed bull released from its pen; it required multiple Colts' linebackers and defensive backs to haul him down or, failing that, to knock him out of bounds.

Namath's extraordinary game preparation and football intelligence enabled him to read the Colts' defense and make proper play calls. Joe, Ewbank, and Rush discovered they could manipulate the Colts' defense with Namath's audibles at the line, shifting Baltimore safeties and linebackers in the opposite direction that the Jets intended to run or pass. (See center John Schmitt's profile for details.) Lance Alworth said, "If I were Joe, I would have thrown more passes to the outside because they [Baltimore] couldn't cover."

During film sessions, the coaching staff, receivers, and running backs had glared at dead spots in the Colts' zone, particularly when Baltimore blitzed. The Jets' running game kept the Colts' defense off-balance, and Namath's pass protection and quick release kept the heat off Joe. When Namath read upcoming blitzes, Jets receivers angled to predetermined spots based on the film, and Namath hit them in stride.

Don Maynard and George Sauer Jr. were a scary one-two receiving duo, with Maynard's breakaway speed and long-ball threat complemented by Sauer's precise routes. In Super Bowl III, Don Maynard's legs were not 100 percent recovered from a December injury, yet his jaunts past Baltimore's deep zone in the first and third quarters gave the Colts the willies. Defensive coordinator Walt Michaels alerted the bench from the press box when the Baltimore zone concentrated to Maynard's side, leaving Sauer with single coverage on the opposite side of the field. Maynard had no catches in Super Bowl III, however Sauer dominated Colts' right cornerback Lenny Lyle, with eight catches for 133 yards.

Baltimore zealously tried to prevent a quick strike by Maynard with its deep zone. So, short passes in the soft part of the Colts' defense to Sauer, Matt Snell (40 yards on 4 catches) and Bill Mathis (20 yards from 3) worked to perfection. Receptions by Snell and Mathis helped fill some of the void left by Maynard. Jets' receivers racked up significant YAC (yards after the catch).

It seemed ironic that Baltimore succumbed to the same loss of poise that had done in Kansas City and Oakland in Super Bowls I and II. Mark Smolinski thought Ewbank's pre–Super Bowl media strategy in telling reporters the Jets were "so darn lucky to be on the field with" Baltimore "snookered them." Smo said, "We slapped them in the face, and they didn't respond."

Football's elite writers and reporters had spent nearly a decade building the case that the AFL couldn't compete with the NFL because of so few experienced players. Super Bowl III turned that argument upside down. These Jets were a young team, far more youthful than many graying Colts at several positions, and the Jets' personnel boasted three to six years of professional experience at nearly every position. Youth and talent served the Jets well in Super Bowl III, particularly in the offensive trenches (Herman and Hill, 27; Schmitt, 26; Rasmussen, 23; Talamini, 30). The Jets' offensive linemen had their way with Baltimore's more established, aging defensive unit.

The Jets became one of the youngest teams in a decade to win a pro football championship.

Finally, the Jets' defense received little acclaim despite leading the AFL in rush defense and starring sack specialists Gerry Philbin, Verlon Biggs, and John Elliott. Linebackers Larry Grantham, Al Atkinson, and Ralph Baker were a tough, swift, steady, strong tackling group. In the secondary, with the exception of second-year right cornerback Randy Beverly, the starters—Jim Hudson, Bill Baird, and Johnny Sample—had extensive experience. The overlooked story in Super Bowl III was the surprising, unanticipated near-shutout by the Jets' defensive eleven.

The Colts hadn't been shut out in four years, nor had they failed to score in the first half of any game in 1968, yet they were blanked until three minutes remained in Super Bowl III. The Jets' defense executed as designed in the team's playbook: it bent several times that day (fighting the Colts drives downfield), but didn't break (permitting only one TD—and that took three plunges from inside the five-yard line). All told, the Jets forced five Baltimore turnovers.

There exists a body of opinion that Joe Namath's "guarantee" of a Jets win had psyched up the Jets and psyched out the Colts. "Namath psyched two teams," the Oakland Raiders' George Blanda, pro football's oldest professional player, said after the game. "He psyched the Jets into believing they could win and he psyched the Colts into doubting that they could win."

An NFL documentary captured the enduring importance of Super Bowl III: "the ultimate example of why the players and not the prognosticators always have the final say, and it remains a source of inspiration for anybody who has been told it couldn't be done. There have been better football games, but Super Bowl III is one of the very few that truly deserved to be called a classic."

PART TWO

PROFILES OF THE 1968—69 SUPER BOWL JETS

Narratives have been written that tell the story, week by week, of how the 1968 New York Jets became the Super Bowl champion Jets.

However, never before has anyone profiled the forty-four members of the fabled 1968-69 Super Bowl team who surrounded, protected, and enabled Joe Namath to reach the zenith of his stardom. Only thirty-nine could take the field with Joe from week to week. Their backgrounds, how they became Jets, their disheartening, and, finally, their exhilarating times in a Jets uniform could have been detailed years ago, but no one thought these other Jets merited such attention.

This book takes you on that ride. We interviewed thirty-five Super Bowl Jets players (and some of their wives); the lone surviving assistant coach; other Jets during the team's formative years; and the families and friends of players, coaches, and owners who are no longer alive. *Beyond Broadway Joe* profiles begin with David A. "Sonny" Werblin, the principal owner, who had the vision and the money, and was the driving force behind the investor team that purchased the New York AFL franchise out of bankruptcy and renamed them the Jets.

Werblin's chapter leads into one for Weeb Ewbank, whose name may have little meaning to pro football fans in the twenty-first century. Weeb was the brains and the architect behind the football organization. He accepted the responsibility of taking over a Jets club with crumbs of talent, and completed the franchise's championship goal in six years.

From there, we go on to discuss all forty-five players, starting with Joe Namath. Bigger than life, Joe was the media's darling for the news and controversy he generated. Namath has credited the men around him for the Super Bowl III victory, but reporters may have been remiss in failing to emphasize Joe's kudos loudly enough. *Beyond Broadway Joe* makes it crystal clear.

DAVID A. "SONNY" WERBLIN

PRINCIPAL OWNER

*He signed and made a celebrity of Joe Namath,
and spent the Jets into relevancy.
To his chagrin, his success forced an NFL-AFL
merger that he opposed.*

Sonny Werblin's name was golden in the entertainment, movie, and television industries during the 1950s. He was a New York Giants fan and had assisted the AFL in landing its first TV contract in 1960, but the original idea of buying the New York AFL franchise wasn't his alone.

Tad Dowd, a young advertising agency exec, and Jimmy Iselin, son of Phil Iselin, the millionaire owner of women's apparel manufacturer Korell Corporation, were at least partially responsible. After chatting with Harry Wismer at a Titans home game, Dowd and Iselin had excitedly brought the idea of someone buying out Wismer to the attention of the elder Iselin. Phil Iselin contacted his friend Sonny Werblin, who reached out to friends Leon Hess and Townsend Martin. Others were considered, but an outsider, Donald Lillis, completed the group.

The five-man syndicate bought the New York Titans franchise out of bankruptcy court, assumed the Titans' $1 million in debt and put an additional $1.5 million into the team's operations. Werblin thought any New York sports franchise was worth a minimum of $1 million.

The myriad obstacles confronting Werblin should have dried up his enthusiasm. Foremost was the Jets' shortage of professional talent. The tough New York media was mostly indifferent about the Jets. The stands in the Polo Grounds, where even the Jets were forced to play for one year, were all but empty. But that didn't slow down Sonny, who worked to attract whatever attention he could to the Jets. "Sonny Werblin would do anything for publicity all the time," confirmed former *New York Times* sportswriter Dave Anderson.

Fortunately for the Jets, Sonny didn't let a dump of a home field and its depressing environment deter him from beginning to renovate the Jets into a first-class organization. He told the equipment manager to toss out all of the Titans' damaged football equipment. Sonny launched a saturation newspaper and TV advertising campaign to attract fans. "We have to make our own stars," Werblin conceded. "We're going first class and we're spending a lot of money. We want the players to feel like they're the Yankees, so that they'll play like the Yankees." (In 1963, the New York Yankees were on their way to winning their fourth of five consecutive American League pennants.)

He kept his eye on the prize: becoming personally involved in importing college talent. First came Ohio State fullback Matt Snell in the first round of the 1964 college draft. He invited Matt's family to be his guest at a game in the relic of a ballpark, and on that freezing day he sent them hot chocolate to make the experience more palatable. Matt became a Jet because of Sonny.

After his historic career in the entertainment industry, during which he had earned the title "Mr. Show Biz," Werblin wasn't looking for just any football talent. As in the television and movie business, his core business strategy was to identify, sign, and manage stars who would attract attention and dollars. He told confidants, "I believe in the star system. It's the only way to sell tickets. It's what you put on stage or the playing field that draws people."

Starting in the 1930s, Werblin had built a management entertainment career at Music Corporation of America, handling film stars and others whom he channeled into programming for the CBS, NBC, and ABC networks' prime-time lineups. When he retired from MCA in the early 1960s, *Variety* credited Sonny with having "helped shape broadcasting perhaps more than anyone else in America," and added "if he was not broadcasting's greatest showman, he certainly qualified as its greatest promoter and salesman."

Even Werblin's wife, the former Leah Ray Hubbard, was a star. She had been a vocalist for the Tommy Dorsey and Phil Harris bands, and a motion picture leading lady. Sonny regularly escorted his stable of stars to his home for dinner. He had three sons, two of whom say they found nothing out of the ordinary for a star entertainer to come over for a meal.

"My dad would tell us that 'so and so' was coming over tonight, and that we should act this way or that way," reminisced middle son Robert Werblin. Those "normal, everyday" guests included Alfred Hitchcock, who read the boys bedtime ghost stories. The kids recall answering the phone and speaking with actress Joan Crawford, newspaper columnist/TV host Ed Sullivan, and comedian Shelley Berman (among others), each looking for their father.

Sonny made no pretense of having an eye for football talent, but he publicly and financially committed to transforming the Jets into an appealing, exciting, and winning football team. Acting on a tip from a popular New York City newspaper sports columnist, Jimmy Cannon, and with the endorsement of Baltimore Colts owner Carroll Rosenbloom, Sonny hired Weeb Ewbank to be the Jets' general manager and coach. Ewbank didn't have pizazz—in fact, he exuded the opposite—but Weeb had an enviable resume and track record of success, having built and guided the Colts to back-to-back NFL championships in 1958 and 1959. Ewbank declared that he could replicate that success with the Jets and Sonny was ready to spend what it took.

After signing Snell in 1964 (he won AFL Rookie of the Year

honors), Werblin geared up to fill the team's biggest need, a star quarterback. Game-changing talent was critical to both Ewbank and Werblin, but for Sonny there was also the PR value of the signing, and a quarterback with personality would be icing on the cake. In 1964, Weeb Ewbank told Sonny and the press that he had his eye on a junior QB at the University of Alabama, Joe Namath. College players were not eligible to enter the pros until after their senior season, so Weeb had to make do with veteran QB Dick Wood and several rookie signal callers (Pete Liske, Mike Taliaferro, and others) for at least one more year.

Even after a 5-8-1 record in 1963, Werblin's marketing and salesmanship paid surprising dividends at the gate. After selling 3,800 season tickets at the Polo Grounds in the Jets' first year, the Jets sold 38,000 season tickets for year one (1964) at Shea Stadium in Flushing Meadows, Queens. Werblin was thinking big: he spoke about limiting season ticket sales to 50,000, so that fans who could only afford $4 to $6 could buy Jets' tickets. Total Jets home attendance in 1964 nearly tripled (298,972) versus the Polo Grounds (103,550) in 1963.

Werblin continued the New York Titans' custom of scheduling Saturday night games to avoid direct competition with Sunday New York Giants' games; he also hoped that some Giants season ticket holders might add a weekend pro football game at Shea to their itinerary. Werblin injected entertainment at Jets homes games, introducing cheerleaders, the Bob Cleveland Orchestra, and a remote-controlled, motorized Jets plane scooting on the ground behind the Jets' bench.

After doling out $140,000 in 1964 to college signees, Werblin told the press and the Jets' players that he was prepared to spend at least $600,000 to land top college players in 1965. That money would be newly available from the five-year, $36 million AFL television deal Werblin helped negotiate for the league with NBC through Sonny's friend, NBC president Bob Sarnoff. Each AFL team received $900,000 each year of the contract, which was to be used to sign star college talent. NBC even tried to help recruitment by telling players their games would be televised in color, a first for football.

Werblin focused on developing influence with New York sports media personalities to further interest in the Jets. He befriended Howard Cosell, executive producer of the Jets' broadcasts and host of the pregame show on WABC. Cosell also did a daily afternoon national sportscast and handled the sports on WABC-TV's six o'clock local news. Another local New York radio figure, Bill Mazer, host on WNBC of the country's first telephone-talk sports program, likewise became a Werblin target.

By late in 1964, Werblin had honed his quarterback choices down to Namath and University of Tulsa's Jerry Rhome, whom the Jets had drafted in the prior year's college draft. Rhome came to New York, but it didn't take long for the collegian and the owner to realize that there wasn't a fit. Rhome said he tried, but Werblin wasn't interested in talking football. Werblin inquired about Rhome's high school days and life off the field. "He was looking for flamboyance; that wasn't me," Jerry admitted. A story made the rounds for years that Rhome had blown it with Werblin by purportedly dashing during a rainstorm into a waiting limousine ahead of Mrs. Werblin. Rhome said he never met Mrs. Werblin, so he couldn't have offended her or Sonny. "And I wouldn't have done that if she had been there. I don't act that way," said the seventy-three-year-old Rhome in a deep Texas drawl when we spoke in 2016.

It was just as well. Ewbank had reservations about any "short" quarterback and Rhome was six feet tall. Weeb said he knew from experience that short quarterbacks could be effective, but not championship caliber. In a steal of a deal, the Jets traded the rights to Rhome to the Houston Oilers for the first pick in the AFL draft. Namath was claimed with that pick. The Oilers thought Rhome, a native Texan, would attract fans, but he ended up signing with the Dallas Cowboys.

Sonny loved stories about Joe's active life on the Tuscaloosa, Alabama, social scene. He also found Joe to be a total gentleman. "We went down to Birmingham to meet Joe and the minute Joe walked into the room and it lit up, I knew he was our man," remarked Sonny. In Los Angeles, Werblin saw the reaction when Namath walked into a restaurant. Sonny told people that only Namath and Clark Gable had the kind of star power that instantaneously turned heads when they entered a room. Sonny wanted Namath to be a Jet; now he had to sign him.

The Jets competed with the NFL's St. Louis Football Cardinals, who gagged at Namath's initial $200,000 contract request, plus a new car. Understanding the composite selling and media opportunity, Werblin dropped tidbits about the Namath negotiations to New York tabloid newspapers. Sonny's interest in Joe was so intense that he and Ewbank completely overlooked the fact that one of Namath's knees had been severely injured his senior year.

Werblin declared to Namath and his attorney, Mike Bite, that he didn't want to quibble over money. The Jets' initial $300,000 bid quickly escalated to $400,000 and, ultimately, to $427,000. Robert Werblin recalled his dad telling him, "You've got to speculate to accumulate"—in other words, take the risk and pay football players with outstanding potential what you think they are worth if they help you win.

As negotiations continued to unfold, something seemed off to Werblin, as well as to Joe and agent Bite. All came to believe that the Cardinals' notoriously stingy brother owners were bidding for Namath's signature on a contract, but they intended to trade him to the Giants. That soured Namath on the NFL, the Cardinals, and, prospectively, the Giants.

Namath had to complete his college career before signing. When his Alabama squad faced Texas in the 1964 Orange Bowl, Joe had a contract with Sonny Werblin's signature on it. Namath's signature was affixed to it the next morning. Though it might have been hyperbole and for PR's sake, Werblin noted afterward that he would have paid up to $800,000 for Namath. "I needed to build a franchise with somebody who could do more than just play," he explained.

Werblin's spending and gamesmanship didn't stop there. After Namath's contract, Heisman Trophy winner John Huarte of Notre

Dame received $200,000 to sign—"insurance" in case Joe's battered knees didn't stand up to the rigors of professional football. Sonny told *Sports Illustrated* he didn't care whether Namath or Huarte became his star QB, as long as one of them filled the bill. Jets QB Mike Taliaferro, who competed with Namath for the starting nod in 1965, said he heard Huarte's signing was a way to deny the New York Giants a hotshot QB to take attention away from Namath.

Sonny Werblin was described by those who did business with him as a gentleman of impeccable integrity, a master marketer and promoter, a father figure to some players, and a go-to guy when individual Jets had a problem. "Sonny used to fly back with the team on road trips, and he'd walk down the aisle and talk with us," Taliaferro related. "One time, we were flying back from Oakland and I was upset because my father had suffered a heart attack in Chicago. Sonny had the flight rerouted there. He handed me a few hundred dollars and told me to rejoin the team in New York after I saw my dad."

Unlike other teams during the signing war that erupted between the NFL and AFL, Werblin didn't hide college players to keep them away from the NFL. "I was in New York for the Heisman Trophy announcement," said Huarte, the 1965 winner. "We met at the Waldorf-Astoria. The meeting was nothing grandiose, but I came away so impressed with Mr. Werblin; a wonderful man, classy, dignified, very kind; his language was never careless or coarse. His wife was classy. I signed with the Jets; they offered me a better deal than the Philadelphia Eagles."

Most of Werblin's big-money signings did not work out. Huarte and 1965 third-round pick, Bob Schweickert, ($150,000) did not become big-time players; neither did 1966 draftees for the defense: Michigan linebacker Bill Yearby ($250,000) and Oklahoma linebacker Carl McAdams ($300,000). Both suffered incapacitating injuries before their Jets careers began. Those four contracts represented almost $1 million in bad football investments.

One collegiate star that Werblin really craved got away. Taliaferro, a former University of Illinois QB, arranged a meeting for Werblin with Taliaferro's Illini college buddy Dick Butkus. The ferocious line-man/linebacker—at the top of every pro team's collegiate draft list in 1965—had been drafted by Denver in the AFL and Chicago in the NFL.

Weeks before Joe Namath became a Jet, Mike escorted Butkus to the Jets' office in midtown Manhattan. Werblin and Butkus sat on opposite sides of a small table in Sonny's office, with Taliaferro seated alongside observing everything. Werblin would tell the press that he had offered Butkus $300,000. However, Taliaferro says Werblin slid a contract across the desk to Butkus that left blank the value of the Jets deal. Taliaferro says Sonny told Butkus to fill in the number—and the Jets would pay it. Only at that point did Butkus reveal he had given the Chicago Bears a verbal commitment and was uncomfortable going back on it. (Butkus was elected to the Pro Football Hall of Fame in 1979.) Years later, Butkus, who starred for poor or mediocre Bears teams during his sensational career, told Taliaferro he should have become a Jet.

There were other misses, too. That same year, the Chicago Bears and Kansas City Chiefs angled for the services of Kansas halfback Gale Sayers. The Chiefs were going to lose Sayers to the Bears over a few thousand dollars and the Jets were willing to blow away the halfback with a huge offer, but the Jets couldn't get Chiefs owner Lamar Hunt's permission to negotiate with Sayers. In 1977, Sayers, too, became a Pro Football Hall of Famer.

According to Jets public relations director Frank Ramos, in 1966 Syracuse all-America halfback Floyd Little was the apple of Werblin's eye. The Jets tried to convince Little to tell interested teams that he wanted to play for the Jets to dissuade other teams from selecting him, but Denver coach Lou Saban wouldn't back off. Little was selected by the Broncos and he, too, was voted into the Pro Football Hall of Fame in 2010.

Werblin spoke to all his players on occasion, but he had an open door for a handful of Jets. Matt Snell and Emerson Boozer both negotiated their second contract with Sonny, then met with Weeb Ewbank to sign their deals. In both cases, Ewbank tried to reduce the payout on their contracts, and Sonny had to tell the GM to honor his verbal understandings with Snell and Boozer.

But Joe Namath was the apple of Werblin's eye. Once signed, Werblin set out to make Namath a celebrity. Sonny told Joe to find a pad in Manhattan with Sonny's friend Joe Hirsch. Sonny began arranging for his quarterback to accompany starlets around the city. Sonny also helped Namath adapt to the city's dressing mores. Namath had the time of his life, and so did the New York tabloids that trailed him in and out of Manhattan's night spots. "He made sure I was getting along well. He told me to get to know New York, that it was the greatest city," shared Namath.

The Werblin-Namath nexus left Coach Ewbank feeling his authority was being undercut, and there were clear disagreements between the owner and head coach about fines for Joe's off-field behavior. From the start, Ewbank was lenient about Joe's behavioral indiscretions; Werblin gave Namath even more room. Joe was a star, he explained, and deserved to be treated differently.

In 1967, the Jets were in the black for the first time. Early in 1968, Sonny reupped with Namath on Joe's second Jets contract, a reported $500,000 package. Executed without the knowledge or consent of his four partners, within days it became a point of contention for them. Their wives were also unhappy that Werblin didn't treat their husbands as his equal in the Jets' public gatherings at Shea Stadium and Manhattan press conferences. Further, Namath's off-field celebrity was rubbing them the wrong way; they questioned if his Broadway Joe persona was negatively affecting his progress as a player.

They were also perturbed that Werblin's penchant for six-figure contracts—many of which had not borne good results—had depressed profitability. In spite of not being involved since 1963 in operation of the Jets, the four formerly "silent" partners felt they deserved the public's attention and demanded that the Jets be run and decisions be made by the group.

It was decided that one side or the other would sell. Werblin offered to buy out the other four. A price was agreed upon, but Werblin wanted to pay it out over time, and Hess, Martin, Iselin, and Lillis insisted on a lump-sum payment. Sonny could not get the money without becoming cash poor, so he sold his 23 percent share of the club. On May 21, 1968, Donald Lillis was named the Jets' team president, but he died that summer. On August 6, Phil Iselin assumed the title. According to son Tom, Sonny never again spoke to his former partners.

No longer involved with the team in 1968, Werblin watched the Jets plow their way to the Super Bowl from his box at Shea. Regarding regrets he had about selling the Jets, in December of the Super Bowl season, he commented, "At least I had the fun and the heartache of helping build the Jets to what they are now."

At his Florida home not far from the Orange Bowl, where Super Bowl III was played, he hosted Jets players the evening before the game and attended the contest, then joyfully celebrated with the players in the postgame locker room. He inferred to *New York Daily News* sports columnist Dick Young before Super Bowl III that, with the Jets an 18-point underdog, he had made a sizable bet on his former team.

Werblin left another mark on New York–area sports by guiding the construction of the Meadowlands Sports Complex and Giants Stadium (where Leon Hess moved the Jets after the 1983 season) and as president of Madison Square Garden from 1977 to 1984. He died on November 21, 1991, at age eighty-one. Some have urged his election to the Pro Football Hall of Fame on the basis of his impact on the Jets and pro football during his abbreviated six-year tenure with the Jets.

WILBUR "WEEB" EWBANK

GENERAL MANAGER AND COACH

*He built the Super Bowl Jets from scratch.
Weeb's confidential personnel and
statistical player evaluations shed light on
how he put the Jets together.*

S econd only to Joe Namath, general manager and head coach
Wilbur Charles "Weeb" Ewbank earned the greatest acclaim
of any member of the Super Bowl III New York Jets. He entered
the 1968 season on the hot seat for failing to deliver on his five-year
plan to win a championship with the Jets. Given a reprieve by frus-
trated Jets management (after trying to replace Weeb with Vince
Lombardi in May 1968), Ewbank finished that sixth year at the top
of the pro football mountain.

It was the cap on a storied pro football coaching career. When
he negotiated away the two remaining years on his Baltimore Colts
coaching contract to come to New York in 1963, he became the first
coach in three leading postwar professional football leagues. (He had
been an assistant with the AAFC's Cleveland Browns beginning in
1949.) Ewbank's two-team, twenty-year, professional head-coaching
career won-lost record was a pedestrian 130-129-7. Still, any judg-
ment about Weeb based solely on that is misleading. He became the

only coach ever to win championships in two different professional leagues with two different teams.

Oddly, although he accepted Sonny Werblin's laissez-faire attitude when it came to Namath's behavior, the principal owner did not think that Weeb was enough of a disciplinarian with the rest of the team. Some Jets players (mostly on defense) believed Namath should be brought under control; however, Weeb didn't believe in fining his players. "It's very difficult to treat a player like a child off the field and then expect him to go out on the field and do a man's job," he said in 1973. The 5'7", 180-pound Ewbank was a comparatively quiet sideline presence, who once said, "I'm a teacher, not a screamer." Weeb believed in giving players responsibility for policing their own behavior.

Many former all-Americans joined the Jets from powerhouse collegiate football programs, leading to comparisons by young Jets of Weeb with their sometimes venerated college coaches. For instance, Bob Schweickert, from Virginia Tech, couldn't understand how so many Jets players were having personal conversations when Ewbank spoke. "There were a lot of players who didn't like some of Weeb's mannerisms," described Bob Talamini, a veteran who only played the Super Bowl season in New York. "Weeb just kept his head down and kept on moving. He was a good coach, very smart."

Weeb's three world championships (two in Baltimore, one with the Jets) resulted from a meticulous roster-building process. With both franchises, he and his staff trained, taught, and coached up young talent into outstanding professionals. In Baltimore in the 1950s, a general manager acquired players for Ewbank; a decade later, he was his own GM. With the Jets, he took on the pressure of working with a low talent base, incorporated his system, scouted, selected, signed, and coached the players.

Ewbank was faced with delicate situations in Baltimore and New York. Both the Colts and Jets had been "reintroduced" in their respective markets and needed to build a fan base. The Colts franchise had been acquired from Dallas ownership and moved to Baltimore in 1953; the Jets' owners acquired the moribund Titans franchise out of bankruptcy court in 1963. That made the promise in his five-year plan very important in the eyes of local fans.

Colts owner Carroll Rosenbloom offered Ewbank an amazing compliment a decade after unceremoniously firing him as his coach. "Weeb Ewbank is the one man in football who's gotten the least credit of all the coaches," he said. "They talk about [Vince] Lombardi, [Paul] Brown, [Don] Shula. . . . Weeb is as fine as any of them. . . . History will evaluate Weeb as a man who in his 20 years as head coach did more with less material than any coach in the NFL." Ewbank viewed his Jets achievement as bigger than in Baltimore, telling reporters after Super Bowl III that he had started with much less to work with in New York than with the Colts. Rosenbloom told Weeb after Ewbank retired in New York that he should never have fired him.

Coaches generally agree that star players deserve and receive some degree of special treatment. Weeb increasingly bestowed that on Namath. Cornerback John Dockery recalled a Jets practice in the post–Super Bowl time frame where nothing was going right for Joe, pass after pass missing its target by a wide margin. When Joe's frustration reached its peak, Namath took off his helmet and announced he was calling it a day. Dockery, taking it all in with the rest of the squad, wondered what Weeb's response would be. Ewbank told everyone the day's practice was over.

Ewbank deserves full credit for developing Namath into an All-Pro QB, but he also merits overlooked acclaim for Joe's signing. As he was choosing between the NFL St. Louis Cardinals and the Jets, Namath's most trusted collegiate advisor, Alabama coach Bear Bryant, put in a strong plug with Joe for Ewbank. Namath shared, "Weeb had impressed the hell out of him . . . his coaching records had been outstanding and . . . he was in every possible way a good football man."

The most vital and underestimated aspect of Weeb's coaching responsibilities came after new players were secured. Ewbank, director of player personnel George Sauer Sr., two offensive coaches, and two defensive coaches toiled for hours, weeks, months—and longer—teaching and training gifted amateur football players how to become steady professionals, some of whom performed at or near the top of their position.

He watched his players in practice and game situations; formulated impressions of their strengths, flaws, and progress; and dictated all that to his assistant. Some of Weeb's most private thoughts about Jets players are available for the first time thanks to the generosity of Jay Pomerantz, a devoted Jets fan and Super Bowl Jets memorabilia collector. Pomerantz acquired the Weeb Ewbank estate and shared all of Ewbank's playbooks, notations, written observations, critiques, and player grades for this book.

It is unclear why Weeb formulated and dictated evaluations for every Jets player in the franchise's first few years. However, New England Patriots coach Bill Belichick put his player observations in writing, too, when he became head coach for the first time with the Cleveland Browns in 1995. In a 2012 NFL Network film, Belichick explained that writing down and sharing evaluations with his assistants, as Weeb had done with the Jets, was critical. Belichick said the printed player logs would emphasize what was most important about each player. Belichick said, "Before we get to all the Xs and Os, we've got to go through each player, (his) strengths, weaknesses, overall physical abilities, what his history is, speed, all that bleep."

A sampling of Weeb's profiles, written after the 1964 season—his second in New York—provide developmental insights about key offensive and defensive members of the Super Bowl team.

Weeb wrote this about the Jets' top defensive and offensive linemen:

GERRY PHILBIN / Left End / 24 / 6'2" / 242

Has the most potential of our defensive ends, and can become an all-pro with time and work, which he is more than willing to spend to reach this goal. He was grading very high until his unfortunate injury. He learns fast, he is very quick and fast. There are times we think of him as a middle guard.

WINSTON HILL / Tackle / 23 / 6'4" / 275

Played in every game, including two as a center. (843 plays) Overall grade was 81%. His grade on runs was 80% and on passes 83%. He made tremendous improvement in his play over 1963 and should develop into one of the best offensive tackles in the League. He was on the kickoff return, punt and place kick teams. He needs to work on perfecting his stance and on exploding with the starting center. He still has a tendency to "open up" when setting for pass protection. Due to inexperience, he will occasionally get excited and lose his poise temporarily. Has potential—was placed on "All-Star" team when Saban invited a Jet lineman. This was his "rookie year" and he should benefit from the experience of playing regularly.

Here's what Weeb penned about his power running back, Matt Snell, comparing the fullback's 1965 performance with his rookie year:

MATT SNELL / FB / 6'2" / 219 / 24 / **(92%)**

Had the impression several times throughout the season that Matt was not performing as well as his previous rookie season. However, after thorough grading and evaluation, it could be summarized that he did perform as well but did not have as many #4's and #5's. He graded out high again—meaning he got the job done—but without as many outstanding individual plays as 1964. I further felt that his concentration in receiving was not as sharp and this is confirmed by the sum of 3 more dropped balls. Matt is still the complete football player with the necessary skills to be considered one of the greats in Professional Football.

Am hopeful that his lack of as many individual big plays was

due to leg and rib injuries obtained in training camp and through-
out the season. Was not timed in 1964 because of pulled muscle
from All-Star game and pleased us all with his 4.6 at 220 lbs. in
1965. A power runner with deceptive speed and maintains bal-
ance for that unusual "break." When well, has been excellent 1 on
1 downfield. As good a blocker for the plunge play as I have seen—
quick and crisp. Better than very good pass protector. Receiving
needs more concentration. Is not a fumbler (had 4) but did so
twice in that 100° day at Houston. There were some indications
for concern of attitude. But it appears that these were spasmodic
and apparently settled and over. Should have a long, successful
and productive future with the Jets.

The bolded percentage in parenthesis on the top line of Snell's
evaluation indicates the Jets' coaching staff's grade for Matt. The
comment on Hill includes his 1964 grade. Player grades were a Ewbank innovation. The effectiveness of each player on each play was
tracked, recorded, and compiled for each game and over the full season. Beginning in 1966, the annual typewritten reviews seem to have
ended, but the analytic evaluations of the players' effectiveness continued. Combined, the written notations and statistical data detail
Jets who became stars or essential contributors in the Jets' Super
Bowl season.

Jets players knew about the grading system but had no idea
about the dictated evaluations or how their grade compared with
their peers. They remembered being graded, but when we showed
a handful of them their individual grades forty-eight years after the
fact, they struggled to make sense of them. (A sample, Dave Herman's 1968 analysis, is shown on page 53.)

Ewbank designed his player analysis system during his coaching stint from 1947 to 1948 at Washington University in St. Louis,
then incorporated it in Baltimore and later with the Jets. It's hard
to know for certain how unique it was in pro football circles, though

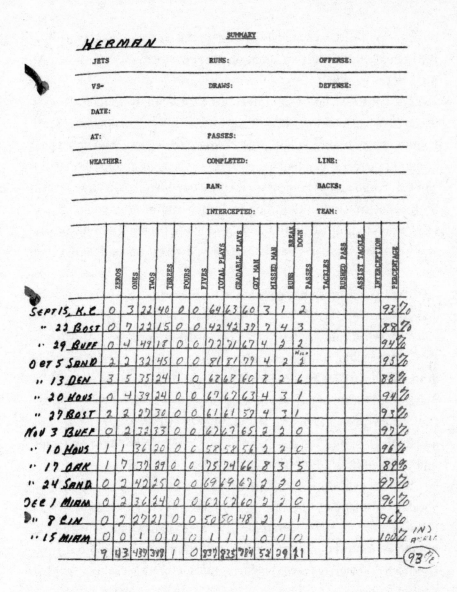

HERMAN   SUMMARY

JETS   RUNS: OFFENSE:

VS-   DRAWS: DEFENSE:

DATE:

AT: PASSES:

WEATHER: COMPLETED: LINE:

                  RAN: BACKS:

                  INTERCEPTED: TEAM:

	ZEROS	ONES	TWOS	THREES	FOURS	FIVES	TOTAL PLAYS	GRADABLE PLAYS	GOT MAN	MISSED MAN	BREAK DOWN	RUNS	PASSES	TACKLES	RUSHED PASS	ASSIST TACKLE	INTERCEPTION	PERCENTAGE
Sept 15, K.C	0	3	22	40	0	0	64	63	60	3	1	2						93%
" 22 Bost	0	7	22	15	0	0	42	42	37	7	4	3						88%
" 29 Buff	0	4	49	18	0	0	72	71	67	4	2	2						94%
Oct 5 Sand	2	2	32	45	0	0	81	81	77	4	2	1 hold						95%
" 13 Den	3	5	35	24	1	0	68	68	60	8	2	6						88%
" 20 Hous	0	4	39	24	0	0	67	67	63	4	3	1						94%
" 27 Bost	2	2	27	30	0	0	61	61	57	4	3	1						93%
Nov 3 Buff	0	2	32	33	0	0	67	67	65	2	2	0						97%
" 10 Hous	1	1	36	20	0	0	58	58	56	2	2	0						96%
" 17 Oak	1	7	37	29	0	0	75	74	66	8	3	5						89%
" 24 Sand	0	2	42	25	0	0	69	69	67	2	2	0						92%
Dec 1 Miam	0	2	36	24	0	0	62	62	60	2	2	0						96%
" 8 Cin	0	2	27	21	0	0	50	50	48	2	1	1						96%
" 15 Miam	0	0	1	0	0	0	1	1	1	0	0	0						100% (IN)
	9	43	437	348	1	0	837	835	784	53	29	22						93%

it was revealed by the *New York Times'* Robert Lipsyte in April 1963 as he reported Weeb's hiring. "When Ewbank was coach of the Baltimore Colts . . . the owner of the club called him 'my crew-cut I.B.M. machine,'" wrote Lipsyte. "After each day's workout, Ewbank would write a report and file it in the basement of his four-bedroom colonial house. . . . He and his assistants would make a play-by-play, position-by-position analysis of every preseason and league game. Individual players were graded on their performance as shown in films of the games."

The impressiveness of undertaking these analyses in the 1960s is elevated by the reality that Weeb and his four-man coaching staff had no computers or calculators. Two offensive and two defensive assistant coaches watched every Jets offensive or defensive play on game film and rated their players' effectiveness on a 0-to-5 scale. "It took a morning out of the week to do the grading. You had to grade each game to know how the guys were doing," commented Charlie Winner, one of Ewbank's assistants in Baltimore. Special teams play was not rated.

The player grading sheets make little sense without input from someone who did them. Winner did that for us. For instance, on Dave Herman's grading during the 1968 season-opening win at Kansas City, he earned a 93 percent effectiveness number from 63 (of 64) gradable plays. Herman received a "0" rating on 0 plays, a "1" for 3 plays, a "2" for 22 plays, a "3" for 40 plays, and zero "4" or "5s." (Author's note: I recognize that the number of evaluated plays does not add up to 63 or 64.) Dave is shown to have "Got [His] Man" 60 times and "Missed [His] Man" 3 times.

Winner explained Weeb's grading system: "A '0' meant you blew your assignment on the play. On offense, a '1' was a very average block, a '2' was a pretty good block, a '3' was an outstanding block, a '4' was an even better block for a lineman (or breaking multiple tackles if you were a running back). A '5' was a superlative, once-in-a-season play.

"On defense, a '0' also meant a blown assignment," detailed Winner. "A '1' was a half-assed job, a '2' meant you did your job well enough that the defense didn't break down because of you. A '3' was a good, solid job on your assignment. A '4' was a sack or fumble you caused and a '5' would be an outstanding outcome—you caused a sack or a fumble, *and* you recovered the football."

Ewbank became convinced that a championship-level team must have great talent and leadership in its QB after being around Cleveland Browns quarterback Otto Graham, who won seven championship games with the Browns in ten tries between 1946 and 1955. John Unitas fulfilled that quarterback role for Weeb in Baltimore from 1956 to 1962. Demonstrating some of Ewbank's genius, Weeb saw no film of Unitas in action before the Colts signed him, but somehow detected high-quality arm action from still photos. Ewbank brought in Otto Graham to help tutor Unitas. Graham was a color commentator on Jets radio broadcasts when Namath signed, though it is not believed that they worked together. After Graham left the Jets' broadcast team, he became a vocal critic of Namath.

Ewbank was one of the last pro football head coaches who understood and could coach any position. Weeb's true calling was offense, but Paul Brown in Cleveland in 1949 assigned Ewbank the defensive line. "He knew I'd have to work very hard at this job and bring a fresh approach," Ewbank said years later. With the Jets, Weeb worked primarily with the quarterbacks, but also on all phases of the kicking game.

Weeb had worked with Cleveland Browns Hall of Fame kicker Lou Groza, even designing Groza's kicking tee (which Ewbank's daughter still has). Ewbank's status as a kicking savant was shown twice with the Jets. Placekicker Jim Turner had significant financial differences with general manager Ewbank about his compensation, but to this day Turner has endless praise for Ewbank's tutoring of kicking mechanics. For a while, Ewbank was uncomfortable coaching soccer-style kickers (who made their debut in pro football in 1964) because of their unique technique. He figured them out, too. The field goal percentage of sidewinder Bobby Howfield, acquired from Denver in exchange for Turner, improved under Ewbank from an average of 50 percent in his three years with the Broncos to more than 73 percent from 1972 to 1974 in New York.

The offensive line received his closest attention in the early

Namath years. To maximize Joe's pass protection, Ewbank resurrected blocking schemes from his days as a Cleveland Browns assistant; improvement also came from blocking tactics that offensive line coach Chuck Knox brought with him from the University of Kentucky. (Jets linemen extended their arms in parallel with defenders' bodies and kept their hands open.) A grade of 90 percent for an offensive lineman was excellent, and how well the O-line blocked is shown below.

Jets 1967 Offensive Line Blocking Grades

LINEMAN	RUN BLOCKING	PASS BLOCKING	OVERALL
John Schmitt	86.3%	95.2%	91.5%
Dave Herman	88.6%	94.9%	92.4%
Winston Hill	90.4%	95.5%	93.5%
Sherman Plunkett	82.0%	94.0%	89.1%
Randy Rasmussen	83.1%	88.7%	86.5%

Notice the across-the-board comparatively better pass blocking than run blocking in these statistics.

Namath's wobbly knees made him what seemed the ultimate QB target for defenses, and a stationary one at that. When it came to keeping pass rushers off Namath, Ewbank was the master, going so far as to provide personal instruction. "Weeb taught me all the basics," said the team's best offensive lineman, Winston Hill. "During the course of a game, I always remember two things he taught me," Hill recalled. "One was balance—keeping your knees bent and finding your center of gravity, finding a comfortable position so your legs aren't bent to extremes. And the other was something I'd never heard before or since. Weeb used to say, 'When you're pass-blocking, always be in a position where you can let the tips of your fingers touch the ground.'"

Ewbank's private records show that sacks of Jets quarterbacks were slashed from 34 in 1963 to 27 in 1964 to 17 in Namath's rookie year. The near-halving of the 1963 number by 1965 came from a combination of an improved offensive line, upgraded running-back blocking from Snell, Bill Mathis, and Mark Smolinski—and, beginning in 1965, Namath's rapid-fire setup and pass release.

Namath's protection got even better. The NFL did not officially record sacks until 1969, but estimates show Joe Namath went down only 9 times in 1967 (none in the first six games, before injuries wiped out Joe's running game), 11 times in 1968, and 13 times the year after the Super Bowl. Unofficially, according to FootballPerspective.com, Namath was sacked a paltry 3.8 percent of the time he dropped back to throw between 1965 and 1974—the lowest percentage among 17 high-profile QBs during that decade and 12 percent better than the quarterback with the next-lowest sack frequency. Joe also registered 15.1 yards per completion in that comparison—the highest average among the 17 and 15.5 percent better than the group as a whole.

Weeb didn't just ensure Namath's safety on the field; he was engrossed in teaching Joe how to maximize his effectiveness. A core element in the Jets' Super Bowl III success was Weeb's checkoff system, which he created in Baltimore and was a clear break with Paul Brown's system in Cleveland. Brown, an acknowledged football genius, called all offensive plays himself for the Browns and shuttled offensive guards in and out on each play to dictate the next pass or run. Not even the great Otto Graham was permitted to change the play call. With the Jets, Namath was trained and encouraged to do so.

In Weeb's offense, the quarterback called his own plays based on film study, the week's game plan, and the QB's reading of the defense at the line of scrimmage. The Ewbank checkoff system trained the QB to come to the line (with or without a play called in the huddle) to analyze the defense, reach a conclusion about what the defense was geared to do, and select a play the defense was vulnerable to. What made Ewbank's "Check with Me" system all the more novel was that all the other offensive players took their cue from Namath's play call decision. They read the defense, too, and made adjustments.

Namath's distinct "Check with Me" utilization was instrumental in the Super Bowl, described in this book's offensive line chapter by center John Schmitt.

Though few of Weeb's choices for assistant coaches had professional coaching experience and none were "name" recruits, Weeb won praise for the quality of those choices throughout the 1960s. He found coaching diamonds in the rough: unofficial offensive coordinator Clive Rush (from University of Toledo), offensive line Coach Knox, defensive coach Walt Michaels (a Cleveland Browns all-star linebacker and a linebacker coach for one year with the Oakland Raiders), and defensive line Coach Buddy Ryan (Vanderbilt and the University of Buffalo). All went on to become NFL head coaches.

According to his daughter, Nancy (who married Weeb's assistant coach in Baltimore, Charlie Winner), her dad's whole life was football. She helped him break down film in their basement and noted, "We talked football all the time because that's all he wanted to talk about. Dad was the same way with me as with the players—if I didn't write legibly I had to do it over and over again until he thought it was legible."

After coaching in Baltimore, Weeb insisted on controlling his situation and became the Jets' general manager as well as head coach. His tightness in salary negotiations fit right in with the AFL's focus on extreme economic prudence; however, it angered most Jets. Weeb was not generous in paying his players, but player treatment was identical even on teams with well-heeled owners (that is, Buffalo's Ralph Wilson, Kansas City's Lamar Hunt, and Houston oilman Bud Adams).

In the 1960s, player pay was not much of a media issue and players did not discuss their paychecks with their buddies. Writers and fans didn't care that perennial AFL all-stars like Larry Grantham or Don Maynard were making $20,000. When sportswriters wrote about player salaries, it concerned how much college seniors were reaping from the NFL-AFL bidding war.

Jets players had good reasons to dislike their GM. The *New York Post*'s Paul Zimmerman noted that although they did not know it, 30 of the 40 players on the active roster for most of the 1966 season made less than the league average at their position. Namath's best-paid bodyguard, right tackle Sherman Plunkett, made all of $15,000. It didn't change until after Super Bowl III, and even then attaining a substantial boost in salary was a grind.

Many Jets players were at the top of their game during that 1968 season, with eleven AFL all-stars and numerous second- and third-team all-stars dotting the roster. Many Jets' contracts expired after the Super Bowl. Those who refused to report to camp the next season until they had a new contract got a markedly better deal than anyone who accepted an offer to negotiate face-to-face with Weeb.

Jets players laughingly recount Don Maynard's salary negotiations in Weeb's office during the team's early years. Seated on opposite sides of a desk, GM Ewbank and Don slid a small piece of white paper—blank side facing up—back and forth across the table, with a suggested price scribbled by Weeb or the star wide receiver on the bottom side of the paper. They each pushed the paper from their side to the opposite side of the table until the two settled on a price. Maynard verbally sparred with Weeb during the process, commenting "the janitor makes that much." Don shared, "When we were finished, Weeb stood up, shook my hand, and said, 'It's great to have you with us. Please don't tell anybody what you're making.' I told him, 'Don't worry, Weeb, I won't. I'm just as embarrassed as you are.'"

Some players could separate how they felt about general manager Ewbank from coach Weeb, while others didn't find it that simple because of how miserly they felt Ewbank was in his treatment of them. Unknown to the players, Ewbank had a distinct information advantage.

Larry Grantham and other Jets recall that Weeb told them that he knew the salaries of every AFL player, on the face of it an outlandish claim. Yet his private papers show that in 1967 he did, in fact, know what every AFL player was being paid by San Diego, Miami, Houston, and Kansas City. So, he knew what the average and best player at every position was earning.

Ewbank's stinginess with his players caused him to be blamed by many on the team for its failure to repeat as Super Bowl champions in 1969–70. The players repeatedly point to offensive guard Bob Talamini, a six-time AFL all-star selection at left guard, as their prime example of how Weeb's cheapness had cost them on the field. In 1968–69, Talamini's professionalism stabilized the offensive line, provided veteran leadership and an AFL championship pedigree, and added depth and flexibility to the unit. After Super Bowl III, Talamini, a devoted family man, quietly retired to move on to his postfootball career. He sent a formal retirement letter to Ewbank that the newspapers picked up.

Still, Talamini's bon voyage morphed into an inaccurate belief by teammates that Weeb had been too chintzy to bring him back, though Talamini then and today never indicated a return to the Jets was possible. Weeb did try to talk other Jets from hanging up their cleats (for example, Bill Mathis did come back, although Mark Smolinski stuck with his retirement decision). The low-ball salaries were so top of mind with several Jets that they firmly believed that Weeb's frugality had to be traceable to a clause in his contract that rewarded him for restraining salaries. However, Weeb's contracts from his estate showed no such stated bonus arrangements.

Ewbank's children shed some light on Weeb's frugality with player contracts. His family didn't have much money growing up, and he was a young adult during the Great Depression. Youngest daughter Jan Hudson, seventy-eight years of age when we spoke in 2016, observed, "My dad really loved the guys. He just liked coaching. [Being general manager] just wasn't his thing. I just know he wasn't as comfortable [doing that]." Jan described her father as a man who carefully watched what he spent on utilities in his home. "He turned off the lights at home to save electricity," she explained.

While players saw Ewbank as holding the line on what they were worth, Weeb was handsomely rewarded by Jets management. His three-year Jets contract in 1963 paid him $50,000 per year (superseding the annual $30,000 for two years remaining on his Colts agreement) and he had the right to purchase Jets stock. In 1965, Sonny Werblin reupped with Ewbank for three more years (through 1968). Jets ownership bought back Weeb's ownership rights when Werblin sold his shares in early 1968. A three-year contract after Super Bowl III rewarded him $60,000, $65,000, and $70,000, respectively, for 1969–71. A final two-year deal in 1972 paid him $75,000 a year. According to DollarTimes.com, the 1963 contract was worth $397,000 in 2016 dollars and the final deal was worth $440,500 in 2016 compensation.

Money aside, Weeb's players respected him and his coaching. Offensive lineman Dave Herman played for Weeb in ten (1964–73) of Ewbank's eleven years as Jets coach. "Weeb Ewbank was like my father, actually my grandfather; a good guy, a head coach, and also a personal advisor," Herman said. The voice of center John Schmitt, a Jets fixture into the 1970s, cracked as he related his post–Super Bowl salary negotiation with GM Ewbank. Weeb and John met in the Jets' Manhattan offices and agreed on a $100,000, three-year deal, but they ran out of time to finalize the contract that afternoon. "Here is a blank contract. Sign it and I'll fill it out and send it to you," Weeb told Schmitt. "I thought he had to be kidding, but I signed it," Schmitt said, "and in my first paycheck a few months later he was paying me $1,500 more than we had settled on. It [being GM] was hard for Weeb, but I loved the guy."

In 1967, winning a championship seemed not that far off and Weeb's ability to round out the Jets roster for a championship run was on the clock. The condition of Joe Namath's knees was paramount in his plans. After Joe's second knee operation in late 1966 to remove torn cartilage, repair a torn cruciate ligament, and transfer a tendon to stabilize his right knee, the Jets asked a specialist to update the prognosis on his football longevity. The diagnosis sent to Werblin and Ewbank stated that the latest operation had improved Joe's condition, but for how long was anyone's guess. With complications from arthritis possibly setting in, the Jets would have Joe at the top of his game for possibly three years. Dr. James Nicholas, the team surgeon, said he had no long-term optimism and cautioned the Jets to keep that in mind in their plans for the future.

There's no written evidence that Ewbank decided it was now or never to grab a championship. However, he made maneuvers that point to such a decision. The next season, even as Namath threw for pro-football-record yardage, he had been pulled off of muddy fields to avoid unnecessary risks. When 1967 had concluded, with one of the three projected years of a top-flight Namath potentially used up and the Jets having finished one-half game out of first place, Weeb may well have decided to go for it all in 1968. He sure acted like it, trading for Babe Parilli, the first veteran backup for Namath, and strengthening his quarterbacks' protection by dealing for all-star guard Bob Talamini. Never before had Ewbank acquired two such accomplished veterans, and it paid off in a Super Bowl–winning season.

It can be difficult to judge the actual coaching of a head man, but Mark Smolinski, who played for Ewbank for two years in Baltimore and six with the Jets, made the case for Weeb's strategic and tactical excellence. "He was most able to prepare an excellent game plan," said Smo. "How he did this, I am not sure. However, I think a lot of it was a natural ability. He could see a team, possibly a player, and evaluate [his] strength & weakness and mold it into a game plan. When people say 'the game slows down to the good ones' or 'they see the whole field,' I believe they are talking about guys like Weeb."

Joe Namath, the most important and challenging player in Weeb's Jets tenure, said every coach he played for after Ewbank added to his sense of how great a coach Weeb had been.

Ewbank was inducted into the Pro Football Hall of Fame in 1978. He died November 17, 1998, at the age of ninety-one.

JOE NAMATH

QUARTERBACK #12

6'2" / 200 LB.

*More than a superstar player and celebrity,
he brought respectability to the AFL,
became a cultural icon, and forced
a merger.*

There are historical reasons why fifty years after Joe Namath led the New York Jets to a Super Bowl III victory, he remains someone the National Football League rolls out with relish whenever it can. Namath was more than a superstar quarterback; he was a compelling sports figure, celebrity, cultural icon, and pro football's single most exciting and important figure of the 1960s, even though he played only for five of those years (1965 to 1969).

Although many NFL owners and some NFL fans thought the Jets' Super Bowl III victory had been an unrepeatable 100–1 shot, Namath won universal pro football respect that day. Joe was the youngest quarterback (25) to win a Super Bowl until Tom Brady guided New England 33 years later to victory in Super Bowl XXXVI. ESPN's Jeremy Schaap dubbed Namath "arguably the single most important player in the history of pro football," in the 2015 NFL Network special *The Merger*.

Some who scouted Namath at Alabama thought he was the greatest quarterback prospect ever to enter pro football. Weeb Ewbank became enthralled with Joe his junior year after viewing his superb technique and majestic football-throwing ability. He also had scary-good running ability until a knee injury his senior year wiped out his mobility and made it Namath's major weakness.

The Jets had to deal to secure Namath's draft rights, but Joe wanted the bright lights of the big city. The Houston Oilers had the first pick in the 1964 AFL draft (courtesy of the Denver Broncos, who traded their first-round pick to Houston in exchange for a two-year lease of the services of QB Jacky Lee). NFL Hall of Famer and Oilers head coach Sammy Baugh ardently wanted Joe, and money was no object to Houston owner Bud Adams, but Joe told Adams he wasn't interested in Houston.

Adams explained, "When I called [Namath], he said, 'I'm a New York man. I want to play in New York. Where the lights are big and fast and everything, or Chicago or Los Angeles.' So, I made a trade when I saw I wasn't going to do anything good with him. . . . I made the right decision because it gave us [the American Football League] the first victory over the NFL in Super Bowl III."

Joe's $427,000, three-year contract with the Jets was a block-buster in 1965—the talk of the sports world all year long. (In comparison, the Detroit Lions awarded veteran QB Matthew Stafford a record five-year, $135 million deal in 2017 that was yesterday's news a week later.) That Namath, a potentially great QB, was heading to the upstart league was a blow to NFL prestige. Much worse for the NFL was the scope of the deal because it eviscerated the NFL owners' limiting pay structure.

There was a potentially huge downside for the Jets. After Namath signed his Jets contract, team orthopedic surgeon Dr. James Nicholas did the team's first examination of Namath's severely injured knee in the bathroom at the site of the press conference, Toots Shor's restaurant. Dr. Nicholas asked Joe to roll up his pants leg, felt around Joe's knee, and told Werblin and Ewbank they might want to get another quarterback.

Joe went under the knife to repair his knee three days after signing his contract. "I thought that even with an operation, he might not ever be able to play," Nicholas remarked. Joe's multiple knee surgeries in succeeding years were unusually complicated. After that first one in 1965, Dr. Nicholas thrilled Joe by telling him that he could play for four years; he fooled everyone by lasting thirteen.

Namath deferred much of the money in his record agreement; his $25,000 annual salary was only $10,000 more than Illinois quarterback Mike Taliaferro's with the Jets one year before. Critics questioned the Jets' pay-whatever-it-took philosophy to land Namath. At first, Jets players did, too. However, once Joe walked onto the practice field, his arm strength and accuracy, plus his personal magnetism and sex appeal, erased any doubt about the shrewdness of Sonny Werblin's investment.

From his very first professional appearance—a preseason tilt against the AFL champion Buffalo Bills—he was treated with extraordinary reverence. Joe engineered a Jets drive to get into field goal range as the first half was running down. He was dumped hard by the Bills defense as the clock wound down to zero, and Bills head coach Lou Saban rushed onto the field, gesturing to Namath. Everyone assumed that Saban was checking Joe's condition. Not so.

As Namath lay on his back, Saban saluted Namath's effort during the half's last thirty seconds. "Kid, that was a brilliant display of both poise and your intelligence," he told the rookie. "The only two quarterbacks that ever did what you just did are in the Pro Football Hall of Fame, my former teammate, Otto Graham, and the Rams' Bob Waterfield.

"Kid, keep listening to Weeb," Saban continued. "I have followed him since the day he got Unitas. Just keep your mouth shut, study tape and listen. . . . Thanks from all the coaches and players who gambled with the AFL for signing with Sonny Werblin and the Jets. You will make more money for all of us who took the risk." Then the Buffalo coach extended his hand to help Namath get to his feet.

Weeb refused to accede to the demands of fans and Sonny Werblin that Joe be rushed into the starting lineup. He relieved Taliaferro in the season's second game, then started in week three. At year's end, Joe became the second consecutive Jet to win AFL Rookie of the Year (after Matt Snell in 1964).

After the 1965 season, Ewbank entered an evaluation of his prized QB into his personnel records. Joe received a 78 percent rating for his physical and mental execution at quarterback, one of the most complex positions on a football field. Dictated Ewbank:

Performed exceptionally well for a rookie at the obvious most difficult position. Has every physical skill necessary to develop into one of the best, if not the very best, in Professional QB history. His development was slightly above normal at the beginning. He experienced the usual first year problems such as defensive recognition, coverage reading, "forcing" a play and coming to secondary and third choices. Also at this early period his accuracy was ineffective and at times poor.

There were probably a series of factors other than some PP's that could have contributed to this: 1) the above mentioned first year problems, 2) trying too hard, 3) the tremendous amount of pressure and expectancy from the public (which he handled perfectly), 4) lack of timing between him and our receivers (which sometimes takes years to develop), 5) confidence and understanding in the play called, the defense and the receiver, 6) confidence in his now proven successful knee operation. This could have affected his setting, delivery and follow through. (We don't actually know what was going through his mind about this.)

Throughout this period Joe's attitude, dedication study and learning could not have been better . . . Joe is very coachable and has been accepted and respected by his teammates. Needs to improve in every area and undoubtedly will.

Namath developed into the typical AFL gunslinger quarterback—but he also took more risks in his throws than his peers. It was a sign of supreme self-assurance in his arm, linked with his inexperience and immaturity in recognizing potential interceptions.

Namath bent other passing rules. For example, for every professional quarterback, 10-yard out-patterns (throws to the sideline) to receivers were the standard. Buffalo Bills defensive back Booker Edgerson remarked that Namath drew gasps from defenders by lengthening those patterns to 20 to 25 yards. Throwing from deep in the pocket to the sidelines, normally simple "down-and-outs" became 40- to 45-yard heaves with impeccable accuracy and timing.

Mike Taliaferro explained the logic of Namath's preference for long throws. "[Cornerbacks] played bump-and-run [from the line of scrimmage and into the secondary]. In the AFL, you wouldn't dare send a receiver or back across the middle because they'd get cold cocked by linebackers—and it was legal. Longer pass patterns were actually safer," Taliaferro said.

From the start of his pro career, Namath's presence captivated sports fans, especially the counterculture group that would later be dubbed "baby boomers." The paparazzi documented Joe's activities to the public at large and football's newest fans, women. As curiosity about Namath pumped up viewership and ratings and watching Namath was becoming must-see TV, NBC's telecasts began to balloon the enormity of the NFL's predicament. Even ten years later, when the World Football League offered Joe $4 million to bolt the Jets and be the linchpin of that new league's Chicago franchise, former Kansas City coach Hank Stram told reporters that the WFL believed Joe's appearance on a telecast added ten million viewers.

Namath's popularity began to move influential NFL owners toward a merger with the six-year-old AFL. When the 1966 college draft took place and the AFL-NFL bidding war led to more Namath-like contracts with fresh-faced collegians (none of whom had Joe's ticket-selling qualities), NFL owners anxiously pivoted to an irrevocable course toward a merger. Namath's physical skills went beyond arm strength. Although limited by battered knees, he somehow backtracked more swiftly and smoothly into the pocket than any other AFL or NFL quarterback. "He has what we call fast feet," observed Colts coach Don Shula before Super Bowl III. "[That gives] him the ability to move back from the center quickly, and once he's in the pocket he can move from side to side to get out of the [pass] rushing lanes." Namath also had a remarkably fast release. "I'd say I save at least two-tenths of a second, and probably even more than that, on a pass play," Joe estimated. "That's worth a lot when you consider that on a pass play, the quarterback would like to have four seconds from the time the ball is snapped until he throws it."

Weeb Ewbank saw something distinctive in Namath's setup in the pocket. Every QB—even Otto Graham and John Unitas—dropped back to pass six to ten yards and then stepped forward to build momentum behind their pass. Joe stepped back "eight-plus, often ten yards. Joe never believed in dropping back and then coming up that step," Weeb explained. "He was ready to throw as soon as he took his first drop; that's a trick of balance you can't teach anyone."

Namath also developed a reputation for avoiding traps set by defenses. Jets all-star offensive guard Bob Talamini theorized that Joe's physical limitations enhanced his ability to read defenses. "Joe had to stay in the pocket and learn how to read defenses and throw into the zone," explained Talamini. "He had to learn to do all that to move the ball. Joe didn't have the liberty of putting pressure on anybody [by running]."

Opposing players became shameless Namath enthusiasts. John Hadl, the San Diego Chargers' starting quarterback, fawned over Joe's form and technique. "Joe had a great delivery," Hadl explained. "I looked at all his film all the time and tried to emulate his delivery. I looked at every game he played, maybe ten times. I focused on how he positioned the ball from the minute he brought the ball up to his shoulder, to the point where he threw the ball. I tried to copy that as best I could."

Namath had the universal respect of AFL players as their "meal ticket"—the one guy who had given the league collective respectability, viability, and star power. They also admired his mettle; teammates recount their shock at seeing Joe having his knees drained and painkillers administered, not to mention the wrapping and braces on his knees so he could play. Opponents heard about it and shook their heads in wonder. Though Namath remained a mostly stationary pocket presence and AFL defenders would hit him as hard as they could, almost no one would belt him below the waist. "If I were to get hit a direct shot to the knee, then I'd be out of the game for good," admitted Namath.

Buffalo Bills all-star linebacker Mike Stratton, whose jarring tackle of San Diego running back Keith Lincoln in the 1964 AFL Championship Game was the most memorable single hit in the history of the league, recounted how at halftime of a Bills-Jets game "one of our assistant coaches encouraged a few of us to do something to get [Joe], to hurt him. I spoke out of turn and said, 'You'll have to find someone else to do that.'"

Buffalo all-AFL guard Billy Shaw witnessed Joe's leadership skills during preparations for the AFL All-Star Game after the 1967 season. In practices prior to the game, Namath continued throwing to his receivers after everyone else preparing for the exhibition had left the field. In the contest itself, with the AFL East squad trailing 24–13, Namath drove his team to a touchdown. The East's other all-star quarterback, Bob Griese, was due to call signals in the fourth quarter, but Shaw remembers Joe walking into the huddle and asking no one in particular, "You guys want to collect the winner's share?" Griese headed to the sidelines and Namath drove the East to the winning score.

The omnipresent aspect of Namath's personal life was his unrepen-tant skirt chasing. Yet, said one wife of a Super Bowl Jets player, "I never met Broadway Joe, but I've known Joseph Namath for a long time." Without exception, the wives of other Jets agree. Safety Jim Hudson's first wife, Wendy, remarked, "Joe was very kindhearted and very respectful to me. My grandmother loved Joe, and she came up to New York for a Jets game. Jim and I and my grandmother and Joe went to dinner, and Joe said to her, 'You haven't seen New York.' With that, he took her bar-hopping for a couple of hours."

Namath's transparency about his sex life hit a new high in a *Playboy* magazine interview during the 1969 Jets training camp. Sex before a game was taboo for athletes. That rolled off Joe's back. He openly declared his preference for blondes and Johnnie Walker Red. "A ballplayer has to be relaxed to play well," he shared with *Playboy*. "And if that involves being with a girl that night, he should do it." It became something of a Namath ritual.

He confessed to having shared his bed the night before the Jets' two biggest games of the 1968–69 season, the AFL Championship Game and Super Bowl III. Asked if he made "a point of doing that on the eve of the game," Joe replied, "I try to; it depends on how I feel that night." Namath even revealed, "One of the Jets' team doctors, in fact, told me that it's a good idea to have sexual relations before a game because it gets rid of the kind of nervous tension an athlete doesn't need."

Most of Namath's offensive teammates had no trouble with two sets of rules—one for Namath and another for them. However, some members of the Jets defense felt differently. Jets' All-Pro defensive end Gerry Philbin, who had the utmost respect for Namath's cour-age and toughness, openly critiqued the Jets' superstar. Philbin was aghast at Joe's lack of dedication to the team. "Joe took money out of my pocket. We should have won [the Super Bowl] in 1967," he stated in an NFL Films documentary. Gerry related how before one home game in 1967, Joe sauntered into the Shea Stadium locker room ten minutes before the opening kick, his arrival so tardy and unexpected that the Jets' backup quarterbacks were fully warmed up and expecting to play.

The dissension from Joe's personal set of rules was resolved in 1968. Namath had been taken aback in finishing a distant sixth in a player vote for the 1967 Jets offensive player of the year. Joe had lost his top runners halfway through the season, all but forcing him to throw on nearly every down. He amassed a pro record 4,007 yards that season, but threw so frequently that every time he called a pass play, it was akin to a bullfighter (Namath) waving a red cape in front of several bulls (on opposition defenses) and his skill somehow helping him avoid being gored.

In the spring of 1968, with Sonny Werblin forced out of ownership, Weeb wanted to resolve the uneasiness between Namath and some teammates, and he opted for a solution that the coach hoped would put Namath on a team-oriented course. Since Weeb's arrival in 1963, he had named Jets team captains game by game. Before the first game of 1968, Ewbank held a secret ballot to select offensive and defensive captains for the year.

Gerry Philbin remembered Walt Michaels instructing every defensive player to vote for Joe. Namath was elected offensive captain. Matt Snell remembered Johnny Sample, who was voted defensive captain, working his way around the clubhouse, asking everyone if they had voted for Joe. Snell laughed and said, "Johnny couldn't find anybody. We all figured that Weeb wanted Joe to be captain, so he named him." Joe was struck then and for years afterward by the vote of confidence, though Philbin presented a nuanced perspective: "Joe thinks he was elected because he was a leader. Just the opposite—he needed to become a leader."

It worked, with a couple of hiccups. Namath showed remarkable flexibility and selflessness in adjusting "his game" several times during 1968. In game one at Kansas City, after flinging two long fly-pattern TD passes to Don Maynard, it was Namath's pinpoint accuracy that helped the Jets retain possession of the ball that sealed a 20–19 win. With minutes to go in the game, Joe's crucial third-down completion from the Jets' four-yard line to Maynard gained a desperately needed fresh set of downs. Matt Snell and Emerson Boozer took it from there with runs that enabled the Jets to run out the clock and keep the Chiefs' deadly long-distance field goal kicker, Jan Stenerud, on the sideline.

Joe's cockiness about his arm strength helped and hurt that year. In game three of 1968, the Jets flew to Buffalo to take on the winless Bills, who had to start their third-string quarterback. Tight end Pete Lammons tells a story about a conversation between Namath and buddy Ray Abruzzese on their way to War Memorial Stadium for the game. "Joe said that he couldn't imagine how the Bills could score against the Jets' league-best defense," related Lammons. After the Bills shocked the Jets 37–35 by picking off five Namath passes and returning three for TDs, Abruzzese kidded Joe in the ride back to the airport, "I guess we know now how the Bills could score."

Namath's arm betrayed him and the team again two weeks later. In game five of the season at Shea against a Denver Broncos team top-heavy with rookies, Joe was picked off five more times due to a heavy Denver pass rush. The two losses in the Jets' mediocre 3-2 record were Joe's fault, and he accepted, unconditionally, the criticism for that from his buddy and roommate, safety Jim Hudson, and the defensive platoon.

During the next four weeks, against mostly weaker AFL opponents, the Jets' offensive game plans put Namath's arm mostly under wraps. The defense set up the Jets' offense (relying on a potent running game and short, low-risk passes) in advantageous field position. Namath's play calling not only became more conservative, but, Matt Snell says, Joe buckled down, spending nighttime hours studying opponent defenses on film instead of sexual conquests in Manhattan.

In game ten, bumping heads with the high-powered offense and aggressive defense of the Oakland Raiders, the Jets took the shackles off of Namath. Although the Raiders levied a gnawing loss in this, the *Heidi* Game, Joe was magnificent. The Raiders put on their typical substantial defensive pressure, but Namath registered 3 TDs, no interceptions, and 345 yards through the air. The next week, in San Diego, he maintained his stepped-up game: 337 yards and 2 TDs. Once the Jets clinched the AFL East, everyone turned their attention to the eventual AFL Championship Game, which the Jets would host at Shea.

Namath displayed unimaginable toughness on that windy, cold afternoon versus Oakland. In guiding the Jets to a 10–0 lead during the first half, he took three ferocious hits. In the opening quarter, defensive end Ike Lassiter belted him so hard that Namath needed smelling salts on the sideline. In the second quarter, one of the Raiders' pass rushers stepped on the ring finger of Joe's left hand; it had to be popped back into place and taped to his middle finger. He later bruised the thumb on his throwing hand. Later still, Lassiter and fellow DE Ben Davidson pancaked Namath; for a second time, he was unsure of his surroundings and felt throbbing pain in his head for the remainder of the game.

At halftime, battling the effects of a concussion, Joe received painkillers for his knees and Xylocaine for his finger. Namath described the Raiders' pounding in the first thirty minutes as the hardest he had been hit since a game at Alabama as a sophomore. Ewbank was advised by Dr. Calvin Nicholas to warm up backup Babe Parilli. Namath considered sitting it out, but somehow pulled himself together and willed his way back onto the field.

In the final thirty minutes, Namath threw an interception (which led to the Raiders taking their only lead of the game), sandwiched between a TD pass to Pete Lammons, a 52-yard hurl to Don Maynard against a howling wind, and, the winning touchdown toss, a six-yarder to Maynard. Off their 27–23 win, they headed to South Florida to prepare to face the NFL champion Baltimore Colts.

The two weeks between the AFL Championship Game and Super Bowl III defined Namath's career. In casual conversation, Joe stated to the media from a chaise lounge that he expected the Jets to win. He matter-of-factly repeated it several more times before declaring his famous guarantee of a Jets victory on Thursday night, January 9, when honored as Pro Football Player of the Year.

Baltimore's defense had pummeled NFL offenses throughout fourteen regular season and two playoff games. However, Ewbank and the coaching staff, Namath, and the Jets' running backs, receivers, and tight ends were licking their chops as they watched game film of the Colts. The Jets perceived Baltimore's supposed strengths—a blitzing defense and workmanlike offense—as made to order for them. Joe wrote after the game, "The only thing that scared me was that [the Colts] might change their defense."

He penned, "Lots of times, just before the snap or on the snap, they moved their two safeties, Rick Volk and Jerry Logan, up to fill in the gaps between the linebackers. Sometimes, one safety would blitz—shoot through and try to get to the quarterback—and, sometimes, the other one would blitz. No matter who they blitzed, they had to leave part of the middle open. I knew I could hit my wide receivers slanting in."

The Colts' reliance on a zone defense was especially vulnerable to Namath's arm strength and speedy delivery. Special teamer John Dockery explained, "Joe had such a quick release and so much velocity on the ball that reaction time for a defensive back playing in a zone defense was a big problem." Reserve Bob Schweickert emphasized that the Colts' defensive backs wouldn't be able to break up Joe's passes. Joe ripped apart the Colts' zone in leading the Jets to victory in Super Bowl III.

There was another, less publicized, off-the-field side to Namath. He was central to easing race relations on the Jets. The locker room was beset with the same racial turmoil that engulfed much of America in the 1960s, but Joe helped alleviate black-white tensions on the Jets. Namath had grown up in integrated surroundings in western Pennsylvania, and at Alabama he couldn't understand separate water fountains for whites and blacks. In New York, he stunned Ewbank in requesting that black offensive tackle Winston Hill be his roommate for a Jets exhibition game in Birmingham. Namath's belief in racial equality was core to the relationship and special bond he had with Hill for more than fifty years.

Paul Zimmerman, the *New York Post*'s Jets beat writer, wrote that more than once he saw "Namath plunk his tray down at one of [the Jets'] all-black tables, and then a few white players join him, and soon it becomes a mixed table. . . . The same thing on buses. I've seen Namath integrate a little knot of black players by his presence."

Weeb Ewbank saw more to like about Joe's arm and clutch play, football acumen, and self-confidence than Namath's unsightly 220 career interceptions versus 173 touchdown passes. His statistics in Super Bowl III don't blow you away, but his masterful performance in dissecting Baltimore's impenetrable defense was a sight to see. On the strength of that, Namath was elected into the Pro Football Hall of Fame in 1985.

Namath was the no-holds-barred leader of the Jets offense, but has repeatedly articulated to have been blessed to be supported by great football players, outstanding coaching, and incredibly supportive ownership. In the recesses of the locker room in the bowels of the Orange Bowl after Super Bowl III, Joe granted a one-on-one interview to WCBS-TV sportscaster Sal Marciano. "Joe, you're the king of the hill," Sal said. "I'm not king of the hill," Joe gently responded. "We're king of the hill. We've got the team, brother."

Joe Namath was the nucleus of the Jets' Super Bowl team and the difference maker, but he had bulwarks on the offensive line, at running back, wide receiver, and tight end, plus the excellence of the Jets' kicking game. As a group, they set the Jets' single-season scoring record that holds to this day.

Add to that the AFL's best defense for 1968 that got Namath the ball in good field position. A great defensive line put substantial heat on rival quarterbacks and stopped the run better than any other team in the league. Talented linebackers filled the gaps that opponents tested. Speedy, resourceful defensive backs kept the AFL's numerous potential game-changing receivers under control. Jets special teamers did not allow cheap touchdowns—they had to be earned.

Here are the untold stories of the forty-four special Jets in 1968 who were instrumental in the Jets winning the Super Bowl, plus the four assistant coaches and player personnel director.

"O" LINE
IT PROTECTED NAMATH AT ALL COSTS

WINSTON HILL	#75
DAVE HERMAN	#67
JOHN SCHMITT	#52
JEFF RICHARDSON	#74
RANDY RASMUSSEN	#66
BOB TALAMINI	#61
SAM WALTON	#71

WINSTON HILL

LEFT TACKLE #75   6'4"   270 LB.

According to his own wishes, the Jets top offensive lineman isn't in the Pro Football Hall of Fame, but he should be.

Winston Cordell Hill was an inaugural member of the Jets' Ring of Honor (joined by Namath, Don Maynard, Joe Klecko, Curtis Martin, and Weeb Ewbank), but the Super Bowl Jets' All-Pro left tackle is not in the Pro Football Hall of Fame. The reason has nothing to do with his qualifications: he received more honors (eight All-Pro mentions) than any Jet in history, even Joe Namath. It's attributable to the soft-spoken, selfless giant's modesty. Winston was a humble, grounded star.

His Christian upbringing preached personal humility. Hill would not tout himself for election to the Hall of Fame; he preferred to let his considerable on-the-field accomplishments speak for him. Nor did he make an effort to have other football personalities and executives (notably Namath) make the case on his behalf to the Hall's electors.

He was great nearly every week, but was at his best in two of the biggest games of the Super Bowl season. In the 1968 AFL Championship Game against the Raiders, which Winston told his family was "the hardest game of 1968," Hill "manhandled that crazy Ben Davidson," observed substitute defensive lineman Karl Henke. Two weeks later, Winston's power, speed, and agility bullied and buried Baltimore Colts defensive end Ordell Braase all over the field in Super Bowl III.

Matt Snell's 121 yards rushing and the Jets' only TD of Super Bowl III came largely on the play known as "19 Straight," the bread-and-butter power run in Ewbank's playbook. The Jets had used it successfully against every AFL team. Snell (or Boozer) would take the handoff, head up the middle, then bounce to the outside, as Hill rode his man off the line and sealed the edge. Once the Jets exposed the right side of Baltimore's defense as hopelessly susceptible to that play, they ran it behind Winston, again and again. The Colts' center, Bill Curry, assessed, "Winston Hill was probably the most valuable player of the game."

Hill's peak years were 1965–75. When *Pro Football Journal* published its All Mid-Decade Team for that era, he was selected as a second-team offensive tackle. Of Winston's eight Pro Bowl/AFL All-Star Game selections, the first five came at left tackle and, after being asked to make a move to accommodate a new teammate in 1971, three more came at right tackle. (Only two NFL Hall of Fame offensive linemen, the Houston Oilers' Bruce Matthews and Baltimore's Jim Parker, ever earned All-Pro distinction at more than one position.)

Linemen in the league who went to war against Hill confirmed the giant tackle's technical skills. "He was very crafty, very knowledgeable, very skillful," described the Denver Broncos' Rich "Tombstone" Jackson. Atlanta Falcons Hall of Famer Claude Humphrey complimented Hill as "one of those guys who sent me back to the film room to study."

Hill was also an ironman, who over 14 seasons played 195 consecutive games for the Jets (174 consecutive starts—the NFL's tenth-longest consecutive starting streak at the time; the current NFL record is 297 by Brett Favre). His consecutive game streak continued unabated in spite of a broken leg in 1965 and someone stepping on his throat in 1974. Many years into his retirement, Winston's internist asked him when he had broken his neck. Hill didn't know what the doctor was talking about; family members, though, had recognized that it had been difficult for Winny to turn his neck very far for years. He left football with cartilage, knee, and elbow damage, and he underwent knee and hip replacements.

New York Post Jets beat writer Paul Zimmerman saluted Winston as a forerunner at his position in the 1960s, writing: "With the merger of the two leagues [in 1970], a new type of left tackle came into existence, and the prototype was Winston Hill, 6'4", 270 pounds, a smooth graceful athlete."

Tall, strong, but also graceful, he was an all-around athlete who could have made a living in tennis (he was a Texas state tennis champion in college and, as an amateur, he once beat Arthur Ashe). Basketball could have also been an option. His agility and quickness on his feet were a textbook fit with the Jets' blocking schemes. "Winston Hill was our best offensive lineman by far, a real All-Star on the pass or the run," summarized Ewbank. "When he blocks, he doesn't just get a stalemate with the guy he's on. He blows him out."

Ewbank's internal game-to-game rating system showed that in 1967—the pre–Super Bowl season—Hill had registered a 90.4 percent effectiveness score on running plays and 95.5 percent on passes

(93.5 percent overall). For the 1968 Super Bowl season, Hill's overall grade was 93 percent. Both years, his offensive line blocking effectiveness was tops on the team. (Dave Herman's rating was equal to Winston's in 1968.)

Recognizing that footwork was one of his best attributes, Hill tried to "suck in the defensive end and let him think he has the edge," noted his grandson, Grant Winston Staffer. "With every move the defensive lineman would make, Winston would be one move ahead of him." Hill tried not to absorb continuing punishment from pass-rushing defensive ends; with the help of his superior footwork, he tried to maneuver his man so far from Namath that the defensive end didn't have the time to pose a threat. Hill's rise to prominence was unexpected.

He graduated from Texas Southern, an eleventh-round draft pick of the Baltimore Colts in 1963. Talented and strong, he was also raw and became embarrassed by Colts veteran defensive end Ordell Braase in the 1963 camp. The Colts saw his potential but couldn't retain Winston and number-one pick Bob Vogel on a cluttered 37-man roster.

"After Don Shula cut me, my dad said, 'Come on home. If you want to go back to school, you can. If you want to go into business, you can.'" Winston was devastated, but Coach Shula set him up for a Jets tryout. "When Weeb cut me from the Jets, I called my dad. 'I'm ready to come home. It looks like I'm not cut out for professional football.'"

His dad's message to Winston on that call changed the course of Jets history. "My dad said, 'Okay, I listened to you, and I want you to listen to me. Don't interrupt me. You go tell Weeb to let you stay on the team until the season starts. Whatever per diem he's paying the other guys, I will pay yours. And if you have not made the team by the time the season starts, I will send you a plane ticket home. [The Jets] won't be out of anything. Don't say goodbye. Just hang up the phone and go tell Weeb.'

"Weeb told me that I could stay on at the Jets' expense if I'd try to learn a second position—center. I centered the ball until I couldn't see," Winston stated. Hill made Weeb's inaugural Jets roster in 1963 as a member of the taxi squad.

His big break came late in 1963 when, with the Jets' starting and backup left tackles both injured, Ewbank inserted him into the lineup against the Boston Patriots. It was the strangest situation in Winston's career. Hill was unaware that a handshake agreement was in place to trade him to the Patriots after the season for a draft pick.

Oddly, the man playing against him—Boston's all-star defensive end, Jim Hunt—had that inside scoop. As the former college opponents squared off, Hunt told Winston not to worry about anything, that he could room with Hunt until Hill found a room. "I had no idea what he was talking about, and he told me to forget it," said Hill. It ended up not mattering, since Weeb saw something in Hill that day and rescinded the deal. Winston found out about it ten years later.

Few Jets were willing to mentor young guys playing behind them for fear of putting their own jobs at risk. "Winston always shared and helped anybody and everybody, during his football career and afterward," said Jets offensive lineman Jeff Richardson. Guard Randy Rasmussen said he couldn't thank Winston enough for volunteering to teach him how to pass block. Winston also spent his personal time squaring off against young Jets defensive linemen (like 1968 second-round pick Steve Thompson), teaching them professional tricks they would face against other top-notch offensive linemen.

Winston ended up blocking for Joe Namath in every game of the QB's Jets career, part of their personal relationship that lasted for more than fifty years. It was an unlikely friendship, forged on mutual respect, between a devout Christian and football's swinging sex symbol.

After having been in poor health for some time, Winston Hill died April 26, 2016, at the age of seventy-four. Clark Judge, who has covered the NFL for thirty-plus years, blogged: "It's not Winston Hill's exclusion from the Hall of Fame that puzzles me. It's the Hall's failure to discuss the guy that I don't get."

DAVE HERMAN

RIGHT GUARD, TACKLE #67   6'1"   255 LB.

Dave's blocking philosophy was to "get right in the middle of them [defensive linemen] and force them to get through me, not around me."

The second most famous phrase associated with the Jets' two weeks at Super Bowl III (after Namath's "I guarantee you") was "Bubba's loose." Dave Herman, the Jets' right tackle, shouted it only once and it was heard only by the few players standing between the Baltimore Colts' pass rushing left defensive end, Bubba Smith, and Joe Namath. That it was yelled once is proof of the success Dave Herman had with the feared Smith.

Football fans today are likely unfamiliar with Dave Herman and his role as the unsung hero of Super Bowl III. Since 1965, Dave had established himself as a top AFL offensive right guard. The esteemed *New York Post* Jets beat writer Paul Zimmerman wrote that Herman played "guard the same way a horse plows a field, doggedly with great determination, from a high-pain threshold. His basic athletic ability was minimal, but he wouldn't let himself be beaten on pass blocks."

Herman had no issue shifting to right tackle at the tail end of the 1968 regular season when the productivity of rookie tackle Sam Walton took a nosedive. In the November 1968 *Heidi* Game, when Walton lost control of Oakland Raiders' left defensive end Ike Lassiter, coach Weeb Ewbank abruptly asked Herman to move from guard to right tackle. Without hesitation, Dave made the move with five minutes left in the contest and immediately neutralized Lassiter.

Winning the AFL Championship Game had been the team's goal since 1963. Six seasons later, a Jets victory at Shea Stadium versus Oakland would achieve it. Too much was at stake to chance another Walton matchup with Lassiter in the Jets' championship bid. Weeb again put Herman at right tackle.

Little about it seemed to make sense. How could all-AFL guard Herman hope to deal with this physical mismatch? Dave, at 6'1" and 255 pounds, didn't have the height or weight of a pro tackle, but he did have the technique, physicality, intensity, intelligence, and laser-like focus. To Herman, playing guard or tackle did not matter. "I had to stay right between my opponent and the football, or the quarterback," he says.

At offensive guard, he operated in the congested interior of the line where multiple big bodies collided; at tackle, Dave would combat a taller, heavier, quicker foe, one-on-one, in a wider area of the field. On top of physical superiority, a defensive end could disorient Herman using an arsenal of legal tactics (head butts and head slaps) that are illegal today. Single-minded on play after play to finish block after block as well as he could, Herman was not going to allow a footwork adjustment and more wide-open spaces to deter him.

In the AFL Championship Game, Herman got off to a bumpy start. In the second quarter, Lassiter hit Namath in the head so hard that center John Schmitt says Joe's eyes rolled up into his head. From then on, Herman blunted Lassiter, a key in the Jets' victory.

When the Jets moved on to the Super Bowl, football reporters analyzed Dave's new task and saw the Baltimore Colts' 6'7", 275-pound defensive end Bubba Smith as a ridiculous mismatch. Herman didn't buy it and was maniacally determined. He also had a conversation with Namath before the game, in which he told Joe not to have any concern about getting hit by Smith. Joe supposedly responded, "That's good to hear." Then Dave jested, "Of course, it's going to be third down and 25 yards to go a lot." (That alluded to the prospect that he might be penalized for holding Smith, *which never happened*.)

Herman told me he preferred to block a bigger guy versus a shorter, quicker opponent. Dave was tougher, ornerier, and more persistent than he was nimble. Pass blocking was his forte. Herman admits Bubba Smith "might have been the strongest guy I ever faced. He was very active and had the quickness of a much smaller player. Like most defensive ends, he wanted to move me out from in front of him. Bubba liked to grab you up high and throw you to the side."

With all the talk about the confidence that flowed through the Jets' coaching staff and players entering Super Bowl III, Herman was the single Jets player to tell us that the team's widespread confidence didn't matter to him that day or before any contest he played in. "I didn't focus on the team effort it would take to win the game, only on my individual task against the one player that I had to take on," he told me in 2016.

How effectively Herman warded off Smith that day is one of the top one-on-one performances in Super Bowl history. On NBC's telecast and the next day in newspapers across the United States, his neutralization of Smith was highlighted, though not showcased as much as the output of skill-position players.

It was then and still is a massive oversight. Adding to the aura around Herman's success was that he took on Smith all by himself. Center John Schmitt pointed out, "We couldn't give Dave help with Bubba; [tight end Pete] Lammons could chip him once in a while, but that was it." Matt Snell peered at the Herman-Smith match-up on every pass play—just in case Dave needed assistance—and says he never had to roll to that side to help out. At the final gun, Winston Hill, Bob Talamini, Randy Rasmussen, and Schmitt helped the exhausted Herman walk off the field.

Bubba did get loose and sack Namath once, but overall the Colts' monster lineman suffered day-long frustration. "Bubba managed to run over him two or three times," reviewed coach Ewbank, "but he was never quite in position to lower the boom on Namath." Bubba had a lot to say about how the Colts should have won that day, but he never complained about Herman holding him.

Herman played five seasons after the Super Bowl for the Jets, chalking up extremely positive grades against defensive tackles at his normal right guard position. Herman's Super Bowl success was no one-off; the best of the NFL's 1970s defensive tackles, Pittsburgh Steelers Hall of Famer "Mean Joe" Greene, told Pittsburgh writers after his final tussle with Herman in 1973: "Only one guy I can't beat in either league, and that's Dave Herman."

JOHN SCHMITT

CENTER #52   6'4"   250 LB.

No Super Bowl Jets player was as unlikely to become a prominent player as the Jets' center was.

Free agent John Schmitt, a 295-pound Little All-American defensive tackle from Hofstra University, was signed to an $8,500 contract in 1964 to play center, and was immediately told he must lose forty-five pounds. At Jets training camp that summer in Peekskill, New York, he counted five other centers, called his wife, and said he'd probably be coming home soon.

"The big reason I didn't get cut was Artie Donovan," says Schmitt. The retired, 320-pound Baltimore Colts defensive tackle was in Jets camp, a guest of his former coach, Weeb Ewbank. Donovan was there to tutor the team's defensive linemen but became an exemplary teacher for Schmitt. "He made me into a center," Schmitt recalled. "Artie strapped on a helmet and came at me in shorts and a T-shirt for a half hour after practice. He beat the s--t out of me, but he told Weeb he had to give me a chance."

John appeared in four preseason games and started his education as a center prospect on the Jets' taxi squad. "Coach Ewbank told me to learn to play center with our minor-league team, the Jersey Jets. It was so low class," Schmitt remembers. "The unprofessional guys playing there beat up and hurt people; it was like gang warfare. I hated it so much that I tried to put it out of my mind."

Late that season, during the Jets' first half of a two-game West Coast road trip, starting center Mike Hudock was injured and Ewbank needed an emergency replacement. With barely one day's warning, Schmitt was instructed to fly overnight to San Diego to snap against the Chargers. With limited game preparation, Schmitt trotted out onto the field with the offense, broke the huddle, jogged to the line of scrimmage, and discovered Ernie Ladd, pro football's biggest, meanest defensive lineman, lining up head-on opposite him.

Schmitt decided to do what his old college coach would have advised: "fire into Ladd with all my might." He snapped the ball, literally bounced off Ladd, and was writhing on the ground. It got worse. Midway through the third quarter, Schmitt snapped for punter Curley Johnson and ran downfield to cover the kick . . . only to have Ladd clip him from behind and tear the cruciate ligament, cartilage, and kneecap in Schmitt's right knee. The season was over and Dr. James Nicholas said that in all likelihood his career was, too. "My wife was pregnant and I had $226 in the bank," a teary Schmitt related.

Dr. Nicholas offered Schmitt a procedure that was a "1 in a 1,000 shot" to revive his football career. With nothing to lose, John okayed the experimental surgery. The doctor took an extra ligament from his right thigh and strung it to create a new cruciate ligament. Schmitt beat heavy odds and ended up playing for more than a decade.

Schmitt worked his tail off to convalesce his recovering knee and cope with a cumbersome brace in 1965 training camp. Once again, he made the taxi squad. With four games left in the 1965 season, Schmitt was activated again and had improved to the point that the Jets exposed and lost starting center Mike Hudock in the expansion draft to the Miami Dolphins.

Continued hard work and focus transformed John Schmitt into a dependable AFL center. "I had the least amount of experience of any guy on the line, so I was quiet," he said. In the next few years, Schmitt and his mates warded off pass-rushing defensive linemen and blitzing linebackers so well that Namath became the least-sacked QB in pro football. By his third year as a starter, John was performing at peak performance, named first or second team all-AFL at center by Associated Press, United Press International, the *New York Daily News,* and the *Sporting News.* During the 1968 season, Schmitt's Jets grade from coaches was a sterling 92.5.

Centers can offer unusual perspectives, almost as much as the quarterback. Like Joe Namath, Schmitt learned how to read defenses. That meant shouting out call-blocking assignments instantaneously in response to Joe's play calls. John also became Joe's on-field bodyguard. "Joe and I, to this day, have a special relationship," says Schmitt. "If Joe got hit and was shaking, I'd talk to him, look in his eyes, take a time-out," he said, then with cascading laughter, added, "You know, a guy has his hands between your legs for ten years, you get pretty close."

Schmitt, among all the surviving Super Bowl Jets, has the finest grasp of how Namath's play calls in Super Bowl III tamed the Baltimore Colts' swarming, supposedly overpowering defense. It's a story that has never been completely told.

Don Shula, after replacing Weeb Ewbank as coach of the Colts early in 1963, retained Ewbank's offensive and defensive systems. In other words, the "hot colors," offensive formations/play calls and numbers associated with each play, went largely unchanged. Shula did reverse the direction of offensive plays, so in Baltimore a running play headed to the right, while the same call on the Jets would veer to the left. For six regular seasons, the Jets and Colts competed in separate leagues and never played each other, so Shula's decision had no impact.

It didn't take long once Super Bowl III started for Weeb Ewbank and offensive assistant Clive Rush to recognize that the Jets' and Colts' offensive plays and signals were identical, only designed to head in the opposite direction. That insight, according to Schmitt, was a key reason why the Jets' offense and Namath implemented "Check with Me." Namath understood the Colts' defense superbly from game film and could accurately read it at the line of scrimmage.

Using "Check with Me," Joe came to the line without a play call, analyzed where Baltimore's defense was loading up, made his play decision, and barked out his play call. Namath's first signals deliberately had the active Colts safety and linebacker shifting in one direction—and once they did, Joe immediately changed his play call to one heading in the opposite direction. For a professional player, even one or two steps in the wrong direction can take them out of the play.

The Colts appeared to sense but did not react to the similarity of the Jets' offense system. Namath began using the Colts' indecisiveness against them. "The Colts knew our check-off colors—Green, Gray, and Gold; Blue, Black, and Brown; or Red, White, and Blue," said Schmitt. "They would hear Joe check off, I would yell out a play to the offensive line (like Blue, Blue, P36T), the Colts would shift in a direction, and Joe would immediately audible, bark out Green P35T—the same play he originally called, but in the opposite direction, and I'd snap the ball. We did it over and over, and the Colts' frustration grew. They never figured out why they were always a step behind us. By the third quarter, we knew we had the game. The Colts started fighting each other."

One Baltimore defensive line tactic had the Jets scratching their heads in pregame practices, but Schmitt and Winston Hill figured out how to blunt it on the Orange Bowl field. "Their defensive tackles, Billy Ray Smith and Fred Miller, would crisscross and one of the defensive ends would circle to the opposite side of their defense and then attack our offense. In practice, we couldn't figure out how to stop that end," Schmitt said.

However, Schmitt detected when the maneuver was coming. "In our film sessions, I had a read on Billy Ray Smith," he explained. "When he was coming down on that tackle-tackle play, he'd set his foot back differently. It wasn't a one hundred percent certainty, but damn near it, and I had a one-syllable call to alert everyone else. Midway through the second quarter, Winston Hill and I agreed that if Ordell Braase, the right defensive end playing opposite Winston, pulled up and circled to the opposite side, Winny would drop back from the left side of our offensive line and circle to the right side, wait for and pick up Braase over there. Solving how to handle the crisscrosses came together on the field."

Super Bowl III was Schmitt's "best day and worst day." He had developed pneumonia after the AFL Championship Game and the Jets, believing he was allergic to penicillin, didn't treat him with that conventional drug. He got sicker with each succeeding day. Schmitt went through the motions during practice sessions, and defensive teammates were not told why, only not to hit him. Three days prior to the game, Schmitt told Coach Ewbank he couldn't walk and his ribs hurt. John insisted on a dose of penicillin. It didn't kick in fully by Sunday, but Schmitt somehow persevered.

"At the end of game, I could hardly walk," John related. "I came into the locker room, kneeled down with everyone else for our group prayer, and my body gave out in front of everyone. Joe was right next to me and said, 'No offense, John, but I'm out of here.'"

JEFF RICHARDSON

OFFENSIVE GUARD, OFFENSIVE TACKLE, CENTER #74   6'3"   250 LB.

Bubba Smith hated being blocked around his ankles. Richardson, Bubba's college buddy, knew that and told Dave Herman, who used it against Smith.

Football fans know that the offensive line has five positions, but no Jets fan has ever known that in winning Super Bowl III, they had the benefit of a sixth lineman. Jeff Richardson didn't play a down as an offensive lineman against the Baltimore defense that afternoon, but he still had a massive impact on the Colts.

"Big Jeff" Richardson, as he was known during his brief Jets career, played special teams that day in the Orange Bowl. Yet he was the Jets' secret weapon because he knew how to neutralize the Colts' feared one-man wrecking crew, Bubba Smith. Jeff taught Dave Herman a method of combatting and frustrating Smith's power and speed—a relatively simple blocking monkey wrench to blunt the 6'7", 275-pound monster.

Richardson and Smith had been friends and teammates in college. In their senior year at Michigan State University, they played side-by-side on the MSU defensive line. "He liked to take some plays off," Richardson recounted, so Jeff became Smith's in-game motivator. When Bubba didn't go all out, Jeff yelled in his ear, exhorting him to put all his physical superiority to work.

Years later, Richardson found out that Sonny Werblin had attended the 1966 "Game of the Century" between Notre Dame and Michigan State. "Sonny came there to scout Bubba. My top college performance came that day against Notre Dame, with 16 tackles and I made the All–Notre Dame Opponent Team that year. The Jets ended up drafting me in the sixth round in 1967. I was told that Mr. Werblin saw me grabbing Bubba in the huddle, shouting at him, and then seeing Bubba take somebody's head off on the next play," Richardson said, "and that Mr. Werblin decided he wanted the guy who made Bubba tick."

No Colts opponent had ever tried to combat Bubba by striking him low. Richardson said forty-seven years later, "I preached to Dave Herman that Bubba's toughest challenge came when the offensive tackle stayed as low as he could and rammed into Bubba's waistline and below. At Michigan State, we had a running back who used to frustrate Bubba in practice by going for his knees. In those days, it was legal in pro football for an offensive player to hit the defensive player around his ankles. I advised Dave, 'If you are losing the block, go down and take him down by the ankles.'"

That counsel may have been the greatest impact that Jeff Richardson had in his Jets career, but he was, at Weeb Ewbank's suggestion, an offensive line fill-in at all five positions. Weeb told him that the more positions he could play the better chance he had at making the team; he became an offensive line swingman, a backup proficient and savvy enough to step in and play in the event of an injury to either Jets' starting tackle, guard, or center John Schmitt.

"I remember Winston Hill got shaken up in one game and they told me on the sideline to get ready to go in for him. On the sidelines, I was thinking to myself, 'Left tackle, left tackle, left tackle.' The very next play, Schmitt went down and I rushed in to play center, instead of left tackle. I had to change my brain to playing center. Joe got sacked a couple of times before I got my head together."

Richardson was unceremoniously and surprisingly traded to Cincinnati in training camp the year after the Super Bowl. "Weeb explained they were looking for experts in one position and that I wasn't expert at one position—after he had told me for two years that my value to the team would come in playing any of the five offensive line slots. I couldn't accept why they had traded me. I'd done everything they had asked, played my heart out."

If Jeff had a grudge with Ewbank, in a matter of weeks he got a taste of greater indignity from two other reputable coaches. The Cincinnati Bengals' Paul Brown and the Miami Dolphins' head coach, George Wilson, both cut him, and neither could be bothered to tell him face-to-face. Jeff's pro football career came to an abrupt end in the fall of 1969 and he moved on and became a top supermarket industry executive.

"I didn't do so when I was much younger, but now I wear my Super Bowl ring just about every day," he said. "I've worn it out. The recognition that I get as a member of the Super Bowl Jets is still there. The first time I took my wife to one of our reunions was the first time that she realized how big it is. Almost fifty years after the game, people still know who we are for having been part of that team."

That brought to mind a Richardson family visit to Hofstra during a Jets training camp. Joe Namath was signing autographs and Jeff and his grandson waited patiently in line with fans, but Jeff realized that they weren't going to get to Joe before he would depart. "I shouted, 'This guy from Johnston [Pennsylvania] has to wait at the back of this whole line?' Joe stood up, spotted me, and yelled, 'Big Jeff, c'mon up front.' He signed my grandson's hat. The next day, my grandson went to baseball practice and showed his hat to his coach, who spotted Joe's signature and asked, 'Do you know who Joe Namath is?'

"My grandson said, 'Yeah, he played in the Super Bowl with my grandpa.'"

RANDY RASMUSSEN

LEFT/RIGHT GUARD #66   6'2"   255 LB.

Projected to be a substitute at left guard in 1968, he was forced to start at right guard and was dominant in Super Bowl III.

Randy Rasmussen's teammates often shook their heads in awe when they saw Randy's odd physical characteristic: massive thighs and calves that gave him a permanent bowlegged walk. Jets center John Schmitt was amazed by Rasmussen's twenty-five-inch calves, which infused him with breathtaking blocking muscle. "He wore a pair of socks that wouldn't stay up on anyone else's ankles," Schmitt noted. "He had a low center of gravity and he could get right under a defensive lineman's chest. You would just try to tie him up—you never could push him back three yards."

Randy's toughness in the trenches helped build a Jets record for player longevity. Randy Rasmussen surpassed all but kicker Pat Leahy in games played (207) and starts (205) for "Gang Green." It wasn't just his length of service that was commendable; he was voted one of the best guards in Jets history. Thirteen years after the Super Bowl III upset, thirty-seven-year-old Rasmussen became the last member of the 1969 squad to retire.

His remarkable story began in the 1967 pro football draft, where the Jets looked for offensive line help. Notre Dame head coach Ara Parseghian urged Weeb Ewbank to use his twelfth pick in the first round to scoop up Fighting Irish center Paul Seiler. The Jets did, and the choice flopped. The Jets also selected guards from Texas and Delaware in rounds eight and eleven. With the draft's 302nd pick in the twelfth round, the Jets grabbed freckle-faced Randy Rasmussen, a guard out of Kearney State (Nebraska).

Randy could have taken a local math teaching job but agreed to a Jets contract for $12,500 in salary, $1,000 if he made the team, $2,000 at season's end if he participated in 50 percent of the Jets' 1967 offensive plays, *and* an additional $3,000 signing bonus (unheard-of for a twelfth-round pick). The latter seems to have occurred because he was late to training camp due to a collegiate shotput competition and the Jets were desperate to finalize a contract with him.

Rasmussen discovered he had a stranger-than-fiction personal advantage: the Jets' offensive system was identical to the one used at Kearney State. On the Peekskill practice field, his run blocks versus first-year and other young defensive linemen opened eyes. Drop-back pass blocking was not going smoothly. "I was being over-aggressive," he said. As a third practice finished up, Randy was hailed by veteran tackle Winston Hill from a few feet away on the sidelines. "Winston pointed at me and said, 'Come here. Son, you've got a little trouble with pass blocking.'" At Kearney State, the QB used a moving pocket—a rollout, sprint-out, or bootleg. Ninety-nine percent of the time, Joe Namath dropped straight back in the pocket.

"Winston instructed me to use my left hand to grab his breast-plate, to pull him towards me and lift. I did it, but he admonished me, 'No, grab it hard.' I did and had him straight up in the air. 'See, Randy,' Winny said, 'I can't do anything.' I let him down and I said, 'That's holding.' Hill slapped me so hard on the shoulder that I almost fell over. 'Son, you're not listening. That's pass blocking in the AFL.' Over the years Winston forgot that little side lesson, but to me it's like it happened yesterday and it was a turning point in my career."

In his next practice, Randy grabbed breastplates, kept his head up and maintained his balance. He moved up the depth chart quickly in the next two to three practices. In the final 1967 preseason game, starting left guard Sam DeLuca's knee got so severely mangled that his career ended. At halftime, Randy saw offensive line coach Ernie Zwahlen, offensive assistant Clive Rush, and Coach Ewbank commiserating. "Weeb came over, put his hand on my shoulder, and said, 'You're going in now. Don't get too excited. You've got Winston on one side and Schmitt on the other side.'" Randy played the second half and started the next week in the opening regular season game in Buffalo.

As the 1967 season progressed, the pressure amped up on the Jets offensive line. In the opening game, fullback Matt Snell left the field with a knee injury, and halfback Emerson Boozer was similarly felled and lost for the year in the seventh game. With the Jets' rushing attack basically wiped out, Namath was forced to pass on nearly every play. He threw for 4,000 yards, but protecting the stationary quarterback, game after game, became tougher and tougher.

"You don't get beat up that badly pass blocking," Randy said, "but mentally I knew that I couldn't make a mistake. I had to be perfect on every play. The few times Joe got sacked, it was shocking to see him on the ground. It instantaneously forced me to be sharper. I couldn't be the guy who allowed Joe to be hit. You get tired of beating yourself up to be perfect."

Rasmussen did well as a rookie—even bested Ernie Ladd, the AFL's best defensive tackle the one time they faced each other—but after his 1967 campaign, the Jets had doubts about him. Years later, Randy was told that there had been a trade in the works to send him to Denver for all-star cornerback Nemiah Wilson. Reportedly, assistant coach Buddy Ryan went to Weeb and told Ewbank not to do it, and the general manager followed that advice.

In 1968 training camp, Ewbank acquired six-time all-AFL offensive guard Bob Talamini to strengthen the line. Rasmussen observed, "Acquiring Tali was a genius move. He was much more experienced than me—a good strong run blocker, but probably better at pass blocking. He blocked for passes differently than I did. He had a quick head-butt; I had to not watch him so I would not pick up a bad habit."

Talamini pulled a muscle his first day in that Jets camp, was sidelined, had to recover, then play himself into shape. He suffered other leg injuries later on, so Randy and Talamini split the position most of the season. Then came an offensive line upheaval late in the *Heidi* Game. In crunch time in Oakland, Rasmussen stepped in at right guard as Dave Herman made a spur-of-the-moment switch to right tackle to protect Joe Namath. The line reverted to its normal starters for the final five games of the schedule. However, in the AFL Championship Game, the three-guard alignment that had worked against the Raiders reappeared.

Rasmussen found the Oakland Raiders a greater challenge in that game than the team's eventual Super Bowl opponent. "We didn't match up as well with the Raiders," Ras recalled. "Their pass rush would get to you. Their three-man line gave us a few more things to look at. We couldn't connect on a quick pass because Joe would drop back three to five steps—and they'd be on top of him. They had really good linebackers, and the stuff we did well—tackle-to-tackle runs—is where they were best." Nonetheless, the Jets held off Oakland, 27–23. Playing that one full game at right guard, with Dave Herman at right tackle next to him, got both accustomed to their new positions. Postgame with reporters, Coach Ewbank credited Randy for his complete control of the Raiders' dangerous defensive tackle Dan Birdwell.

Super Bowl III presented Rasmussen with a personal and personnel concern—the Colts' left defensive tackle, Billy Ray Smith. "I grew up the biggest Baltimore Colts fan in high school and through college," Randy said. "I was, man oh man, Colts all the way. I adored Billy Ray and Ordell Braase; they were my heroes and now I was blocking them. On film, I didn't think I was looking at Billy Ray, but reality set in when we came out on the field and there he was.

"Once Super Bowl III began, there were so many things to think about in our preparations that Billy Ray Smith having been one of my idols went out the window." Randy shocked the football world (and maybe himself) by dominating his childhood hero.

The Colts had thrived against NFL opponents with their stunting–tackle-end and tackle-tackle games with defensive linemen crisscrossing from their positions to confuse and get an edge on an off-balance offensive lineman. Randy noted, "All of the Colts' stunts, we saw every week in the AFL. The one way that Baltimore was different from AFL teams actually made their stunts easier to spot. With the Colts, there was not a lot of jumping around. When they were in a certain set, it was an indication that it was coming."

Paul Zimmerman wrote in the *New York Post* about Super Bowl III: "The Jets threw a child at [Smith]—a freckle-faced youngster off the Nebraska prairies named Randy Rasmussen. . . . There's no logical reason why Rasmussen should have wiped out Billy Ray Smith yesterday, but it happened. . . . Smith never even threw a shadow on Joe Namath, and when the Jets decided to run, Rasmussen drove him straight back on blasts that jolted him like electric shocks."

With a Super Bowl III world championship in only his second year and considering the youth of the Jets' squad, Randy expected to make a Super Bowl return. He didn't. "It had been so easy; I thought that we'd do it every year," he said. "Then I found out what football really was."

The Jets' elimination in the 1969 AFL divisional playoff by Kansas City was the closest Randy ever came to another Super Bowl appearance. He experienced one lone winning season after 1969, four 7-7 or 8-8 teams, and seven dismal losing seasons, (six with only three or four victories). "There's not much difference between winning and the bottom," Randy observed.

Walt Michaels, who coached the Jets during the last six years of Randy's career, said he was the team's most consistent player; Weeb called Randy his most coachable player. Upon retiring, Rasmussen became a Jets radio color commentator. While calling a game only a few years removed from the Super Bowl, Randy mused about the struggling Jets squad and how the team's attitude had changed. "When we walked on the field our Super Bowl year," he said, "there was no doubt we were going to win. It was just what the score would be."

BOB TALAMINI

LEFT GUARD #61   6'1"   255 LB.

One of eleven players to be part of three AFL champions—and the first to earn a Super Bowl ring.

Bob Talamini had competed in four AFL Championship Games—winning three—conditioning him to treat pressure-filled contests as routine. At Super Bowl III, he was enjoying the Florida sun, his wife, and four kids. However, Talamini remembers something being whispered through the Jets' locker room that drew the players' attention.

"We were told that if we weren't competitive in this Super Bowl, there wasn't going to be a Super Bowl any more," he recounted. Talamini, whose AFL career dated back to the league's first year, was distressed that the NFL would sideline AFL teams from the Super Bowl and convert the championship into a game pitting two old-line NFL teams against each other.

Bob Talamini had worked almost a decade to mold himself into one of the AFL's most respected offensive linemen. He had signed with the Houston Oilers in 1960 as a 190-pound, twenty-second-round draft choice out of the University of Kentucky. He joked that his draft slot was all that anyone needed to know about how unimpressive a prospect he was. The Oilers told him to bulk up, so Talamini headed to "the grunt room" in the basement of Kentucky's student union. "I asked the three guys down there what to do to put on some quick weight," Bob said. "They said, dead lift, press, bench press, and squats. I did it for four months, got up to 245 pounds, *and then* I thought about whether I wanted to play pro football. I told the Oilers I needed a bonus; one week later, I received an envelope with two hundred fifty dollars in cash. I thought, 'That was easy,' and signed the contract for seven thousand dollars, payable if I made the team. Turned out, they took the two hundred fifty dollars out of my first paycheck."

Talamini became a steady AFL all-star at left guard, but never felt respected as his pay barely budged, $1,000 at a time, year to year. Things came to a head after the 1967 draft. Houston drafted and signed Notre Dame guard Tommy Regner, a consensus all-American, for more than Talamini was making. Bob asked for a $3,000 raise on his $16,000 salary, pointing out his latest AFL all-star honor and his need to take care of his wife, who had been badly hurt in an auto accident. When the Oilers turned him down, Bob told Houston management that he wasn't interested in playing there anymore. Luckily for Talamini, the Oilers were open to trading him and he had a friend talking him up to the Jets.

Joe Spencer, Houston's offensive line coach from 1961 to 1965, had become fast friends with Talamini. "Joe Spencer was my Pygmalion," said a clearly moved Talamini. "He saw more in me than I saw in myself. I was lucky to have a coach like Joe, and really wanted to live up to his expectations." Spencer molded Bob into an all-league offensive guard, swift and adept at leading sweeps, as well as a tactical, physical rock that could match the muscle of any AFL tackle.

In 1968, Spencer became the Jets' offensive line coach. "Joe put the bug in Weeb's ear about me," remarked Talamini. Spencer called Talamini and asked if he would play in New York for $19,000 if a trade could be negotiated. After some wrangling, a 1969 third-round draft choice was sent to the Oilers and Bob flew to New York.

That a player of Talamini's quality would be available was unusual. On the ceremonial all-time AFL squad, Talamini was selected for the second team. Jets defensive end Verlon Biggs greeted Bob, voicing his pleasure that he wouldn't have to bump into the tough Talamini anymore. So did DT Paul Rochester. Talamini was a force, and the cool, calm way that he handled every situation impressed many teammates.

Talamini was a Jet to provide immediate all-star-caliber play at left guard. The Jets had landed, in Bob's own words, "a powerful, strong" lineman who "no defensive lineman could run over." He plied his craft on the offensive line like "a Sicilian Buddha or a waterfront enforcer," described the *New York Post*'s Zimmerman. "He plays football like a guy driving a stake into the ground—unemotionally but thoroughly competently. And you never lose track of his tremendous hitting power at work." Bob once told the *Post* columnist Larry Merchant that he liked "to hit [opponents] and hard [so] that, like the fellow hit by a truck, all they want to do is get his license [plate] number."

But his Jets career got off to a tough start. When Talamini sauntered onto the practice field at Hofstra for the first time, he pulled a quadriceps muscle, which shelved him through training camp. He was limited to studying the Jets playbook, so when the season started Randy Rasmussen and Talamini shared the position.

The Jets offense hit some bumps but generally got the job done early in the season. Then, as the season hit its do-or-die phase, rookie right tackle Sam Walton, who had replaced retired Jets legend Sherman Plunkett, experienced some rough games that deflated his confidence. Protection for Joe Namath weakened. Three changes would be made on the offensive line.

Talamini's presence made them comparatively effortless. As Dave Herman moved to right tackle and Rasmussen shifted from part-time left guard to full-time in Herman's vacant right guard spot, Bob Talamini took charge in his AFL-honored left guard role.

Talamini's optimum playing weight with Houston had been a firm 255 pounds, which gave him the maneuverability and flexibility to lead sweeps and still effectively pass block. Joining the Jets, Bob added pounds, figuring that 260 pounds in the trenches would work better with the Jets' greater emphasis on slant passes, trap blocks versus sweeps, and long pass plays. He played Super Bowl III at 270.

A true believer in learning from his mistakes, Bob said, "The only way you get to be a great player and good enough to have somebody vote you for All-Pro is to learn from your mistakes on the field." However, weekly reviews of the last game in the film room at Shea were a humbling experience for the lineman at the top of his game. "Coaches would run any bad plays forward and back, and forward and back, and forward and back," he said without a chuckle, indicating the seriousness of the exercise.

Talamini displayed unusual composure heading into Super Bowl III. He said real pressure was finding diapers when they sold out near the team hotel, and watching over his kids. Asked what the Jets' 1968 postseason games meant to him, he glibly noted "more money than I made in my first three years in Houston."

For him and his buddies on the offensive line, there was humdrum reaction to what analysts feared about Baltimore's defense: plentiful stunting. "We'd seen it in the AFL for years; the AFL invented that," declared Talamini. "[Baltimore's] whole defense is predicated on stunting and trying to get the offensive line confused. When we watched the three films of Baltimore's defensive line looking for tendencies, strengths, and weaknesses, we walked away believing they weren't as tough as the Oakland Raiders."

Of all the Super Bowl Jets, only Talamini makes the case for divine intervention in the victory. "Michaels missed a chippy field goal; they [the Colts] threw an interception from the six-yard line that hit a receiver's shoulder pads and Beverly intercepted," he said. "Morrall, near halftime, threw the ball away from a wide-open man. Michaels missed another field goal. There were things going on that weren't supposed to happen. [Baltimore] looked good, but didn't play good that day."

But after the Jets victory, as the team hooped and hollered on the Orange Bowl field, Bob Talamini felt a mixture of exuberance and gratification that the AFL finally showed competitiveness with the NFL, plus sadness. "I knew it was my last game. I made over forty-five thousand dollars that year, and I told the Jets I didn't think I wanted to play in 1969. It wasn't a negotiating ploy; there never was a discussion for me to return. Commuting every two weeks from New York to Houston and back, for two days at a time that 1968 season, was brutal."

As time has passed, Talamini has never tired of reminiscing about his final professional game. "It's like a fine wine: the older it gets, the better it gets. A lot of Super Bowl games have been lackluster. Our game delivered," he said.

SAM WALTON

OFFENSIVE TACKLE #71   6'5"   270 LB.

In training camp, Weeb Ewbank praised him again and again, but as the season went on his failures created a QB protection crisis.

Of all the stories about the forty-five players who appeared in a Jets uniform in 1968, none is as perplexing and tragic as Sam Walton's. He grew up in the projects of Memphis, Tennessee, and according to his son, Marlon Beloch, was a great basketball player who was scouted and recruited to play football for Texas A&M–Commerce (now East Texas State) in Commerce. He was a consensus all-American his senior year (1967).

When Walton, the Jets' third-round pick in the 1968 college draft, reported to Hofstra University training camp, Weeb Ewbank's compliments flowed like a waterfall. Veteran right tackle Sherman Plunkett had slowed down from age and weight issues he could no longer overcome. Plunkett had to lose thirty pounds, insisted Weeb Ewbank, and he huffed and puffed trying to get in shape. Walton ran off competition for the offensive right tackle spot from Jim Harris, a defensive tackle trying to make the transition to offense. Plunkett couldn't drop the weight, asked for his release, then retired.

Walton was the lone rookie starter in the Jets' Green-versus-

White intrasquad game and won more praise from Weeb. Starting at right tackle was his job to lose and by the end of training camp he was considered the best rookie on the squad. In his pro debut, he butted heads with Kansas City Chiefs defensive end Jerry Mays, an eight-year pro and perennial first- or second all-AFL selection. On the game's first play, Walton drove a forearm into Mays' neck—and Sam had the advantage the rest of the day. Joe Namath personally complimented Sam's play.

He played well the following week versus Boston, but then Walton had a reversal of fortune. Ron McDole, the Bills' accomplished 6'4", 260-pound left defensive end, recorded four Namath sacks and pressured Joe into making numerous ill-advised throws in a loss at Buffalo. Five interceptions ensued and three were converted into touchdowns.

At one point late in the going, Walton panicked when McDole eluded him and he grabbed McDole's jersey, a professional no-no. Walton chalked up his poor day to part of his "education ... [McDole] was a lot smarter than I was, and I got rattled when I realized I was being outsmarted," he told reporters.

The Jets simplified their offense and deemphasized passing in the next game, a victory over San Diego and an easier time for Walton. However, the Denver Broncos invaded Shea Stadium the week after that, and Walton's man—the agile, 6'3" 255-pound left defensive end Rich Jackson—overwhelmed him. Jackson seemed to be in the Jets' backfield all afternoon, harassing Namath, and leading Denver to a stunning 21–13 upset. Five more interceptions that day "were not Joe's fault," Weeb Ewbank said. "We couldn't stop that Jackson all day."

In the next four weeks, twice against Houston, plus Boston and Buffalo, Walton registered average outings. The Bills' annual visit to Shea Stadium prompted a slight sense of relief as Walton, in his second confrontation with Ron McDole, improved his "game grade" by 13 percent over what he had been rated in Buffalo.

However, in the *Heidi* Game at Oakland, Namath was again battered and Walton was the clear culprit. A two-touchdown sequence in the game's closing seconds and NBC's cutaway before completion of the telecast to most of the U.S. audience left football fans shaking their heads. But something far more important was brewing inside the Jets' organization. Of all the mistakes Sam made that afternoon, he had twice been outmaneuvered and overpowered by a defensive end his own size—6'5", 270-pound Ike Lassiter.

It got so gruesome that late in the game, Weeb could no longer stand and watch the carnage. The Jets had spent years constructing the league's best QB pass protection for Namath. On the sideline with five minutes to go, Ewbank asked right guard Dave Herman to go in for Walton, and instructed Randy Rasmussen to shift from his normal left guard assignment to Herman's position. Once the pair were in place, the pressure on Joe deescalated. A spur-of-the-moment decision had prompted a desperation revamp of the Jets' offensive line. No one knew it then, but the Jets' season had just been saved.

Preparing the next week for San Diego, Ewbank ran Herman and Rasmussen through drills at right tackle. Ewbank strongly advocated maintaining the confidence of all his players, so his rookie tackle's starting role wasn't over. Sam started the last four games of the Jets regular season. He acquitted himself very well in the first and fourth versus San Diego and Miami on the road, but there was no consistency. In the second and third games (Miami and Cincinnati at home), Walton turned in his second- and fourth-worst outings for 1968.

With the AFL Championship Game a few weeks away, Ewbank's mind worked overtime because the Jets' opponent, either Kansas City or Oakland, each had veteran, take-no-prisoners defenses that would go right at the offensive line's weak link and pummel Walton, then Namath. Ewbank kept his starting right tackle decision under wraps, and sent Herman out to face Ike Lassiter. "It hurt at first when they said I wouldn't play [on offense]," Walton commented afterward. "But now I realize how important it was to use someone with experience." Weeb didn't try to hide that Herman would replace Walton in the Super Bowl.

Walton's teammates were uncertain what to make of the once-promising rookie's deterioration during the season. "One pro season is almost like two college seasons, and rookies sometimes wear out mentally, especially someone playing the offensive line," assessed Dave Herman. "Though Sam had talent, he [Walton] sometimes lost concentration in games and even on the practice field."

Al Atkinson remarked, "They said Sam Walton's nightlife caught up to him. He wasn't even getting into his stance properly." Jeff Richardson was more descriptive: "Sam was a great ball player, but he let his partying take over. He was going to have his New York adventures. [He] started to screw up, [was] late for practice and smelling of booze." Sam's son, Marlon, who was born in 1964 while Walton was in college, said, "He talked to me about the Italian guys and the Jewish guys that he met in New York, and how they taught him a lot of stuff that he didn't know coming from the South. We wondered but he never talked about why he hadn't played much in the AFL Championship Game or the Super Bowl."

The Jets, looking to strengthen the right tackle position, drafted Ohio State offensive tackle Dave Foley with their top draft pick after the Super Bowl. Foley and Walton competed in 1969 training camp, until Foley was lost for the season with an injury. Walton won the job by default but again showed little consistency from week to week, and lost his starting position after four games.

Roger Finnie, the Jets' fourteenth-round 1969 draft choice from Florida A&M, took over at right tackle on October 12. On November 16, Walton, who had gone missing for a week, was suspended by the Jets, the first time that Weeb Ewbank had taken such a stern measure against any Jets player. Walton was out of football in 1970, then was traded to the Houston Oilers, where he played fourteen games in 1971. Sam tried out with the New York Stars in 1974 but didn't make the cut. That led to his retirement.

Walton returned home to Memphis and years later was rumored to be living on the streets. Larry Grantham, living in the town, was enlisted to find him and help Walton out. Grantham did spot him once, but Sam ran away. Walton was found dead in 2002 of a heart attack in a vacant Memphis apartment, his body in a deep state of decay, surrounded by liquor bottles. Money raised by his Jets teammates helped pay for his funeral. As preparations were made to put his comrade to rest, Grantham said, somberly, "He wouldn't let any of us help when he was living; now, we will finally be able to help him."

RECEIVERS
SUNSHINE, THE FAST RAY BERRY, BAKE, AND BIG BOY

DON MAYNARD	#13
BAKE TURNER	#29
GEORGE SAUER JR.	#83
PETE LAMMONS	#87

DON MAYNARD

WIDE RECEIVER #13   6'0"   180 LB.

This rail-thin, blazing-fast wide receiver, whose long strides helped him race past the fastest defensive backs, is one of three SB Jets in the Hall of Fame.

Forty-five years after being released by the Jets, Don Maynard still holds team records for career catches (626), receiving yards (11,732), and touchdowns (88). Still, in the case of Maynard, who was known as "Sunshine," there is a more telling standard for his excellence.

Maynard's greatness at the flanker position and the deep threat he posed to defenses came into perfect focus in Super Bowl III, a game where, for one of probably two times in his Jets career, *he failed to make a catch.* He was coming off one of his best professional seasons (57 catches, 1,297 yards, 10 TD catches, a career-best 22.8 yards per reception, and an average 99.8 yards per game). In the 1968 AFL

Championship Game, Don had registered 6 catches, 188 yards, and 2 touchdowns (including the winning TD). The cover of the official Super Bowl program depicted him, in full stride, extending his arms for an over-the-shoulder catch.

Don was still recovering from a pulled leg muscle that dated back to the next-to-last game of the regular season six weeks before. He had skipped game fourteen of the regular season in Miami, which likely cost him the AFL yardage receiving title to Lance Alworth by 15 yards. "I told Weeb, 'I want to play . . . but I'm looking down the road [at the postseason]," he said.

When the Jets returned to Miami for the Super Bowl, Maynard limped around Jets practices for two weeks, out of the sight of media. During the week, Dr. James Nicholas administered a cortisone shot in Don's left hamstring. Backup wide receiver Bake Turner mentally prepared himself to start the game. The Jets were uncertain about Maynard's limitations even as the game kicked off; Baltimore was certainly in the dark about Maynard's availability.

"I kept a heating pad on it [the hamstring] real low all Saturday night, and early Sunday I was limping," Maynard said of his pregame preparations and status, "but I jumped in a whirlpool at one hundred degrees and got my leg loose. I did all the stretching exercises, administered analgesic balm on my leg and wrapped it good. I never felt tightness or a tingle. My hamstring was as loose as could be." One account of that day said a muscle relaxant, Xylocaine, was injected into the area of the pulled muscle. Jets team physician Dr. Calvin Nicholas advised Weeb Ewbank to start him.

Don shocked the Colts in the first quarter: he outran its impregnable deep zone. Maynard darted straight downfield past the Colts' plodding left corner, Bobby Boyd (with 5.9 speed!), then got a couple of steps past deep safety Jeff Logan. Namath's heave was just barely beyond Maynard's fingertips. "Probably would have had a TD if I was entirely healthy," he stated. According to Namath, Don apologized to him after Super Bowl III for not hauling it in.

"Some writer later said that was the most important incomplete pass in Super Bowl history," observed teammate George Sauer Jr., because the play sent a shiver down the spine of the Colts' defensive brass. Fearful about Maynard doing it again—next time for a long touchdown—the Colts shifted their zone coverage to Don's side of the field for the rest of the game. In the third quarter, Maynard beat the deep zone again and grabbed Namath's toss just a step beyond the backline of the Colts' end zone.

"Joe only threw a few passes to me, but I lined up so wide right that Baltimore's safeties had to show their coverage," Maynard said. "I had learned as a rookie from Kyle Rote on the Giants that there's lots of times you're not supposed to catch the ball. You entertain the corner and the safety, weave at 'em and make one commit and then the other, and you can make 'em play your game. Take 'em deep, and the tight end or the swinging halfback or the fullback, can catch the pass underneath."

The Colts' special attention to Maynard left George Sauer Jr. one-on-one against right corner Lenny Lyles, whom Sauer outfoxed and outmaneuvered on the opposite side of the field. It also opened Maynard's side of the field for short, underneath passes to TE Pete Lammons and the Jets' running backs.

Postgame, Maynard professed no frustration with his zero yards on the score sheet. The prestige of the world championship, Don's revenge against the NFL and the New York Giants ten years after they had callously cut him, and the $15,000 winner's share were sufficient.

Maynard's career was an ongoing battle to prove his critics wrong. In 1958, the New York Giants drafted the football and track star out of Texas Western University. Don was the only rookie on the star-laden squad; he backed up halfback Frank Gifford and receiver Rote, learned their tactics, and was a spare defensive back.

In 1959 training camp, new Giants offensive assistant Allie Sherman, who had replaced Vince Lombardi, admonished Don to dispense with his long sprinter strides, saying they were suitable for track, not the gridiron. Sherman also told him to shave his sideburns. Maynard shrugged off both instructions, and shortly thereafter the dreaded Turk came for his playbook. "I could run faster backwards than [some of the guys they kept] could run forwards," Maynard said. He never talked about it, but never forgot the putdown.

Don headed north to the Canadian Football League's Hamilton Tiger Cats for the 1959 season, after which he enthusiastically returned to New York as the first signee with the AFL's New York Titans. A short bridge over the Harlem River separated the Titans' home field, the Polo Grounds, from the Giants' home, Yankee Stadium, and Maynard quickly moved into the same hotel where he had lived as a Giant. Ex-Giants teammates welcomed him back to town.

From 1960 to 1962, Maynard and the Titans' other wideout, Art Powell, tore AFL secondaries to shreds. In 1960 *and* 1962, Don and Powell became the first professional tandem to each gain 1,000 yards through the air.

New York media paid scant attention to his remarkable AFL pass-catching numbers. His AFL statistics didn't mean much to Weeb Ewbank either when he became coach in 1963. Weeb thought Maynard was talented, but that he needed more consistency. In Weeb's personnel evaluation of Maynard following the 1965 season, the coach spelled out his concerns dating back to 1963:

DON MAYNARD / 6'0" / 185 / 29 / 84%

Finally performed in a manner approaching excellence and his potentials. Has always been a consistent deep threat when he felt like it. Is still not as consistent overall as he could be. His pattern running improved considerably, however he probably will never be a crisp pattern receiver. Has tremendous deception with his outstanding speed. His hands are good but needs to improve, if not eliminate, cradling (doesn't appear to do this when operating on the left side). His blocking is only fair (not strong physically

*like so many flankers) but Don did "get in the way" more this year
and actually helped a few running plays. His overall improvement
began with a fine training camp including an excellent attitude.
Did not have the "odd ball" remarks and actions as he had experienced in the past. This good quality plus his performance made
him more of a "regular guy" and was therefore respected more by
his teammates.*

*Reads coverages very well and adjusts patterns satisfacto-
rily. Can improve in every area and if he does, he could be the
best flanker in the business and should play for several more
years. Improved all receiving categories (number caught, yardage, TD's, average and total points). Improved percent grade
considerably. Had 5 less dropped balls and reduced the number
of poor patterns 50%.*

As a Jet, Maynard became a recognized threat who regularly
faced double teams. For half the decade of the 1960s, Don had latched
on to passes from second-rate QB talent (the Titans' Al Dorow and
the Jets' Dick Wood being the best). Once Namath hit the scene in
1965, Maynard finally had a genuine All-Pro caliber quarterback.

From the moment that Namath got to his first training camp,
Maynard set out to make the most of his relationship with Joe. Don
told him: "I'm going to make you a better quarterback, and you are
going to make me a great receiver. We're going to have the timing
down so good, you are going to be able to make it blindfolded." Namath was assured that it was impossible to take the snap from center and throw it quickly enough to Maynard. "The minute I turn my
body and head, I want the ball there to catch," he said. "Throwing
it early was something many quarterbacks are never taught." That
season, Namath's 14 TDs to Maynard made him a pro football star.

Maynard claimed that he taught Namath something else that
few coaches train a quarterback to do: read the defender. Don analyzed the opposition defense and would hand-signal Namath about

breaking the planned pass pattern to do further damage. Maynard estimates he broke patterns approximately 10 percent of the time, but never on third down because of the specific yards to keep a drive going. Related Namath, "Every time Don's broken a pattern, he's had a damn good reason."

Part of Maynard's success came from the hours spent paying attention to his body and its condition. Case in point: when he sought out Jeff Snedeker about the pulled muscle in his left leg the week before Super Bowl III, the trainer was astonished to find that Don could pinpoint "the sore spot on his leg the size of a pinhead." His week-to-week resilience and tenacity from football's pounding led to thirteen years of eye-popping pass-catching production. Despite his light frame and fearlessness on the field, he didn't miss games, much less practices.

Matt Snell laughs about his 1964 rookie season having been his best because of the weak competition that he faced. The opposite is true of Maynard; his numbers never sagged and his overall game improved: his route running, communication with Namath, and his ability to get open got better even as AFL defenses tightened up. In 1967, Jets teammates elected Don the team MVP, a level of excellence that he sustained beyond the Jets' Super Bowl season.

Maynard performed best against the better competition. He actually preferred to square off against veteran defensive backs because their reactions to Maynard's fakes, cuts, etc. were predictable; he said he didn't know what to expect from a rookie. In 1968's opening game in Kansas City, Don broke free for long- and medium-distance touchdowns. In the *Heidi* Game at Oakland, Don accumulated 10 catches and set a new Jets single-game reception yardage record (228) against first-year corner George Atkinson. The Raider DB was no match for Maynard in the AFL Championship Game, either. Don made a fourteen-yard touchdown catch in the first quarter, then what Don called his "greatest catch ever."

Don had confided in Namath early in the contest that he could run past Atkinson when it was needed. As the Jets, trailing for the first time, awaited the Raiders' kickoff in the fourth quarter, Maynard reminded Joe about the big-play option: "Anytime you want it, I'll get a step on my man, and you let me have it." Having just thrown an interception deep in Jets territory, Namath admitted that "[Don] said that with such confidence it made me feel better." On the second play from scrimmage, Namath came to the line and saw Atkinson, lined up to play "bump-and-run" on Maynard on the right flank. Joe changed his call to a bomb to Maynard.

Namath took the snap and Don galloped to a step or two lead past Atkinson. Namath hurled his pass across a strong gusting wind, aiming for Maynard's left shoulder. The ball was blown by Shea's powerful winds to Maynard's right shoulder. Sprinting at top speed, Maynard tracked the spiral's redirection, adjusted his route, fully extended his arms, grasped the football over his right shoulder, and was spun out of bounds at the Oakland six-yard line.

"I don't think because of the situation and the outcome that there was ever a catch as important to me as that one," said Maynard. On the very next play, Don was Namath's intended target, but Oakland's defense prompted a play-call change at the line. Don became the number-four option, but with the first three blanketed by Raiders, Joe spotted Maynard in the end zone and buried a six-yard bullet barely above the ground into Don's chest, his legs kneeling underneath his outstretched body.

Experts said Maynard's speed was deceiving. Wrote Jets beat writer Paul Zimmerman: "Maynard [ran] three patterns half-speed, then six points." Teammate Jim Hudson, who practiced hundreds of times against Maynard, noted, "Don was long-gaited and he could fly. . . . It was hard to tell if he was going fast or slow. He'd sort of lull you to sleep. By the time you figured out which way he was going; he was gone."

He was the first pro receiver to amass 10,000 yards and eclipsed Raymond Berry's NFL record 631 career receptions. Averaging 18 yards per catch each season was almost a norm. According to the Football Database, in terms of yards-per-catch Maynard is third, all-time among the NFL's top 50 career-yardage receivers. Only Stanley Morgan (19.2) and Lance Alworth (18.9) finished better than Don at 18.7. Maynard was named to the All-Time All-AFL team in 1970 and he entered the Pro Football Hall of Fame in 1987, two years after Namath.

D on's frugality earned him some playful pokes. On road trips, Maynard filled an empty suitcase with rolls of hotel toilet paper. For all his gridiron brilliance, he felt continually underpaid. His $7,500 rookie salary with the Giants in 1958 was on par with first-year player pay in the time before there were minimum salaries. Respected by Weeb Ewbank and excelling at one of football's high-skill positions, in 1967 Maynard had a $26,000 salary that exceeded Namath's ($25,000), but without the QB's bonuses and deferred payments.

Some of his eccentricities turned out to be way ahead of their time: long sideburns; a "dress code" that brandished Levi jeans, cowboy boots, a cowboy hat, and a country-and-western belt with a huge brass buckle. (His son, Scot, told us the character in the 1970–77 NBC TV series *McCloud*, about a New Mexico sheriff who relocates to New York City, was based on Don.) Maynard put his engineering skills to work, retrofitting a 1955 Ford coupe to function on propane and gasoline for vastly improved gas efficiency.

Maynard's unconventional football approaches fused his rare ingenuity, his speed-based skill set, and specially modified pro football equipment. Don caught tennis balls in practice with one eye closed to improve his concentration. He rounded pass patterns to maintain his pass pattern momentum. On a sloppy field, he donned short-cleated foot gear, took pronounced shorter steps, and ran in a straight-up position for optimum traction.

His game-day white Puma cleats were customized with twenty-four spikes and he ordered football's first V-neck uniform top and first mesh uniform (both a standard today). Don had equipment manager Bill Hampton order specialized shoulder pads that dropped down to his rib cage and a custom-molded helmet with extra padding around the cheekbones so Maynard wouldn't need a chin strap. He was fitted with an individually molded mouth guard, and an elastic belt and jock strap for more effortless movement.

Maynard primed himself for football's winter weather with a nylon uniform and a detachable white shirt collar for extra warmth, plus two long cleats screwed into the heel of his short-spiked white Pumas for an icy field. "I don't remember slipping one time in the [AFL championship] game. . . . I was in perfect control even with a bad hamstring," Don said.

Maynard told Jets beat writers that he intended to play "until they run me off." At the end of 1973 training camp, Weeb Ewbank traded Don—the last Titan on the Jets' roster—to the St. Louis Football Cardinals, where he played two games before retiring at age thirty-eight. But he has never forgotten the exhilaration of Super Bowl III. "Just playing in it was amazing," he declared.

BAKE TURNER

RECEIVER #29   6'1"   179 LB.

For the first Jets' teams, he was a star. Afterward he was a backup to Don Maynard and George Sauer—and there was little talent drop-off.

Bake Turner didn't start Super Bowl III, ran only a pass pattern or two in the game, and toiled most of the afternoon on special teams, but his story typifies the saga of Jets players who persevered from the team's 1963 introduction to the promised land in Miami. So, not surprisingly, when NFL commissioner Peter Rozelle entered the winner's locker room, Turner acknowledged him, yelling, "Welcome to the American Football League."

Robert Hardy Turner's anointed nickname, Bake, grew out of his childhood fondness for bacon. He was a gifted offensive player who fought his way on to professional football rosters with his speed, slipperiness in the open field, and preparedness to play special teams. Turner's swiftness made him a natural on kickoff and punt returns, plus a legitimate deep-ball wide receiver threat. Yet, regrettably, football's crunching body hits and jolts to the skull overwhelmed his slender, small, 175-pound frame. He was selected as the best player ever to wear number 29 for "Gang Green" by Bleacher Report.com in 2012.

Bake was born in Alpine, Texas, and still resides there. An all-state Texas football, basketball, and track star (he ran a 4.7 40-yard-dash), he attended Texas Tech. He had three solid years playing halfback, averaging 4.1 yards per carry and 19 yards per reception. His 20.2 yards per catch as a sophomore in 1959 led all of the NCAA, and his 444 yards was fourth best in the country among independent schools. Bake made All–Southwest Conference in 1961, his senior year.

He was the twelfth-round pick of the Baltimore Colts in 1962, and returned kicks and punts his rookie season for Coach Ewbank. Bake learned the ropes from stellar NFL wideouts Raymond Berry and R. C. Owens, but it was apparent that Bake's backup position was jeopardized when the Colts made Willie Richardson their 1963 college draft first-round pick, and, sure enough, Turner was released midway through that year's training camp. "When Weeb went to the Jets, he told all the Colts players he'd be looking for us; when I got cut in Baltimore, I called him," Bake said.

It was random good fortune for him and the Jets. Bake made a sensational debut, returning the opening kick of his first preseason game 95 yards for a touchdown, then scored again on a fourth-quarter, 78-yard catch-and-run. In practice the week before game one of the season, Don Maynard watched Turner practice at Don's position and told Ewbank: "He ain't gonna beat me out. He's too good to be my number two. Stick Bake Turner on the left side." Weeb did.

Maynard and Bake formed one of the AFL's dynamic receiving duos even before Joe Namath's arrival. With Bake and Maynard split wide on opposite sides of the field, defenses decided to double-team Maynard and signaled to the unfamiliar Turner to "go ahead and try to beat us." Bake became the favorite target of strong-armed Jets QB Dick Wood. He set the Jets' single-game receiving yardage record, 210, which held up until 1968. His 71 catches were third best in the league in 1963, Bake was voted the Jets' team MVP by fellow players, and he went to the AFL All-Star Game.

Turner said, "I was quick—not fast straightway, but I changed direction quickly, and Clive [Rush] taught us some really good pass patterns. I liked to run small post, corner post, and standard post patterns. I didn't like to go across the middle against zone formations; I did catch a lot of balls there, but I suffered broken ribs and concussions."

Bake hooked up with Wood 58 times in 1964 (sixth best in the AFL), plus scored 9 TDs. His third Jets season (1965) was less productive; he was victimized by injuries that first forced him from the lineup and then hampered his productivity when he played while on the mend.

Weeb's assessment of Bake after the 1966 campaign was complimentary:

BAKE TURNER / FLK / 6'0" / 180 / 26 / 85%
Perhaps Bake has hit the skids, but feel he is still capable of being the fine flanker he had already proven. As mentioned in previous annual reports, he has all the skills—speed, hands, moves, attitude, and age to play well for a long time. His lack of concentration and carelessness has resulted in too many dropped balls. He

*is our best pattern runner, however, careless in this area at times
too. Reads coverages well and is always a threat deep and has always scored deep.*

*Turner is effective as a returner on teams and could be a
"get-by" punter. If our other flankers come through as expected,
we could possibly consider Bake as one of our better trading
strengths. Played 408 snaps less than previous year and therefore
caught less, scored less, and had fewer dropped balls and fewer
poor patterns. Led team in K.O. returns but was not ranked in
AFL K.O. returns.*

In 1966, Bake didn't complain when second-year receiver George
Sauer took his spot in the starting lineup. Turner became a valuable,
on-demand replacement part, but was not diminished in the minds
of coaches or teammates. Turner had developed calcium deposits on
his Achilles' tendon, and was happy just to be on the team. Clive
Rush's son, Doug, says his dad felt "Bake didn't have the skills that
Maynard and Sauer did, but my dad had a strong affinity for him. He
was an overachiever, and dad loved his hustle and heart."

Although his playing time at wide receiver had been drastically
reduced, Bake proved that he could fill in with skill and precision
with little notice. He displayed exemplary skills in two memorable
fill-in appearances at the tail end of the 1968 regular season. One was
a 40-yard, one-handed TD hookup with Babe Parilli at Shea against
Miami (it earned him a game ball); the other came two weeks later,
versus the Dolphins in Miami—a 71-yard touchdown on a flea-flicker.

He loved returning kicks, which he and Maynard handled as a
tandem in 1963, and with other Jets through 1969. In 1966, Turner
set a team—and tied an NFL—record with seven fair catches in one
game. "I had dislocated a shoulder in one game when I didn't fair
catch," explained Turner, who was unaware of his place in the record books.

In the post–Super Bowl season, Bake's last before a trade that shipped him to Boston, Turner continued to chip in with impromptu professionalism. When George Sauer Jr. was sidelined for the Jets' 1969 preseason opener in the College All-Star Game, Turner grabbed 8 passes for 145 yards. Bake incurred bruised rib cartilage the next week in an exhibition contest in St. Louis and missed a handful of games. Turner scored 3 touchdowns on just 11 catches that year.

Bake had led the nation in punting his senior year (1961) at Texas Tech and had been Curley Johnson's punting backup since 1963. It was finally his turn on November 10, 1969, when Steve O'Neal, the AFL's leading punter, suffered a bruised pelvis. "Weeb told me that I should kick a ball into the stands for practice and he wouldn't charge me $100 (the automatic league fine for tossing a ball into the stands after a touchdown). My girlfriend was sitting in the stands behind the bench, and I tried to kick it to her," he explained with a dry laugh. That attempt fell far short of the target, but he averaged a professional-grade 44.5 yards on two punts in the second half against Buffalo.

Bake revealed that Ewbank never liked to run substitutes into a game when players were at full strength, yet Turner played most of the game in his final Jets appearance, the 13–6 AFL divisional play-off loss to Kansas City. Don Maynard, whose broken bone in his foot was only partially healed, courageously hit the field. Turner got the bulk of the playing time that day, catching two Namath throws for 25 yards.

In 1970, Bake was in Boston with a handful of other Super Bowl Jets and head coach Clive Rush. Turner collected his last 28 professional catches, good for 428 yards (15.3 yards per reception). Bake said he retired while he could still stride off the field in one piece. "There were a lot of tough guys—physically and mentally tough—on the Jets, but I was more of a lover than a fighter," he said. Putting his body on the line, absorbing hard hits week after week, Bake had always felt it unlikely that he would have a lengthy football career. "I was not big enough, though I was there nine years—four years as a starter and hung on for another five years," he said. "If I had started for ten years in the AFL and NFL, I probably wouldn't be able to walk."

From his early days in pro football, Turner was taking steps to use his athletic fame to ease into a music career. In Bake's rookie year, his guitar and vocals ingratiated him with Johnny Unitas in training camp. "The one year I played with the Colts, Johnny would have me come to his room with my guitar and play country music after the lights went out," recalled Bake. "I thought we'd get in trouble, but I should have known better. It's probably the reason I made the team that year. Johnny was a solitary person, but he had an entourage. He and I had a closer relationship than most of the other guys on the team."

As Turner engaged in football's weekly battles, he dedicated his free time cultivating his post-football music career, a physically safer proposition. Handsome, unassuming, honest, and the epitome of "cool," Bake very quietly became a fixture on Manhattan's social scene. His secret? "I always had my guitar," he said. In 1966, he cut two songs in a New York recording studio. A clever marketer, he began picking his guitar and singing at Namath's ballyhooed nightclub, Bachelor's III. "I think I got about one hundred dollars a night to entertain. I remember Tom Jones and Johnny Carson at the club," he said. "Out front, all the ladies would be making passes at Joe and in the rear, I would be singing and picking my guitar."

When the Jets became world champions, Bake's music career blossomed. Invitations to perform grew and his earnings from commercials took off. "Before long, I was making more money doing ads than I was playing football," he revealed. Turner formed "the Four Jets"—himself, "Country" Don Maynard, "Mr." Jim Turner, and "Brother" Matt Snell—for a Score hair dressing commercial in which they sang an adapted version of Johnny Nash's tune "Hold Me

Tight." Turner was the "DQ Dude" in a Dairy Queen spot and there was a Rango after-shave TV ad that won a Creative Excellence Award in the personal products category.

Bake was welcomed by Johnny Carson to *The Tonight Show* with Namath and the Four Jets. On the 1968 *Ed Sullivan* Christmas show, Bake sang and played the guitar, joined by Namath and Maynard. Bake overlooked a red flag when, after his performance, Sullivan asked Namath, "What kind of music is that?" Joe answered, "That's 'country,' Ed." Sadly for Turner, it would be a few more years before country music caught on across much of the United States.

Bake signed a recording contract with Kapp Records, but his music aspirations never approached his expectations. A couple of promising songs that he recorded on 45s were also released by big country stars (Dottie West and Charlie Pride, respectively) only a few months later. Pride actually apologized to Bake, but the damage was done.

In his late seventies, Bake can still saunter around a room like few men his age, and he is still singing and strumming his guitar for appreciative Alpine, Texas, audiences.

GEORGE SAUER JR.

WIDE RECEIVER #83   6'2"   195 LB.

His Super Bowl III starring role was one of many highlights in his six-year Jets career. On a path to the Pro Football Hall of Fame, George bid adieu to the Jets in 1970 at age 27, explaining he had other life goals.

George Sauer Jr. was the son of the Jets' player personnel director George Sauer Sr., whose gridiron feats as a player and coach had enthralled football fans since the 1930s. Writing after Navy's shocking 21-all tie with Army in 1948, United Press sports writer Carl

Lundquist noted how much the coach of Navy, Sauer Sr., had hoped that his first offspring would be a boy. He planned to name him after his legendary University of Nebraska coach, Dana X. Bible, and "train [the boy] to be a grid star."

Lillian and George Sauer's first child, born in 1942, had been named Dana, but *she* had no football road to follow. However, in November, 1943, George Sauer Jr. was born and a letter soon arrived from the same Dana Bible, at this point the athletic director at the University of Texas, informing the proud parents that a Texas football uniform and scholarship would be waiting for George Jr. in 1961.

The Sauer name had so much power and prestige in football circles that George Jr. could have tied himself in a psychological knot trying to match his dad's reputation. It didn't happen, and the elder Sauer's fondest football hopes for his boy were exceeded. George Sauer Jr. became an AFL All-Pro in three of his first four Jets seasons and twice he was a first-team All-Pro.

In January 1969, as the Jets prepared for Super Bowl III, Weeb Ewbank was asked by NFL reporters, "How good is George Sauer Jr.?" His response paid the ultimate compliment for any wide receiver at that time: "I would describe George as a fast Ray Berry," Ewbank said. "Berry was not fast, but he ran great patterns. George is fast and also a master at patterns."

The name Raymond Berry may not ring a bell to twenty-first-century gridiron fans, but from 1956 to 1966 he was the NFL's receiver par excellence. He had been drafted by the Colts and coached by Weeb. Berry's flawless pass patterns shook him loose from defensive backs, and his unrivaled sticky hands corralled any throw within reach. Both made him the prototypical "possession receiver." He had the added advantage of being paired with the NFL's best quarterback, John Unitas. Ray Berry retired in 1967 with an NFL record 631 catches.

Sauer saw his skill set similarities with Berry and studied and replicated Berry's practice habits, for example, doing game preparation in full football gear to prevent unforeseeable injuries.

Dana Sauer Keifer, George Sr.'s daughter, says, "As a youngster, George loved to run, but he wasn't obsessed with sports. George was very bright. He was interested in and questioned everything, like why the sky is blue and the grass is green." Everything George did, she added, he was determined to do remarkably well.

George pursued track until he realized that he didn't have sprinter speed, then he turned to football. "George sat on the bench until his junior year in high school," remembered Keifer. "I felt George didn't show interest in football earlier because he wondered how good he'd look compared to Dad." She also speculated that her brother might have taken a shot at football as a way of pleasing their father. When a college decision needed to be made, George learned from his Mom about the long-ago promised Texas football scholarship, and he headed to UT in 1961.

It was not a serene fit for the player or UT. George Sauer Jr. was born to catch footballs; Texas coach Darrell Royal's offense was a grind-it-out, wing-T rushing attack that all but disdained the forward pass. Ironically, circumstances in key games over the next few years forced Texas to throw the football, which saved the team and spotlighted Sauer.

Freshmen weren't eligible to play varsity football in the 1960s, and in 1961 Royal talked George into being redshirted, so George did not play in 1962, either. That extended George's football eligibility into 1965. When George finally got on the field in 1963, his play at split end helped Texas capture the NCAA football championship.

College football's one-platoon football system in 1963 forced players to play offense and defense. To stay on the field for sixty minutes, the 205-pound Sauer played split end and stand-up defensive end. "He didn't particularly like playing defense, but back then you had to," said the Longhorns' other receiver/linebacker and future Jets tight end, Pete Lammons.

In 1964, college football substitution rules loosened and Sauer focused on his offensive game. George played well, even with limited opportunities to catch the ball, but Texas' single loss (versus 10 wins) knocked the Longhorns out of the national title picture. In Texas' 1964 bowl appearance, Sauer's 69-yard catch-and-TD run produced Texas' winning points in the Orange Bowl against NCAA champion Alabama and Joe Namath.

According to Lammons, George Jr. didn't care for Coach Royal, so he departed for the professional ranks a year earlier than Royal had planned. George was the first redshirt Texas football player to leave UT early, and an unhappy Royal closed his practices to the Jets. George Jr. was not drafted by the NFL, whose scouts assumed he would join the Jets, where his father was personnel director.

The Jets already had a pair of top receivers in Don Maynard and Bake Turner, but Weeb Ewbank, recognizing Turner's small frame and proclivity for injuries, wanted another tall, sure-handed target for Joe Namath. George Sauer Sr. assured Ewbank that his son would latch on to any spiral thrown near him. George Jr.'s 1965 rookie season was unspectacular, but he earned his stripes as an emergency late-season fill-in at tight end. When injuries sidelined starting TE Dee Mackey and backup Gene Heeter, George, twenty-five to thirty pounds lighter than a normal TE, started the Jets' final four games there.

Coach Ewbank dictated a glowing evaluation of Sauer's first campaign in his personnel notes:

GEORGE SAUER / 6'2" / 206 / 22 / 78%

Has all of the skills to be a great receiver: great hands, fine moves, good speed and size and strength (rare for a flanker). I believe there were definite factors that thwarted his performance development: 1) came to camp with a pull and missed 11 days (over 20 sessions). Although he learned all the mental work he still wasn't "doing it" in this difficult position. 2) Throughout an early tempo-

rary general receiving problem on the squad, George was forced to become a starter before he was ready and did not have the opportunity to "grow" into it smoothly. 3) About the time he began to come along as a flanker, it was necessary to switch him to the injured TE position. He made the adjustment to TE extremely well because of intelligence and an excellent attitude. . . . His best position is still outside.

Most telling about George Jr. was Weeb's declared faith in the receiver's future prospects:

Must and will improve in every category including his blocking which is not adequate. Because of the person he is I am confident George will come to camp with some of the rough edges already knocked off and will improve skills to greatness in the future. Is already effective on [special] teams.

George blossomed in his second season, with a contact lens in his right eye to correct twenty-two hundred vision. He replaced Bake Turner in the starting lineup, grabbed 63 passes, and averaged 17.1 yards each. In 1967, his 75 catches led the AFL and he added 66 more in 1968. So magnificent were his hands that the *New York Times'* Dave Anderson ended one game story after a rain-soaked afternoon at Shea Stadium reveling that Sauer "probably could catch a pass while scuba diving."

Off the field, Sauer was an easygoing guy who enjoyed the company of teens and other young people. Dr. Cal Nicholas' daughter, Connie, spoke warmly about the star receiver hanging out with her as a teenager and blending in with other Jets at the team physician's home. He made it a habit to bring along his guitar. Dana Keifer said, "Kids loved him; he could get down to their level with very little effort. George never had guitar lessons, but could play it by ear, and he could play beautifully."

George Sauer Jr.'s contributions to the Jets' offense extended beyond statistics. Sauer's off-the-field horn-rimmed glasses and blond facial hair reminded his sister of Albert Einstein, an apropos comparison because George's football thought process was zealously analytical. He filled his playbook with notations about one-on-one match-ups with defensive backs and was exhaustive about fixing flaws in his route running. Sauer asked Joe Namath to stay after practice to refine his moves and improve their timing. That kind of over-the-top commitment became contagious. George's personal drive got the attention of Pete Lammons and Don Maynard, who began staying late as well.

"One of George's favorite patterns was a corner post," depicted teammate and friend John Dockery. "He'd go down ten or twelve yards, break hard to the middle like he was running a post pattern, take three steps, Joe would pump-fake, and George would break his pattern hard to the corner, maybe twenty yards downfield. It was about impossible to cover because of his great quickness and body control, plus the timing between Joe and George. The defensive back would be turned around, he'd often be off-balance and arrive late to the sideline."

All the Jets receivers learned how to read defenses. The preciseness of Sauer's routes enhanced his ability to find the seams between linebackers and defensive backs. He was even more dangerous in that he could read coverages at full speed. His concentration was so acute that he claimed to see the grain on the ball, "even the printing" on its way into his hands.

Before the Super Bowl, George was nervous but confident. He told the *Times'* Anderson, "My problem this week is not to be overwhelmed by the situation. Like today, when we got back from practice, the kids were waiting for us to get autographs. It suddenly struck me why I am here. I began to realize that this is the biggest game in pro football. . . . My problem this week is keeping my cool."

To put the game in context, George Jr. remembered how his dad had somehow coaxed the winless, 21-point underdog Navy team in 1948 into tying an unbeaten, untied, eight-win Army powerhouse, 21–21. Twenty-one years later, George Jr. was on a club that bookies had made a 17- to 21-point underdog. The longshot similarity between the two games was obvious.

Sauer Jr. became Namath's favorite target in Super Bowl III. Johnny Sample had passed on personal tips about competing against Lenny Lyles, who defended Sauer that day. George caught passes in front of the Colts' corner and deked him to break loose on midrange patterns. A double move twisted Lyles around, clearing George on a post pattern that led to a 39-yard gain, the Jets' longest of the game. He also fumbled a second-quarter pass on the Jets' twelve-yard line that proved one of the turning points in the game when Baltimore failed to convert it into any points. Seeing George continuing to brood about his miscue at halftime, offensive tackle Winston Hill told his teammate, "Thank you, George. You showed me you were human."

No one could have guessed that the 16–7 Jets win would spark the beginning of the end of Sauer's Jets career. He felt his career had peaked and he acknowledged that his dedication to football fell after that. In the locker room after Super Bowl III, George recollected, "My dad was there. We shook hands. He said, 'Thanks.' I said, 'Thanks.' I don't know exactly why it was we were thanking each other. . . . I think all of us have a need to feel as competent as the person who is our example in life. Well, I think I had finally done that because my dad had played in an NFL championship in 1936 with the Green Bay Packers and they won the game. I didn't have anything more to prove in football."

He didn't retire for another two years, but bereft of his drive, Sauer's game deteriorated. It became noticeable to the opposition. His pass patterns, always unpredictable with double moves and sharp permutations, became more conventional. Buffalo Bills cornerback Butch Byrd noticed it. Byrd had figured out a few things about covering Sauer. "I remember [Weeb] Ewbank yelling and screaming at George from the sideline because he wasn't getting loose. I actually felt kind of sorry for George because things had changed so dramatically," Byrd said.

George Sauer Jr.'s statistical grade in 1969 was a glossy 91 percent, yet his production clearly had dropped. After averaging 68 receptions from 1966 to 1968, he caught only 45 that year and 31 in 1970. At age twenty-seven, Sauer retired with one year left on a $40,000 contract.

It turned out that Ewbank's comparison with Raymond Berry was spot-on. In George's six years—less than half the thirteen played by Berry—George Jr. gained 4,965 receiving yards (53.5 percent of Berry's total). Sauer had 49 percent the number of catches registered by Berry (309, versus 631). George averaged 59.1 receiving yards per game versus Berry's 60.2 and exceeded Berry's yard-per-catch (16.1 versus 14.7).

In walking away from pro football, George shared with Jets beat writers his discomfort with football's intense, militaristic style and dehumanizing discipline. He told the *New York Times* that "for me, playing pro football got to be like being in jail."

Yet Sauer Jr. never completely left football. In 1973, he volunteered to coach at tiny Oberlin College. Head coach Cass Jackson says George guided everything on the team's offense. Away from practices and games, he still demonstrated amazing intensity. "He ran five or six miles every day to stay in shape," Jackson remembered. "We'd stop and talk and then George would run pass patterns over and over. He was like a kid; he almost wore my arm out."

In 1974, Sauer returned to pro football to play for the World Football League's New York Stars. His playing days ended after that season and in 1979 he became an assistant coach with the American Football Association's Carolina Chargers. He was later its head coach for two seasons.

He worked assiduously for decades toward his goal of publishing a book, finally submitting a novel that a publisher told him was a little dense. His sister read it and had the same impression. She said George had spent years collecting unfamiliar words that he had stored in a green box. Keifer said of his writing, "I needed a dictionary to read something in four hours that should normally take thirty minutes." George's fondest wish—to have a book published—never came to pass.

George Jr. told former Jets publicist Frank Ramos that one of his life's most moving moments came when he represented his late father at a U.S. Naval Academy ceremony in the late 1990s. George Jr. said he was overcome with pride as dedications were made about his father, who had coached at the academy in 1948–49.

George suffered from what he had long feared, the same Alzheimer's disease that killed his father. George Sauer Jr. died on May 7, 2013, of congestive heart failure.

Dane Knutson, who stocked shelves with Sauer at a grocery store in Sioux Falls, South Dakota, in the 1990s, called his late companion "the most interesting guy I've ever known. It always amazed me that . . . I had gotten to be such a friend to a Super Bowl hero. . . . He was an incredible man who could never overcome his demons. I think [he] wanted to achieve greatness and, at the same time, was scared to death of the greatness that he wanted to achieve."

PETE LAMMONS

TIGHT END #87   6'3"   230 LB.

Pete caught few passes in Super Bowl III because he was busy blocking Baltimore's vicious blitzing linebacker, Mike Curtis.

"I didn't know where New York was when they drafted me," Pete Lammons said. "Heck, I didn't know if I was good enough to play in the pros." His two University of Texas buddies, free agent quarterback-turned-safety Jim Hudson and receiver George Sauer Jr., were waiting for him to join them after the Jets made Lammons their 1966 eighth-round draft choice. "I asked them after their rookie year if I was good enough to play, and they said, 'For sure you can play here [on the Jets].'"

As an offensive end and linebacker for Texas, Lammons made headlines in the 1964 Orange Bowl by intercepting Alabama's Joe Namath twice in Texas' win. Texas Coach Darrell Royal's belief in an offense oriented to three-yard runs and a succeeding cloud of dust made it unusual for Texas to chuck the football. However, Lammons set and still holds the Longhorns' record for touchdown receptions in one game (three). "It was against Baylor and I didn't play the second half because we were beating the hell out of them," he cackled.

Jets defensive coach J. D. Donaldson had come down to Austin, determined to sign Lammons; he offered him $13,000 on the spot, a bonus, and a no-cut contract, and Pete told Donaldson to drop the no-cut. "I wasn't going to waste my time if I couldn't play," he explained, before his mom recommended, "You better sign this," and he agreed that day to the salary and a bigger bonus.

Lammons had no idea that the no-cut was a sign of the Jets' desperation for a tight end and belief in his ability to fill the slot. In Weeb Ewbank's personnel evaluations the year before Lammons arrived, the coach had noted the team's dire need for a tough tight end who could block and catch. Lammons fit immediately in offensive assistant Clive Rush's system. Entering the lineup to start the second half of the first preseason game, Lammons blocked like a demon and was in synch with the offensive system. Pete became an immediate starter.

In addition to solid blocking, during his rookie season Pete grabbed 41 of 81 passes thrown to him by Joe Namath for 565 yards (a 13.8-yard average). In his second season, he gathered in 45 passes for

515 yards (11.4-yard average). Picking up the nickname "Big Boy" from Namath, Pete provided steady, reliable play and toughness, missing only one game in his six seasons in New York. In 1967, he, Don Maynard, and George Sauer Jr. were named to the AFL All-Star Game, the first time in pro football history that all three receivers from the same team appeared together in an all-star contest.

Playing with pain became a trademark and a source of pride for Lammons. In 1968's third game, he had been too lame to start against San Diego at Shea, but torn leg muscle and all he somehow pulled himself off the bench to make a last-minute, straight-ahead, goal-line block that got Emerson Boozer into the end zone with the winning TD. Not keen about any sort of surgery, Lammons missed only that first half of that one game that season. Dr. Jim Nicholas, who knew more than anybody on the Jets about injuries and pain thresholds, told Pete he "was a medical phenomenon."

According to Don Maynard, Pete's presence at TE on the same right side of the field as Don was one of Pete's unsung contributions. "Every time I made a catch on the strong side, I had to thank him and compliment him for entertaining the linebacker there," Maynard elaborated. "I caught a lot of passes because Pete was drawing coverage. A lot of times, Namath would call a play, Pete would react to Joe's call and the defensive coverage, or he'd split out a little wider to get the linebacker to come out with him. The linebacker didn't know whether the pass would go to Lammons, Boozer, Snell, or Mathis on a little curl pattern and it kept extra coverage off of me." In Super Bowl III, Maynard drew almost game-long double zone coverage, leaving empty spaces underneath for tosses to Pete and the Jets backs.

Showing up for fourteen games each season wasn't commonplace for any pro football player. In the Jets' fifteenth game of the 1968 season—the AFL Championship Game—Pete caught a 20-yard touchdown. Game sixteen was, of course, the Super Bowl.

Jets fans with only a passing familiarity with Super Bowl III know two things: (1) the Jets won, and (2) Namath guaranteed the victory. But they should also know a third: that Pete Lammons half-jokingly pleaded after a film session to Weeb Ewbank days before the game to stop showing footage of the Colts against Cleveland and Minnesota because the Jets were getting overconfident. "That may have been the smartest thing I ever said . . . and at the time we were eighteen-point underdogs," Lammons chuckled.

That eighteen-point spread colored everyone's expectations. Pete got a call from his Texas high school coach the night before Super Bowl III. "I was surprised," Pete related. "I talked to him for a while and I told him, 'We're going to win this game tomorrow.' He said, 'Hmm,'" Lammons recounted and laughed about his old coach's discouraging reaction.

On Tuesday, January 7, 1969, the receivers, quarterbacks, Weeb, and Clive began looking at film of the Colts. Weeb had gone to school on Baltimore the week before, telling his coaching staff that there was no reason the Jets couldn't pull off the upset, and that the Jets' ability to throw the ball against the Colts' vaunted defense was about as sure as anything.

"The film showed what the Colts' defense did in certain situations, and they mostly ran a zone [passing] coverage," Lammons remembered. "They thought zone was the best deal in the world because their defensive backs were all old and they hadn't been beaten deep all year. Maynard looked at the film and said he'd beat Bobby Boyd.

"Baltimore really loved to blitz, too—and our backs loved when defenses blitzed. Snell, Boozer, and Mathis were always ready for it, and the rest of us were great at taking on blitzers. When a team blitzes, somewhere your receivers have one-on-one coverage. Joe and us could take advantage of that every time a defense blitzed." Weeb Ewbank confidently told reporters the weekend of the game that he welcomed Baltimore blitzing. But the film study was more intensive than that.

"As we watched the film, it wasn't so much the defense of Baltimore that got our attention, it was the Colts' playoff opponents, the Vikings and Browns. They ran the play called in the huddle, refusing to make an adjustment. Even if their play call was a bad deal, they kept running into the strength of the Baltimore defense," Lammons said. "We also saw that neither team's quarterback, Joe Kapp for the Vikings or Bill Nelson of the Browns, threw the ball well."

The Jets scoffed about running an offense that didn't adjust with the defense it was up against. "We never did that," said Lammons. "We'd read the defense and run particular patterns based on zone or man coverage. The Colts mostly played zone and we'd beaten teams to death all season who played zone because we studied and knew where the holes were downfield."

Lammons didn't have a lot of passes thrown his way in Super Bowl III, but one of his three catches continued a drive that led to a Jets field goal. Pete punished the Colts with his blocking. Lammons continually faced off against the NFL's 1968 cover boy for vicious play and blitzing, left-side linebacker Mike "Mad Dog" Curtis. As the two butted heads over and over, Lammons said he learned what he couldn't see on film: Curtis was also "a cheap shot kind of guy" and a supreme trash talker.

On one of the first series, Curtis blitzed and was greeted by Matt Snell, who dumped Curtis far from Namath. Not long after that, Lammons remembers, "I was blocking Curtis and he brought an uppercut under my chin. It was real chickens--t play, trying to intimidate. The next time we lined up across from each other, I came out of my stance and hit him right in the jaw, knocked him on his back, and he never touched me the rest of the game."

AFL all-stars from the Super Bowl Jets were showered with thanks from other AFL all-stars the week after the game. Expressions of gratitude continue to this day. Pete says for years players have approached him to express gratitude for what the Jets did to bolster the reputation of the league with that one win.

Lammons has outlived former Texas teammates Hudson and Sauer, as well as linebacker Larry Grantham, so he (in 1963 for Texas) and Joe Namath and Paul Crane (1964 at Alabama) are the only surviving Super Bowl Jets with a professional and college championship ring.

RUNNING BACKS
POWER, SPEED, AND A LOT OF BLOCKING

BILL MATHIS	#31
MATT SNELL	#41
EMERSON BOOZER	#32
BILLY JOE	#35
LEE WHITE	#34

BILL MATHIS

RUNNING BACK #31   6'1"   220 LB.

Bill was always called an original Titan, but actually he started 1960 with Houston and was acquired from them.

Bill Mathis never wowed scouts or fans with flashy moves, breakaway speed, or bruising runs over defenders, but under the tutelage of Weeb Ewbank and Clive Rush (and with family encouragement) he developed into a valued pro running back. In his ten-year Titans/Jets career, Mathis became known for consistency, willingness to undertake what Bill made seem an effortless transition into changing backfield roles, a positive team approach, and loyalty. His blocking, catching, and short-distance running became so reliable that when Bill tried to retire in 1969 after Super Bowl III to work on Wall

Street, Mathis was asked by Weeb Ewbank to delay it. He cheerfully obliged.

The Denver Broncos won Mathis' AFL draft rights when his name was literally plucked from a container filled with the names of senior running backs during the AFL's inaugural college allocation draft in November 1959. Also an eighth-round choice by San Francisco of the NFL, Mathis noticed the 49ers' backfield had legends Hugh McElhenny and Joe "the Jet" Perry. It convinced him to head to the AFL.

But Mathis signed with the Houston Oilers when Houston owner Bud Adams approached him. According to America.pink in a posting about the 1960 AFL draft, "AFL teams cooperated in signing draftees, allowing other teams in the league to sign their choices, to keep the players in the AFL." Bill told the Oilers to top the 49ers' $5,000 offer, and Adams tripled it: an $8,000 contract and $7,000 bonus. Mathis got a better deal, but then he had to compete with the AFL's star signee, Heisman Trophy winner, running back Billy Cannon. Mathis' stay in Houston was short.

Acquired by the Titans after the second game of the 1960 preseason schedule, Mathis guessed that New York became his next stop due to the 1959 Blue-Gray All-Star Game, where an assistant coach on the Gray squad had been Sammy Baugh, who months later became head coach of the Titans.

Mathis said that he had little trouble with the jump to the pro ranks. "I had never seen a pro game, but thought I was good enough to make the pros when I reported to Titans camp," recalled Mathis. "I was bigger than the other guys. I saw myself as a reliable short-distance back and I picked up what I needed to be a good receiver. I ran a ten-second one hundred but I was quick cutting into holes. There was no position coach on the Titans, so I picked things up myself, and Sammy Baugh would run plays over and over until you got it right."

Mathis played special teams most of his rookie year, after which he spent the off-season lifting weights. Bill gained sixteen pounds, mostly muscle, and became the Titans' 1961 starting fullback. Mathis had quite a coming-out party: the team's leading rusher (846 yards), the AFL's leader in carries (202), Titans MVP, and an AFL All-Pro.

Despite that sterling 1961 season, Bill told Titans historian William Ryczek that he tried to forget the franchise's early years and its series of problems. At the Jets' first training camp in the summer of 1963, Weeb Ewbank chose to retain Mathis along with more than one dozen ex-Titans on the squad, and Bill became a personal favorite of Sonny Werblin.

However, Weeb was not bowled over by Mathis. Ewbank was desperate for a complete back with power, speed, catching, and blocking ability, a role Mathis couldn't fill. After the 1964 season, with two years of Mathis' work as a Jet under his belt, Weeb wrote in Bill's talent evaluation:

> Has been a get-by performer for two years with limited all-around ability. . . . Has been a consistently good pass protector, better than average blocker. . . . A below-average receiver, with below-fair hands. Hard runner, but lacks speed. . . . A hypochondriac and will not play hurt.

Weeb wrote in his next Mathis review that he believed that Bill's pro career turned around after he mentioned retirement to Ewbank and Mathis' mother. Weeb surmised that something clicked after the family tête-à-tête. Mathis returned to the Jets in 1965 and his performance bore no resemblance to what Ewbank had seen before. His belief in Mathis took a sharp turn for the better.

After 1965, Ewbank dictated:

> Improved in total yards and average per try, as well as considerable improvement in pass receiving, which, the two previous years had been poor. Continues to be a consistently good pass protector and above-average blocker.

Weeb also praised Mathis' "favorable attitude, which has been questionable in the past . . . overall improvement in areas such as extra effort in running, breaking tackles, and concentration for pass receiving even with poor hands. Practiced harder, complained less."

Mathis had actually begun to show himself as a keeper beginning in 1964. When the Jets signed Ohio State fullback Matt Snell, Bill welcomed the bigger, faster rookie, tutored him on the finer arts of blocking, and transitioned to halfback, alongside the 1964 AFL Rookie of the Year. Mathis pooh-poohed any real adjustment, saying, "They [fullback and halfback] were essentially the same position."

After the slippery, speedy Emerson Boozer joined the Jets to play halfback and added an entirely new backfield dimension in 1966, Bill's role was altered again. Boozer cut into Mathis' time in the backfield, yet Bill was one of several teammates who stayed after practice to teach Emerson how to block. Through 1969, Snell, Boozer, and Mathis became the Jets' revolving rushing threesome, with Mathis the multidimensional, third-down contributor. He would report into the lineup, block for Joe Namath in passing situations, occasionally catch, and sometimes make a surprise run.

As Mathis grew into his new role, his number of receptions markedly improved. Bill's 22 in 1966 came with an impressive 17.2 yards per catch. It jumped somewhat in 1967, with a career-high 25 catches and 429 receiving yards, and the same 17.2 average. In 1967, with Snell injured in game one and Boozer shelved for the year in game seven, Mathis was the only healthy member of the running trio for the entire campaign.

Mathis' contributions evolved again in 1968. Boozer came back from his torturous 1967 knee injuries and, for his own protection, was confined to first- and third-quarter play by Jets surgeon Dr. James Nicholas during the regular season. That pushed Mathis on the field for extra playing time in the second and fourth quarters of games. With three healthy runners in 1968, the Jets pounded the ball on the ground 467 times, 20 percent more than any earlier season.

Bill contributed four catches in the Jets' 1968 AFL Championship Game victory and four more in the Super Bowl, and had 6 rushes in each game. In 1969, Bill's final year with the Jets, he recorded his best rushing totals since 1965 (96 carries and an average 3.7 yards-per-carry). When Mathis retired after 1969, he was the second-leading rusher in team history (3,589 yards) and had a respectable 3.4-yard average.

Weeb's faith in and reliance on Mathis came to light when he assigned Bill to be Joe Namath's first road roommate. He recalled, "I was supposed to keep Joe from going astray. In New York, I spent a lot of time out with him, a lot of time at Toots Shor's. I hope I did good—Joe didn't miss a game and I don't think [when we roomed] that Joe showed up with a hangover."

Bill also learned firsthand about Namath's prolific sex appeal. "I had a promotional deal that got me a *Buick* to drive. Joe and I went everywhere in it. So many fans recognized the car that I had to park it inside Shea Stadium during practice because fans were stealing everything off it," he related.

When Mathis wasn't on the town with Namath, he rollicked around New York with roommate Tucker Frederickson, the 1965 first-round pick of the New York Football Giants. The two running backs remained the best of friends, to the consternation of the Giants. Tucker watched Super Bowl III from a seat provided by "Birdie," as everyone called Bill. (It was a reference to the Thunderbird that Mathis had lusted for during his Titans' days and eventually bought.) Frederickson expected a Baltimore blowout. "I couldn't get out of the Orange Bowl fast enough at the end of the game," he said of the ordeal of watching the NFL champions get taken to school by Bill and the Jets that afternoon.

Mathis, seventy-nine as this was written in 2017, lives in an assisted living facility, suffering from Alzheimer's disease and dementia, symptoms consistent with chronic traumatic encephalopathy and peripheral neuropathy. Monthly, he collects $3,000 from the

NFL retirement plan and legacy benefits, and he is awaiting a settlement with 4,000 of his former NFL alums for willful deception about the effects of concussions and collisions. The NFL also covers up to $130,000 annually for Bill's medical issues related to neurocognitive issues through the 88 Plan. His family considers it a true blessing.

MATT SNELL

FULLBACK #41   6'2"   219 LB.

George Sauer Sr. brought Matt a defensive playbook to the Southwest Challenge Bowl. After the game, he never saw one again with the Jets.

Matt Snell holds a number of distinctions in Jets lore. He was one of the cornerstone college stars that the NBC television network demanded the AFL sign when the Peacock Network doled out $36 million in 1964 for its American Football League coverage. The first number-one pick ever to sign with the Jets, he earned the Jets' first AFL Rookie of the Year honors, led the team in 1964 in rushing, and finished second in receiving. The fourth-leading rusher in Jets history (4,285 yards), he is not only synonymous with the Jets' Super Bowl III victory over Baltimore, but in the minds of many, deserved to be named MVP in that epic win.

But Matt's first mark in Jets history occurred in 1963, the only time both the New York Jets and New York Giants made the same player a high draft pick (the Jets' number-one selection in the AFL draft on November 30, 1963; the Giants' number three in the NFL draft, three days later). When they didn't ignore them, Giants ownership publicly sneered at the Jets until after Super Bowl III.

A Giants fan growing up on Long Island, Matt was the first member of the Snell clan given the opportunity to attend college. His mom became sold on Ohio State when Matt was offered a full scholarship that was not dependent on him playing football. Coach Woody Hayes promised Mrs. Snell that Matt would earn his B.A. if he was a serious student, accepted tutoring if needed, attended classes, etc. That established college as a Snell family goal for his siblings and, later in life, his own children.

It's hard to fathom that during Matt's college football career, he was never timed in the 40-yard dash. (Jets' notes show he ran a 4.6 in the pros.) "At Ohio State," Snell admitted, "all the skill position players had to do was run a mile in less than seven minutes." Also surprising: as Matt finished his senior year at Ohio State, he didn't know what it meant to be drafted.

Matt's Mom heard from a newspaperman shortly after the Jets selected him. Snell approached head coach Woody Hayes and his position coaches (he played running back and stand-up linebacker), and they calmly explained that he should sit back and wait for the NFL to hold its draft. He couldn't bring an agent on campus without jeopardizing his full scholarship, so Hayes became Matt's pro football career advisor. "Get the Jet and Giant offers, bring them to me, and we'll evaluate them with you," he was instructed.

The Giants had just lost the NFL Championship Game to the Chicago Bears. They sent scout and Giants legend Emlen Tunnel to Columbus, Ohio, to meet Matt. Old and rebuilding, the Giants offered Snell a multiyear contract but said he should expect to sit for a few seasons and learn from veteran Giants running backs Alex Webster, Dick James, and Joe Morrison. Later he met a member of the Mara family, owners of the Giants.

Matt next got together with Jets principal owner Sonny Werblin, who needed to make a splash in New York. Werblin promised Matt that he'd start immediately for the Jets and he shared the Jets' five-year plan to build a championship team, telling Matt that he would be a cornerstone. Then came the teams' offers.

"My father had a fifth-grade education and never made more than fifteen thousand dollars; my mother graduated eighth grade and, as a woman, made less than that. I couldn't imagine the kind of money the Giants and Jets offered me," Matt remembers. Snell weighed the Giants' $12,000 salary and $12,000 bonus versus the Jets' offer of $20,000 salary and a $30,000 bonus, and inked a one-year deal with the Jets due to personal attention from the Jets' head man.

His contract settled, Snell was invited to Corpus Christi, Texas, to play on January 4, 1964, in the Southwest Challenge Bowl, pitting Texas' senior college all-stars against all-stars from the rest of the country. "The Jets had drafted me as a linebacker and that's where I was going to play in the game. But our team's fullback didn't show up," Snell recalls, "and the Thursday before the game the coach of the National All-Stars, Oakland's Al Davis, asked me to play fullback with halfback Butch Byrd. Davis told me, 'You'll mostly be blocking.'" Snell's play that weekend altered his professional career.

The National team slaughtered Texas, 66–14. Snell ran for 117 yards and 4 touchdowns. Al Davis was smitten, but was rebuffed when he called the Jets about trading for Snell. Matt wasn't carried away by his performance, saying that it was "just one of those fluke games. Everything I did turned out right." Maybe so, but Jets' plans for Matt Snell at outside linebacker went into the dumpster. "Jets player personnel director George Sauer Sr. came to Texas to give me a defensive playbook to begin studying," Matt said. "After the game, he told Weeb Ewbank, 'If you don't put this guy at running back, you're crazy.'"

Matt's transition to the professional game was more of a challenge off the field than on. He had been exposed to segregationist attitudes when Ohio State hosted Texas Christian's lily-white squad in Columbus in the first game of his senior year. "The guys on TCU had never played against a team with black players," recalled Snell. "One said, 'You *guys* are pretty good.' I asked them a couple of times, 'What do you mean, "You guys?" Who's "You guys?"'"

The United States was convulsed by turbulent racial issues, and

Peekskill Academy, site of the Jets' training camp, wasn't inoculated from them. The Jets had a number of southern white players. When in 1965 a rookie black wide receiver, Alphonse Dotson, was invited by a group of white Jets for a night out, Matt says he warned Dotson to be careful. Sure enough, after too many drinks at a bar, things got out of hand. They all returned to the dormitory and, in what the veterans thought was a joke, they cut eyeholes in sheets, pulled the sheets over their heads, tied up the helpless receiver, and hung him up from beneath his arms from a light fixture. Studying the playbook up in his room, Matt heard screams, rushed down the stairs to the source of the commotion, saw Dotson, and freed him.

Matt insisted Clive Rush call Weeb. The next morning, Sonny Werblin forcefully communicated his intolerance to his team for any racist behavior. Only Matt and rookie Joe Namath were assured jobs, Werblin stated; everyone else was expendable and could be replaced. "I can have a new team here by Saturday," Matt recalls Werblin saying. Snell said that "didn't necessarily change the way some guys may have felt, but after Sonny spoke out, they wouldn't act on it in a way that would affect the team."

In Snell's rookie year (1964—the Jets' inaugural season at Shea Stadium), the back he was replacing, Bill Mathis, took Matt under his wing. Mathis became a halfback in the Jets' split backfield and improved Matt's blocking. Matt's 941 rushing yards that year were second only to AFL leader Cookie Gilchrist and he was fourth in the league in yards from scrimmage (1,341). Matt agreed it was his finest overall Jets season, but in his self-effacing way noted how tougher the competition became in succeeding years. "Look at who I was facing in 1964," he said with a laugh.

Snell's soft hands made catching the ball part of his game, but it needed to be honed. Matt estimated having caught 20 passes in three years in Woody Hayes' offense, a run-dedicated attack. Snell became a Jets receiving threat—sure-handed, quick, powerful, difficult to take down in the open field. After 56 receptions, good for seventh in the league and second to Bake Turner on the Jets, Matt learned why he had so many chances: a clause in Jets quarterback Dick Wood's contract. Wood was ponderous in dropping back in the pocket and his knees rivaled that of the more famous quarterback who would replace him, Joe Namath. "I found out Weeb put an unusual clause in Dick's contract. He wouldn't be paid if his knees were injured, so when Dick went back to pass and saw no one downfield to throw to, he always flipped it to me or Mathis in the flat," Snell said with a chuckle.

Bobby Bell, the Kansas City Chiefs' Hall of Fame linebacker and 1960s AFL All-Pro, went to war against Snell and described Matt as a "tough, tough guy. Trying to tackle him was like tackling a rock. I'd hit him with everything—and there was no change in his expression. I don't know what it was about him; he shot back to me the funniest look. He pissed off [Mike] Curtis in the Super Bowl; Curtis wanted to fight him."

Blocking became essential in 1965 when Namath joined the Jets; building a wall around Joe and keeping blitzers off the AFL's new star (to protect his fragile knees) became a core part of the offense. Snell's blocking was so good that it became Ewbank's standard for every running back. If you couldn't effectively block, you couldn't crack the Jets' lineup.

In a scrimmage, linebacker Paul Crane learned about Snell's blocking. He saw fellow linebacker Larry Grantham rush into the Jets backfield on a blitz, only to pull up and grapple with Snell in hand-to-hand combat. Crane couldn't understand why Larry had not barreled into Snell. Perhaps determined to impress, when it was Paul's turn to blitz, Crane ran full-speed into Snell and was thrown in a heap to the ground. "I learned why Larry didn't waste his time trying to get past Matt," Crane said. St. Louis Cardinals Hall of Fame safety Larry Wilson would say after facing the Jets in the 1969 preseason that no running back hit harder than Matt.

When Emerson Boozer, with his speedy, shifty, electrifying,

high-kicking running style, joined the Jets in 1966, Snell smiled at the new explosive outside running threat. Boozer didn't know how to block, but Matt saw that Boozer had the tools. With Weeb's approval, Matt took Boozer under his wing and taught him. After Snell was done coaching up Boozer, Jets left guard Bob Talamini said he never saw a tandem who could block like the twosome.

Snell was the first Jet to hold out for a better contract. After his rookie contract, he dickered with Werblin on a new pact and agreed to $25,000 for 1965 and $30,000 for 1966. He earned $30,500 in 1967 but tore the cartilage in his left knee in that season's first game. After working his tail off to get his knee back into playing shape (and with Werblin having sold his interests in the team), Snell had to negotiate with GM Ewbank. He was offered a $2,500 raise; Matt was determined to get $5,000. For added leverage, Ewbank signed fullback competition: free agent and former AFL Rookie of the Year Billy Joe and 1968 first-round draft pick Lee White from Weber State.

During training camp, White seemed a natural future replacement for Snell, so Ewbank's bargaining position stiffened. Ewbank told Matt he wouldn't play without a contract, yet Snell dressed for games and stood on the sideline. The season kicked off in Kansas City and White wrecked his knee. Weeb couldn't keep Snell, in uniform and ready to play, planted on the sideline. Matt carried the ball ten times that afternoon. After the game, Snell said, "Two hours ago, the club was in the driver's seat. Now, I'm behind the wheel."

The next Sunday against the Boston Patriots could have been another tense situation with Snell suited up and the Jets' starting fullback not running or blocking. Matt's contract situation was resolved in the midst of the game with an assist from . . . Joe Namath. At a key juncture during the second half, Joe told Weeb that he needed Matt in the lineup for the next drive. Weeb approached Matt; GM Ewbank gave him his $5,000 raise and Coach Ewbank sent him into the game.

Snell ended up having his third-best rushing season (747 yards, sixth in the AFL) in 1968, and the Jets captured the AFL championship in December. Snell barely had time to celebrate when odds maker Jimmy "the Greek" Snyder made the Baltimore Colts a 17.5-point Super Bowl favorite based on position-by-position superiority. Snyder gave the Colts two points for the Colts' superiority with Tom Matte and Jerry Hill versus Snell and Boozer.

Matt took personal umbrage over that slight. "I knew how good Matte was; I was a sophomore when he was a senior at Ohio State," explained Snell. He and Boozer had even stronger convictions about the strength of the Jets' running game. All season long, the play the Jets called 19 Straight had worked against every opponent. Watching the Colts on film convinced Matt and Boozer that Baltimore would be no exception. "The Friday before the game, Boozer and I made a pact in our hotel room: We'd go on the field Sunday," Snell related, "and whoever's running play was working, the other would block like they'd never done before."

Matt said the Jets knew they had to set the tempo for the game. "On the first play from scrimmage, Joe checked off at the line of scrimmage to run a sweep, a call Boozer and I didn't expect. I had to shift to my right, then run the sweep to the left behind Emerson." The play proved pivotal. Hill and Talamini executed their blocks. Leading Snell into the hole, Boozer blasted feared Colts' linebacker Mike Curtis, and as Snell turned the corner, his knee struck Colts All-Pro safety Rick Volk in the head. It concussed Volk. "I remember coming out of the pileup and saying, 'These guys aren't so tough,'" shared Snell.

All game long, Matt ran with unstoppable fury, blasting through and bowling over single Colts tacklers. Boozer and Bill Mathis picked up yards on the ground, too, and all three blocked like demons. At game's end, Snell had a Super Bowl record 121 rushing yards. Matt and Emerson's Super Bowl rings both say "19 Straight" on the inside, the play that met little Baltimore resistance that day.

Snell had one more productive season following the Super Bowl

(695 rushing yards in 1969), before injuries sidelined him and eventually closed out his career. In 1970, torn knee cartilage ended his season after three impressive games (281 yards—93 per game, exceeding his 1964 career-best 67 per game). In 1971, Matt ruptured his Achilles and in 1972 on the kickoff return team he broke a rib that ruptured his spleen.

Snell was escorted to the sideline, where he told team surgeon Dr. James Nicholas, "When I got hit, it felt like someone spilled hot water inside my belly." Matt was sent home, unaware that he was slowly bleeding to death. That night, he fell down the stairs and was unconscious. Matt's wife called an ambulance that took him to Lenox Hill Hospital, where he was tended to hours after his life-threatening injury.

Matt retired at age thirty-one, ready to move on with his life, which he had every reason to believe included a direct association with the Jets. "Sonny Werblin promised in presenting the five-year plan that if we won a championship, there would be a place for me with the team for life," explains Snell. "I was a local boy, from Long Island, who made good. I don't think that Sonny forgot our understanding; he came into our locker room after Super Bowl III, gave me a big bear hug, and kept telling me, 'We did it. We did it.' Two weeks later, I got a call from a New Jersey Cadillac dealer, who told me to come over and he gave me the keys to a 1969 mint-green Cadillac. 'This is from Sonny Werblin,' I was told. 'He thinks you were the Super Bowl MVP.'

"I don't know if Sonny ever communicated what he had promised me to the other owners. I know there were people around the organization that were not happy that Sonny and I were friends, and some of them jumped on the opportunity to say bad things about me when Sonny was gone. It may be that no one in Jets management knew about Sonny's promises to me, but in 1974, there was a recession and I was in line for a construction job. I asked the Jets for a reference. They told me they didn't do that for players. They said they couldn't do it! Can you believe that? I can't prove it, but I don't think any of that would have ever happened if Sonny were in charge. That's why I don't get along with the organization now."

EMERSON BOOZER

HALFBACK #32   5'11"   195 LB.

Fans never took their eyes off Boozer because on any carry he could make a startling move, break tackles, and race into the open field.

Emerson Boozer was an unheralded 1966 sixth-round draft choice out of Maryland State (now University of Maryland Eastern Shore) who had been pointed out to Jets scouts as one of the team's offensive solutions by Jets right tackle and fellow Maryland State alumnus Sherman Plunkett. The Jets' backfield desperately needed a fast, elusive, breakaway runner to diversify the attack and amp up the offense.

Rookie tailback Emerson Boozer banked his combined $110,000 salary and bonus and had what he thought was "a great [1966] preseason." Ewbank wasn't ready to insert Boozer into the lineup until, of all things, a defensive coach spoke up. "I happened to be on my way to the training room and I'll never forget hearing a very loud conversation Walt Michaels was having with Weeb," Boozer related in his familiar deep voice. "The two of them were going at it in Weeb's office about how little playing time I was getting. Walt told Ewbank, 'You've been looking for a breakaway back—and you've got him and you're afraid to put him on the field!'" From then on, Emerson had a steady role.

Emerson knew his blocking needed work and refinement; it was a matter of learning the basics and practice. "I needed more work in technique and timing than I could get in training camp," he said. "So, once the season started, I dedicated myself to work on my run blocking, pass blocking, and receiving before practice. Matt [Snell], Bill [Mathis], Mark [Smolinski], and Curley [Johnson] helped me with my blocking. After practice, I'd ask a linebacker to work with me on blitzes."

Learning how to effectively block involved, he said, "first taking the proper steps so you're not weak on the inside. Second, there was closing the gap between you and the oncoming 240-pound linebacker so that he couldn't come in full steam and bowl you over. It took time and it wasn't easy, but I got the steps down and I got used to head-on collisions with my eyes open."

Boozer's blocking improved so much that right guard Dave Herman complimented him saying, "He takes the romance out of the blitz." It was lofty praise given Matt Snell's reputation.

Boozer put a big smile on Weeb's face his rookie year with 455 yards and an average 4.7 yards-per-carry; he also returned one of 26 kickoffs 96 yards for a touchdown. Emerson's high-knee-action running style, a tactic taught in high school by coaches Jim Daggett and David Dupree, made defenders miss. No individual tackler could get Boozer off his feet. Even when surrounded, he found ways to squirm free from groups of tacklers.

To pro football fans in the 1960s, the descriptions "elusive" and "breakaway speed" instinctively brought to mind the Chicago Bears halfback Gayle Sayers. (Today it might be Patriots running back Dion Lewis.) Each time Boozer carried the ball, something startling could happen—and often did.

His "spin move" left would leave tacklers in the dust or mud. "I had to make contact with a defender before I began my spin. Young running backs want to spin before they get hit, but you can't do that. With the spin, you attack them—not the other way around," Emerson explained.

Boozer's favorite running call—"I could jitterbug on any play"—was a "34" or "35" call, where "I'd be running inside and had the option to turn it outside. One play I really liked was a quick trap. We ran a lot of those behind John Schmitt."

Emerson worked to improve his game in the 1966 off-season, but even with all his preparation his responsibilities became unexpectedly heavier when Snell was injured in the first game of 1967 and lost for most of the year. Boozer suffered from bilateral bunions on his toes but got off to an electrifying, record touchdown pace (10 on the ground and 3 through the air) in six-plus games. Sayers' pro record of 23 touchdowns was in his sights. "Frankly, that start even frightened the dickens out of me," he remembered. "It seemed too easy, so to speak. It reminded me of my high school and college days, where you wonder how the hell something happened. When you start off that fast against pro competition, it's just like a gift and you make the best of it."

In the first half of the seventh game, however, Emerson suffered a devastating knee injury. Fans were sad about the termination of Boozer's quest for the TD record, but it didn't come close to doctors' concerns about Emerson's football career. He had broken his tibia in high school, but this was far more serious: he had blown out the posterior cruciate of his knee, both meniscuses and his medial and lateral ligaments.

In his recovery, Emerson needed to overcome painful physical knee soreness and block out subconscious psychological doubts. "It took time because the ligament inserted in my knee was doing something it wasn't designed to do. I got used to it, and got past the adhesions and soreness from the surgery," Boozer recalled. "I also had to get used to not having full flex extension of my knee. I still don't, but my knee had the stability it needed." He also had to get reaccustomed to the punishment on his body and legs. The only remnant from the operation on his running was an inability to "stop fast," to not be able to "put on the brakes."

Some key plays rebuilt his confidence. In the fourth game of

1968, the offense went on a game-winning drive and reached the San Diego one-yard line. Joe Namath called Boozer's number on a play that would test his surgically repaired right knee. "I told Joe I wasn't too confident having to make a sharp cut. He said, 'Okay,' and changed the play. We went to the line, Joe looked at the defense, audibled, and checked off to run P34, the original play.

"'Oh s--t,' I thought, and I prepared for the snap on Joe's first sound. He handed off to me, I made the strong, sharp turn inside, jumped across the goal line, and scored. Joe forced me to have confidence. As we ran off the field, Joe told me he 'didn't do it for me. 34Power was part of our game plan.'"

Another play at another game at Shea instilled a different inward confidence. "I took a handoff, broke free, and scampered across the field," Emerson recalled. "The safety lined me up to make the tackle, but before he expected we were running almost side by side. I heard him curse because I blew right past him. Another time, I got hit hard and feared I had blown it out again, but Dr. Nicholas told me on the sideline that I had just torn some surgical adhesions. I limped to the locker room, extremely sore, spent a lot of time in the whirlpool, and a day later I was like new again.

"Late in the '68 season; I felt that the leg was sound, would not give out on me, and that I should just go out and do what my mind told me to do." Weeb Ewbank thought Boozer regained "his old flash" as a runner in the last game of the regular season. Boozer rushed for 83 yards, playing with agility and explosiveness on the Orange Bowl's "firm, fast turf" versus Miami.

"Before the operation, quickness was my game more than anything else, a highly unusual asset for a two-hundred-pounder. I had a lot more power than people thought . . . and I had speed. The surgery more than anything else deprived me of a lot of my former quickness. I came back as an elusive power back, perhaps with more power than before, still some elusiveness and no less speed. I had to change my running style—no more total high-knee action—but I was a more complete back, contributing with my blocking, catching, and running because I had time to work on all the other areas."

Weeb Ewbank later said that he never saw a player work as hard as Boozer to change and elevate his game. Boozer's determination to revive his career and his performance that Super Bowl year would have won him the AFL Comeback Player of the Year for 1968 if there had been such an award. UPI (United Press International, a news service) had discontinued its award after 1963, and the Associated Press did not give out an award from 1967 to 1998. Emerson had almost as many rushing yards, more carries, and as many catches in 12 games in 1968 than in either of his first two 14-game seasons.

Emerson attended both of the first two Super Bowl games. He told the *New York Times*' William Rhoden in 2010 that as he watched those contests, Green Bay's victories in Los Angeles and Miami, respectively, he wondered, "Will I ever get to this ballgame?"

A year later, he did make it. Boozer tried to tamp down roommate Matt Snell's emotions about oddsmaker Jimmy the Greek's superior rating for the Baltimore Colts' starting running backs. "Matt didn't understand how writers could write such a thing. If you knew both clubs, you would know they might be equal, but certainly not better than us," stated Boozer. "We thought in establishing an eighteen-point spread that the prognosticators didn't understand the game."

Boozer, freed by the doctors from playing restrictions in the playoffs, carried the ball only three times for 14 yards over four quarters in Super Bowl III, but his blocking in front of Snell's punishing runs enabled the Jets fullback to gain 121 yards that afternoon. Boozer recalls the Colts' All-Pro linebacker, Mike Curtis, pleading with his defensive teammates to stop the Jets' offense. It went for naught. Weeb Ewbank called Boozer "perhaps the best I have ever seen leading the running play as a blocker."

Emerson's most personal post–Super Bowl III recollection was feeling "totally exhausted from the work, training, and the game . . . the effort from doing everything we had to do . . . Oh, and Weeb forgot to order champagne. Our traveling secretary, John Free, went next door and borrowed the champagne the Colts had on ice for their expected victory."

Forty-eight years after the fact, the humble, eloquent tailback remains totally comfortable with his place in pro football history, as well as his understated but essential role in Super Bowl III. The 2010 electee to the College Football Hall of Fame for his Maryland State running exploits (2,537 yards and 22 touchdowns), Emerson also retired as the Jets' all-time leading rusher (5,135 yards); yet he was a generally unheralded Super Bowl superstar as a blocking back.

Boozer's complete recovery from 1967 surgery took three years. It's shown in his annual rushing totals, which year by year exceeded the 441 yards of his Super Bowl comeback year. He averaged nearly 625 for the next six years (topped by a career-high 831 in 1973). Emerson became a TD-scoring threat again in 1972, with 11 in 11 games. He retired after the 1975 season.

We learned from the wife of the Jets' halfback, Enez, that she and his teammates have always called him simply "Boozer." While she does not remember much about the game, Enez does remember being high in the stands as the Jets won Super Bowl III. "Over the years, Boozer and I have met so many sports, TV, and movie celebrities," she said with a sense of wonder, "all because he played in that game."

BILLY JOE

FULLBACK #35   6'2"   235 LB.

The 1963 AFL Rookie of the Year made special teams and running back contributions—and became one of college football's greatest coaches.

The highs and lows that beset William "Billy" Joe's AFL playing career from 1963 to 1969 were unique among Super Bowl Jets. Yet, his career highlights—Rookie of the Year, Pro Bowl player, member of two AFL Championship teams, and, of course, member of a Super Bowl winner—were unmatched not only by Jets players but by 99 percent of everyone else who donned an American Football League uniform. And he topped that, after hanging up his cleats, by becoming the second-winningest coach in the annals of black college football.

Billy Joe's collegiate career was highlighted in the 1961 Sun Bowl (where, as the game's "Outstanding Back," he shook off three tacklers on a 19-yard TD run) and the 1962 Liberty Bowl. In the 1963 college draft, Joe was the NFL Washington Redskins' ninth-round pick and the AFL Denver Broncos' eleventh-round selection. Redskins owner George Preston Marshall was a reputed racist, so despite promises from Redskin Coach Bill McPeak that the organization was changing, Billy opted for Denver's two-year, no-cut contract. It paid him a $6,000 signing bonus, $17,000 in salary in 1963, and $18,000 in 1964.

Joe was part of a short-lived era of giant running backs, exemplified by 235-pound Jimmy Brown and 240-pound Cookie Gilchrist. Heavier than most linebackers and the equal of some linemen at 250 to 260 pounds, the 6'2" Joe had a bruising, punishing running style—and when Joe got into the secondary, he could unleash an unusual burst of speed that permitted him to outrace defensive backs.

Billy won AFL Rookie of the Year in 1963 with the two-win Broncos, and after his sophomore year in Denver, in one of the biggest trades in AFL history, he was dealt with a substantial amount of cash to Buffalo for Gilchrist, the league's leading rusher in 1963 and 1964. Buffalo coach Lou Saban thought Joe would take direction better than Gilchrist, and continue to pound defenses like Cookie had. But there was a miscommunication between Saban and Joe. Billy had decided before the trade to follow his doctor's suggestion and drop thirty pounds. "My battered legs didn't permit me to carry my natural 250 to 260 pounds," Joe conceded. He also assumed the weight loss would boost his speed and elusiveness.

In retrospect, Joe questions that decision. "Losing that weight was my career's Achilles' heel," he said. "If my legs had been healthy, I'd have put the weight back on because big backs were very popular. Weighing less, I didn't have the size to run and block as they envisioned." He did, however, become a top receiver among AFL running backs.

Joe won a ring in 1965 as part of the second consecutive Buffalo AFL Championship squad, but it wasn't a banner season (only 377 yards, an average of 3.1 yards per rushing attempt). In the off-season, Joe was made available to the Miami Dolphins in the expansion draft and became the first selection. His rushing numbers slipped again (232 yards) for Miami in 1966 and he was released during training camp by the Dolphins in 1967. Joe, receiver Bo Roberson, and defensive lineman Al Dotson—three black players—went public about the racism they were encountering in and around the Boca Raton training camp. Weeb Ewbank signed Joe and added him to the Jets' taxi squad in early September.

When knee injuries sidelined Matt Snell for much of the 1967 season and Emerson Boozer was lost for the entire campaign, Joe became the Jets' lead back for a short period. He ran the ball 37 times, averaging 4.2 yards-per-attempt and caught 8 passes (with a career-best 10.6 yards per reception). "I had a lot of fun on the kick-off and other special teams," noted Joe, who took on the notoriously dangerous job of wedge buster. He fell prey to bruised ribs while running the ball and was lost for the season.

Joe returned to New York in 1968 to back up Matt Snell. The highlight of his season came October 27 against the Boston Patriots when Joe tied an AFL record with three touchdown runs (7, 15, and 32 yards) in a single quarter (the fourth). He spent most of his time on special teams and lasted ten games. Joe knew the dangers of being part of the Jets' suicide squad. "It worries you to death," he said. "Get hit from the side while you're chasing somebody with the ball, get blindsided and you're out of business." He was carted off the field in the closing minutes of the *Heidi* Game on a play most of the country never saw because NBC had switched to the movie. "All I saw was a blur coming at my knee," Billy recalled. "[Wayne Hawkins] hit me low and tore up my left knee," which was diagnosed as combined ligament, cartilage, and tendon damage.

Dr. James Nicholas performed a "Slocum operation" on Joe, a procedure similar to what had worked for Emerson Boozer in 1967. After three weeks at UCLA Medical Center in Los Angeles, Billy was moved to Lenox Hill Hospital in New York, where he recuperated from the injury and a subsequent staph infection. In his rehab, Joe "spent eight months squatting 350 times a day, walking with two pounds of metal attached to his knee and doing increasingly strenuous calisthenics," reported Bill Surface in the *New York Times Magazine*.

Joe couldn't watch the AFL Championship Game from his hospital room because it was blacked out in New York, but he was on the sideline in civvies at Super Bowl III, with a full leg cast from his hip to his toes, and crutches. He recalled seeing Colts open receivers in the game "that their quarterbacks didn't hit because of our rush. We just befuddled them. It was a real good game for us in terms of execution, game plan, and our players being fired up and ready to play. To those who think it was lucky, I've seen enough to understand that there's no luck in football, but things happen. Of course, luck is when opportunity meets preparation."

Billy returned to Jets training camp at Hofstra University in the summer of 1969, uncertain that he could play again. Billy limped around, then after several weeks progressed to running, though not up to professional caliber. He played an exhibition game against Oakland, lugging the ball twice and not answering his or the Jets' questions about his ability to play. Still, Ewbank hung on to Billy the entire season and activated him to play in the last game. The knee never responded sufficiently to allow him to play in the Jets backfield and, at age twenty-eight, Joe retired.

The Billy Joe football story didn't end there—it became increasingly better. In 1970, he was a volunteer backfield coach at Cheyney State University of Pennsylvania. That led in 1971 to a paid coaching position at Maryland. He was named head coach at Cheyney State in 1972, which he held until 1978. For two seasons (1979–80) Joe served as the Philadelphia Eagles' running backs coach and he was part of the losing Super Bowl team in 1981.

From 1981 to 1993, Joe was head football coach at Central State University (Wilberforce, Ohio), and from 1986 to 1990 Billy's teams won five consecutive black college football national championships. In 1990 and 1992, he led Central State to NAIA football championships. Florida A&M hired him to coach in 1994 (through 2004), where he won a sixth black college football national crown. Coach Joe wound up his coaching career at Division II Miles College (Fairfield, Alabama) from 2008 to 2010.

Joe's college coaching career boasted 243 wins, 133 losses, and 2 ties—second, all-time, to Grambling great Eddie Robinson among historically black colleges and universities. In 1995, he was the second black college coach elected president of the American Football Coaches Association. In 2007, Billy was inducted into the College Football Hall of Fame (with Florida State coach Bobby Bowden and Penn State coach Joe Paterno). Ten years later, Billy became the ninth coach elected to the Black College Football Hall of Fame, a very special tribute, he said, because "they only elect coaches every other year and I preferred not to receive the honor posthumously."

Super Bowl III had a lasting impact on him personally and professionally. "I can't remember specifics, but over my thirty-four-year coaching career I know I mentioned Super Bowl III to my players," he said. "It was the old David-versus-Goliath syndrome. We were just about everybody's underdog—but we prevailed. Being part of Super Bowl III led to quality jobs and recruitment of excellent players."

LEE WHITE

FULLBACK #34   6'2"   232 LB.

White was destined to be the next great Jets fullback, until a knee injury in his very first professional game did damage he never recovered from.

In 1968, Lee White wasn't recognized by football fans as a top pro rushing prospect even though he had amassed 3,062 yards and 34 touchdowns in three years at tiny Weber State (Ogden, Utah) in the Big Sky Conference. "When I look back at my college days, I do it with pride," White noted. "We had a great team." The Wildcats won their conference his senior year and were ranked number five in the nation). *Deseret News'* sportswriter Dan Pattison said White "always walked like a king."

Lee's combination of size and 4.7 speed had pro scouts salivating. The Jets hoped "a big, fast running back" would be available when they picked seventeenth in the first round in 1968, and White and Syracuse's Larry Csonka were reportedly one-two on Weeb Ewbank's wish list. "Many pro scouts prefer Lee White [to Csonka] . . . Remember the name," penned Dave Anderson in the *New York Times* one month before the draft. On January 28, 1968, Miami selected future Pro Football Hall of Famer Csonka with its pick in round one and White fell to the Jets nine spots later.

In training camp, Ewbank praised Lee, comparing him to Cleveland Browns' Hall of Fame running back Marion Motley. After White returned from the College All-Star Game, Ewbank laid more compliments on White for his "sharpness and willingness to learn and work." Teammate Earl Christy remarked that White "looked like he was carved out of stone."

White saw significant preseason playing time and thrived, leading the Jets in running yardage (115). Then came the 1968 regular season—and White's career hopes were left shattered on the field at Kansas City. In the opening minutes in his first official pro contest, White sustained torn knee ligaments playing special teams. It was the first time he had ever been hurt playing football. No one could have foreseen that the Kansas City Chiefs' clipping infraction that destroyed his knee and sent White's tall, speedy, powerful body hurtling to the ground would be so utterly destructive to his career.

White's 1968 season was over, and he strenuously worked to strengthen his knee for a 1969 return. Lee wasn't in New York as the Jets clinched the AFL Championship in the last days of December 1968, so he sent Weeb Ewbank a postgame congratulatory telegram. Teammates awarded him a Super Bowl ring, reportedly three-fourteenths of an AFL championship share (about $1,714), and 50 percent of a Super Bowl share ($7,500).

Once the 1969 regular season began, White's backfield playing time was an afterthought. He played special teams in fourteen games. White's best chance to prove that he had come all the way back from the 1968 surgery surfaced in 1970 when Matt Snell incurred a torn Achilles tendon and White took over at fullback for seven games. He ran the ball 63 times for 188 yards. It didn't impress. Snell's return to health and the arrival of the 1971 first-round draft pick, Kansas' John Riggins, ended Lee White's Jets career in 1971 training camp.

THE KICKERS
"KING OF THE 43-YARD PUNT," TANK, AND "GOLDFINGER"

CURLEY JOHNSON	#33
JIM TURNER	#11
BABE PARILLI	#15

CURLEY JOHNSON

PUNTER #33   6'0"   215 LB.

A top AFL punter, Johnson was crucial as the guy who kept everybody loose—and the prankster for whom every Jets player was fair game.

Curley Johnson was one of the top punters in the American Football League during its ten-year existence. Eight times he was one of the top five. He led the combined NFL/AFL in punting once (1964), finished second twice (1962, 1963), was third best on three occasions, and fourth best twice. His career yard-per-kick average was 42.3, and in his very best season averaged 45.3. Curley's eight years with the Jets also stand out. Only two other punters (Steve Weatherford and Ben Graham) had higher Jets career punting averages, both over three years.

Curley was famous for his high, booming kicks. Randy Rasmussen admiringly called him the king of the 43-yard punt. "Every punt would go exactly 42 or 43 yards, with good height," Ras elaborated. "There were always kickers who could kick it 60 yards, but they would shank it here and there; not Curley."

Weeb Ewbank was somewhat less upbeat about Johnson's skills. He commented that "Curley took a little too long getting rid of the ball. A punter should get the ball off in about two seconds. He got off some long kicks for us and always had a good average, but we had to block a little longer for him and that left us susceptible to the good punt return."

Safety and punt returner Bill Baird emphasized that Curley and his punting excelled when the Jets most needed him, saying, "When we were backed into our end zone, he'd get off a fifty-yarder. He could move and execute under pressure." Indeed, in Super Bowl III, he got off a 40-yard punt to midfield from the back of the Jets' end zone against a ten-man Baltimore rush. When it was called back for offsetting penalties, Curley boomed the next one 46 yards from the backline.

As was required, Curley was a jack-of-all-trades on offense. Besides backup fullback and tight end, Curley was one of Jim Turner's holders for field goals and extra points from 1965 to 1967. Turner praised Curley as the best of the Jets' bunch of holders prior to Babe Parilli's 1968 arrival. Nobody in pro football compared with Parilli, but Turner said "there was probably no more than a millisecond difference" between Babe and Curley in how long they took to place the ball down.

Jim Turner's kickoffs were invariably short, so Curley got that assignment as well. He devised a means to get more foot into the ball, gluing a wide plastic insert underneath the front tip of his kicking shoe. Curley would tie a thick shoelace around the front end of the shoe and pull it back hard so that he could strike the ball directly with the insert. Records weren't kept for how far kickoffs traveled, but Curley's state-of-the-art kicking boot had to work well—he couldn't run very well to cover his own kickoffs with the kicking contraption on his right foot.

Weeb's private notes about Johnson, composed after the 1965 season, showed general satisfaction with Curley, that his punting had "gotten the job done." With tight roster space, specialists like Curley and field goal kicker Jim Turner had to be able backups at one or more other positions. Ewbank wrote that Curley had been "an average or 'get-by' performer when playing RB or TE." In spite of having led the AFL in punting for all but one of the league's fourteen weeks in 1965, Weeb hoped that Curley's punting would become more consistent, especially when he had to step in at tight end.

But Curley's backup responsibilities were nowhere as important as his contributions in keeping everyone on the roster loose and smiling. Only those who wore a Jets uniform and their immediate families knew about that side of Curley. He generated rollicking off-field chemistry and helped maintain the squad's morale. Don Maynard noted Curley's special nicknames for players that broke up the room. At a time of severe racial tension across America, even black teammates accepted Curley's verbal pokes. "Curley was really a big factor on our team for a long time," affirmed linebacker Ralph Baker. "He was loved by every Jets teammate."

In spite of Ewbank's punting criticisms of Johnson, John Schmitt spotlighted the harmony between the two. "If any player and coach on our team were at all close, it was Curley and Weeb." Curley knew it, too. "I loved Weeb and he loved me," he shared in his last interview. Curley's wife, Janet, tells a story that demonstrates her husband's goodhearted impishness and Ewbank's willingness to be Johnson's target. Weeb's given name was Wilbur, but no player dared to address him by that name, except as it turned out, Curley. He used it behind Ewbank's back with a select number of Jets.

Janet Johnson recounted that after a home game, she and son Curley Jr. were waiting outside the Jets' locker room for Curley when Weeb popped out. He greeted them and was introduced to eight- or nine-year-old Curley Jr. Weeb leaned over and said, "Hello, young man," to which Curley Jr. innocently replied, "Hello, Wilbur." Caught entirely off guard, Weeb had no comeback. Weeb's daughters laugh heartily at the story, commenting that their dad was only called "Wilbur" when their mom was mad at Weeb.

It would be an understatement to say that Curley was an independent sort, and he showed it if he didn't like a rule. Playing for the AFL's Dallas Texans, Johnson reviled head coach Hank Stram's "rah-rah" coaching style and resented the coach's no-smoking policy. After practice, Curley would find an out-of-the-way place to light up and not be hassled. In the Texans' 1961 training camp, Johnson walked into a bathroom and entered a stall when, by chance, Stram ambled in, smelled burning tobacco, saw smoke wafting from Curley's hiding place and spotted Curley's feet. Busted, Stram issued a $1,500 fine. Curley, making around $10,000, said he wouldn't pay it and challenged the coach to trade him. By the time he had driven home, he was a member of the New York Titans.

The Titans, hot for a professional punter, were glad to acquire Curley. Coach Sammy Baugh, a fellow Texan and Pro Football Hall of Fame QB, was one of Curley's football idols. Johnson wore Baugh's famed No. 33 in college and took the number with the Titans and Jets. Curley and Janet Johnson flew to New York and met the unassuming Baugh in the coach's apartment. The living legend greeted them in his underwear, smoking a stogie.

Curley told William J. Ryczek for his book, *Crash of the Titans*, how Baugh, a freak of nature who excelled at quarterback, safety, and punter during his playing days (he led the NFL in passing, interceptions, and punting in 1943), taught him the finer points of punting. Curley marveled as assistant coach Bones Taylor threw a long pass in practice to Baugh, who would punt it back within five to ten feet of Taylor. Baugh stressed to Curley how to avoid shanks by always aiming his kick toward the center of the field.

Curley remained the punter when the Titans became the Jets.

Johnson wasted no time razzing his new teammates and coaches, with no one immune from his mischief. "He built unity," emphasized Bill Baird. Joe Namath noted in his first book how Curley was one of the few Jets to welcome him in his first Jets training camp. "He kidded me just as cheerfully as he kidded everybody else," wrote Namath.

In probably his last interview in 2016, Curley admitted pranking Namath during that training camp, calling Joe on the phone from his room, putting on a falsetto voice, and arranging to meet Joe for a date. Namath wrote, "'She' talked a pretty good game, and I agreed to meet her downtown in Peekskill. When I showed up at the meeting place, there was no girl around. There were just a few guys—and Curley Johnson. 'Hi, dahlin',' he said."

Don Maynard became Curley's target after a game in Oakland. With the team plane delayed for hours after the game, Weeb Ewbank bused the team to San Francisco, where they could kill a few hours and have a good time. Maynard, typically watching what he was spending, asked Weeb for money to rent a room instead of exploring the city with the boys. Curley grabbed Ewbank's hat and started passing it around the room, asking the team to throw in some of their money "to help ole Don." They did, to Maynard's embarrassment.

Even Jets coaches treasured Johnson's personality. Weeb Ewbank accepted his status as a recurring target of Curley's good-natured humor. When Ewbank wasn't around, Curley flipped a baseball cap on his head, positioned it slightly sideways, got down on his knees behind a podium to underscore Weeb's short 5'7" frame, and barked out the coach's oft-repeated, cliché-rich pre-game comments. Weeb took it with good spirit and laughed along with everyone else.

For instance, the day the Jets players received coaches' intensive film study notes about the Colts, Carl McAdams remembers Curley holding court before his teammates "as Weeb." McAdams said, "As always, he had everybody laughing and in a great mood. All of a sudden, Weeb walked through the door and barked, 'What's going on here?' Curley didn't miss a beat, replying, 'I've just been getting them ready for you.'"

McAdams also remembers Curley announcing to his teammates, "We don't win many games, but we never lose a party." Jeff Richardson said Curley was always in finest form on the team plane on the way home after a road win. "With a captive audience, when he started talking, we stopped and waited for the punch line we'd heard many times before," shared Richardson.

Ralph Baker pointed out the obvious: some people can tell any joke and get a laugh, while other people tell a story and hope for a positive reaction. In spinning his yarns, Curley exaggerated his already pronounced Texas drawl, which all by itself cracked everyone up, every time. Pete Lammons said, "It wasn't what he said, it was how he said it." The best evidence of that came when Curley, accompanied by a teammate or two, approached complete strangers of the opposite gender in a hotel or restaurant. Lammons remarked, with a loud giggle, "He'd tell a crude joke, and this good-looking guy would get away with it. The women would laugh. If any of the rest of us had said the same thing, we'd have had our faces slapped."

Curley could take it as well as dish it out. Backup QB Mike Taliaferro remembers when Johnson flew into New York and was picked up by Bill Mathis and the pair headed into Manhattan. "Mathis parked his car on the street, and when they returned to it they found somebody had broken into Bill's car. They stole everything," Taliaferro said with a laugh, "except one of Curley's ties. Curley took an awful razzing about that."

Curley, the morale builder, was put to his biggest test after the *Heidi* Game in Oakland in November 1968. "The way we had just lost that game really threw us," John Schmitt related. The Jets had been called for a number of bad penalties, and defensive standouts Jim Hudson and John Elliott had been thrown out. Walt Michaels and Dr. James Nicholas were so upset with the officials that after the game they were banging on their locker room door. "It seemed like our forty guys were going in different directions," Schmitt said.

"We stayed on the West Coast in Long Beach to play San Diego the next week," Schmitt continued. "The hotel had a cocktail lounge on the second floor, and every night that week Curley told jokes, Clive Rush played the drums, Bake Turner sang and strummed his guitar, and George Sauer Jr. played the piano. Every night, Curley loosened us up, brought the team back together."

Many times, Curley's utterance was, frankly, incomprehensible. Rochester recalled Johnson exclaiming, "There are chickens and there are eggs." Rocky said he didn't often "understand what Curley was saying, but we always laughed." Curley's pet expression in the two weeks leading up to Super Bowl III was "Chicken ain't nothing but a bird." In "Curley talk," that translated to "The Super Bowl is just another game."

Curley's Jets career came to a sad, surprising end in the 1969 training camp, six months after the Super Bowl. He was the victim of Weeb's decision to replace several older Super Bowl Jets. Aside from age and issues with his punting, Curley's value had been lessened when the league ruled his special kickoff boot illegal, neutering his role on kickoffs.

To the obvious disappointment of his Jets teammates, Weeb awarded the punting job to rookie Steve O'Neal, a specialist with a booming leg who could not play other positions. Curley's absence in the locker room left a notable void. He served as an emergency fill-in punter for the New York Giants later that season before retiring. More than a decade later, at Weeb Ewbank's tearful, last reunion with the Super Bowl team, Ewbank told Curley he had made a mistake ever letting him go.

Curley's playful personality remained intact to his dying day. Shortly before he had to enter hospice in 2016, he watched a Texas Rangers game one night with son Curley Jr. The old man declared, "Time for bed check." As he was wheeled into his bedroom, Curley Jr.

kidded his dad, "Didn't you used to sneak out after bed check?" Curley responded, "You're correct," specifying Lammons, Jim Hudson, Larry Grantham, and Paul Rochester as his running mates.

Curley Jr. asked why they broke curfew. With no hesitation, Curley said that Marilyn Monroe wanted to meet him. When Curley woke up the next morning, Curley Jr. asked his dad, "Did Marilyn show up last night?" Curley told his son, "No . . . and I wouldn't know what to do with her if she had."

Janet Johnson said Curley had suffered from problems associated with his football career since age sixty when ultrasensitivity to sunlight made it difficult for him to venture outside. Things got progressively worse from there. Johnson died June 15, 2016, at 3:33 P.M. (33 was his uniform number). Suffering from Parkinson's disease and dementia, he was eighty years young. Janet, his wife of sixty-one years, dictated that the memorial service not be a downer. "I didn't want it to be so very sad. He was a happy person and I wanted that to show."

JIM TURNER

KICKER #11   6'2"   205 LB.

Jim had no use for GM Ewbank's tightness with player salaries, which even got him traded. But he thanks Coach Weeb profusely for his kicking career.

The Jets' Super Bowl III squad performed so well individually and as offensive and defensive groups, yet only placekicker Jim Turner rewrote the record books that season, establishing pro standards for field goals (34) and points scored by a pure kicker (145). In fourteen games, he was a perfect 43 of 43 on extra points and 34 of 46 on field goals.

Turner produced 9 points in the AFL Championship Game and 10 in Super Bowl III. Eleven kickers went on to surpass Jim's 145-point mark (Stephen Gostkowski did it five times)—all in sixteen-game regular seasons. To show how remarkable a season Jim Turner had fifty years ago, since 1968–69 the NFL single-season record for points by a kicker is 166 by San Francisco's David Akers in 2011. Add Jim's 19 points from the 1968 AFL Championship Game (no. 15) and 1969 Super Bowl III (no. 16) and he's at 164—two less than Akers and tied with Minnesota's Gary Anderson for second all-time.

Turner was such a great athlete that he played QB, safety, kick returner, kicker, and punter at John Swett High School in Crockett, California. It won him a football scholarship at Utah State. In college, Turner said he was a functional backup quarterback, a good leader (Utah State was 24-6 during his time there); he kicked extra points and played with future Pro Football Hall of Famer and actor Merlin Olsen and future NFL first-round pick QB Bill Munson. For a future star kicker, his kicking wasn't consistent. "I might have tried six field goals at Utah State. There were limited opportunities because we led the nation in scoring [31.8 points per game] in 1963," Turner said.

The Washington Redskins made him their 1963 nineteenth-round draftee, but Turner was cut in training camp. That fall, the Jets came west to play the Oakland Raiders and Weeb Ewbank, who had put up with putrid field goal kicking all season, invited Turner to come out to Oakland's Frank Youell Field for a tryout. Assistant coach Clive Rush gave Weeb a positive report after Jim booted three of four 52-yard field goal attempts.

Turner had a highly unorthodox, punch-kicking approach using square-toed kicking gear. Straightaway kickers predominated in pro football in the early 1960s, and two of the best were the Boston Patriots' Gino Cappelletti and the St. Louis Cardinals' Jim Baaken. "They had perfect follow-throughs. Nobody taught me my style," Turner said. "I kind of developed my style on my own. Maybe I didn't follow through because of tight back muscles."

Turner says that to this day he is indebted to Ewbank for the tryout. Weeb immediately recognized Jim's superiority to the 1963 Jets kicker, defensive tackle Dick Guesman, who was 30 of 30 on extra points and a lame 9 of 24 on field goal attempts. Turner actually rejected Weeb's on-the-spot contract offer, leaving his options open for 1964 pro camps. He ended up signing with the Jets.

In the summer of 1964, Jim won the Jets kicking job with his leg, plus his serviceability as a third-string QB, backup punter, and more. Both Jets tight ends were sidelined at times that season and Turner filled the void. In succeeding years, he took turns at quarterback, halfback, fullback, and even wide receiver. "I played receiver with Joe at quarterback. I had no moves. Joe called a pass play for me," Turner vaguely remembers. "I ran straight downfield as fast as I could . . . and ran over the cornerback."

Jim looked good enough at quarterback during practice that Ewbank wrote in his personal player notes that Turner could play the position in a pinch:

> One of our most valuable men. A fine all-around athlete and fairly good QB. Could finish a game at QB and not embarrass us. His throwing in training camp has always been fairly good with real good accuracy short.

Turner became Namath's emergency replacement when regular backup Mike Taliaferro injured his right collarbone versus Houston during the 1967 preseason. Bringing in a seasoned backup for Joe would have been extremely costly. "I'm not concerned with Turner," Ewbank told reporters. "I think he can play quarterback." Jim took over (hitting 1 of 4 throws versus Houston) and the next week against

The Jets were forced to spend their first year of existence at the antiquated Polo Grounds in Manhattan. It hadn't been updated since the early twentieth century. *AP Photo/File*

In 1964, the Jets moved into Shea Stadium in Flushing Meadows, Queens. The team immediately began recording sellouts like this one for the 1969 division playoff against Kansas City. *AP Photo/Spencer Jones*

In February 1966, the contract of Weeb Ewbank (left) was extended as general manager and coach by principal owner Sonny Werblin. *AP Photo*

Signed Players
1965

Player	1965	Bonus	50%	EDC	Pro Bowl	Misc	1964
Allen, Troy	11,000	2,000				1,500 - MI Kick 500 - Cash (3 x5000) NC Chev Grand Prix	1000 See Additional Agreements
Biggs, D.	12,500	10,000	2,000	500			
Cartwright, S.	10,000	3,500				Scholarship Not in writing See CHR	200
Dudek, M.	10,500	1,500	1,000				
Farmer, R.	11,500	2,500	1,000			750 - Scholar	
Finamore, R.	11,500	3,500	1,000	500		500 Cash to Sign	
Gordon, C.	10,000	2,500	500			Scholarship to either Univ. or the Kid.	
Gray, J.	12,000	4,500	1,000			NC	1,000
Harris, J.	13,000	21,000	1,000				
Hoovler, D.	11,000	7,500	2,000			NC	
Huarte, J.	40,000(2)	50,000				Scholarship to either Univ. or the Kid	
Hudson, J.	11,500	3,000	1,000				
Kearley, G.	11,000	1,000	1,000			250 Against Pre-Season	
Mayne, M.	11,000						1,000
Namath, J.	25,000(3)					Scholarship to either Univ. or the Kid	
Plumlee, G.	10,000	2,500	1,000				
Roberts, A.							
St. Victor, M.	13,500	3,500					
Schweickert, R.	30,000	20,000				(3 x 15000) 2000 - Mrs.	Sodom
Iacavazzi, C.	14000	7500					
Sauer, G.							

The 1965 Jets draft and free agent signings were the most successful input of talent for one year in the team's history. Shown is the rookie salary and bonuses for every first-year player except George Sauer Jr. The "misc" column, second from the right, indicates additional contractual promises made to the players. *Courtesy Cradle of Coaches Collection, The Walter Havighurst Special Collections, Miami University Libraries*

- 3 -

scored from the left side and nothing deeper than 30 yards completed. In the last four games, when it was necessary because of injury to start him again, he scored twice one of which was 62 yards. The first two years I felt we had the rare good fortune of almost equal threat and scoring from either left or right flanker. This year the left flankers did not score as they had and therefore we became "right handed" in flanker scoring and obviously more pressure on Maynard. The following is a breakdown that few teams have enjoyed. (Most have had only one high scoring flanker).

	Left Flanker	Right Flanker
1963	71-6 (Turner)	38-9 (Maynard)
1964	58-9 (Turner)	46-8 (Maynard)
1965	3 a) 31-3 Turner	68-14 (Maynard)
	b) 1 Sauer	

With the addition of Colclough and the expected development of Sauer, I hope we shall regain this almost equal scoring threat and balance. (However, Colclough's scoring is 3-5-3 for the same 3 year period).

Turner is effective as a returner on teams and could be a "get-by" punter. If our other flankers come through as expected, we could possibly consider Babe as one of our better trading strengths. Played 408 snaps less than previous year and therefore caught less, scored less and had fewer dropped balls and fewer poor patterns. Lead team in K.O. returns but was not ranked in AFL K.O. returns.

Joe Namath - QB - 6' 2" - 190 - 23 - (78%)
Performed exceptionally well for a rookie at the obvious most difficult position. Has every physical skill necessary to develop into one of the best if not the very best in Professional QB history. His development was slightly above normal at the beginning. He experienced the usual first year problems such as defensive recognition, coverage reading, "forcing" a play and coming to secondary and third choices. Also at this early period his accuracy was ineffective and at times poor. There were probably a series of factors other than some FP's that could have contributed to this: 1) the above mentioned first year problems, 2) trying to hard, 3) the tremendous amount of pressure and expectancy from the public (which he handled perfectly), 4) lack of timing between him and our receivers (which sometimes takes years to develop), 5) confidence and understanding in the play called, the defense, and the receiver, 6) confidence in his now proven successful knee operation. This could have affected his setting, delivery and follow through. (We don't actually know what was going through his mind about this). Throughout this period Joe's attitude, dedication, study and learning could not have been better. And about half way through the season everything began to jell for Joe and ultimately our offense. Most of the above mentioned factors or problems began to unfold - particularly passer-receiver timing and "reading". This total improvement was far ahead of schedule for beginning QB's. Joe is

Jets coach Weeb Ewbank kept extensive notes throughout each season for a postseason written evaluation of all his players between 1963 and 1966. This is part of Weeb's dictated notes about Joe Namath's 1965 rookie season. *Courtesy Jay Pomerantz*

Coach Weeb Ewbank knew what the starters on four other AFL teams (Kansas City, San Diego, Boston, and Miami) had made in 1966. That information is at the lower left of this document for offensive players and kickers. Defensive player salaries, by position, appear on the lower right. In the middle, at the bottom, are the team payrolls for Kansas City, Boston, the Jets, San Diego, and Miami. Across the top two-thirds of the page are the salaries of Jets starters and backups in 1966 and a second number indicating what they would make in 1967. *Courtesy Jay Pomerantz*

The Jets had run "19 Straight" all season long and did it extremely effectively in Super Bowl III. Here Namath hands off to Matt Snell, who had lead blocker Emerson Boozer and left guard Bob Talamini in front of Boozer. Not seen was the key blocker on "19 Straight," left tackle Winston Hill. *AP Photo*

Jets coach Weeb Ewbank's power running play, "19 Straight," was effective throughout the 1968 regular season and lethal against the Colts in Super Bowl III due to the blocking of left tackle Winston Hill, left guard Bob Talamini, halfback Emerson Boozer, and the running of Matt Snell. Snell gained 121 yards on the ground in the game. *Courtesy Jay Pomerantz*

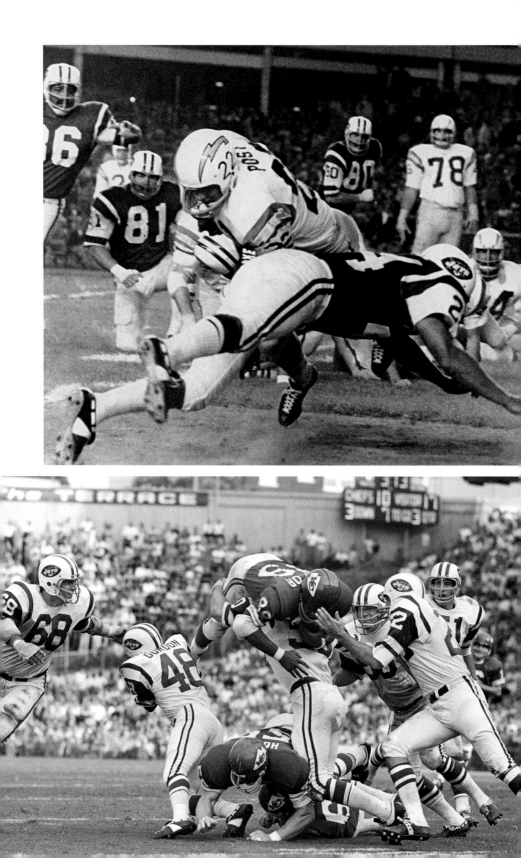

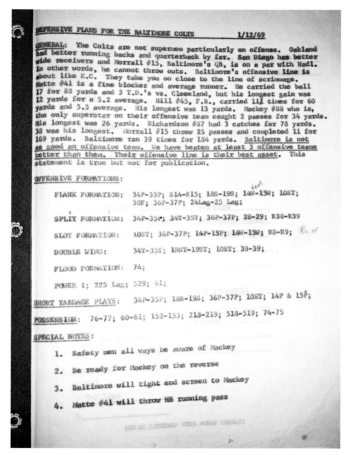

DEFENSIVE PLANS FOR THE BALTIMORE COLTS   1/12/69

GENERAL: The Colts are not supermen particularly on offense. Oakland had better running backs and quarterback by far. San Diego has better wide receivers and Morrall #15, Baltimore's QB, is on a par with Hadl. In other words, he cannot throw outs. Baltimore's offensive line is about like K.C. They take you on close to the line of scrimmage. Matte #41 is a fine blocker and average runner. He carried the ball 17 for 88 yards and 3 T.D.'s vs. Cleveland, but his longest gain was 12 yards for a 5.2 average. Hill #45, F.B., carried 11½ times for 60 yards and 5.5 average. His longest was 13 yards. Mackey #88 who is, the only superstar on their offensive team caught 2 passes for 34 yards. His longest was 26 yards. Richardson #87 had 3 catches for 78 yards. 38 was his longest. Morrall #15 threw 25 passes and completed 11 for 169 yards. Baltimore ran 39 times for 134 yards. Baltimore is not as good an offensive team. We have beaten at least 3 offensive teams better than them. Their offensive line is their best asset. This statement is true but not for publication.

OFFENSIVE FORMATIONS:

    FLANK FORMATION: 34P-35P; S14-S15; 18S-19S; 14W-15W; 10ST; 30F; 36P-37P; 24Lag-25 Lag;

    SPLIT FORMATION: 34P-35P; 34T-35T; 36P-37P; 28-29; R38-R39

    SLOT FORMATION: 10ST; 36P-37P; 14P-15P; 14W-15W; R8-R9; Run

    DOUBLE WING: 34T-35T; 18ST-19ST; 10ST; 38-39;

    FLOOD FORMATION: 74;

    POWER I; 225 Lag; 529; 61;

SHORT YARDAGE PLAYS: 34P-35P; 18S-19S; 36P-37P; 10ST; 14P & 15P;

POSSESSION: 76-77; 60-61; 152-153; 218-219; 518-519; 74-75

SPECIAL NOTES:

    1. Safety men always be aware of Mackey

    2. Be ready for Mackey on the reverse

    3. Baltimore will tight end screen to Mackey

    4. Matte #41 will throw HB running pass

    (TO BE RETURNED WITH SCOUT REPORT)

Coordinator Walt Michaels' defensive game plan for Super Bowl III (from Weeb Ewbank's playbook) shows the very high regard the Jets coaching staff (Michaels and defensive line coach Buddy Ryan) had for Colts tight end John Mackey—and the fewer concerns they had about everybody else on the Colts offense. Standout first line: "The Colts are not supermen particularly on offense." *Courtesy Jay Pomerantz*

Opposite page, top: San Diego halfback Dickie Post is taken down by Johnny Sample (24) in game three of the 1968 campaign at Shea Stadium. Watching are (left to right) Verlon Biggs, Gerry Philbin, and John Elliott. *AP Photo/Marty Lederhandler*

Opposite page, bottom: Carl McAdams stops the KC Chiefs' Otis Taylor in game one of the 1968 season at Kansas City, with Jim Hudson (22) and John Elliott (80) ready to help. At left is Mike Stromberg (68) and Cornell Gordon (48). Ralph Baker (partially obscured) is on far right. *Rich Clarkson/Rich Clarkson Associates via AP Images*

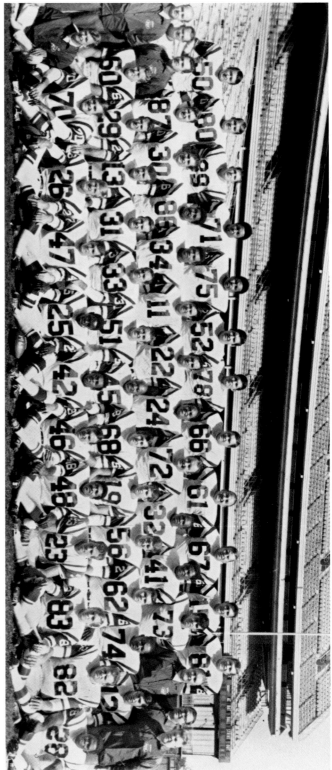

Front row (L to R): Trainer Jeff Snedeker, Karl Henke, Jim Richards, Mike D'Amato, Harvey Nairn, Randy Beverly, Bill Baird, Cornell Gordon, Bill Rademacher, George Sauer Jr., Hatch Rosdahl, and Robert Taylor. *Row 2:* Larry Grantham, Bake Turner, Don Maynard, Bill Mathis, Curley Johnson, Ralph Baker, Earl Christy, Mike Stromberg, Tommy Burnett, Paul Crane, Al Atkinson, Jeff Richardson, Joe Namath, and coach Weeb Ewbank. *Row 3:* Assistant coach Clive Rush, equipment manager Bill Hampton, assistant coach Walt Michaels, Pete Lammons, Mark Smolinski, Verlon Biggs, Lee White, Jim Turner, Jim Hudson, Johnny Sample, Paul Rochester, Emerson Boozer, Matt Snell, Tony DiMidio, assistant coach Joe Spencer, and assistant coach Buddy Ryan. *Row 4:* Carl McAdams, John Elliott, Ray Hayes, Sam Walton, Winston Hill, John Schmitt, Steve Thompson, Randy Rasmussen, Bob Talamini, Dave Herman, Babe Parilli, and Gerry Philbin. *AP Photo/NFL Photos*

Buffalo (4 of 10) in the exhibition season. Jim completed 2 of 4 passes in the regular season, until Taliaferro recovered.

Turner, who received the nickname Tank, knew nothing of Weeb's personal evaluations, but Jim had the utmost self-confidence in his quarterbacking, even the cerebral side. "There wasn't anything you could throw at me that I couldn't handle," he commented. "I'd been coached well in college, and other than a certain defense that no one would have seen in school, you couldn't confuse me. With the Jets, I knew I wasn't going to play, but I was in every meeting as the third quarterback and always knew our game plan."

The 1964 season was a major learning experience for Turner's kicking game. He was perfect on extra points and successful on 13 of 27 field goals, including 11 out of 16 from 39 yards or closer. He was far less successful beyond 40 yards, some of it attributable to Shea Stadium's unpredictable swirling winds.

During Turner's eight-year Jets career, he hit 40- to 49-yard field goals at a 32 percent clip and 18.2 percent when 50 or farther. "I wasn't the strongest-legged guy," Jim acknowledged, "but the wind at Shea Stadium made long kicks futile. There were times that gusts blew the football away from the goal posts by twenty yards. In 1969, when Kansas City came into play us, Jan Stenerud, a kicker who became a Hall of Famer, asked me, incredulously, 'How do you kick here, in these conditions?' I told him, 'I don't know.'"

Turner was fibbing. He knew more about kicking at Shea than anyone, except perhaps Weeb Ewbank, who trained Turner and taught him how to use Shea's winds to his advantage. "Nobody took care of my career like Weeb," declares Turner. "He was the best coach I've ever been around."

The Turner-Ewbank alliance might have created the Jets' biggest home-field advantage. The two charted the actual impact of Shea's winds week to week in practice. Turner and Weeb attempted field goals from varied distances and angles with and against Shea's gusts. Turner's study of the impact of wind currents at Shea gave him a leg up as fall and winter conditions set in. In comparison, opposition kickers left the visitors' Shea locker room for warm-ups and had scant minutes to assess Shea's winds.

It made a huge difference in the 1968 AFL Championship Game. Jim converted a 33-yard field goal with the wind at his back and a 36-yarder against the swirling gusts. "The one against the wind, I had to aim inside the right upright and hook it in. It went up, and hooked and stopped, like it always did in Shea's winds, and dropped over [the crossbar].

"I may have been the first kicker who was told by a coach that it is okay to kick it outside the goalpost and let the football roll through. Weeb would encourage me during games at Shea to 'Just do it like we did it at practice. Kick it out a few yards and it will roll in,' and it did," said Turner.

Like a baseball pitcher who is coached to repeat his delivery exactly over and over, Ewbank emphasized a consistent, exact, repetitive approach to booting the football. "One day, he told me, 'I've got an idea; we did this with [the Browns' Lou] Groza.' Weeb got a piece of chalk and chalked the front of my kicking toe. I made a kick, Weeb brought the ball back, and we saw where I had hit it. For me, it was two finger lengths below the middle with a tilt back towards me. We practiced it and practiced it until I was consistent.

"Another time, he examined my footing on a half-dozen kicks. Weeb pointed to the turf. He said, 'There are five or six different sets of footprints there. There has to be one footprint; there can't be any change in your stride.' Another time, he got a cameraman to take film of me from behind. 'I want to see if you are stepping straight or leaning left or right,' he explained. Weeb also figured out where we could place a flag to track the wind to see how hard it was blowing and its direction. I think Curley put a flag in the upper deck to help with his punting."

Jim had to practice in unusual locations. "A couple of times, the grounds crew at Shea wouldn't remove the tarp because the Mets didn't want us on the field," he disclosed. Practice relocated to the former World's Fair grass fields near the stadium. There was no football field, just a wide expanse of browning lawn—and no goalpost, either. "Weeb told me, 'S--t, kick it at a tree.' Imagine, a tree was my goalpost. We also practiced in Shea's parking lot until one of our guys fell down on the asphalt surface," Turner said.

Turner lost his job in 1967 training camp to Booth Lusteg, but Jim's replacement developed a sore foot. It reopened the door to Turner and he took full advantage, cementing his position with solid early season kicks. His potency made a startling improvement in 1968, elevated from a "good" to an All-Pro kicker by his new holder, Babe Parilli.

"He'd been holding for Gino Cappelletti in Boston, one of the greatest kickers of all time," said Turner. "When we acquired Babe from Boston for Mike Taliaferro before the 1968 season, I knew my game would get better. I made All-Pro the moment he came here. Babe never dropped the ball, and he and our center, John Schmitt, stayed after practice as long as I wanted. We got our snap and my kick off in one-point-two seconds. Any longer, it would be blocked."

Aside from his prodigious 1968 scoring, Turner's greatest satisfaction came from the close professional relationship he developed that year with Joe Namath. Following Joe's pair of five-interception games, the Jets offense turned conservative. Turner's consistent kicking made it easier for Joe to accept his reduced throwing role. "I gained Joe's confidence that he didn't have to squeeze in a pass and risk an interception," related Turner. "He saw how hard I was working and that he could trust me. We were not 'settling' for a field goal; Joe felt good taking the three points. Joe would ask me about field conditions before each game; he knew that I preferred to kick the ball from the right and he set me up."

Turner's reliability reached a crescendo with six field goals in a Shea victory over Buffalo. He missed two kicks at the especially kicking-tricky open end of Shea that afternoon. Eight would have set a pro record for one game at that time.

Even when his days as a backup fullback or tight end were over, Turner carried himself like a complete, strong, and tough football player. For instance, the Oakland Raiders' kick return team took obvious shots at him, hoping to knock him out of the game. Jim said, "Bring it on." When they didn't injure Jim, Oakland part-owner Al Davis tried to psych him out. Before the *Heidi* Game, "Al asked a game official to check my kicking shoe for an illegal weight," Turner explained. Nothing came of it and Turner never held a grudge.

Turner kicked three field goals (in five attempts) and an extra point in Super Bowl III—the game's nine-point differential. "Turner was the hero of the Super Bowl game," says offensive guard Bob Talamini. "He should have gotten more praise than he got." Turner remarked about the game, "There will never be another Super Bowl played with the importance and tension of that one. We saw panic in the Colts. It was interceptions and panic, then despondency, then history."

When the Jets cut Curley Johnson in 1969, Turner was given kickoff responsibilities, but he recoiled at Ewbank's orders to squib-kick. That, his drop-off from 34 field goals in 1968 and 32 in 1969 to 19 in 1970 (when Babe Parilli was gone), and Turner's unhappiness with his contract, led Weeb to trade him to Denver. "My problems were with general manager Weeb Ewbank, not coach Ewbank," Turner said of that moment in time. "Years later, he ran into me at a Super Bowl and said, 'Jim, I made a mistake. I shouldn't have traded you, and I didn't mean to piss you off.'"

Turner is a member of the Denver Broncos' Ring of Fame for his nine years of solid placekicking. The case is easily made that he likewise deserves to be elected to the Jets' Ring of Honor at MetLife Stadium.

BABE PARILLI

QUARTERBACK #15   6'1"   196 LB.

The veteran QB was the best holder in his era for place kicks, earning the nickname "Goldfinger." He turned Jim Turner, a good kicker, into an All-Pro.

"Babe" Parilli got his nickname at birth ("What a babe," a neighbor told his mom), but many Jets teammates called him by his given name, Vito. He was the oldest Super Bowl Jet (38) and Joe Namath's backup, but his skill as a holder on point-after attempts and field goals was his overriding contribution in 1968. The press never made a big deal about Babe, but Jim Turner did.

Parilli was born in Rochester, Pennsylvania, four miles from Joe Namath's hometown. In the early 1950s, he was the star QB for Paul "Bear" Bryant at the University of Kentucky. In Parilli's three years as a starter—perhaps the Kentucky football program's shining moments—Babe led the team to the Orange Bowl, Sugar Bowl, and Cotton Bowl. The Sugar Bowl victory over undefeated Oklahoma could be the biggest in the history of Kentucky football.

He had immediate professional success as MVP in the 1952 College All-Star Game against the reigning NFL champion Los Angeles Rams. Parilli played for four mythic coaches: Bryant and Pro Football Hall of Famers Paul Brown, Vince Lombardi, and Weeb Ewbank.

Despite being the fourth pick in the first round of the 1952 NFL draft by the Green Bay Packers, he didn't get a legitimate starting QB shot for a decade. As a Boston Patriot from 1961 to 1967, he racked up 132 touchdowns and 16,747 yards. His 31 TD passes in 1964 was a Patriots record for forty-three years until Tom Brady broke it in 2007.

Ironically, the Namath and Parilli pairing on the Jets was not the first time the QBs had crossed paths. As a ten-year old, Namath had been fascinated by "Babe Parilli" footballs in shops around Beaver Falls, Pennsylvania. In the late 1950s, Parilli shared his University of Kentucky/Bear Bryant offensive playbook with the new Beaver Falls High School football coach. For two weeks, Parilli and Larry Bruno reviewed it, then Bruno began teaching it to his hot-shot teen quarterback prospect, Joe Namath.

Parilli, a three-time AFL All-Star Game selection, could step in without a hitch if Namath was injured, but Babe's most vital Jets partnership was with Jim Turner. Parilli says he isn't sure if Weeb had backup QB or holder foremost in his plans when he traded Mike Taliaferro for Babe. In the end, Parilli's preeminent contribution in the Jets' 1968–69 Super Bowl season took place on fourth downs and after TDs—and it grew increasingly important as the season wore on and the Jets' quick-strike offense turned conservative.

"When Joe and the offense stalled in the Red Zone that year," Parilli recalled, "Jim Turner put points on the scoreboard." Turner's 73.9 percent field goal accuracy in 1968 was the second best of his career (topped by 75 percent with Denver in 1975), and Turner's two campaigns with Parilli were the kicker's sole 30-plus field goal seasons and two highest point production years. Admittedly not a long-distance kicker, thanks to Parilli, Turner hit 5 of 9 from 40 to 49 yards in 1968.

Babe said positioning his leg for his hold was key. "Most holders set up with their right leg extended and their left knee down. I put my right knee down instead of extending it and put the ball down six inches from my left toe," he explained. "Because of Shea Stadium's swirling winds, Jim would sometimes tell me to tilt the ball one way or another way."

Parilli also recommended to Schmitt and Turner that his spotting of the ball be shortened a few inches. "That way, the ball will be coming into my hands with the laces facing the goalposts and I won't have to waste time spinning the ball," he added.

The high-quality spotting by Babe was authenticated by his

status as the only placeholder in the 1960s on two different teams whose field goal kicker booted 6 field goals in a single game. Gino Cappelletti was 6 for 6 for Boston against Denver in 1964 and Turner booted 6 out of 8 versus Buffalo in 1968. (The NFL record at the time was 7.) Parilli was nicknamed "Goldfinger" for the incredible quickness with which his hands caught the snap from center, spun it (if necessary) so the laces faced the goalpost, and placed it at the best possible angle for a kick. He doled out credit to center John Schmitt. "John consistently snapped the ball to me fast, straight, right where I wanted it, and softly. It was easy for me to handle, compared to other centers I worked with."

Namath and Parilli loved to throw the ball downfield (few dinks and dunks for them) and prepared studiously to read defenses. The Jets' quarterback protection amazed Parilli. "With the Patriots, the rule was to get the ball out in two-point-eight seconds," Babe recalled. "Weeb told me that with the Jets, I had four seconds . . . an eternity. At thirty-eight, if I was going to be a backup, Joe was the guy to play behind."

Babe's Super Bowl reflections ("the top moment in my career") focus on his collaboration with Turner that day. "Jim's three field goals were the difference in the 16–7 game," he said. Baltimore's suffocating blitz was supposed to discombobulate the passing game, but Parilli also understood that a good blitz could take a toll on the running game. "Baltimore blitzed so much and from all different angles without disguising them—and still no one had run effectively against them all year," he said. "Matt [Snell] got over 120 yards behind our great offensive line. That's what separated the Jets from Kansas City and Oakland in the first two Super Bowls."

Parilli was part of a weird situation before the game: "The Jets had three footballs to kick during the game, and during warm-ups. With no nets behind the goalpost in those days, Jim kicked one through the uprights and into the stands. We needed the ball back. The guy who caught it refused to return the ball, so I promised him a football after the game. He relented, and in all the commotion after the final gun I forgot about it. Twenty years later, at a personal appearance in Concord, Massachusetts, the same guy came over to me and said, 'You still owe me a football.'"

Babe entered Super Bowl III in relief of Namath when Joe jammed a finger on his throwing hand when it struck the helmet of a Baltimore lineman in the fourth quarter. Parilli threw an incomplete third-down pass to George Sauer. "I didn't know that Joe and George had agreed that Sauer would go a step deeper than usual when Joe called a quick slant. I called that play in the huddle, George took a little longer to break, and to make sure I didn't get sacked I threw the ball away, and we kicked the field goal," said Parilli.

Parilli's smarts and leadership led to a lengthy coaching career. There were assistant coaching stints with Pittsburgh and Denver. With the Steelers, he tutored young Terry Bradshaw, Joe Gilliam, and Terry Hanratty. As quarterback coach for Denver from 1977 to 1979, he resurrected the career of twelve-year-veteran Craig Morton, who took the Broncos to their first Super Bowl.

Honored with a spot on the All-AFL 10-Year Anniversary team, he was inducted into the New England Patriots' Hall of Fame in 1993. Babe was a head coach in the World Football League and USFL, start-up pro football leagues that tried—and failed—to emulate the AFL's successful merger with the NFL. He also coached for six indoor Arena League teams. Parilli passed away on July 15, 2017, at age eighty-seven from complications of multiple myeloma.

DEFENSIVE LINE
DOMINATING AGILITY, QUICKNESS, AND SMARTS

GERRY PHILBIN	#81
PAUL ROCHESTER	#72
VERLON BIGGS	#86
CARL MCADAMS	#50
JOHN ELLIOTT	#80

GERRY PHILBIN

DEFENSIVE END #81   6'2"   245 LB.

"We're wearing white [uniforms] today."

The typical pro football roster has at least one overachiever, a person whom the TV cameras can't help but highlight. However, even the top overachiever tends to burn out in a season or two. The Super Bowl Jets' colossal overachiever was Gerry Philbin, though he wasn't just an overachiever for long.

Permanent laurels came his way, like "most consistent" and "inspirational," and later, "intense," "studious," "quick," a "sponge," and "dedicated." Philbin became a leading symbol of the Jets' defense, and as the merger with the NFL brought down the curtain on the AFL, the strength and quality of his play for seven years in the decade earned him election to the American Football League's All-Time Team.

"Gerry Philbin was a student of the game," says Larry Grantham. "As a result, he didn't line up wrong, he didn't make mistakes. Gerry gave us one hundred percent on every play—and made plays the entire game." After one game, his effort and defensive ferocity were described as "resembling a bull charging out of a rodeo stall."

The Rhode Island–born Philbin attended the University of Buffalo, a school not known for producing pro football talent. Gerry developed pro football aspirations as a junior, so local sportscaster Bill Mazer hooked him up with weight lifter Ken Stoller. Gerry spent the summer in a weight-training regimen to transform his quickness at 210 pounds into an even more agile 240-pound defensive end—and a legitimate pro prospect. Mazer took a special liking to Philbin (he all but adopted him), and when Bill moved to New York City in 1964 to become the country's first radio sports talk show host, he gave the Jets and listeners an earful about Philbin.

The Jets selected Gerry in the third round of the 1964 AFL draft; the NFL Detroit Lions took him in round three. Lions GM Russ Thomas told Gerry he might not be big enough for the NFL, souring Philbin on Detroit. Though he was offered 40 percent more by the Canadian Football League's Toronto Argonauts than the Jets' combined $12,000 salary and $6,000 bonus, Philbin followed his heart to play in New York. "I grew up a New York Giants fan; they would have been tougher for me to walk away from," he admits. Ironically, five years later, after winning the Super Bowl, "beating the Giants bad" in a preseason game became his, the Jets', and their fans' shared obsession.

Philbin joined veteran Paul Rochester on the defensive line in 1964, and for the next eight seasons he was sometimes underpublicized, but always a categorical front-four standout at left end. Gerry grappled with much larger offensive linemen, blocking tight ends and sometimes a running back, but he used brainpower—intelligence and film study—to diagnose plays so he could put the heat on quarterbacks and stop rival ball carriers.

Weeb Ewbank was entranced. At the conclusion of Philbin's rookie season, he penned in his private player notations:

Has the most potential of our defensive ends, and can become an all-pro with time and work, which he is more than willing to spend to reach this goal. . . . He learns fast, he is very quick and fast.

After the 1965 season, Weeb praised Gerry even more highly:

Our most consistent defensive lineman. . . . Played more than any of the primary linemen . . . scores higher against the running game than against the passing game, however, he is improving on his pass rush and should become equally proficient. He can and should become one of the finest players in the league. 11 players on the field with an attitude and desire to win comparable to Gerry can make us a winner.

Gerry met Ewbank's hopes. John Dockery, who played left corner behind Philbin, said, "He brought unbelievable spirit and energy, and he was inspirational. Do you realize how small he was, and how tough? I'd come into the huddle and see blood and sweat dripping off his face. One time, he dislocated his shoulder and I figured, okay, he'll be off to the locker room—then he came back to the huddle with a sling on his shoulder."

Remarkably, all of Philbin's extraordinary physical and mental effort to become a dominant defensive end did not quench the fire in his belly. During his first five years in the league, Gerry insisted on being part of the kickoff and punt-return special teams. He collected game awards regularly during his rookie season for special teams tackles and quarterback sacks. In November 1968, he was awarded a game ball for his standout play after a crunching special teams' tackle that induced a fumble and closed out the Jets' win over the Houston Oilers. In 1969, after an AFL all-star season, he was dropped from kickoff and punt return duties, but insisted on blocking for field goals and point-after TDs.

Gerry harmonized his grit and focus with savvy. Philbin savored tutoring from retired Baltimore Colts defensive lineman Artie Donovan, a four-time NFL All-Pro and special Ewbank guest at 1964 and 1965 training camps. For two weeks each of those years, over a case of beer after practice, Donovan lectured about the physical nature and sophistication of the pro game, and the intelligence of the best pro players from film study.

Even after weight training added heft, Philbin was still considered undersized. But compared to the prototypical 6'4", 260-pound defensive end, Philbin's productivity put most rangier, bulkier defensive linemen to shame. A Green Bay Packers fan during the Lombardi era of the 1960s pointed out to me how Gerry would have fit perfectly in the Packers' physical, agile, and quick defensive alignment. Philbin was nearly the identical size and weight as the Packers' five-time All-Pro left defensive end, Willie Davis.

What Gerry lacked in size, he more than made up for in aggressiveness, tenacity, and desire. He once commented about Verlon Biggs, at 6'4", 275 pounds the Jets' biggest defensive lineman. "If I was that big, people would have to pay me to let them live." Regardless, from 1964 through 1972, Philbin was the Jets' stalwart tackler and QB sacker.

Perhaps his tolerance for punishment came from being the son of an alcoholic father who died at fifty-five and a mother who, for twenty-two long years, toiled overnight from 11 P.M. to 7 A.M. to support four boys and four girls. Gerry's personal motivation was to play extremely well—combined with his determination to be recognized for it. "I wanted to win; I wanted to get as much credit as I could possibly get—and to be known for doing all the things that a player can do," he said.

Because Philbin played in the AFL and—outsmarting and outmaneuvering offensive linemen, rather than physically dominating them was his modus operandi—he was easily overlooked in conversations about football's top defensive linemen. "I didn't have a power move, but my footwork and quickness worked for me on the pass rush," he said. Yet it was not hard to make the case about his elite stature.

Quarterback sacks were not tracked in the 1960s, but no defensive lineman back then came close to the 19.5 sacks Gerry was unofficially credited with by *New York Post* Jets beat writer Paul Zimmerman during the 1968 season. Still, Philbin said the previous 1967 season was his personal best, although the AFL's writers did not vote him to the AFL All-Pro team. Gerry admitted that after receiving that deflating news the Saturday night before the final game of that season, he headed to his San Diego hotel room in tears. He had led the Jets in sacks and graded the highest of any Jets defensive lineman. He didn't sulk very long—positively channeling it into "extra determination for the next season," he remarked.

Because he wasn't physically overpowering and not spotlighted by the electronic media, Philbin was not seen as a superstar in the mold of Joe Namath. However, as the ultimate sign of his stardom, after Super Bowl III Gerry became the second-highest-paid player on the team. He injected into the Jets' defense the leadership, energy, and motivation that Namath did with the offense.

Pro football discouraged weight lifting when Gerry played, yet he was a workout demon. Philbin still keeps himself in shape; he was and remains today the epitome of the word *tough*. (His own son told us, "I wouldn't want to fool with him.") Namath continually spoke his mind, and Philbin was no verbal wallflower—he just didn't get the degree of attention the press afforded a $400,000 quarterback. He raised concerns inside and outside the team structure early in 1968. Joe's risky deep downfield passes had created friction between Jets' defensive coaches, players on the defensive side of the ball, and Joe. It was worked out, but only after two calamitous losses due to Namath interceptions.

Philbin got in Namath's ear about it the following year. When the Jets opened the season in Buffalo, Philbin stood in the tunnel with the entire Jets squad, waiting to be introduced. Gerry leaned toward Namath and, in a dig about his forgettable five-interception game the year before versus the Bills, he whispered in the QB's ear, "We're wearing white [uniforms] today." Gerry says Joe didn't laugh back then, but today even he likes to tell the story.

Ewbank's description of the team's 1968 defensive style implemented by Michaels and new D-line coach Buddy Ryan—"bend, but don't break"—was in force for the football world to see in Super Bowl III. Baltimore went up and down the field several times but was regularly stymied as the Colts neared the Jets' goal line. Philbin made one of the first Jets' defensive stops of the game—a tackle for a loss in the first quarter, deep in Jets territory. "They ran the ball pretty good; the game started off like a romp in their favor til on a key play they tried to trap us, and I stopped it," Gerry remembers.

That the Jets only sacked Baltimore quarterbacks once during the Super Bowl is somewhat misleading. Philbin missed tackling quarterback Earl Morrall for a loss in the opening quarter, but throughout the contest, Gerry, John Elliott, Biggs, Paul Rochester, and Carl McAdams consistently pressured Morrall and, later, John Unitas. Four interceptions are testimony to that.

Even as his body aged and his Jets career was winding down, Philbin's perseverance never eased up. During his last Jets season in 1972, determined to show Coach Ewbank his still powerful motor, Gerry refused to be sidelined by serious injuries. The harness on his busted shoulder or the brace on an injured knee would have derailed most players. At year-end, he asked for a $5,000 raise and Ewbank stung Philbin in private when he said that he wasn't in the business of giving charity, a remark that later became public and hurt Gerry deeply.

"I gave my body to the Jets; I had five major operations, but no regrets about my Jets career. I love the Jets," he says of his time in

New York. Documenting Philbin's contribution to the franchise, only Namath, Ewbank, Don Maynard, Winston Hill, Curtis Martin, and Joe Klecko (in 2010) preceded him into the team's "Ring of Honor," which took place in 2011.

PAUL ROCHESTER

DEFENSIVE LEFT TACKLE #72   6'2"   255 LB.

Buddy Ryan told Paul that his play at defensive tackle in Super Bowl III was the best game he had seen played by a defensive tackle.

Paul "Rocky" Rochester's ten-year pro football career was marked by rebounds from down moments. He was drafted and cut by the Dallas Cowboys in 1960 after playing in the College All-Star Game, but his anger was alleviated when he found work locally with the AFL Dallas Texans. He was voted an AFL all-star in 1961 and won a championship with the Texans in 1962.

In 1963, his fortunes seemed to turn sour. Paul was dealt by an up-and-coming Kansas City team (relocated from Dallas) to the downtrodden New York Titans "for a bucket of old socks," jokes Rochester. To add to his woes, his reputation was dragged through the mud. "[KC coach] Hank Stram talked down my ability to Weeb Ewbank." But Rochester had two things going for him. Paul was returning to his hometown; he had grown up in Floral Park, Long Island, where as a high school defensive lineman he had picked up the nickname "Rocky" for his heavy quarterback hits. And, it didn't take long for Paul to get a degree of revenge against Stram. Rochester briefed Weeb before the Chiefs and Jets met in New York that stopping KC's star halfback Abner Haynes from being able to run wide took the air out of the Chiefs' offense. The Jets keyed on that, leading to the franchise's first shutout.

Paul established a reputation as a tough, durable, stay-at-home run-stopper, a thinking man's defensive tackle with the Jets. Paul admits, "I tried to outthink, outmaneuver the guy on the other side of the line." Middle linebacker Al Atkinson credited him with "keeping a lot of offensive guards off me." Paul, who weighed 255 pounds because that's what Weeb demanded, said, "I could have been three hundred pounds. Every one of us was smaller than the linemen today; none of us had big bellies and we played every down on defense."

Rochester's contributions at defensive left tackle expanded to a tutoring role, injecting attitude and imparting game experience to young developing linemen. His tutelage specifically helped mold Gerry Philbin and John Elliott, both natural linebackers in size, into stout defensive linemen and, as a bonus, into all-stars.

In both cases, Rocky said his biggest advice concerned stopping a trap play. Early in his Jets career, "a guy trapped me and the runner went up through the hole," said Rochester. "In the film room that week, Walt Michaels ran that one play, back and forth, back and forth, I'll bet you forty times. I got trapped and trapped and trapped, again. Everyone laughed, and I'll tell you after that I never got trapped in a game again."

Rocky worked with Philbin during his early years as a Jet. "Gerry couldn't take a trap straight on," Rocky explained. "I helped him understand the problem and if a trap was coming, I could stop the guy blocking down on me and trapping on Gerry." Paul also took great pride in perfecting the "tackle-end game," a pass-rush strategy effective in obvious throwing situations.

Ordinarily, Philbin battled the offensive right tackle, while Rochester fired out on the offensive right guard. In a tackle-end game, Philbin and Rochester crisscrossed and Gerry followed Rocky, who charged the offensive guard. "I'd hook the right guard's arm," related Rocky, "with my strength and cunning to take him out of position so he couldn't move to block Gerry, and Philbin's quickness gave him a wide-open shot at the quarterback. I don't remember ever having one blow up." Paul claims some credit for Philbin's 19.5 sacks in 1968.

Rochester's guidance to Elliott, also on avoiding being trapped, turned the second-year linebacker in his first full year at DT into a superquick lineman. Rocky lectured Elliott to pull back a bit on his pass rush, "to look inside as each play was developing. I told him that if a guy is coming at you, you better take him on because the offense is trying to trap you." It took a half season of mentoring to instill Rocky's prescribed discipline into Elliott ("Big Bad John," as he was called). Many Jets teammates say John could not be blocked.

From 1964 to 1969, as the defensive line pieces were put in place, Rochester, Philbin, Elliott, and defensive right end Verlon Biggs jelled into a unit that controlled the line of scrimmage, habitually held running backs under 100 yards a game, and harassed and sacked pass-happy AFL quarterbacks.

The AFL Championship Game at Shea Stadium was made to order for Rochester. It was cold and windy and Rocky was central to the Jets' defensive game plan to prevent Oakland from running the football. Five times Raiders running backs were thrown for a loss and three times they barely got back to the line of scrimmage. Of Oakland's fourteen running plays for positive yardage, nine pushed the football forward only one or two yards.

Rochester had no fear of playing the vaunted Colts come the Super Bowl. The NFL's convincing wins over Kansas City and Oakland in 1967 and 1968 mattered little to the twenty-nine-year-old defensive tackle. "I had gone through many a battle and had pretty much seen everything; I'd had every injury. I wasn't afraid of anybody, anything," Rochester explained. How loose did he feel during the Super Bowl festivities? Joe Namath missed a scheduled morning press event, so Paul grabbed Namath's No. 12 jersey, pulled it over his head, and, as "Joe," went out to meet the assembled reporters.

"I played out of my gourd in Super Bowl III," stated a very serious

Rochester. "I was as motivated as you could get; I was out to prove a lot of things to a lot of people. Everything I did that day against [the Colts' offensive guard] Dan Sullivan seemed to work. I did a spin move on him and he fell on his face. I did a false forearm shiver and he backed off. I thought to myself, 'I own this guy.'" As was true of many of the Super Bowl Jets players, Paul grew up admiring Colts QB John Unitas, so he speaks with special delight about "smacking Unitas down" just as Johnny U released a late-game toss that fell harmlessly to the turf.

As the sun was setting on the most shocking upset in Super Bowl history, Buddy Ryan, the Jets' defensive line coach, took Paul aside to tell Rocky he had just played the best game Ryan had ever seen a defensive tackle play. When the gun went off in Miami that late January afternoon, Rochester and teammate and offensive guard Bob Talamini stood out as the first players to boast of a Super Bowl ring on one hand and an AFL championship ring (from earlier in the decade) on the other.

Rochester probably would have taken one thing back in his career. He was taught to tackle using his head at Michigan State University. During his freshman year, Paul said defensive line coach Lou Agase "pointed at my head and asked, 'What's that, Rocky?' I replied, 'That's my head.' Agase said, 'Not as long as you are here. That's your weapon.' Agase told that to all the players; I think Dave Herman, who graduated from MSU after me, led with his head more than I did." That coaching hurt many players later in their lives.

"Leading with your head" today would certainly produce a wince from anyone even partially aware of its association with concussions and brain damage. At the end of each season, Rocky said his helmet had deep impressions from helmet-to-helmet hits; each season's helmet was retired and became a ghastly souvenir. He has given away all of the dented helmets, except one that he keeps in his Jacksonville, Florida, home. "That's where I place all the obituaries of the guys who hurt me—and I'm waiting for some more of those guys," he explained.

Seventy-seven years old and working out three times a week when we spoke with him in 2016, Paul has suffered a heart attack, copes with type 2 diabetes, and has had a broken foot and fingers. Both of his knees have been replaced and he and wife, Nancy, cope with his memory loss, and Rocky lives with a cochlear implant to offset significant hearing loss. He relies on a captioning telephone that transcribes on a computer screen what a caller says. Rochester is part of the players' concussion lawsuit. He's a recovered alcoholic who hasn't had a drink since the 1970s. "My birthday is July 15; my AA birthday is January 21," he says with pride.

He loves to tell stories, like mingling with members of the 1969 Amazing Mets at Shea Stadium. "We had a sauna in the Jets' locker room, and the Mets didn't," he remembered. "Well, Tom Seaver, Jerry Koosman, and Tug McGraw asked if they could join us. Our defensive linemen sat there and I don't know who said it, but one of us remarked, 'If we can win the Super Bowl, you can win the World Series.'" We all know what happened later that fall.

VERLON BIGGS

DEFENSIVE END #86   6'4"   275 LB.

Verlon had such an abundance of natural talent that it sometimes appeared that he was not hustling, but he had a knack for making big plays.

A powerful force at defensive right end, Verlon Biggs was a big-play performer, both in the 1968 AFL Championship Game and Super Bowl III. He helped snuff out Oakland's last big drive in the AFL Championship Game with a late-game sack. Two weeks later, in the third quarter of Super Bowl III, he halted Baltimore's hopes for second-half momentum when he stripped the football from Colts halfback Tom Matte on the Colts' first play from scrimmage.

Yet Biggs, the most physically impressive and talented defensive player ever drafted by Weeb Ewbank, was frequently a frustrating enigma to Jets coaches. Walt Michaels considered Verlon his finest scouting discovery; however, during Verlon's seven years as a Jet, neither Coach Ewbank nor Michaels was ever completely satisfied with his effort and production.

Jets defensive coaches never discovered the on/off switch to un-leash all of Verlon's ability all the time, which they felt could have opened the doors of the Hall of Fame for Biggs. Larry Grantham commented, "If we could have instilled Gerry Philbin's desire in Verlon, he would have rewritten all the record books."

Yet what the coaches saw as disappointing about Biggs could be perceived much differently by his teammates. Defensive lineman Steve Thompson sort of agreed: "He played kind of average half the time. When he had a fire under him, Verlon was amazing." And Ver-lon Biggs in a critical game situation would and did turn it on and blow up a play. Emerson Boozer and Snell didn't see any lack of effort. Boozer thought Verlon "a very talented defensive end. He did not like formations where the running backs and tight ends—with the offen-sive tackle—would double-team, even chop-block him. Because of rule changes concerning chop blocking, Verlon would be a monster defensive end in today's game."

Snell conceded, "He didn't know how good he could have been," and believed that Verlon wanted to avoid an injury. "He saw it hap-pening all around him with Joe, Boozer, and me. There wasn't a better gamer than Verlon Biggs. Some of the league's coaches had a crazy theory that black players from small black colleges were lazy. Verlon wasn't lazy; he was so talented that everything appeared to come easy to him."

Biggs' sheer size was always a point of discussion. "He was built like a Clydesdale," remembers Al Atkinson, but a Clydesdale that "could flat-out move," observed Matt Snell. "Verlon lined up right in front of me," said lightweight linebacker Paul Crane. "He was such a big guy, and he knocked everybody down so I could make the tackle. I felt I could hold my own out there with the help of guys like Verlon."

Larry Grantham, the Jets' starting right side linebacker (who was lighter than Crane) was central to Biggs' play. Weeb Ewbank wrote in his personnel notes, "He [Larry] was valuable in helping Biggs with his play where it was badly needed." Grantham added, "Verlon was one of my best friends, but he only knew how to line up one way, so I had to slap him to move him over."

Big and fearsome on the field, Biggs was playful, friendly, and a practical joker off the turf. Said Jeff Richardson, "Verlon was some-times something of a clown prince. He loved to play cards—and to cheat. They were playing for money, and Verlon always seemed to have a couple of extra cards." Defensive back and buddy Cornell Gor-don admitted that Verlon would "tie people's clothes up, put gum in people's jock straps and shoes . . . then, he'd just start laughing." Matt Snell commented, "He was a lot of fun to be around, always smiling with a very nice disposition."

Verlon attended Jackson State, a small black college in Missis-sippi that flew under the radar in pro football circles until Willie Richardson (Baltimore in 1963) and Speedy Duncan and Ben Mc-Gee (San Diego and Pittsburgh, respectively, in 1964) burst onto the scene in the NFL and AFL.

In 1965, Biggs didn't have an agent to represent him in NFL and AFL negotiations, but he was far from a hayseed who could be taken advantage of. According to members of his family, his mother preached about being paid what he, as an all-American invited to participate in the College All-Star Game, was worth. His pro choices in 1965 were juicy: the Jets (their third pick) or Vince Lombardi's Green Bay Packers (in round two). The Packers "wanted him real bad," according to Verlon's youngest brother, Dennis. He opted for the Jets' three-year deal, which included a signing bonus and 1965 Chevy Malibu.

Biggs made a big impression on the AFL in 1965. The *Pittsburgh Courier*, a leading African American newspaper, named him the 1965 AFL Rookie of the Year. When Joe Namath was informed that he had been selected the league's Rookie of the Year, the QB expressed surprise in learning Verlon had not received a single vote in the official AFL rookie of the year tally. A few years later, Namath went a bit further: "I knew the voting didn't mean too much because my teammate, Verlon Biggs . . . deserved the award just as much as me."

Jets management was impressed by how much Verlon was living up to their first-year expectations and noted it internally. Ewbank graded Biggs' effectiveness in his rookie season at 84 percent and wrote:

> Probably has more potential than any rookie lineman coming into the league in 1965. He can be "great" and go into the books as one of the greatest. His biggest problem was learning formations and how to adjust to these formations. . . . As a pass rusher, he was one of the best in the league and gave us more "big plays" than any other lineman. However, he still needs to become more clever, instead of trying to over-power his opposition. Against running, he made mistakes but his quickness and second effort compensated for this.

Verlon's play in 1966 was considered his best by the *New York Post*'s beat writer Paul Zimmerman. Two different news services named Biggs a first-team AFL all-star. Verlon was also named MVP of the 1966 AFL All-Star Game. After that season, his 270-pound playing weight ballooned all the way up to 300. Verlon dropped the thirty pounds and went on to a very good 1967 season—a second-team all-AFL selection. Neither the AFL nor NFL tracked "sacks," but in 1968 Verlon was credited, unofficially, with 12.

Four days before the Super Bowl, DL coach Buddy Ryan challenged Dave Herman, who was prepping to take on the massive Bubba Smith in the game. Ryan had Herman go mano a mano with Biggs, the Jets' biggest, fastest, most physical lineman. Dave asked Biggs to "try to come over the top of me and try to grab hold of me and throw me, like Bubba tries to do." According to the *New York Times'* Dave Anderson, who saw the practice field match-up, Verlon yanked him aside. "'Is that how he [Bubba] does it?' Biggs asked in all seriousness. 'He better not,' replied Herman." Bubba was less of a problem for Herman in Super Bowl III than Biggs was in that practice.

Biggs fully expected to win Super Bowl III. "When the Jets got to Miami to practice for the Super Bowl, Verlon called our brother in California and told him, 'Bet the kitchen sink on the game. We're going to beat them.' Verlon told me two months before Super Bowl III that Oakland was as good as, or better than, Baltimore," said his brother, Dennis.

In the Super Bowl game, after some early Colts success, Verlon helped the Jets control the line of scrimmage. Aside from his tackle of Matte that forced the third-quarter turnover, he had one other memorable near-sack. On a second quarter play, first Philbin and then Biggs literally missed sacks of Earl Morrall. "Verlon often laughed about it," admitted Dennis. "He said he 'had' Morrall, but Earl stopped, leaned forward, and Verlon ran right over the top of him."

The day after the game, interspersed in pages of celebratory Super Bowl Jets stories, Biggs, who had played out his option that year (playing for 90 percent of his prior year salary to gain his freedom), said he wanted to leave the Jets. He ended up reupping with the Jets for 1969 and 1970. They finished second in overall team defense in 1969 and led the NFL in rushing defense in 1970.

In 1971, according to the Jets, Biggs agreed to a two-year contract. But when it was time to sign, he asked for better terms. That request was denied and Washington obtained him and two future draft choices for a first-round pick and an unspecified second pick or player.

An unexposed side of Verlon Biggs was his deep compassion for the less fortunate: friends, neighborhood children back in Mississippi, acquaintances, and complete strangers. For example, as Biggs left the Jets' team bus at the Orange Bowl for Super Bowl III, he gave two game tickets he hadn't disposed of to a young boy. "As I got older, I began to understand that he didn't have anybody looking out for him when he was young," remarked his brother Dennis. "My gift to the world would be that everyone in the world would have a big brother like Verlon."

On June 7, 1994, at fifty-one years of age, Verlon Biggs became the youngest player on the Super Bowl Jets to pass away. He succumbed to leukemia, an illness his brother, Charles, told mourners Verlon had battled quietly for four years. "We inscribed on his headstone: 'Never lose the common touch,'" said Dennis Biggs. Eighty-seven-year-old Weeb Ewbank spoke at the funeral, eulogizing his former defensive end as "a great team player who was always where he was supposed to be in the defensive alignment. He had the keen ability to make the big plays."

CARL MCADAMS

DEFENSIVE TACKLE #50   6'3"   228 LB.

Ankle injuries robbed him of his plans to be a perennial All-Pro linebacker, so he contributed as a specialist pass-rushing defensive tackle.

Carl McAdams grew up in White Deer, Texas, and was a superstar high school linebacker. The Texan anxiously awaited an invitation to play football for the University of Texas, but UT coach Darrell Royal never came calling. Carl ended up at Texas' biggest rival, the

University of Oklahoma, where his brilliant linebacking became the talk of college football. On top of 1964 and 1965 all-American honors, McAdams was voted MVP in the 1964 Gator Bowl and was selected captain of the West squad in the 1965 East-West Shrine Game.

Professional scouts evaluated McAdams as the equal of the University of Texas' more heralded Tommy Nobis. Nobis went number one in the NFL draft; the St. Louis Cardinals made McAdams the eighth pick in the NFL first round. One year earlier, St. Louis had selected and lost their first pick, Joe Namath, to the Jets in a $427,000 deal. In 1966, Sonny Werblin's $300,000 offer outbid the Cardinals for their first pick again. *New York Times'* football scribe William Wallace wrote after Werblin announced McAdams' contract: "The . . . Jets accomplished a coup equal to the acquisition of Joe Namath when Sonny Werblin . . . signed Carl."

Per the Jets' request, McAdams reported to 1966 training camp 25 pounds heavier than his 6'4", 215-pound collegiate frame. "I was very self-motivated," McAdams said. He also set sky-high expectations "as I had set in grade school, high school, and college: (1) to make the team and start and (2) to be the best player on the team. Considering how much the Jets had invested in me, I also wanted to be a multiple-time All-Pro at linebacker."

The rookie began showing every sign of fulfilling all those hopes on the practice field in Peekskill. Third-year left linebacker Ralph Baker and second-year player Al Atkinson, the leading middle linebacker candidate, watched in awe as McAdams used his speed and range to make tackles all over the field. Unfortunately, within weeks, all of Carl's plans went poof.

McAdams flew to Chicago to play in the annual College All-Stars against the prior season's NFL champion. McAdams didn't play in the game and, worse, his career was nearly snuffed out by a hideous injury a few days before on a Windy City street. Carl told the Jets that on July 30 he had hurt himself slipping off a sidewalk downtown. McAdams inwardly struggled with the embarrassing truth.

"A player from the Chicago Bears bumped into me in a bar and spilt his drink on me," said McAdams, who was initially dumbfounded by the intentional act. But the Bears player didn't stop there; he ripped the front of Carl's shirt and then the shirt's back for good measure, before leaving the saloon. As the quiet, poised, and gentlemanly McAdams slowly came to grips with what had happened, his anger began to surface.

Provided the whereabouts of the Bears player, McAdams headed there to settle the score. "I found him," McAdams continued, "and I wound up to belt him with a surprise roundhouse right. As I stepped off the sidewalk and into the street, I swung but I missed, and I completely lost my balance. My body's momentum twisted me entirely around and put so much pressure on my left ankle that I dislocated and fractured it. I kick myself to this day for my immaturity."

McAdams underwent ankle surgery in a Chicago hospital. On the mend for three weeks and unnerved by his plight, he stopped eating and his 235-pound frame plunged to 190. When he was released from the hospital, he flew home to Oklahoma. A family doctor examined his ankle and detected a staph infection that required a specialist's urgent attention. McAdams dashed up to New York to see Dr. James Nicholas. The Jets' surgeon dealt with it and told Carl he needed to cut the ligaments in McAdams' damaged left toes. Later, he grafted skin from Carl's right thigh onto the damaged left ankle. He went on to remove a pin that had been inserted in McAdams' left ankle. McAdams spent the 1966 pro football season recovering and rehabbing four operations over a few short months. That included a punishing six to eight hours daily of exercising and conditioning.

McAdams returned in 1967 with a burning desire to live up to his Jets contract. After the hundreds of hours of punishing rehabilitation, his left leg and ankle felt great. That ended on the first play in the first preseason game without any serious contact. Debilitating pain flared through his foot, diagnosed by Dr. Nicholas as bone spurs, a boney growth that forms on a normal bone as the body repairs itself.

His left ankle continued to throb, but McAdams, deprived of much of his lateral movement, dragged himself onto the field. "During another exhibition game in 1967, the ankle started to hamper me after three plays," said McAdams. The sudden resurgence of ankle pain so discouraged Carl that he nearly lost interest in rehab.

McAdams' diminished maneuverability lost Carl a spot in the linebacker rotation. Special teams—a meat grinder and one of the severest challenges for a healthy player—became his goal. He had been timed at a 4.6 or 4.7 40-yard dash at Oklahoma. "Coach Michaels said he'd time me and I'd be activated if I broke five seconds," he recalled. "I ran the forty and didn't do it in five. They let me try again—and this time I did it."

On October 29, 1967, he made his Jets debut with two tackles on special teams, earning a Weeb Ewbank salute: "He died a thousand deaths when he couldn't play, but he never stopped working to get back in shape." McAdams replied: "I didn't want anybody to call me a quitter." Dr. Nicholas, who regularly interacted with Carl, observed: "That kid is in tears with pain almost every game, but he never whines about anything."

Meanwhile, Dave Herman detected unknown pass-rushing skills in McAdams when the two lined up against each other in a 1967 practice. "I put a move on Dave and got around him real quick," remembers McAdams. "He told the coaches about it." Carl received playing time at tackle during the final pair of West Coast games that season. At the start of 1968, Carl was in the defensive line rotation, considered part of the "Front Five," along with Verlon Biggs, Gerry Philbin, Paul Rochester, and John Elliott.

When Karl Henke was injured prior to the tenth game of the season (the *Heidi* Game), Buddy Ryan elevated Carl's role. Competing as a 229-pound defensive tackle (he tried but couldn't gain weight), Carl trotted on the field against Oakland as a pass-rushing substitute for Rochester. "I didn't even know I was going to play tackle until the game started. I think I probably was in for ten plays," he says. Oakland tried to take advantage of Carl and his small size for a defensive tackle, but McAdams thwarted the Raiders' attempts to run right over him.

Carl played a good number of defensive snaps in the final four regular season games of 1968. Regarding his position shift to the D-line, Carl said, "It wasn't that hard. Paul Rochester stressed that most of all, I needed to think. It didn't sink in right away. We played Cincinnati, and the Bengals ran a sucker play two times in a row. On the first one, I caught the ball carrier for no gain. They ran it again, I moved down the line again to make the tackle—only they handed the ball off, I got blocked, and the runner ran straight through the hole I had vacated."

Because the AFL Championship defensive game plan was predicated on stopping Oakland's rushing attack, Ryan had to take McAdams out of the defensive line rotation. "I was told that if I was in there, the Raiders would really come at me," Carl said. He would play in the Super Bowl.

The highlight for Carl during the two weeks before Super Bowl III was about something he didn't do. The NFL ordered Weeb Ewbank to fine Joe Namath and Matt Snell for failing to appear for a media photo session. McAdams wasn't there, either; he slept through the mandatory appearance, too, but avoided a fine. "Nobody noticed I wasn't there," Carl admitted. "Sometimes it's good not to be a star."

McAdams earned his Super Bowl III ring. "I hadn't done it for any game that season, but I took shots in my ankle prior to the Super Bowl to get rid of the pain," he said. McAdams played quite a bit, with noticeable efforts in each half.

In the closing seconds of the second quarter, he almost wrecked the Colts' infamous flea-flicker. On the play, Earl Morrall handed the ball off to Tom Matte, who started a power sweep to the right side. A side-angle view of the play shows McAdams came close to blowing up the play at the line, lunging at Matte and wrapping both arms around the halfback. Somehow Matte slithered through Carl's tackle and the play proceeded. Matte stopped in mid-run, whirled, and tossed it back to Morrall. The Colts QB looked downfield and was supposed to hit on a deep pass. Morrall's pass, however, was intercepted.

Carl nearly became a second-half starter at linebacker when middle linebacker Al Atkinson damaged his shoulder near the end of the first half and was escorted to the Jets' training room. When Atkinson was injured, Paul Crane entered the lineup at weak-side linebacker, pushing Larry Grantham to the middle for the remainder of the second quarter.

"In the locker room, as Walt Michaels spoke out loud about Carl taking Atkinson's place at middle linebacker, Larry told me not to be concerned about assignments," McAdams said. "He said, 'I'll tell you what you need to do before every play.'" McAdams emotionally braced himself for the role he had dreamt about since signing with the Jets. In an adjoining room, Atkinson told Dr. Nicholas he had to play the second half. Al received an injection to numb the discomfort in his aching shoulder and Michaels made no change.

In the second half, McAdams performed as well at tackle as he had in the four games after the *Heidi* fiasco. In the third quarter, he had the Jets' only takedown of a Baltimore quarterback that day. Earl Morrall dropped back to throw, had no open receiver, and scrambled sideways along the line of scrimmage toward the left sideline. Morrall tiptoed his way until he ran out of room at the left sideline. McAdams put him in a bear hug and dragged him down.

Due to the Miami heat, Carl put in some time at defensive end, relieving Verlon Biggs. NBC analyst Al DeRogatis described McAdams' entry in the lineup in the fourth quarter as a way to supplement the Jets' pass rush.

The next season, 1969, Carl's spot on the D-line was given to Steve Thompson. McAdams' left ankle never fully healed, and was weaker and more painful as he played special teams. After the Jets lost to Kansas City in a 1969 divisional playoff game, McAdams was without a contract and faced the prospect of more surgery. The thought of a fifth operation, torturous rehab, and little assurance that he would be his old self persuaded the twenty-six-year-old McAdams to wrap up his career.

He had played only twenty-six AFL games in four years, about half the Jets' games. "After the ankle injury, I was never the same player," McAdams concedes. "The Jets didn't get the player they expected. I don't think I ever reached sixty percent of my playing ability. I never reached my professional football goals, which made me feel like a failure—and still does."

JOHN ELLIOTT

DEFENSIVE TACKLE #80   6'4"   244 LB.

Only three new Jets broke into the 1968 lineup; John was one of them and he became an AFL all-star.

As the 1967 season closed, it was irksome to some Jets, like Don Maynard, that third-year defensive tackle Jim Harris had not been in shape at the end of the schedule. Warned by Weeb Ewbank to spend the off-season doing something about it, Harris reported overweight to 1968 training camp and immediately lost his starting job.

First up with an opportunity to replace Harris was Dennis Randall, a 6'7", 250-pound 1967 third-round draft choice out of Oklahoma State. He had suffered a season-ending knee injury his rookie year, showed up at Hofstra training camp, and left in July 1968 without a public explanation. Next up could have been 1968 second-round draft choice Steve Thompson, an angular 6'2", 240-pounder out of the University of Washington, but he injured a knee in a controlled rookie scrimmage with the Baltimore Colts.

Darrell John Elliott, the Jets' seventh-round 1967 collegiate pick, was the next option. A Texas high school high hurdles champ, John had been a respected University of Texas offensive lineman and linebacker. Pro teams didn't drool over him, but at Jets camp, his speed, quickness, and hustle at defensive tackle were numbing. It didn't surprise Carl McAdams, who remembered playing against Elliott in college. "I intercepted a pass for Oklahoma against Texas and cruised towards the goal line on my way to a touchdown," he recounted. "I was shocked to be caught from behind *by John Elliott.*"

As something of a tryout, Weeb had thrown Elliott into the Jets' defensive line—replacing Harris—in the team's final games of 1967. That postseason, Elliott put on twenty-five pounds, raising his playing weight to 246. Elliott started the second half of the Jets' first 1968 preseason game and was so effective that by the second exhibition, he had sealed the deal for a starting DT role.

His rapid ascent in the lineup was completely unforeseen. At the end of the preseason, Ewbank told the New York media, "We've really got something in this kid. He can be an All-Pro." John's insertion improved a defensive unit with tremendous unity, pride, and continuity, plus familiarity with everyone's role from years of playing together. Not far into the 1968 season, the Jets' defense leaped to the top of the AFL rankings and Elliott began to be known on Jets broadcasts as "Big Bad John."

Paul Zimmerman wrote, "John Elliott's meteoric and unexpected rise at right tackle threw the whole operation into high gear." Three-quarters into the 1968 season, Zimmerman selected John to his personal 1968 all-AFL team, and wrote, "He pursues better than anyone at his position, rushes the passer and won't get caught on traps." In the days leading to Super Bowl III, defensive line partner

Gerry Philbin credited Elliott's season-long improvement for the defense's year-end number-one AFL ranking.

Elliott's partner at defensive tackle, Paul Rochester, gets a lot of the credit for John's improvement. Rocky recognized John's natural talent but shook his head about Elliott's technique. Elliott's stance before the snap and how he attacked the offensive line after the snap "were terrible," according to Rochester. "John wasn't the only guy on our line to need that help. Verlon's three-point stance was also terrible," he added.

Rochester elaborated: "I learned at Michigan State to keep your feet, toe-to-heel, as wide as your shoulders. John and Verlon both set their back foot way behind them, like a sprinter. You can't 'explode' against the offensive linemen when you set up that way. At the snap, instead of driving towards the guard or center—and going as low as you can—driving from that extended back leg forces you to straighten and stand up, which slows your momentum and makes you easier to block."

Elliott's quarterback pressures from the middle of the defensive line created an awesome pass-rushing dimension for the Jets. John underwent more training with Rochester. John regularly beat the guard or guard/center combination and he was actually in the offensive backfield too quickly. Competitors used Elliott's super aggressiveness against him until Rocky showed him how to not get trapped.

In barely half of the 1968 season, that Elliott weakness became a non-issue. He stopped over-pursuing and he became an unblockable force, solid against the run, and a hustling 245-pounder who made tackles far from the line of scrimmage. "I remember one time when John had rushed the passer, and the throw went into the flat and John was in on the tackle down the field," reminisced linebacker Ralph Baker. Top AFL competition—All-Pro guard Billy Shaw and Kansas City hulking left guard Ed Budde—complimented him to the hilt for his quickness, elusiveness, and strength.

Elliott became an even more effective defensive weapon when Walt Michaels and defensive line coach Buddy Ryan resorted to an "overshifted" defensive line, a basic part of Michaels' repertoire that hadn't been effective before Elliott. Appearing on film as a "5–2" alignment, the Jets' four defensive linemen were joined by one of the linebackers on the line of scrimmage.

Most teams are right-handed; in other words, the opposition's tight end sets up on the right side of the offensive line. It leaves only two offensive linemen on the weak (non–tight end) side. Elliott's quickness, strength, and toughness boosted the power of the overshift. John positioned himself head up over the center, with Al Atkinson standing directly behind him. John could attack to his left (take on the center and/or right guard) or to his right (moving against the left guard). Guessing which direction John would go confused the opposition's center and both guards.

"The offense didn't know which way I was going," confirmed Elliott. "If I went left, I tied up both the right guard and center. If the center hesitated a second, it gave Al a step advantage to go where he wanted. We always got that half-step because we relied on our quickness." Grantham disclosed that he knew Elliott's target—the center or which of the offensive guards—on each play. "He would signal us by patting himself on the side he was going," he said.

Larry noted that Walt Michaels' overshifted defensive formation attempted to force competitors' offensive lines to double-team Elliott or left tackle Rochester, depending on which side of the line the tight end set up on. Grantham noted that the overshift attack scheme had the added benefit of helping the Jets' linebackers find who had the ball.

"John wasn't the meanest guy; if he had that streak in him, he would have made All-Pro more often than he did," observed Gerry Philbin. John elevated his standing with teammates by volunteering to join starters Grantham, Philbin, and Al Atkinson on special team kickoffs at the finish of important, close games. What he lacked in experience, John more than made up for with apparent extra effort and pure tackling ability.

The *Heidi* Game was among the Jets' most memorable match-ups in the 1968 season, but Elliott had little effect that day. He's half of the answer to the trivia question: Which two Jets were ejected from the game? John was tossed by officials in the second quarter for decking Raiders center Jim Otto. He protested, unsuccessfully, that Otto had been the instigator.

In the Super Bowl, Elliott quickly established his strengths. On the Colts' first play from scrimmage, John ran down Baltimore TE John Mackey on a swing pass. Mackey had evaded the normally un-flappable Grantham and bulled over the sure-tackling Jim Hudson. Elliott pursued him over 20 yards and knocked the All-Pro TE out of bounds after a 19-yard gain.

Later on that same Colts drive, with a first down on the New York 37-yard line, Elliott executed a superhuman defensive play. Halfback Tom Matte was going to run up the middle between the Colts' center, Bill Curry, and the left guard, Dan Sullivan, directly at Elliott.

At the snap of the ball, left guard Sullivan launched his 6'3", 250-pound frame at Elliott, who warded off the block. A fraction of a second later, right guard Glenn Ressler (likewise 6'3" and 250) charged diagonally at John, who evaded the full impact of Ressler's block. In the next instant, fullback Jerry Hill burst through the line, leading Matte—and also targeting Elliott. John threw Hill to the side. Finally, Matte came through the hole, where Elliott, still upright, wrapped his arms around the Colt ball carrier and stopped him after a 1-yard gain. It was one of his four tackles that afternoon.

Elliott had foiled three blocks and blown up the rush attempt *on his own*. In the Jets' internal statistical ratings system, it would have earned a "4" rating (on a 0–5 scale), possibly a "5" (defined as a once-in-a-season effort by a defender on a single play). Whether a 4 or 5, Jets defensive mates like Grantham and Rochester said this one effort was vintage Elliott.

That single Baltimore running play became emblematic of the emerging dominance of the Jets' defense. Midway through the first quarter, the Jets' D-line had established control of the line of scrimmage. Colts QB Earl Morrall was never dumped, but he was ceaselessly chased, hurried, and harassed. "We knew that the Colts' two quarterbacks couldn't throw a twenty-yard out and couldn't throw deep downfield with any zip on the ball," noted Elliott.

As for Baltimore's running attack, except for a couple of long runs, the Colts couldn't mount a ground game against a Jets defense that had led the AFL in rushing yards per game (85). "If we shut down their running game early and made them pass, we were pretty sure we had them," added Elliott. As the Jets extended their halftime lead from 7–0, to 10–, 13–, and finally, 16–0, the Colts had diminishing time on the clock to try and catch up and had to pass.

The Super Bowl win had one humorous postmortem. Jets' brass forgot to pick up the Super Bowl trophy from the hotel safe before they checked out, so John grabbed it as he made his way to the team bus. "That was the only time I ever held it," he admitted. In the postgame Super Bowl locker room, John learned firsthand from other AFL stars how much the game meant to Daryle Lamonica, Ben Davidson, and Kansas City's Buck Buchanan, AFL players who had failed to get the job done in Super Bowls I and II. The appreciation of other AFL players cascaded when Elliott got to Jacksonville the following weekend to play for the East in the AFL All-Star Game. The Bills' Billy Shaw told him he had been so pumped that he not been able to sleep the night of the Jets' victory.

Elliott's salary for the Super Bowl season was $16,000. He was second among team defensive linemen in tackles and led the team in assisted tackles that season. His 118 tackling points (55 unassisted and 63 assisted) trailed only Al Atkinson on defense. His total compensation worked out to $26,700 for the 1969 season. His paycheck did steadily increase ($35,000 in 1970, $42,500 in 1971, and $45,500 in 1972), but John tired of his contract squabbles with Ewbank. After the 1973 season, he departed the Jets for the World Football League's New York Stars. Elliott was named an all-WFL defensive tackle his only year in the league.

John Elliott was a "gentle giant, a man's man," according to his wife, Nancy. A loving father and grandfather also devoted to his friends, Elliott was "calm, laid-back and relaxed, seldom ever lost his temper," she said. Nancy noted John's humanity, remembering: "We watched him carry a crippled elderly man into the baptistery waters so he could be baptized before he died." She added that John's most cherished honor was a bronze Jets 1970 MVP trophy voted on by his teammates.

He died at age sixty-six from cancer on November 11, 2010.

LINEBACKERS
THREE DIFFERENT STYLES CAME TOGETHER

LARRY GRANTHAM	#60
RALPH BAKER	#51
AL ATKINSON	#62
MIKE STROMBERG	#68

LARRY GRANTHAM

RIGHT LINEBACKER #60   6'0"   210 LB.

The off-season weight-training regimen of the Jets' defensive signal caller was lifting twelve ounces at a time (beer).

Larry Grantham was honored more times in his Jets career than anyone else on the Super Bowl III Jets, and in the 1960s no other AFL defensive player had as distinguished a decade as he did. He was a first-team all-AFL linebacker from his second year with the New York Titans (1961) through the team's early Jets years (1963 and 1964), and Larry's excellent linebacker play continued even as the league's talent level took larger and larger leaps from 1965 through 1969. Year after year, week after week, Larry battled bigger, more physically gifted opponents. He foiled the plans of opposing offenses and earned second-team All-AFL honors each of those five years.

Based strictly on achievement and tenure with the team, Grantham could have been, but was not, the face of the franchise. When the AFL wrapped up its existence in 1970, the AFL All-Time Team included Grantham at second-team outside linebacker. Writing about the Jets' celebration of the fortieth anniversary of their Super Bowl Jets team in 2008, Dave Anderson commented in the *New York Times*: "Joe Namath will surely get the loudest cheers, but Larry Grantham deserves as many decibels, if not more."

Those honors and the Super Bowl win supplemented Larry's sterling college career and generally overlooked national college football championship at Ole Miss. The 1959 University of Mississippi squad, 10-1, was voted national champion by the Clyde Berryman College Football Ranking, the Dunkel College Football Index, and Jeff Sagarin College Football Ratings. (Syracuse was the choice by some other services.) Ole Miss' opponents scored only 21 points.

Grantham was a terrific athlete; he went to Ole Miss on partial baseball and football scholarships. College Football Hall of Famer Charlie Flowers played linebacker behind Larry at defensive end at Mississippi and said, "I played linebacker on Larry Grantham's side, so I never got a chance to make any tackles. Grantham always got there first. All I got to do was jump on a few piles." Larry played end on offense and defensive end and learned the value of studying opposing offenses on film. He capped his college career at the Hula Bowl All-Star Game in January 1960, where he was named Most Valuable Lineman and, for good measure, caught an 11-yard TD pass.

He never made it into the College or Pro Football Hall of Fame—astounding dual oversights. Larry was named to the 1950s' SEC Football Team of the Decade and was honored as a member of the Ole Miss Team of the Century in 1993. "Larry should be in Canton," believes Gerry Philbin. "He made All-Pro so many years, our Super

Bowl defense never got the credit it deserved and he was the leader of our defense." Only twenty players lasted all ten years of the AFL and Grantham was one of only five defensive players on that distinguished list. Of the twenty players, only Buffalo Bills offensive guard Billy Shaw is in the Hall.

Larry Grantham, at right side or weak-side linebacker, consistently tackled as well as any defender. He wasn't scary or mean like others in his time (that is, Philadelphia Eagles legend Chuck Bednarik or Chicago Bears famed middle linebacker Dick Butkus). He did not call attention to himself, like Sam Huff of the New York Giants. Every offensive coordinator tried to attack Grantham, to run the sub-200-pounder over—and they invariably failed.

Grantham was only 6'0" tall in an era where 6'2" was the pro scout's minimum linebacker standard. The football program listed him at 210 pounds but he cackled that he came to training camp at 190 and was worn down to 175 by the end of most seasons. Larry wasn't fast but had enough quickness to run step for step with all but the fastest backs. As for strength, the 1960s were mostly the pre-weight-lifting era in football. He described his off-season weight training as "lifting twelve ounces at a time"—beer.

"He knew the game, was very quick mobility-wise, and he never let blockers get a real good shot at him," assessed Ralph Baker, Grantham's bookend left-side linebacker. "He ducked under blockers, got by them without actually taking them on. Larry was also a sharp blitzer; he timed the snap very well and, with his quickness, made a lot of plays by squeezing through whatever little hole there was." Middle linebacker Al Atkinson said, "Larry didn't blow assignments; he was reliable and played through injury. I remember against Denver he broke his bridge on a tackle, spit his teeth out, and kept on playing."

Grantham took much bigger and heavier guys down, despite his size. "I led with my shoulder on tackles—the way I was taught in college," Grantham said of his style. "You don't tackle by putting your head down the middle of a guy. You put your head on the out-side of the ball carrier. If he is running to his left, you drive your shoulder into his left side. If he's running to his right, you do the opposite."

Larry's mental capacity helped overcome any size and strength deficiencies. His knowledge of opponent offenses was complemented by his experience versus AFL linemen, backs and ends. He loved the detail in his work and possessed extraordinary vision. His time in-vestment and mental capacities instilled in Larry instantaneous on-field comprehension of opponent play calls. From there, *all Larry did* was shout to Jets defenders the offensive play about to unfold, bodily nudge teammates into proper position, and put into motion his own immediate, instinctive reactions.

"I tailored my assets to my game. I was told my whole life that I was too small," Larry related. "I was fast enough to get to the spot on the field I needed to be at when a back came out of the backfield. After watching game film, I always liked the whole play unfolding in front of me just like on the film. I pretty much knew what to expect." Watch film of Grantham in action and you see his feet and fingers in motion, Larry having diagnosed the play and preparing to launch himself toward the appropriate location. "Larry always played like a heavyweight," summed up Walt Michaels.

The Baltimore Colts had drafted him in the fifteenth round of the 1960 draft, but coming off consecutive NFL titles in 1958 and 1959, they told him that no more than one or two rookies would crack the squad. The New York Titans' owner, Harry Wismer, offered "a little more than the Colts," Larry says ($10,500 overall), and the best chance of playing professional football.

Grantham reported to the Titans in the summer of 1960, pre-pared to play offense. Titans coaches quickly determined that his fu-ture was elsewhere; head coach Sammy Baugh turned Larry over to defensive coach John Dell Isola. "John and the other defensive coach, Dick Todd, took me under their wing," Larry says fondly. "John saw me studying film and in 1961 he designated me to call defensive signals," an assignment he maintained through his years with the Weeb Ewbank–coached Jets. He retired in 1972.

Larry says everything in the Titans' inaugural season seemed up in the air. Head coach Sammy Baugh's offensive playbook was composed of handwritten notes on a chalkboard, which the players penned into spiral notebooks. Larry gained acclaim during his rookie campaign, and he credits the projector he was permitted to take home with him every night with earning him 1961 all-AFL honors.

Grantham estimates he spent twenty-eight to thirty hours each week poring over game film. By the time he became a Jets linebacker, his son was old enough to run the machine back and forth, providing Larry with more time to concentrate on opponents' plays and the idiosyncrasies of backs and quarterbacks. Studying for the benefit of the Titans/Jets defense, Larry thought that 60 percent of those weekly hours benefited him personally.

The other 40 percent of his viewing time helped him grasp and identify the upcoming opponent's preferred offensive play calls in regular-, long-, and short-yardage situations. That was widely shared with everyone on defense. Larry explained, "Most teams like one formation. You count how many times they are in that formation and how many times in a different formation. The Kansas City Chiefs, who shifted in and out of formations—showing all kinds of looks—were attempting to confuse defenses more than anything else.

"Wide-angle film gave me a lot of important tips about individual players," said Grantham. "When you are as close as I was to the line of scrimmage, you can read a lot of things. A halfback coming out on a pass pattern sits back on his haunches a little bit; when he's going to come straight ahead on a handoff, he has his weight forward. I keyed on that. I also studied quarterbacks. Out of force of habit, with a certain foot up he was going to his right and if he lifted his other foot he was going to his left."

When the Titans became the Jets, Weeb Ewbank hired Walt Michaels to handle the Jets linebackers. Michaels adjusted Grantham's role from weak-side linebacker (the side of the line opposite the tight end) to right-side linebacker. "Walt emphasized intelligence and athleticism in the players," Larry explained. "Even after we all learned the playbook, things on the field moved so fast that all of us had to be smart enough to know what the other team was trying to do—and to react immediately." Each player on the Jets defense had to know the defensive playbook so thoroughly that he knew his responsibility and those of every one of the other ten for the Jets' three defenses—and instinctively carry out his assignment.

Larry was a specially interested bystander when the Jets signed Joe Namath to his $427,000 contract in 1965. Jets players realized their sudden good bargaining position. Weeb Ewbank wanted Larry, whose contract had expired, to be happy. "I asked for more of a raise than I ever had—I think it was five thousand dollars—and he gave it to me real quick," Larry remembers. "I realized later I could have asked for a lot more."

The opening game of 1968, the 20–19 upset at Kansas City in which the Chiefs offense didn't score a touchdown, was memorable for Larry because it tested his signal calling in the AFL's noisiest stadium. "The Chiefs' tricky offensive formations forced us to relay defensive changes across the field, from player to player, above the crowd's whooping and hollering. The Chiefs were still the class of the league, even after they lost Super Bowl I. It was a big win for us—and on the road," he said.

Larry tried to mind his defensive business after controversial losses to Buffalo and Denver in games three and five. In Buffalo, when Joe Namath tossed five interceptions, Grantham didn't put much blame on Namath: "Joe was one of the youngest quarterbacks in the league and Buffalo used some defenses that Joe hadn't seen before. We didn't kid ourselves; our offense wasn't about controlling the ball and keeping the defense off of the field." After the Denver five-interception debacle two weeks later, Grantham admitted, "There was some resentment from the defense, but I was into doing my job, and not worrying about doing someone else's."

Grantham was all in with Walt Michaels' three goals for every game—limiting opposition backs to under 100 yards, holding passing yards to 200, and limiting the opponent to 17 points or less. It was common for Jets starters on offense and defense to volunteer to play special teams in crucial situations. Grantham was one of them.

The 1968 AFL Championship Game, played in the bitter cold and whipping winds of Shea Stadium in late December, was as pleasurable an experience for Grantham and the Jets as the last-minute *Heidi* Game loss to the Raiders had been unsettling. "Taking Oakland on in temperatures twenty degrees colder than the Raiders were accustomed to . . . they didn't like the cold. They had only a short workout the day before because of the weather," Larry remarked. "We keyed our D to stop the run more than the pass because [Raiders QB Daryle] Lamonica had long arm action and he had to deal with Shea's strong, unfamiliar, swirling winds." The plan worked. Lamonica threw for over 400 yards, but not effectively, and the Raiders' running attack was even less of a factor.

Larry said the Jets were certainly confident about winning Super Bowl III, but Grantham said he and his teammates felt disrespected when the Colts didn't compliment them. "We led the AFL in defense that year. We watched the Colts talking on TV about us, never mentioning any of our players' names," Grantham recalled. "We felt they didn't know who we were." The Jets defense figured it would hold the Colts to fewer than 20 points. (They held Baltimore to 7.)

After toiling in obscurity with the Titans and being branded as inferior with the Jets, Super Bowl III represented payback. In the game's closing minutes, Grantham, Atkinson, and Baker were serenaded by NBC Super Bowl III color analyst Al DeRogatis. "The Baltimore Colts have always praised the linebackers of the New York Jets," he told the TV audience. "They said their linebackers are like having seven halfbacks. And these boys have done an outstanding job."

The Colts' last-gasp drive in Super Bowl III ended with 2:26 left in the game, when John Unitas' fourth-down red zone pass was tipped away by Larry, who had a perfect angle to deflect and tip the throw over the head of the Colts' Jimmy Orr. In an exhibition of exhilaration that didn't receive the same attention as Joe Namath's number-one finger salute, Larry removed his helmet and tossed it skyward. It let out two weeks of frustration with the media's contempt for the Jets. Simultaneously, Grantham's nine-year quest for respect and recognition from the football world was also now over.

On the Jets, Larry led in other important ways. Black members of the 1960s Jets confirm racial tension in the early part of the decade from explicit remarks and behavior of some veteran southern white players. Grantham, a native Mississippian, made an impassioned speech to Jets teammates in 1963 that won him election as a founding member of the AFL Players Association. He discussed his southern upbringing and personal evolution concerning race relations and strenuously committed himself to representing the interests of all Jets.

"Growing up, my dad, Carl, emphasized that loyalty was an important part of living," said Grantham. He fulfilled that in his dealings with the Jets, wearing his Super Bowl ring every day and slipping on the Jets Ring of Honor band that had been bestowed on him in 2011. You might conclude that the ultimate sign of loyalty was returned to Larry in spades. Every January 12, the date of Super Bowl III, the townspeople in his hometown of Crystal Springs, Mississippi, celebrated Larry Grantham Day.

Larry Grantham, the Super Bowl Jets' field general on defense, died at age seventy-eight on June 17, 2017, from complications of chronic obstructive pulmonary disease.

RALPH BAKER

LEFT LINEBACKER #51   6'3"   228 LB.

There are no good reasons why Ralph hasn't been dubbed "Big-Game Baker" after fumble recoveries in the AFL Championship Game and Super Bowl III.

To Weeb Ewbank and the Jets, Ralph Baker's play over a decade-plus was what every professional coach craves: solid and reliable. Ralph wasn't flashy and he knew his strengths—and identified and worked on his weaknesses, making it a point to improve upon and compensate for them. Middle linebacker Al Atkinson saluted Baker as "smart, consistent, durable, didn't blow an assignment."

Baker says the seeds of the greatest season in Jets history were planted at the conclusion of the 1967 season, which, with the Jets at 8-5-1 and in second place, ended with collective sadness and deep disappointment. Numerous Jets channeled their personal frustration into incentives to make things right for the team and their fans in 1968.

According to Pro-Football-Reference.com, Ralph recovered only two fumbles in 142 regular season games stretched out over his eleven years as a Jets linebacker. But Baker had two others in the two biggest games the Jets ever played. Curiously, the strong-side left linebacker was never elevated onto a pedestal by the Jets for his two game-changing, backbreaking postseason defensive plays in 1968–69.

In the AFL Championship Game, Baker instantaneously recognized in its closing minutes that Oakland Raiders QB Daryle

Lamonica's swing pass to halfback Charlie Smith inside the Jets' twenty-yard line was thrown behind Smith and thus a lateral. Ralph pounced on it at the two-minute warning, essentially putting the finishing touch on the Jets' 27–23 victory.

Two weeks later, in Super Bowl III, on Baltimore's first play from scrimmage in the second half, Ralph recovered a fumble torn loose by Verlon Biggs from Tom Matte. Baker threw his body on top of the loose ball at the Colts' 33-yard line. (He was so keyed up, Ralph said he didn't know the identity of the Jet who knocked the ball loose until we told him.) Baker's recovery led to a 32-yard field goal, which gave the Jets a 10–0 lead.

Interceptions and fumble recoveries put linebackers and defensive backs on highlight reels, especially in postseason games. So how is it that Baker's recoveries in the two championship games never earned him tributes, either from Jets or NFL media? No one ever nicknamed him "Big-Game Baker," but it fits given the two fumble recoveries.

The soft-spoken Baker didn't put much thought about not being honored as a difference maker. Pro football historians haven't, either, probably because Ralph didn't convert either recovery into a touchdown. He was a quiet, fundamentally sound player, gifted with above-average intelligence and great analytical capability, and he held himself to a very high standard. The best example: in 1964, after a personally disappointing performance, he tried to return his game check to Weeb Ewbank.

Ralph knew the lateral rule, so he knew that after grabbing the loose ball, he couldn't run with it. However, in the heat of the moment, he recalled the Jets' second game of that season when a Joe Namath swing pass had been ruled a lateral by officials. A Boston Patriot lineman picked it up, danced into the end zone, and was awarded a touchdown. Later that week, the AFL league office confirmed it should have been a recovery, dead ball, and no TD.

In the AFL Championship, Ralph retrieved the lateral, tucked the ball away, and, remembering Birmingham, started to jog down the left sideline, just in case. It took a few seconds for officials to blow the play dead. "Charlie Smith came after me," Ralph recalled. He doesn't remember the three-man Jets convoy—Gerry Philbin, Jim Hudson, and John Elliott—who ran and were escorting Ralph to the end zone.

If that fumble had led to a virtual game-ending TD, the jubilation and teammates pounding Ralph in celebration would have been witnessed by a national TV audience and created a memorable video for the ages.

Ralph's Super Bowl fumble recovery was a momentum swinger, but the Jets' four interceptions in that game completely overshadowed it. All five turnovers happened at critical junctures, but all four pickoffs turned back Baltimore inside the Jets' red zone.

Baker graduated in 1964 from Penn State, which years later would become known as "Linebacker U" for the number of quality linebackers it sent to the pro ranks. Baker opted for the Jets over the NFL's Pittsburgh Steelers. He reasoned that Pittsburgh was a bad team with strong linebackers; Ralph saw Larry Grantham and openings at the other two Jets linebacking spots. Ralph wanted to play middle linebacker and Weeb Ewbank promised him he would play there to get his signature on a contract. "Two weeks after I signed, the Jets traded for Denver middle linebacker Wahoo McDaniel. My guess is they humored me until I signed," said Baker, without a ripple of anger.

Ralph's pass defense was a concern because he wasn't fleet of foot. Bizarrely, in the 1964 preseason, Ralph said, "I had five interceptions in four games. I never had that kind of success again." But Ralph's weakness was exposed early once the regular schedule began. One instance sticks in Ralph's mind to this day. "We were in a man-to-man against Boston," Baker recounted. "Their halfback, Ron Burton, ran towards me and I tried to meet him head-on, expecting him to block me. Instead, he sidestepped and ran past me, caught a

Babe Parilli pass on the run, and raced down the sideline sixty-seven yards for a touchdown. That was one of the key teaching moments in my career. I was determined it wouldn't happen again. I told myself that if I didn't correct this mistake so it didn't happen again, I wasn't going to last with the Jets. I think I only got beat one more time on a long pass in man-to-man coverage in my eleven years."

You get a sense of Baker's year-to-year progress from Ewbank's private personnel evaluations. After the 1964 season, he cited Baker's "respectable rookie year" and his development:

> Was an improvement over our linebacking. Size and toughness adequate. Speed and agility his limiting factors. If progress continues at same rate, can become good pro linebacker . . . Must improve and become meaner.

After Baker's sophomore year in New York, Weeb saluted Ralph as "the most improved [defensive veteran]" and said that he had shown "more knowledge of defenses." Ewbank took a more pragmatic view about Baker's pass defense:

> His execution on pass coverage was substantially improved. He will always get beaten occasionally on pass coverage due to lack of speed, but this is true of most linebackers in strong side coverage . . . Still needs to recognize and play screens more effectively . . . He will never be an effective blitzing linebacker due to lack of good quickness, but played with authority and he and (Gerry) Philbin worked together well . . . They could be a tough combination on our left side on defense.

Weeb praised the Jets' Grantham, Baker, and Al Atkinson linebacker tandem, which took the field between 1966 and 1972. Ralph says their success came from above-average intelligence and "us having been together so long. It was more of an on-field together thing than sitting down and talking about it. We got to know where everybody was on every play, knew instinctively where our help was, and took advantage of it."

Baker shared a prescient conversation he had in 1968 before the Jets had any thoughts about a Super Bowl appearance. Team surgeon Dr. James Nicholas told Ralph he had studied the experience of players on Green Bay's two winning Super Bowl teams. "He figured out that the majority of the Packers' roster averaged out to about five-years playing experience," Baker recalled. "He thought that was the magic number for a Super Bowl run. Many of us were hitting our individual peaks and were at that five-year mark."

After an 11–3 regular season record and an AFL East Championship, Baker has vivid memories of the AFL Championship victory on December 29, 1968: "Freezing cold, very gusty winds, paper blowing around the parking lot. I hate the cold; I do not respond well to it, so it was not my kind of day," he said. "We were very confident we could beat the Raiders."

Watching game film for Super Bowl III, Baker, like nearly all his teammates, gained confidence. "Originally I thought the Colts must be a super team, but I saw that we deserved to be on the field with them," he said. Ralph recalled that Walt Michaels' game plan only had a wrinkle or two from the Jets' normal defensive scheme.

He was less sure about the plan when the game began. "My confidence was shaken when the Colts went right down the field at the start of the game; they came up with some good plays against our unorthodox defense," he said. "Somebody had figured out some good things to do against us, and they hit us with all of them on those first plays. They hit us in some very vulnerable spots.

"As a professional you do tell yourself, we'll get 'em on the next play and make sure they can't do that again, but the problem was on the next play they were making another eight or ten yards. In the long run, it worked for us. We were lucky we got those five turnovers. It is skill, but a certain amount of luck."

Perhaps the only black mark on Ralph's career came from center John Schmitt. "Ralph got an extra five hundred dollars a year for ten years to be my backup field goal and extra-point snapper," Schmitt said. "Early in the 1969 playoff game against Kansas City, the Chiefs' players told me they were going to rough me up to stop Jim Turner's kicking game. They sent three guys after me on every field goal snap. We made a field goal and they buried me, and the next time we lined up for another field goal, one of the Chiefs stepped directly on my right hand. They broke it and three of my knuckles.

"I went up to Ralph on the sideline, with my hand wrapped in dry ice so I could still snap for Joe. I told him, 'My hand is broken, I can't snap for field goals. You're going to have to snap the next time we get in range'—and he looked at me and said in a panic, 'I can't snap under pressure,' and walked away. I unloaded on Ralph, 'Son------ch... One time I ask you to do something... You are the lowest," Schmitt blurted out, heartily laughing as he shared his story.

AL ATKINSON

MIDDLE LINEBACKER #62	6'2"	230 LB.

Al, at middle linebacker, was the cement in a stout Jets linebacking corps that had a seven-year run.

The Jets' 1965 college draft, the soundest and deepest in the franchise's history, got an unexpected bonus from a signing by another team. It came during that year's training camp when the two-time defending AFL champion (and linebacker-rich) Buffalo Bills waived third-round draft choice, Al Atkinson. The Bills hoped he would sneak through unclaimed, but the Jets, who had faced Buffalo twice in the 1965 preseason, wasted no time making a hundred-dollar waiver claim on the former Villanova all-America lineman.

"The Bills had a good core all across their defense; the Jets didn't know what they were getting in me," admits Atkinson, who had elected to go to Buffalo rather than the Baltimore Colts. "Playing for Villanova, I had no expectations about being drafted. I was a lineman in high school and college, and I was better suited to play linebacker in the pros, although it was completely different," he added.

Walt Michaels had scouted Al at Villanova, and Atkinson said that during their limited interaction he sensed the Jets' coach could teach him the art of linebacking and get the best out of him. It was one of the reasons he was happy to join the Jets. "Buffalo didn't have a linebacker coach. Walt taught me a lot of things, like that most guys are physical, but a lot of them aren't that mentally prepared—and that's when a team gets upset. You have to keep your mind on the game," he said.

With veteran middle backer Wahoo McDaniel in place, Weeb Ewbank didn't need to throw the rookie into the frying pan in 1965. Wearing No. 88, Atkinson proved his mettle as a rookie special teams wedge-buster, blowing away the coaches with his fearlessness, toughness, and tackling. In one game, he was credited with an incredulous five unassisted tackles. Special teams captain Mark Smolinski sarcastically saluted the rookie: "We all resent Al. He doesn't give the rest of us a chance." Gerry Philbin called Atkinson an uncommonly "reliable, good tackler."

Two games before the end of the 1965 season, Wahoo McDaniel was nicked up, so J. D. Donaldson and linebacker coach Walt Michaels threw Al into the deep water. Atkinson's small sampling at middle linebacker was not a tour de force, though the Jets saw enough to interest them in what Weeb described as the "large, rough rookie."

Atkinson had a good reason to remember the last game of 1965. "The Bills' center, Al Bemiller, hit me with a forearm elbow that shattered the middle of my double-bar plastic face mask. His elbow went into my nose, fracturing it. I came into the huddle and was spitting blood in every direction, and Paul Rochester yelled at me to get out. It taught me pro football was a tough game, but we upset Buffalo so it was a good way to end my first season," said Atkinson.

In Coach Ewbank's 1965 postseason, private breakdown, Weeb wrote:

> Played outstandingly on special teams throughout the season. When given the chance to play regular at middle guard, he did not perform as we had hoped for and expected. The rawness of a rookie was very apparent. His ability to tackle and diagnose plays, playing pass defense as called upon, still makes him a good prospect for next year. Even if he were a back-up linebacker, I still feel that we would be wise to keep him. He is good for a team and is such a solid citizen on and off the field that he is most worthy of having around.

Atkinson didn't know the good fortune that was soon to smile down on him. Wahoo McDaniel, whose nickname had given the Jets good PR value for two years in New York, had slowed down, become lazy in pass coverage, and had lost the stamina necessary to be an every-down player. He was earning more on the professional wrestling circuit than in football. The Jets put Wahoo and center Mike Hudock on a list of players the Miami Dolphins could select in an expansion draft. They took both, creating a hole on each side of the ball. John Schmitt took Hudock's spot and Atkinson would compete to fill the defensive void.

After rookie linebackers Carl McAdams and Bill Yearby both were injured during training camp, Al was the last man standing and the starting middle linebacker with a new number, 62. He grew into and held that position through 1972, and continued special teams duty in 1966 and 1967.

While Al never was on the receiving end of favorable comparisons with the NFL's star middle linebackers of the time—Joe Schmidt, Dick Butkus, or Ray Nitschke—Larry Grantham said "most of the other middle linebackers, including the big-name ones, couldn't hold Al's jockstrap. Believe me, I know, because I watched the film." Matt Snell played against Butkus while at Ohio State and observed, "Al could play with any of the NFL's name linebackers."

Atkinson lacked distinguishing characteristics, like Nitschke's missing front teeth and nasty growl. Schmidt was a thinking man's linebacker—like Al—but Schmidt was also publicized for the hurt he put on QBs, carriers, and receivers. Butkus was Butkus, simply the best to anyone watching pro football.

Atkinson, according to teammates, was the hardest hitter on the Jets defense, but he didn't run all over the field looking to lay people out. Coach Weeb Ewbank labeled him as "a steady, hard-nosed . . . an exceptionally good . . . pass defender." Walt Michaels stressed, "When I look at films of a game, I can't hardly ever recall him making a serious mistake. . . . Some linebackers like to gamble, but I don't want mine to. . . . Al Atkinson might not be spectacular, but he doesn't make that big mistake that can cost us a touchdown."

Never blowing his own horn, Atkinson said he thought his nickname, "Hombre," had to do with his ability to play despite injuries: torn cartilage in the rib cage, a bruised rib, a cracked wrist, and a couple of concussions—none of which caused him to miss a game. Paul Rochester, who played directly in front of Atkinson, said, "You could hear when he smacked a guy and he was as tough as they come." Earl Christie said Al's competitiveness on the field "was second to none." Grantham saluted Al for having "come of age" in 1968.

Atkinson was eerily quiet on and off the field because, he said, "nothing made me mad on the football field. I always felt the game was fifty percent mental and fifty percent physical. I had a little spring to my body, which is maybe where my hitting came from. But I was pass conscious on every play because I was scared of chasing a guy eighty yards on his way to a touchdown, so I focused more on the pass, except on the most obvious running downs."

Plaudits for Atkinson's pass coverage weren't meant as a slight to his tackling. The Jets liked to set their defensive ends extra wide, forcing the opposition to run to the inside. That's where Al (or Grantham or Ralph Baker) was waiting, ready to make the sure tackle designed in Walt Michaels' defensive scheme. "I learned to try and hit the offensive lineman with my shoulder, so he couldn't get to my chest area," Atkinson said. "After the lineman, the lead back came to block me; if I was still standing, the runner was directly behind. On any given play, you take three shots in three seconds. Hopefully, playing linebacker you can maintain it for three hours."

It didn't take the AFL long to take the measure of Atkinson and give him a roaring thumbs-up. Before the 1968 season—Atkinson's third year as a starter—a *Sport* magazine poll of AFL players named him the league's "most underrated player." Considering the young talent spread throughout the American Football League, it was no small honor. Jets statistics for 1968 illuminate Atkinson's top-notch play the Super Bowl year.

In 1967, Al was the only Jets player to record a triple-digit number of unassisted tackles (100—next on the list was Grantham's 68). The Jets led the AFL in rushing defense in 1968, and in spite of missing two of fourteen games, Atkinson led the Jets in tackles (144). In 1969, Atkinson finished second behind Elliott.

Al looked forward to playing the Oakland Raiders for the AFL Championship and he played his normally sturdy game, but he stretched calf muscles in his left leg that afternoon. During Super Bowl III preparations, Dr. Cal Nicholas warned him to stay off his feet a few days "or you might not be able to play next week. What you have can lead to a ruptured Achilles' [sic] tendon." Kicker Jim Turner noted Atkinson's courage and heroism in both postseason contests. "Al played hurt during the AFL Championship Game and the Super Bowl, and never complained."

The Jets' turnover fest at the expense of Baltimore in Super Bowl III got its start with Al's almost imperceptible tip of Colts QB Earl Morrall's toss from the Jets' six-yard line. It slightly altered the football's direction; the ball deflected off the right shoulder pads of backup tight end Tom Mitchell in the end zone and popped softly into the air toward the left corner of the end zone. Jets left cornerback Randy Beverly chased the flight of the ball, then waited for the fluttering spheroid to descend and softly secured it in his arms.

The play ended the Colts' first drive inside the red zone. Credit for the tip wasn't mentioned that day on the telecast, and Al said nothing to reporters of his effect on the throw. "I hate to say anything about myself," he related, in character. The swerving football due to Atkinson's fingertip was finally highlighted and credited to Al months later in the official NFL Super Bowl III promotional film.

Atkinson suffered a severe shoulder injury in Super Bowl III making a tackle just before the end of the first half. John Elliott piled on a downed Colts runner and landed on Al's shoulder. "Just my luck with our Texas players," Al commented about the incident. "In our last preseason game that year, Jim Hudson wanted to lay a cheap shot on the Lions' tight end, but he ran into my knee and I incurred a hairline fracture of the fibula, which caused me to miss the first game of the 1968 season against the Chiefs."

He left the field under his own power but clearly in distress. At halftime, Al ordered the Jets' team physician to get him ready to play. He wouldn't allow the injury to take him out of the lineup. "I'm going to play if that arm falls off," Atkinson told teammate Johnny Sample at halftime. Despite being diagnosed with a shoulder separation, Atkinson told Jets trainers there was no backup middle linebacker, that he needed to play the second half and told Dr. Nicholas to hide the extent of his injury from coaches.

Dr. Nicholas numbed his shoulder with Xylocaine and instructed trainer Jeff Snedeker to tape Al's shoulder pads to his skin. "Normally, I would have taken him out," the doctor later explained, "but his absence would have jarred the team in the most important game it'll ever play." Al played the entire second half, with one good arm.

Because he was being attended to by the doctors, Al probably didn't know that the Jets were making a defensive adjustment to force Colts backs to run inside. That would give him added unwanted tackling responsibilities given his shoulder woes. Walt Michaels adjusted the Jets' defense in the locker room. "Let's space the ends a little wider. Force [Colts runners] to the inside more," Walt directed.

As it turned out, the altered Jets defense had minimal impact because the Jets offense controlled the ball almost all of the third quarter. Al and the defense were on the field for only seven plays. Playing catch-up as the Jets' lead ballooned to 16–0, the Colts had to fling the ball—not run it the entire fourth period.

"My adrenaline was flowing and I was relatively pain-free. I could have taken a hit on the shoulder—which I didn't the entire second half—but raising or stretching my arm felt like it was being torn off. When the final gun sounded, the shot was wearing off," Al reminisced. The next week he played in the AFL All-Star Game without an injection, gave little or no thought to his injury, jerked his arm in the air during the second quarter, and was jolted by agonizing pain.

The decidedly unemotional Atkinson is one of the few Jets who say winning the Super Bowl didn't change their life. One of just five Jets linebackers to ever participate in the Pro Bowl, he emphasized as we closed our conversation: "Remember this: we won it all because we had Joe."

MIKE STROMBERG

LINEBACKER #68   6'2"   235 LB.

Self-deprecating about his ability, the numbers show how well Mike played in two games as Al Atkinson's stand-in early in 1968.

In speaking about being a Super Bowl Jet, Mike Stromberg's candid verbal comebacks sway between genuine surprise at having been drafted out of Temple University to pride in his steady performance filling in for Al Atkinson as the team's middle linebacker in the first two games of the 1968 season. "In college, I was 6'1" and about 220 pounds, playing defensive end and offensive tackle," Stromberg explained. "It wasn't great football; we played Bucknell and Lehigh."

The Jets grabbed him in the 1967 draft's fourteenth round. "My mom called me and said she thought she saw my name on a blackboard on TV," he said. Stromberg got a $1,000 bonus on top of his $12,000 salary. In training camp, Mike was on the roster in the final week. "I stayed in the bathroom the whole morning of the final cuts, figuring they wouldn't cut me if they couldn't find me," joked Stromberg. "They cut me anyway."

Though axed, he had a spot on the Jets' taxi squad and drove to Connecticut to play linebacker for Saturday night games with the Atlantic Coast Football League's Waterbury Orbits. The semipro players' willingness to deliberately injure opposing players made it tough to physically survive—and to accomplish his learning goal. Mike showed enough on special teams and linebacker to be invited to the Jets' 1968 training camp.

All camp long, Mike was Al Atkinson's backup. While no regular season starter today gets close to the playing field in the last preseason game, the opposite was true in the 1960s. "If they didn't play you in the last exhibition game, they were going to cut you," Mike said. It was a tune-up for the starters. Atkinson had an unlucky habit of being injured in the final exhibition, and it happened in the closing minutes of the 1968 exhibition wrapup.

The beefed up 6'2", 235-pound Stromberg had a temporary starting spot in game one against the Kansas City Chiefs. Preparing to take on one of the AFL's best teams, he received minimal mentoring from other players. "They feared being replaced," he observed, a perspective shared by other backups.

The Chiefs, two years after their Super Bowl I appearance, "had a huge team and a very complicated I-formation offense," described Stromberg. It confused defenses with shifting backs and receivers. The Jets' defensive linemen were supposed to take on offensive linemen, leaving linebackers to make plays against runners, so the pressure was directly on Stromberg to be in position and make tackles.

Kansas City's multifaceted running back contingent would have been a load for a veteran like Atkinson. Stromberg, starting in his first professional game at linebacker, held up in the Jets' 20–19 triumph over Kansas City. The Chiefs ran for only 118 yards on 28 carries. Stromberg was named the Jets' Defensive Player of the Week on Kyle Rote's weekly Jets highlight program.

Stromberg says he doesn't "remember the game at all. As a rookie, it was so confusing." However, Joe Namath complimented Stromberg, saying, "Mike Stromberg playing middle linebacker . . . was actually a defining moment for us. Mike played a helluva game. Right then, I knew this team was going to be something special." Walt Michaels observed, "I . . . knew he could play. He was thrown into a very tough situation . . . but he played extremely well."

Atkinson was again unavailable in week two, so Stromberg got ready but still felt nervous. "For me, the twenty-nine thousand people who showed up to the game was huge," he remembered. "I threw up before I waited in the tunnel. I said to myself, 'Mike, this might never happen again.' I had enough intelligence to know this was going to be short-lived. I had never expected to be drafted or to play. I didn't think I was big enough and I was injury prone. I played on instinct and a high."

Stromberg performed well again against the Boston Patriots. He threw a key block on a Randy Beverly interception that became a 68-yard touchdown return. In the second half, the Patriots' all-star center Jon Morris got tangled up with Stromberg, causing ligament and cartilage damage to Mike's left knee. Stromberg's season was kaput. Because for some reason Dr. Nicholas was not at the game, the normal medical process that involved immediate surgery did not occur. His knee was put into a cast and he rehabbed after it was removed. The Jets tried to rush him back into the lineup at the tail end of the season, but the knee wasn't ready to withstand all maneuvers. He ended up being operated on in November, but he had made a good impression.

The Jets' internal tackling data was favorable for Mike in those two games, with 9 tackles and 15 assisted tackles. Comparisons of those two contests with Al Atkinson's 1968 stats are not completely comparable, however, Atkinson led the Jets' defense in stops that season, with 76 tackles and 60 assists in 12 games. That's an average of 6.3 tackles per game for Atkinson versus 4.5 for Stromberg in his not-quite 2 games, and 5 assisted tackles per game for Atkinson versus 7.5 for Stromberg.

Stromberg attended the AFL Championship Game and worked the sideline for the Super Bowl. He received half of a Super Bowl and AFL Championship share, and the irreplaceable Super Bowl ring.

Stromberg was pronounced "fit" for 1969 training camp, but took an awkward step in a hole during his second practice. "I bent my knee way back and it swelled up," he told reporters afterward. "The coaches know I can play . . . but I don't know if they will wait for me to get well. I also know that you can't rest on your laurels in this game. You've got to produce." He couldn't and was waived from the squad on August 26, 1969, then again retained on the taxi squad. Come 1970, he fought for a Jets roster spot one more time, pulled a hamstring in practice halfway through camp, and was let go in late August.

The Super Bowl victory helped Stromberg maintain his personal visibility and attract attention after his retirement to his Great American Art Company graphics business. "You don't want to be defined by being on the Super Bowl team, but I have been," he says. When his son, Matt, was young, Mike liked to drive past Shea Stadium, point at it, and tell him that he used to work over there. Stromberg was the first Temple Owl, as well as Jewish player, to be part of a Super Bowl team.

DEFENSIVE SECONDARY
IT THRIVED WITH FREE AGENTS & FORMER QBS

BILL BAIRD	#46
CORNELL GORDON	#48
JIM HUDSON	#22
JOHNNY SAMPLE	#24
RANDY BEVERLY	#42

BILL BAIRD

WEAK-SIDE SAFETY #46   5'10"   180 LB.

Cut by the Colts in 1963, he joined the Jets, played every season in the secondary through 1969, and set a team record that remains today.

Bill Baird was the one Jets holdover on the starting defensive unit from 1963, when Weeb Ewbank took over the team, through their Super Bowl III victory. As such, he was the only player who can recount the trying journey as Walt Michaels built his defense from one of the AFL's worst to the league's best by 1968.

Baird was one of the Baltimore Colts' final training camp cuts in the summer of 1963, and he was advised to ask Weeb for a job in New York by Colts defensive coordinator and Ewbank son-in-law Charlie Winner. Weeb had scouted Baird, a physical education teacher on the West Coast, in a Colts' tryout in the fall of 1962. Bill felt embarrassed attempting to stay stride for stride with star receivers Raymond Berry, R. C. Owens, Lenny Moore, and Jimmy Orr, but Weeb had a good feeling about him and signed him.

Driving up from Baltimore to Peekskill, New York, only days before the start of the 1963 AFL season, Baird's head was filled with the Colts' defensive schemes. To his delight, Bill discovered that Don Shula had retained Ewbank's defense, so the Jets' system terminology and coverages were identical to the Colts, enabling a smooth transition. "There might have been a wrinkle here or there, but so much was the same and I was able to play half of our first game in Boston a few days later," related Baird.

Baird's height and weight had worked against him in Baltimore, but the size of his head was the big problem with the Jets. "They didn't have a small enough helmet for me because I had arrived so late," he recalled. "I am a size six and seven-eighths; a normal size is seven and one-quarter. Weeb took an old Baltimore Colts helmet from his car, replaced the Colts decal with a Jets decal, and that became my helmet that season."

From 1963 to 1969, other than for injury, Baird was a fixture in the Jets' defensive secondary. As Walt Michaels judiciously built his defense with tough *and* smart athletes, Baird's intelligence, swiftness, and reliability helped him move, year to year, all over the defensive backfield, usually as a starter. He played safety in 1963 and 1964, then each of the cornerback positions in 1965 and 1966, respectively, before finally resettling at his preferred position, weak-side safety in 1967.

Undersized (5'10") and light (168 pounds when he joined the Jets and later a "bulked-up" 180), Bill underwent six years of physical and cerebral development. League-wide, the AFL had limited interest and luck in developing defensive backs, and the Jets churned through dozens of guys who had mixtures of size, speed, determination, and/or football intellect, but rarely all four. Every off-season, writers looked at the Jets and suggested that the physically unimposing Baird would be replaced that year.

Faster, bigger rookies came to Jets camp every summer, but Bill's fortitude, flexibility, understanding of Michaels' system, and instincts earned him a roster spot. Baird reminded Jets coaches about his combined skills and physical capabilities every time a potential replacement came to camp. "A new DB would come in, run an impressive four-point-four, forty-yard dash, and I'd point out to Weeb that he tended to take a misstep on defense a lot of the time. I'd crack, 'He's going the wrong way that much faster.'"

The 1964 season was a tremendous year, statistically, for Bill. "I played left safety; Dainard Paulson, our right safety, and I set an NFL record with a combined twenty interceptions, twelve by Dainard and eight from me," Baird stated. Weeb wrote about Baird after that campaign: "Size will always be a limitation but his dedication and attitude is exceptional. . . . Can win with Bill Baird."

Weeb was less enthused in his 1965 evaluation. Baird had played sparingly in the defensive backfield that year, although he had contributed as a special teams punt and kickoff returner. Ewbank had thrown Bill in at left cornerback for the two last games after an injury to starter Willie West.

Of Baird's cornerback execution, Ewbank wrote:

Inconsistent, but adequate. Good knowledge of the game and competitor. Size is a handicap for tackling from the outside but doesn't seem to hurt easily. Will play when hurt. As safety he seldom gets to the ball as he should. . . . It would appear that he is at the point of no return—to make the team as a starting cornerback this year if ever. Has had quite a few big plays and can go all the way but does not have great speed and quickness.

As it turned out, Baird wouldn't get that planned cornerback shot. Johnny Sample was signed to play left corner and Bill still started, sharing the right corner in 1966. Baird's diminutive frame was a deterrent at cornerback, but he says that his speed (in spite of Weeb's comment) made him one of the three or four fastest Jets and a good fit at safety. "Playing the corner was a physical challenge because of the size of the receivers. The good thing about playing cornerback is that when the game was over, you knew how you did by looking at the stat sheet," he remarked.

That wasn't true at safety, where he settled in as of 1967. Passes batted away or intercepted were only a small aspect of the Jets' evaluation of the safety position. "A safety is a helper; you've got to be able to key and read different things going on all over the field," Baird explained. "I could compensate for my size with good football sense, diagnosing plays and feeling out what the offense was trying to do in each situation. Not only did we practice on the field, I 'practiced' over and over in my head what could happen and what I had to be prepared to do.

"Broadcasters said I was playing free safety, but that's not completely accurate. I never sat back twelve to thirteen yards, like a free safety does, and roam," Bill explained. He covered receivers who set up in the slot. He became so sharp and well versed in Walt Michaels' defensive schemes that Bill became the defensive backfield signal caller. His seven years playing with defensive unit signal caller linebacker Larry Grantham put the pair in complete synch.

Baird conceded that defensive game planning was exceedingly easier in the 1960s. "The size of the rosters, thirty-three in 1963 and only forty in 1968, simplified offensive formations," he said. "Most of the time, the other team put a tight end, two wide receivers, and two backs on the field. By the 1980s, when I coached for Walt with the Jets, rosters had expanded to fifty-three and the formations were much more complicated. So did the internal battles between the coaches for territory."

In the 1960s, Baird and his teammates were a tightly knit defensive group. The players spent a lot of time together, discussing the game, game plans, tendencies, etc. with themselves and the coaches. Grantham and Baird drove every day to and from the stadium with wide receiver Don Maynard and punter/tight end/fullback Curley Johnson. "We talked a lot of football, so Larry and I knew our offense pretty well, too," commented Baird.

"Walt's defense was predicated on each of the eleven players knowing what everybody else on defense would do on each play," Baird added. "That's why intelligence was so important—and why it made so much sense that three members of our 1968 secondary, myself, Cornell Gordon, and Jim Hudson—had been quarterbacks in college. In a game against Buffalo in 1963, I was the third quarterback behind Dick Wood, and he got hurt on the first play."

Bill elaborated how his quarterback experiences translated to his role as a defensive back. "Quarterbacks call plays and read defenses for idiosyncrasies," he said. "On defense, you must instantaneously transfer your understanding of what the offense is trying to do to beat your coverage—and react." That was reinforced by one particular Jets training camp drill. "Our offense would select a play and we had to figure out how to cover that pass or running play," Baird continued. "As a result, we on defense got to know our offensive plays as much as our defensive plays."

The players' familiarity with the Jets' offense and defense came in especially handy in the Super Bowl game as it became apparent that the Jets and Colts were essentially running identical systems and schemes. It enabled Joe Namath on offense and Larry Grantham and Bill Baird on defense to anticipate what was coming next from the Colts.

Baird played a central role in one of the most memorable plays in the *Heidi* Game in Oakland. During the practice preparations, Walt Michaels decided that for one particular Raiders offensive formation, Bill would signal through a check off of strong safety Jim

Hudson's normal coverage. But Hudson was thrown out of the game in the second half, forcing rookie backup Mike D'Amato to take over for Hudson.

It didn't take long for the Raiders to come out in that specific formation. "I checked out to Walt's preferred coverage, but D'Amato hadn't been exposed to it in practice and didn't respond as Jim would have," Baird explained. Charlie Smith got a step on and outran D'Amato on a 43-yard catch-and-run for a touchdown that put Oakland in the lead late and ended up the winning points.

Baird prepared mentally for the Super Bowl somewhat differently than his Jets teammates, with a quiet self-assurance that he said helped overcome nervousness about facing an NFL team again. "What helped me the most," Baird reminisced, "was remembering my rookie year in Colts training camp, where I had played against Jimmy Orr, Willie Richardson, and John Mackey. I'd be facing them again in Miami."

Center John Schmitt's profile in this book describes how the Jets realized early on that they and Baltimore were using almost identical offensive systems, color codes, formations, and signals. Baird indicated that the Jets' defense also took advantage of the commonality of the Baltimore and Jets offenses, although not as directly and powerfully as Namath did on offense.

The Jets' defense had practiced against the Jets' offense every day for several years. Although it was not apparent until the game started, the offensive play calling similarities between the two teams made defensive execution easier and stronger. Grantham and Baird felt those factors gave the Jets' defensive eleven an on-the-spot edge. "We pretty much figured out what they were likely to run from their formations," said Grantham. As the game wore on, you can clearly see Grantham's feet and hands in motion as Earl Morrall or Johnny Unitas barked out signals, indications that Larry knew what was coming.

The Jets' defensive game plan focused special attention on one Baltimore skill position player, John Mackey—pro football's best tight end. Baird and strong side safety Jim Hudson would double-team Mackey, and they shared the burden of shadowing Mackey depending on his pass patterns. "Basically," explained Baird, "if he went straight down the field or inside, I would take him. If he went outside, Hudson would take him. They [the Colts] ran a lot of doubles [pass patterns in the same area], trying to isolate Mackey." The TE did some damage early in the game, turning short passes into long gains on the Colts' first few series. One scouting report said Mackey didn't have very good hands and, in fact, Mackey dropped some medium- and long-range passes.

Baird was in the middle of one of the turning points of Super Bowl III. On the final play of the first half, from the Jets' forty-one-yard line, Baltimore QB Earl Morrall took the snap and ran a gadget play, a flea-flicker. His handoff to halfback Tom Matte was lateraled back to Morrall. The Jets' right cornerback Randy Beverly saw Matte sweeping in the opposite direction, and Randy mistakenly allowed split end Jimmy Orr to race uncovered down the left sideline. Beverly was in big trouble when Matte threw the ball back to Morrall.

The play was designed for Morrall to throw to Orr near the Jets' goal line. Orr was wide open, but human error on both sides of the ball worked in the Jets' favor.

Morrall took Matte's return toss 10 yards deeper than at the snap, barely on the Colts' side of the field. Morrall said that his head had rotated to the right because of the angle at which he regained the ball from Matte. He never looked to his left toward the intended target, Orr; instead, he peered down the center of the field.

Morrall set his feet and wound up to throw to a secondary target, fullback Jerry Hill, inside the Jets' fifteen-yard line. By the time Morrall let it go, the Jets' strong safety, Jim Hudson, had read Morrall's intention and cut in front of Hill and intercepted it.

The Colts' flea-flicker became the talk of the first half. A completion to Orr could have resulted in a Colts touchdown and a 7–7 halftime score. For the Jets, the immediate issue was what had happened to pass coverage. Michaels and assistant coach Buddy Ryan asked that out loud to no one in particular as the team entered the locker room.

Almost five decades later, Baird is one of the very few defenders who can explain all the dimensions of what happened. He makes the case that despite statements from the game announcers that Jimmy Orr was wide open, a completion to Orr and a sure touchdown were far from a sure thing.

"We were prepared for the flea-flicker. We would go into a 'flow' coverage if Matte moved into the flat on Jim Hudson's side, which he did. On this play, I was to take Mackey coming up the seam [running down the center of the field]. Hudson, on the strong side, would force the sweep. But as Morrall handed off, I had picked up Jerry Hill, who was coming up the seam. John Mackey, Hudson's man, did an out [pattern] on the strong side. When Matte stopped, I instantly remembered the flea flicker from game film and I wheeled off of Hill.

"My heart sank when I saw Matte throw back to Morrall because he could be throwing to my man, Hill. Luckily, Hudson's play recognition led him to drop coverage on Mackey and sent him to Hill, and the interception. Everyone made Morrall the goat, but if Hudson hadn't recognized what was happening, I could have been the goat."

But what if Morrall had thrown to Orr? Baird also asserts that he or Randy Beverly (who had raced back to cover Orr) could have stopped Orr from scoring: "I was probably fourteen yards from Orr when I spotted Hudson on Hill," he said. "Orr was standing stationary near our goal line, waving his arms. I believe if Morrall had thrown to him, I could have gotten to him."

Paul Rochester, Morrall's Michigan State teammate more than a decade before, thinks Baird would have reached Orr. A Morrall pass to Orr, Rochester maintains, would have had a lot of hang time because of the Colts QB's lack of arm strength, giving Bill time to reach the open receiver. "I can believe that Bill would have prevented that completion," Rochester noted. "He was small, but he was fast." Grantham, after viewing the game film, observed that Beverly was only ten yards from Orr and could have thwarted a pass.

Don Maynard also saw the wide-angle view of the play in training camp seven months later and had no doubt that Baird would have derailed a connection to Orr. "Billy was the second-fastest man on the team," Maynard said. In 1990, Ewbank told football reporter Ed Gruver that too much had been made of "the Baltimore touchdown that wasn't" from the flea-flicker. "We had the play covered," he asserted.

The exhilaration of 1968 turned into frustration in 1969. The Jets were 10–4 and AFL East champions, but with a decimated, disoriented defensive backfield. After player cuts and numerous injuries, Baird was the only experienced DB, flanked by second-year John Dockery at left cornerback and Jim Richards at strong safety. A Beverly–Cornell Gordon combination (whoever was healthy) manned the right corner.

Baird was back in a world similar to his early Jets days. "As a defensive back, you have to do your own job. You can't worry about the other guys back there once a play starts. After [Jim Hudson] got hurt in San Diego, I was trying to help Jim's replacement, Richards. I looked to see if he was going the right way, but when I did that, I tried to do too much," he explained. "Having confidence in a new man takes time to learn his style, and no two players react to a play exactly the same."

Noting that his legs could no longer take the pounding, Bill retired after the Jets' 1969 playoff loss to Kansas City. After some college jobs, he returned to the Jets as Michaels' secondary coach from 1981 to 1984. Almost fifty years after his retirement, Bill Baird remains the Jets' career interception leader for defensive backs, with 34.

CORNELL GORDON

DEFENSIVE BACK #48   6'0"   187 LB.

Cornell's highly unusual skill set made him productive at all four defensive back positions. He played them all in 1968.

Cornell Gordon joined the New York Jets in 1965 along with Joe Namath, Verlon Biggs, Jim Hudson, George Sauer Jr., and others—the team's best draft year ever. Gordon had been redshirted at North Carolina A&T, then selected in the twenty-third round in 1964 by the Jets. He completed his senior season before coming to New York. He was one of the breakthrough players who emerged from small black colleges in the tumultuous 1960s, and while starring for North Carolina A&T he was the first black football player to be named to North Carolina's all-state team. As the top athlete on the two-way squad, he crossed over from QB to cornerback to guard the opponent's top receiver.

In 1965 Jets training camp, Jets player and assistant scout Clyde Washington, who while injured had scouted him in college and signed Cornell to a contract, tutored Gordon. "Clyde taught me to take two little shuffle steps back in a way that maintained my balance and let me see whether there was a run or a pass, so I could react properly," Gordon said. The speed of pro receivers was startling and gave Cornell more trouble than crafty wideouts. He cited the troublesome Elbert Dubenion in his first start of 1967 in Buffalo, and later, Oakland's Warren Wells. Gordon keeps an action shot in his home that shows Wells with a step on him after catching a pass.

The Jets secondary had severe problems during Gordon's first season; thereafter, the Jets' pass defense made great strides annually and Gordon was an instrumental reason why. At the end of Cornell's 1965 campaign, Weeb Ewbank evaluated his talented rookie:

CORNELL GORDON / #48 / 180 / 6'1" / 1st Year

Has fine speed, quickness, and attitude to become a good corner-back in the AFL and for the Jets. He was replaced early in the season by [Clyde] Washington due to his frequent and costly er-rors. He is capable of the big play and can go all the way with an interception. His performance the last two games of the season revealed more confidence and knowledge. Playing as a backup man did help him but he needs the experience badly. A very good tackler and durable. Two interceptions in 1965. I definitely feel he has a future with us and should become a fine cornerback.

In the offense-heavy AFL, Cornell was a crackerjack defensive back. He was gifted with an unusual combination of football intel-lect and speed, augmented by size, strength, and hitting ability. That made him effective at all four defensive backfield positions. His pri-mary position was right cornerback, but he moved from week to week to the left corner and he effortlessly shifted to free and strong safety. The positions required wholly different physical and mental skills.

"The corner was natural for me, but I played all four positions in 1968," Gordon noted. "Free safety, you have to be alert, see the things that are happening, you have to think and read the offense. At strong safety, you need to come up the field pretty quickly. If you see them blocking down, it's a run. I would have needed to be bigger than I was to play it consistently."

As a pro defender, Cornell—like Bill Baird and Jim Hudson— used his college quarterbacking experiences to help him match wits with AFL quarterbacks. "Being a quarterback takes a lot of thinking; you need to figure out exactly what you need for a first down," Cornell explained. "I thought like a quarterback while I was on defense."

Gordon took a while to establish himself due to injuries. He lost four games playing special teams in 1966. "The first or second time I went to receive a punt, I caught it, dropped it, and it rolled through my legs. That was the last time I was on the punt team—and the best thing that ever happened to me. On a kickoff return, somebody got me from behind and cost me the four games." In his ten games during his second season, his primary playing time came at corner.

Cornell made headlines in the 1967 preseason in the Jets' inaugural contest against an NFL team. After the Philadelphia Eagles' Timmy Brown unloaded a succession of cheap shots, including jamming an elbow into the back of Sample, Gordon, in retaliation, punched TE Mike Ditka. When an on-field imbroglio was over, the officials tossed Sample, Gordon, Brown, and Ditka.

In 1967, after finally earning a starting corner spot, he was badly hurt in the Jets' opening game against the Buffalo Bills. Gordon intercepted a Jackie Kemp pass in the third quarter, looked downfield for blockers, and was cut down from behind by Elbert Dubenion. "I wore green shoes that day, and Matt Snell did, too—and we both ended up in the hospital with knee injuries," Gordon remarked. Cornell didn't return to the Jets' active roster until late that season, when he played one game and grabbed a second 1967 interception.

He started four games in 1968, two at safety and two as a fill-in at one of the corners. The only game Gordon missed that season was the *Heidi* Game. It mattered because the Jets had to press inexperienced rookie safety Mike D'Amato into service when officials gave strong safety Jim Hudson the heave-ho. Ordinarily, Hudson's departure would have sent Gordon in to replace him. Instead, it was D'Amato, who surrendered the winning fifty-ninth-minute touchdown. "I was on the sideline, talking to someone who I didn't know was a reporter," said Gordon. "I said to him that if I had been playing we wouldn't have lost that ballgame. The next day, he reported that. I learned an important lesson."

The following week in San Diego, Cornell started for the ailing

Sample at the left corner. It turned out to be the shining moment for the Jets' top-ranked league defense. The Chargers' league-leading offense was throttled in a 37–15 Jets victory. However, Cornell was injured in the second half, forcing a less-than-full-strength Sample back into the lineup.

Five weeks passed before the Jets were again pitted against Oakland, in the AFL Championship Game. Cornell had to relieve Sample at left corner. Coach Ewbank had warned Sample not to let Fred Biletnikoff, who was lethal on post patterns, hurt the Jets. If Sample allowed Biletnikoff to run free on a post, he would be pulled from the lineup. In the second quarter, Biletnikoff ran a post, Sample surrendered a TD, and Gordon took the field. Cornell remained at the left corner for the rest of the half and the third quarter. "Sample was good at taking away the outside from receivers; I tried to take away the inside," shared Cornell. Although both were picked on, the Jets held off the Raiders.

In Miami, preparing for Super Bowl III, the Jets and Colts both practiced in virtual seclusion. Cornell says Sample was still in Ewbank's doghouse, leaving real doubt who would man the left corner. Sample got the nod. "Johnny got it, which was good. He knew what each of the Colts would do," Gordon explained without a hint of dissatisfaction. As the first substitute for every Jets DB, Cornell watched patiently from the sideline. Beverly, Sample, and Hudson all had interceptions.

Except for a pair of altercations between Sample and Baltimore's Tom Matte that the Colts hoped would lead to Johnny's expulsion, there were few opportunities for Gordon to get on the field because he didn't play special teams. Cornell Gordon ended up winning Super Bowl III without ever participating in a play. "I didn't have any problem with it," he said.

Gordon had an up-and-down year in 1969, which was true of the entire secondary. He began the season at right corner when Beverly pulled a groin muscle, and Cornell had some rough outings.

When Randy returned to health, Cornell moved to the left corner, but a pulled groin muscle sidelined him. When Cornell returned, he shared the right corner with Beverly. In the last regular season game before the 1969 playoffs, left corner John Dockery was sidelined, forcing Cornell to switch sides of the field again.

Cornell was burned for Kansas City's winning touchdown in the AFL Divisional Playoff game. But his mind had been made up to play out his option and seek better pay elsewhere. He became the fifteenth Super Bowl Jet set adrift when Ewbank traded him to Denver for safety Gus Holloman late in Jets training camp in 1970. After years of bickering with Weeb and having no choice but to accept lowball offers, he sat down with the Broncos' general manager. He was asked for his salary demand. "They tripled my Jets salary," Gordon disclosed, "without a question."

JIM HUDSON

STRONG SAFETY #22   6'2"   210 LB

His time with the Jets was short, but Super Bowl III was the cherry on the top of a football career that also included a national college championship.

Super Bowl III was supposed to inflict the harshest pressure on the 1968 New York Jets, but it rolled off the back of many players. Jim Hudson was part of that group of Jets because they had big-game experience. He saw Super Bowl III as no more imposing than winning the national championship at the University of Texas in 1963. He advised a grandson years later that "pressure is just a matter of not being prepared. Don't get caught up in the crowd's cheers or boos—they don't define you." He was also a member of the Texas squad that won the 1964 Orange Bowl and he asked his wife to bring the pair of red shorts that he had worn in that game to Miami for Super Bowl III.

Jim Hudson was a multi-sports high school hero. Perhaps more talented in basketball than football, he turned down a scholarship offer from UCLA coach John Wooden in 1961. Instead, University of Texas football received the benefit of Hudson's extraordinary athleticism at wingback, punt returner, and wide receiver before he settled in at defensive back and quarterback. Hudson missed parts of all his college seasons, particularly in his senior year in 1965, but starred in his final college game. In the Orange Bowl, he opened the game at safety for the Longhorns and took over at QB in midgame, then hurled the 69-yard game-winning TD. It established a UT bowl game record for longest completion and touchdown pass.

Considered by Texas coach Darrell Royal as one of his most talented natural athletes, Jim still went undrafted. His injuries had limited his exposure, but Jets scouts saw something in the Orange Bowl. Jim accepted a $12,500 free agent contract, plus a couple-of-thousand-dollar bonus, to be a defensive back.

Wearing uniform number 44, he made the roster but got a quick dose of the greater physicality of the pro game. Jim's first wife, Wendy, remembered: "During a preseason game, he came to the sidelines all cut up and bruised. Jim told me that when he ran back on the field, he looked on the Jets bench. 'There's $600,000 worth of ballplayers [Namath and QB John Huarte] sitting there,' he said afterward, 'and I'm out on the field and my $12,500 body is just getting beat half to death.'"

In an exhibition game, Hudson was simultaneously belted high and low, cracking his ribs, puncturing his lung, and shifting his heart out of its cavity. Jim came back from that pounding weeks sooner than doctors projected, but he only trotted on the field for two regular season games after more injuries. Somehow he impressed the heck out of Weeb Ewbank, an exacting critic, who after the 1965 season extolled Hudson's future with the Jets. Based on those two appearances, he wrote:

Has all the qualifications for a fine strong safety. . . . Played only token amount the entire season but when healthy was very impressive. . . . He should be capable of covering any tight end in the AFL. Good speed for his size. A strong competitor with whom we should win the division.

Living up to Weeb's hopes, in 1966, he played fourteen games (wearing number 22) and, in spite of his inexperience, assumed a leadership role. Hudson's aggressiveness led to collisions and more injuries, but his toughness, tenacity, high tolerance for pain, and desire to play helped him overcome nagging hurts. Before 1968 training camp, he dealt with a black widow spider bite. UT and Jets buddy Pete Lammons joked that Jim survived, but the spider died.

Hudson became a sure-tackling strong safety who played with abandon, smashed opponents like a linebacker, and "ran like a deer," observed center John Schmitt. Wendy Hudson noted how "in his training, Jim ran backwards as much as he did forward." A committed student of Walt Michaels' defensive philosophies and game plans, he became a defensive leader and the vocal guy in the Jets' secondary. Hudson regularly corrected the other DBs in the saltiest of language when they screwed up. Defensive signal caller Larry Grantham said Hudson talked so much and so loudly in the huddle that "I had to tell him to shut up, so I could call the defense."

Cornell Gordon recalled, "For all practical purposes, Jim [thought] he could do no wrong on the field. If anybody made a mistake, Jim asked, 'What are you doing?' He was a coach on the field—the only guy who got on us, not the coaches, or anyone else. He made us better. I knew I must have played pretty well when a game ended and Jim hadn't cussed me out once."

San Diego Chargers QB John Hadl, who became one of Hudson's business partners after football, described Jim as "probably the smartest defensive guy I ever played against. I had to look at the defense for pre-snap reads, but Jim would line up and screw me up because his alignment didn't coordinate with what I had seen in film and what I saw in the rest of the Jets secondary."

Jim's game reached its zenith in 1968. He led the secondary with 51 unassisted tackles, grabbed 5 interceptions, and was voted an AFL all-star. Hudson could be volatile, such as in the November 1968 *Heidi* Game in Oakland. He intercepted a third-quarter Daryle Lamonica pass, and Joe Namath converted the turnover into a TD-scoring drive. On a subsequent Oakland possession, Jim was penalized for a face-mask penalty. He swore to the field judge he wasn't guilty of the infraction and was ejected when he got too vociferous. "I remember [the expulsion] well," recalled Wendy Hudson. "The TV cameras were waving up and down, and I assumed, correctly, that they were doing all they could to avoid showing Jim giving 'the bird' to the official."

Jim's tackling was the defensive highlight of the Jets' AFL Championship Game victory. In the middle of the third quarter, the Raiders, trailing 13–10, had a first-and-goal from the Jets' six-yard line. "Run support was Jim's forte," stated safety partner Bill Baird. "When he hit you, he didn't give ground." Oakland ran to its strength—the right side of their offensive line—and the left side of the Jets' defense three times.

On first down, Hudson and left linebacker Ralph Baker stopped 230-pound fullback Hewritt Dixon after a three-yard gain. On second-and-goal from the three-yard line, Hudson stood up Dixon after a one-yard gain. On third-and-goal from the two-yard line, Jim dropped Dixon again after one yard. The Raiders settled for a field goal and a 13–13 tie at that point. Preventing that TD denied Oakland four points that ultimately separated the two clubs in the Jets' 27–23 victory.

In the two weeks before Super Bowl III, Jim was characteristically cool. He sat poolside next to Joe Namath when the QB first told reporters he expected to win Super Bowl III. After watching film, Jim was in full, though hushed, agreement. Hudson had the huge defensive assignment no one thought the Jets could manage: controlling the Colts' All-Pro tight end John Mackey, who had bowled over defensive backs like bowling balls all season long, leaving low expectations for Hudson.

Ewbank and Walt Michaels saw Jim as the strong safety with the will and physical prowess to curb Mackey. Ewbank described Hudson as "a very smart player and a good leader of our deep secondary." Michaels told reporters before Super Bowl III that Jim was "as good a tackler as I've ever seen." As one film session focused on Mackey wound up and the lights came up in the room, Michaels attempted to whip up some extra motivation. He said to Jim, "Mackey went to Syracuse, didn't he? Don't tell me that Texas can't beat Syracuse every time."

Hudson was unemotional about the impending confrontation. "Best way to handle him is try to keep him from getting the ball, but that's impossible. He's gonna catch some," Hudson admitted. "The thing to do is keep him from going 100 yards after he gets it. Hit him high or hit him low, not in the middle where the center of gravity is."

Hudson had other believers. "That's one reason why I think the Jets will win," former principal owner Sonny Werblin said the week before Super Bowl III. "Hudson can handle John Mackey because Hudson is bigger than most strong-side safetymen. He's fast, he's strong, and he hits hard. Pete Rozelle once told me that he had reports that Hudson takes pills, but I told him that it wasn't so, that if Hudson took pills he'd be in orbit. He's just one of those wild-eyed Texans."

Hudson proved up to the task. After two rampages by the tight end off short flips early in the contest, Mackey was otherwise quite ordinary. He had 3 catches for 35 yards along with several drops.

One of Joe Namath's lasting recollections as he jogged to the locker room was of Hudson kicking himself for a second quarter miscue. "Jim was practically sick after the game because he'd missed a tackle . . . when Matte got off a long run," said Joe. "'I had him at the line of scrimmage,' Hudson told Namath. 'I was gonna kill him and I closed my eyes and I missed him. Damn.'"

In addition to outstanding coverage on Mackey, Hudson broke up the Colts' gadget call on the last play of the first half. Jim stunned everyone by stepping in front of fullback Jerry Hill and intercepting QB Earl Morrall in the Jets' red zone. Hudson never made a big deal out of the big play, but it is still talked about today.

After the clock ran out, as everyone headed to the locker room, like most of the Super Bowl Jets not named Namath, Hudson's moment of glory—and, ironically, his final professional starring performance—got minimal press attention. In the wild scene surrounding all the Jets' players, Hudson, like many of his teammates (the entire offensive line, George Sauer Jr., Randy Beverly, and others) was individually treated like a showbiz bit player competing for attention in the presence of a Hollywood superstar, Namath.

"After the game, we headed back to our hotel to watch TV and see what they were saying about the game," Wendy Hudson recalled. "We weren't planning to go out and celebrate that night, and Jim looked over at me and said, 'This is kind of a letdown, isn't it?'" Wendy replied, "It sure is, but all the energy for the Super Bowl game was concentrated in the anticipation before it took place."

By the time the Jets' 1969 training camp came around, the cumulative effect of three years of physical punishment that Hudson had delivered and absorbed had worn Jim's body down. Though only twenty-six years old, back and knee injuries curtailed his next two seasons to only 11 of 29 games. Restricted to four games in 1969, he was sidelined by knee injuries to each leg. A collision with Cornell Gordon caused a left-knee ligament tear on September 28. Jim declined surgery, opting to rehab through intolerable pain to return to the field. In his first game back, after missing three games, Jim collided with Larry Grantham; Jim suffered torn ligaments and sustained cartilage and hamstring damage in his good knee.

He returned to the Jets in 1970, but after the season opener at

Cleveland, coaches and the media questioned whether he had lost a step or two. In succeeding contests, he understudied Gus Holloman and other replacements at strong safety, played in seven games, and then retired.

"I quit while I could still walk," he said. Jim's second wife, Lise, remembered that Jim told his loved ones that he thought he "had been totally blessed," was amazed that he got where he did in his sports career. "How do you get that lucky to play for two Hall of Fame coaches [Royal and Ewbank], be on a national championship team, and Super Bowl winner?" Hudson asked.

When Hudson died in 2013, Joe Namath, his roommate for several seasons, said at the funeral, "Jim was a much better roommate for me than I was for him." Wendy Hudson interpreted, "Jim would get Joe out of trouble, if Joe was anywhere close to trouble." A hush-hush story about a scary night in their St. Louis hotel room during the 1969 preseason revealed a lot about their relationship.

The night before the 1969 exhibition game against the St. Louis Cardinals, Hudson was suddenly awakened by a pounding on the hotel room door. Namath was reportedly in the bathroom. When Jim answered the door, he encountered an agitated guy with a beer bottle in hand, looking for his girlfriend and assuming she was with Namath. The intruder barged his way into the room and cut Hudson's jugular vein. Hudson was bleeding profusely and Namath took steps that saved Jim's life. The incident was covered up, reported as Hudson having slipped in the shower, aggravating his spinal disc problem, and receiving several stitches to close lacerations on his jaw.

Jim Hudson died June 25, 2013, of chronic traumatic encephalopathy, or CTE, a progressive degenerative disease found in people who have had a severe blow or repeated blows to the head. Jim had been subject to its effects since the late 1990s. He'd gotten lost driving home from a local high school game, forgotten his son's room in their home, and become increasingly agitated and angry. Thankfully, he was never violent. A year before he died, he was in such a state of delirium that when asked the date he told a physician: "It's the seventh of New England 1934."

His brain and spine were donated to Boston University for its continuing study into the link between head trauma and neurological disease. The autopsy revealed Jim Hudson had level 4 CTE, the most advanced stage of the disease. "He aged thirty years in the last ten years of his life," said Lise Hudson.

At his funeral, in her eulogy to her husband of twenty-eight years, Lise explained Jim's complexity: "Fiercely loyal, laid-back, and, at the same time, cantankerous. . . . He didn't believe in sugarcoating or beating around the bush. . . . He was not for the faint-hearted. . . . If he called you a name, teased you, or yelled at you, he loved you," she said. "Still, he was kind, gentle, and generous."

She said that a famous Erma Bombeck quote captured Jim's earnestness about life: "When I stand before God at the end of my life, I would hope that I would not have a single bit of talent left, and could say, 'I used everything you gave me.'"

JOHNNY SAMPLE

LEFT CORNERBACK #24   6'1"   203 LB.

He was renowned for instituting into the arsenal of defensive backs physical and psychological intimidation, trash-talking, and ratings for each receiver.

Except for Joe Namath, no Super Bowl Jet player was more familiar to football fans than Johnny Sample, the Jets' defensive captain and left cornerback. Football executives who signed him, coaches who put him in their starting lineup (only to wish him gone a few years later), and players who lockered with him or battled Johnny on the field each highlighted something different about Sample. To say he was a complex personality is an understatement.

Those who worked in various NFL and AFL capacities used descriptive words like *intelligent, controversial, personable, outspoken, audacious, fearless, dominant personality, infinitely charming, witty, leader, student of the game, talented yet troubled, hard hitter, intimidating tackler, vicious, violent, cocky, arrogant, hothead, loudmouth, showboat, crazy, cheap-shot artist, trash-talker,* and *rogue.* Overall, they seemed to agree that Sample was the football version of Pete Rose. If he played for your team, you loved him—if he was on the opposition, you likely hated him.

Perhaps that's why Joe Namath's comment said it best: "A teammate a lot of people don't understand. . . . His one goal is to win, and I respect him for that, and his teammates respect him . . . and we don't care what anyone says about Johnny." Billy Joe thought it critical to note that Johnny, his friend and teammate, "wouldn't let coaches, management, or anyone else take advantage of him or his teammates. Johnny refused to take any guff. All players were taken advantage of, but black athletes were especially maligned and mistreated. When something bad happened, a player considered what could be said or done that wouldn't put their job in jeopardy. Conversely, Johnny Sample would speak up or act, even if it wasn't prudent and might lead to his release. His self-respect was more important to him."

The only adjective we can be confident that Sample would agree with was the one he embraced in the title of his 1970 memoir, *Confessions of a Dirty Player.* In it, he details his thoughts around race and culture. Sample wrote that growing up in Cape Charles, Virginia, the fact that his dad, the neighborhood barber, didn't cut the hair of white people taught him never to feel inferior or beholden to whites for a job. Johnny began his process of mentally preparing himself for football games in sixth and seventh grade by secluding himself to focus on being his best and winning. As a ninth-grader, Sample played rough and his goal to win was reinforced.

Jets PR director Frank Ramos remembered watching Sample,

a three-time all-American halfback for Maryland Eastern Shore, play like a one-man gang against a deep, very talented Florida A&M team in the 1957 Orange Blossom Classic. According to Ramos, Johnny "played running back, caught passes, punted, and returned punts and kickoffs . . . one of the greatest individual performances I've ever seen." He also played defense, since every collegian played both ways. Drafted by Baltimore in the 1957 NFL draft, Sample was the first black player from a predominantly black college to play in the annual College All-Star Game where top college seniors faced the NFL champion.

That was a good and bad experience for Sample. He brooded on the all-star bench until Coach Otto Graham finally put him in late in the game against Baltimore, the team that drafted him. He played special teams most of his rookie year, but in the 1958 NFL Championship Game injuries forced him to step in at right cornerback in the closing minutes. In 1959, his reputation as a fast, brash, taunting, hard hitter at safety began to take shape. He had two fourth-quarter interceptions in the Colts' second consecutive NFL Championship Game victory over the New York Giants in 1959, one for 42 yards and a touchdown.

Big and stocky, versus prototype long and lanky defensive backs, Johnny imposed his size and aggressive tactics. Some saw him as vicious, violent, cocky, and arrogant. "[Johnny] was one of the first to use the distracting tactics of talking to you during the game," remarked Colts teammate Raymond Berry. New York Giants fullback Alex Webster, whom Sample had kicked in the head in a game, declared Johnny was "a dirty player."

The year after Sample's hit on Webster, Johnny got his comeuppance. When the Colts and Giants met, Johnny called for a fair catch on a punt return, but a young Giants special teams player decided to exact retribution on Webster's behalf, and purposely propelled himself into Sample. Johnny conceded, "That was the hardest I had ever been hit, and yeah, I deserved it."

Johnny started recording ratings in a little book for each receiver (on a one-to-five scale) regarding speed, running patterns, toughness, blocking, and intimidation. That and his trash-talking caught on with some around the NFL. Sample began to keep his distance from opponents' receivers off the field, admitting, "I'm not so rough on a guy I like."

Johnny's role expanded beyond the secondary; he handled punt returns and kickoffs, and actually led the NFL in several special teams return categories between 1959 to 1961. However, Sample wore out his welcome in Baltimore's locker room. He was suspected of and was then caught stealing money from the wallets of teammates, although Weeb Ewbank accepted owner Carroll Rosenbloom's decision to largely ignore the behavior and play Sample as if nothing had happened.

But Sample crossed the coach. A dispute about paying a hundred-dollar fine by Ewbank caused the Colts to ship Johnny to Pittsburgh in 1961. There, he made NFL All-Pro and all-League with nine interceptions that year. A midseason back injury prematurely ended his 1962 campaign and he was traded to Washington, where he played from 1963 to 1965. When Otto Graham became the Redskins' coach in 1966, Sample's salary became an issue and Johnny was sent to the Chicago Bears. Owner George Halas wouldn't meet Sample's contract demands either, and released him.

Johnny looked for another NFL team and said he learned in a private conversation with the brass of an NFL team that the league was blackballing him. For a twenty-first-century fan, think of Colin Kaepernick's supposed blacklisting by NFL teams—only in the 1960s. A half-century apart and for different reasons, Sample and Kaepernick had each gone too far for conservative pro football managements. To them, Sample's bold personality, especially as a black athlete, was unpalatable. There was also pushback about paying a black DB as much as a white player.

After Sample was advised by Redskins personnel exec Timmy

Temerario to consider the American Football League, Johnny contacted his original NFL coach, the Jets' Weeb Ewbank, in the summer of 1966. All too familiar with Sample's personal baggage, Weeb was apprehensive. But he was also pressed by Sonny Werblin, who wanted to win football games. Desperate to upgrade one of the AFL's worst pass defenses, Weeb told Werblin, "He'll end up suing you and he'll cause you a hell of a lot of trouble, but he's better than what we've got."

Johnny's wife wrote a letter to Weeb, begging that her husband get another chance. Ultimately, the decision was left to the Jets' four assistant coaches, who read Mrs. Sample's letter and unanimously voted to sign Sample. Johnny became one of the team's highest-paid players.

Ewbank told his new veteran cornerback, "You can help us mold the defensive backfield, which has been one of our big problem areas." He did. Most members of the Jets' 1968 Super Bowl III defensive backfield were on hand in 1966 training camp, although some were playing different positions than they would two years hence. Jim Hudson, Dainard Paulson, and Bill Baird were at safety; Baird, Cornell Gordon, and Sample were the corners. Johnny made the group better, individually and collectively, even extended himself to assist special teams returner Earl Christy.

Sample committed himself to get even with the NFL in a future AFL-NFL Championship Game and maintained most of his NFL tactics. In practice, when Don Maynard tried to create space between himself and Sample, Johnny roughed him up. Weeb reminded Johnny he was toying with the Jets' top receiver and told him to save it for the regular season. Sample couldn't wait that long. At a preseason game with the Philadelphia Eagles, he approached Eagles coach Joe Kuharich during warm-ups and told Kuharich to remove the dark glasses that he always wore in a game. Sample told him, "We're going to kick the hell out of you today, and I want you to see every play." Sample was among a few Jets tossed from the game that evening.

He made a pair of interceptions in his Jets debut versus Miami, and throughout the season put the clamps on many dangerous AFL pass catchers. He had less luck with San Diego Chargers' flanker Lance Alworth; the receiver known as "Bambi" was unstoppable in any single-coverage setting. Billy Baird remembered that Alworth totally ignored Sample's on-field banter.

Alworth shared his first encounter with Johnny. "We had this running play to the left. I was on the right side of the field, and I cut diagonally across the field to make a potential block. The next thing I know, I was skidding across the field. I looked up, and there's Johnny Sample, who said, 'Welcome to the NFL.'

"Of course, we were going to run that play again. When we did, I cut across the field, got right behind Sample, and I nailed him. And he sat on the ground, looking back at me, and said, 'Peace.' I looked at him, nodded, and we respected each other after that."

Buffalo Bills wideout Ed Rutkowski had fits contending with Sample's babble. "You'd come to the line of scrimmage, thinking about the route you are going to run, wind conditions, position of the DBs . . . and there's Sample," Rutkowski said. "He'd chirp, 'We've watched you on film the last three games; you're a helluva receiver. Don't burn me, I don't want to get cut.'

"I'd run my pattern, might have been open, but the QB didn't throw the ball to me. Johnny would say, 'Tell him to throw you the goddamn ball. You could be All-Pro; I'm not kidding.' This guy was in your head. It was almost impossible to focus."

Rutkowski continued, "The talk was incessant. You'd go to the line, tell Johnny, 'Shut the f--k up,' and he'd respond, 'Don't go nasty on me, I'm trying to keep you alive.' You'd try to block him out, but he'd keep running off at the mouth. 'You got a wife and kids,' he'd tell me. 'Don't get me cut; I'll help you and you help me.' And after the game he'd come up to you like you were his best friend."

Sample slightly altered his tactics as a Jet: still a trash-talker and pugnacious defender, but, according to Larry Grantham, chippy, cunning, and irritating, rather than bruising. His counseling to members of the secondary led the penurious Ewbank to award Sample a $1,000 bonus. Team defensive data show his categorical impact. The Jets' pass defense, last in the AFL in 1965, took a baby step in Sample's first year, 1966, moving up to fifth; it made a significant leap to second in 1967 and an even stronger number-two ranking in 1968.

Johnny was elected the Jets' defensive captain in 1968 a few hours before the first game of the season. Hours before that, Sample threatened not to take the field without a new contract. Sample inked a three-year deal that morning. With his captaincy, Johnny took on a stronger leadership role and the similar outspoken, brash, and controversial pair of captains, Sample and Namath, developed a deeply respectful camaraderie.

Though respectful of Johnny's 1968 performance, Grantham nonetheless thought "[Sample] was the weak link" in the Super Bowl Jets' secondary. Paul Zimmerman of the *New York Post* disagreed, writing that Sample "had his finest year since his early NFL days." Sample claimed he had surrendered only two TDs and that he had shut out his man in six games in 1968.

Not even Lance Alworth did his normal damage in 1968. The Jets swept two outings with San Diego. At Shea, Alworth grabbed 8 passes—including a TD (against Randy Beverly)—for 137 yards, but Sample snuffed out a last-minute rally with a game-ending interception. In November, in the Jets' West Coast romp over the Chargers, Alworth grabbed only 3 for 33 yards against Sample and Cornell Gordon.

Fred Biletnikoff was Sample's key tormentor in 1968. He caught 7 (for 120 yards) in the *Heidi* Game and 7 more for 180 in the AFL Championship Game. Sample was easy pickings for Oakland's Pro Football Hall of Fame split end. "Sample would come out of the huddle and make the sign of the cross, but he didn't say much to me," Biletnikoff shared. "He was a very talented guy—one of the AFL's best . . . always a challenge and he had a sneaky personality. For me and Sample, it was a real one-on-one battle between two individuals. I didn't have speed, but I could get behind him with double moves that got him stuck."

In the AFL Championship Game, Biletnikoff ate Johnny alive with a touchdown catch and a fourth-quarter 57-yard catch and run. Ewbank benched Johnny for Cornell Gordon in the first half, then reinstated him in the lineup in the fourth quarter. The Raiders threw for over 400 yards through sweeping, swirling winds that sailed passes all over Shea Stadium, but Oakland's inability to mount a running game cost them the game.

Sample was probably the happiest member of the Jets to be playing in the Super Bowl. After three years, he could exact revenge on the NFL. Weeb Ewbank invited his team to bring their families to Miami, figuring it would keep them out of trouble. Johnny's wife said to him over dinner, "John Sample, I don't think I've ever seen you look so evil." Sample told reporters, "Grade school, high school, college or pro, this game means more than anything that ever happened to me in sports."

Sample thought his skills and style would work better against the Colts in Super Bowl III than they had against Oakland. Baltimore ran a conservative offense and Johnny was especially familiar with Baltimore receivers from his time in the NFL. Ewbank made it a point to tell Johnny that "this is your time to get even."

He became the man in the spotlight on two second-quarter plays. First, Baltimore halfback Tom Matte broke a 58-yard running play, was caught and run out of bounds; then Sample enraged Matte, calling him old for being caught from behind. For good measure, as the pile unfurled, Johnny stepped on Matte's hand.

Moments later, Sample jumped in front of Willie Richardson, who had run a slant inside the Jets' 10-yard line, for an interception at the Jets' 2-yard line. Johnny tapped the ball on Richardson's helmet, exclaiming, "Is this what you're looking for?" It didn't sit well with the Colts. Two years after the contest, Baltimore's NFL All-Pro linebacker Mike Curtis remarked, "I hate guys who steal a pass and then stuff it in their victim's face, humiliate them. It's . . . the act of an incompetent and a loudmouth, and Sample is a perfect example of both."

In the fourth quarter, with the Colts down 16–0, when Sample pushed Willie Richardson out of bounds after a completion, Johnny's momentum carried him onto the Colts' sideline. Baltimore backup TE Tom Mitchell swung his helmet at Johnny; Sample kept his professional cool and headed back to the defensive huddle rather than take the Colts' bait and react. A few plays later, Randy Beverly made his second interception of Super Bowl III. An exuberant Sample made a comment to Tom Matte and the halfback pursued Sample, at full speed, from behind. An official intervened.

Sample's man-to-man, single coverage held Richardson, the Colts' top receiver, to a few inconsequential catches. Looking back about a half-decade later, Sample said "It was a high point for me. . . . I didn't care which NFL team we played. But it made it a lot sweeter, it being the Colts. There were still a lot of guys on the Colts who I had played with . . . that made it better, us beating them."

Super Bowl III turned out to be Sample's next-to-last pro football appearance, but his Super Bowl ring created a remarkable record for Johnny: the only player to be part of NFL, AFL, and Super Bowl championship teams. That distinction led a *Philadelphia Tribune* sportswriter to promote Sample for the Pro Football Hall of Fame. His career ended in 1969.

Sample died at age sixty-eight, a victim of heart disease, on April 27, 2005.

RANDY BEVERLY

CORNERBACK #42   5'11"   190 LB.

Undrafted because he was too small, his speed earned him the Jets' right corner spot in 1967. In 1968, he was one of the unexpected stars of Super Bowl III.

The Super Bowl Jets' secondary was still being pieced together in 1966: Veteran Johnny Sample was the new left corner. Bill Baird and defensive captain Dainard Paulson supplemented second-year DBs Cornell Gordon and Jim Hudson. Behind the scenes, things were changing, chief among them Weeb Ewbank's determination to import young blood with size, speed, and intelligence in the defensive backfield.

In 1962, at Wildwood High School in New Jersey, Randy Beverly had earned all-state honors in football, track, and basketball. On offense, he rushed for 3,236 yards and scored 52 touchdowns, leading the *Sporting News* to name him a high school all-American. He enrolled at Trinity Junior College in Colorado and in 1964 transferred to Colorado State. In his final game for CSU, Beverly ran back a kickoff 98 yards for a TD, returned an interception 65 yards for a second touchdown, and returned a punt 74 yards for a third score versus New Mexico. A Jets scout at the game forgot all about New Mexico's QB, whom he was there to evaluate.

Reportedly sized up by scouts as too short, Randy went unselected in the 1966 NFL and AFL college drafts. San Diego, Denver, Houston, and the Jets made contact with the free agent, and Beverly signed a $12,000 contract, plus a $500 bonus with his local AFL team in New York.

New York Post's columnist Milton Gross exaggerated after the Jets' Super Bowl III victory that so little had been expected of Randy in the 1966 Jets camp that he was last on a list of twenty-four potential defensive back candidates. The Jets gave Beverly a shot at the same three assignments—kickoffs, punt returns, and secondary—that had wowed the Jets' bird dog against New Mexico. Above all, Randy's speed excited Jets coaches. "Randy runs the 40 in 4.5. You can't get speed like that," gushed Walt Michaels.

On August 16, 1966, Randy was cut, but the Jets asked him to join their taxi squad. Beverly spent weekends learning how to play cornerback for the Atlantic Coast Football League's Jersey Jets. The right cornerback position remained shaky throughout 1966. An exasperated Weeb Ewbank told Randy in 1967 training camp he would only make the roster if he beat out an incumbent starter.

In an intrasquad game before 14,000 fans in Jersey City in August 1967, Beverly was spotlighted as one of the impressive second-stringers based on their speed. Two-year veteran Cornell Gordon won the right corner job, only to suffer a knee injury in the opening game in Buffalo. Former Kansas City Chief Solomon Brannan took over for Gordon, but was torched for the winning Buffalo points in that game. It happened again the next week in Denver as the Broncos ran off to a 17–0 lead. Beverly was inserted to hopefully stop the bleeding. That and a suddenly revived pass rush turned the game around as the Jets came from behind to win 38–24.

The Jets defense made strides in 1967 and Beverly was partly responsible. On October 1 at Shea versus Miami, Randy had one of the Jets' three interceptions. On November 13, he squelched Buffalo's late-game rally with an interception at the Jets' 1-yard line with 1:22 left. "Beverly broke up passes, tackled like a man possessed and racked up pass receivers the few times [Bills QB Jackie] Kemp connected," reported the *New York Times*. Beverly grew into one of the young, bright spots on defense. The proof came in the college draft after the season—the Jets went after help at safety, but not at cornerback.

Michaels thought Randy was perfect for the Jets' defensive system. "It's hard to explain Beverly. He comes across like someone who just woke up," Walt commented, but added you had to be impressed with Beverly's physical attributes and aggressiveness when the whistle blew. "Randy could outrun anybody," Michaels remarked. "A lot of people said he appeared scared on the field, and I'd say, 'Why don't you try running some patterns against him?'"

Entering the 1968 campaign, for the first time in team history the Jets were all but set in every defensive position. Beverly had all the physical tools, but his preparedness on the mental side was a work in progress. He needed more familiarity with AFL receivers and a fuller understanding of the Jets' defensive system and how to mesh with the three veteran DBs—Sample, Baird, and Hudson. Only playing time would provide the experience and inculcate an ability to react instinctively. The other DBs needed to become comfortable with Beverly as well.

Because Johnny Sample could usually handle his receiver all by himself, the Jets felt free to concentrate on helping Randy with extra guidance and special physical support. "I told Randy before a play, 'I'm going to help you with this and that, and I reminded him of his responsibilities,'" Baird told us.

The Jets' defense leaped to the top of the AFL rankings early in 1968. It held Kansas City without an offensive touchdown in the first game—something the Jets had not accomplished since shutting out the Chiefs at the Polo Grounds in 1963. It limited KC to only 83 yards on 20 attempted passes and 118 yards on the ground. Gaining number-one defensive status had not been a preseason goal, but once it came about, maintaining that top spot was on everyone's mind.

In game two against Boston, Beverly opened the scoring with a 69-yard interception return for a TD. Johnny Sample had worked with Randy to refine his skills, and some writers believed that Beverly's playing style began to resemble Sample's. At Buffalo, in game three (a 37–35 loss), Beverly displayed his Sample alter ego by flattening rookie wide-out Haven Moses with a forearm chop near the end of the game. He wasn't flagged, but the NFL took note of it and imposed a one-hundred dollar fine.

San Diego came to Shea in week four and Beverly yielded three TDs to one of the AFL's most dynamic offenses and two of the league's superstar receivers, Gary Garrison (two touchdowns) and Lance Alworth. "I was kind of careless in that game," said Beverly.

The 43–31 *Heidi* Game loss in game ten was the last time that season that the defense was tested and found wanting. Beverly yielded yardage, but his man didn't record any of Oakland's 4 TDs through the air that afternoon. The following Sunday, San Diego put up only 15 points and 190 yards in the air, with Beverly snatching 1 of 3 Jets interceptions.

When Oakland and the Jets met again for the AFL Championship on December 29, Raiders quarterback Daryle Lamonica put up a dizzying 400 yards and 1 TD, but the material aerial damage was done on the opposite side of the field by split end Fred Biletnikoff against Johnny Sample and Cornell Gordon. Oakland's speedier flanker, Warren Wells, caught 3 on Randy for 81 yards in New York's 27–23 victory.

The Jets' pass defense was considered suspect before Super Bowl III even though the defensive comparisons between the Colts and Jets were close. For the season, the Jets had allowed opposition QBs to complete 46.4 percent of their passes for 2,168 yards. The Colts had allowed a 51.8 percent completion rate, surrendering 130 fewer yards (9 per game). "From our one look at the Jets, cornerback appears to be their weakest position," opined a *Chicago Tribune* sportswriter after the AFL Championship Game—and Beverly was anointed the Jets' weak link.

Yet for Beverly, the two-week prelude to Super Bowl III was like every other game preparation. Johnny Sample, a teammate as well as defender against the Colts' wide receiver Jimmy Orr in the past, shared his scouting report on him with Beverly. "Orr has great hands and great moves, but he's a little guy and doesn't like to get roughed up," was Sample's top-line description. Orr, he added, used friendly trash-talking to throw off a cornerback's concentration. He'll "come out and say, 'How you doing? Nice weather we got. If you don't hit me, I won't hit you.'" Sample counseled, "He's trying to lull you and then, zip, he'll make a cut on you and you're beat. He's tricky."

Beverly showed his cool about Orr's verbal tactics when he asked Sample: "Will it be all right if I tell him I'm an orphan and a bachelor?" To which Sample responded, "Yes, but only once." Beverly shot back, "A receiver can only do so many things," as if to say Jimmy Orr wasn't Superman.

Beverly was targeted in the Baltimore offensive game plan, but the Jets and Randy were ready. They knew from game film that neither Baltimore quarterback had a strong arm. Earl Morrall's throwing ability had always been rated average and Johnny Unitas had a bad wing. On certain plays—particularly long throws—neither Morrall nor Unitas could consistently hit open receivers with the football.

Beverly was ready to battle and made two end zone interceptions, the first one early in the second quarter. Earl Morrall's toss over from the Jets' 6-yard line was barely redirected by Al Atkinson. The pass was behind backup tight end Tom Mitchell, bounced off his right shoulder pads, and careened into the air in the opposite direction—wobbling high and back toward the left corner of the end zone. Beverly tracked the flight of the ball and calmly, gently embraced it with an over-the-shoulder catch.

In the fourth quarter, Johnny Unitas threw a fluttering post to Jimmy Orr near the Jets end zone. The slow flight of the ball gave Beverly time to catch up to the shifty Orr and grab the ball almost literally out of the receiver's outstretched hands.

Randy's effectiveness convinced one blogger to designate Beverly's play in Super Bowl III as the fifth most surprising effort in Super Bowl history. The two thefts made Randy the first of twelve players in Super Bowl history to achieve that feat. "Beverly just might have been the biggest hero on a dominating defense in Super Bowl III," reviewed a Jets blogger in 2012.

Randy said in 1996 that he had long felt underappreciated. "We were the forgotten few," Beverly commented. "People don't remember us. They remember the win." Even if that is so, Beverly still glows about the two interceptions. "That never gets old. . . . It's a part of history," he said. "My grands and great-grands can see that now, hear about it, and read about it."

In a 1976 retrospective of Super Bowl III, Randy intimated that he had a chance at a third interception in the game. He didn't specify when, but in reviewing the game play-by-play, he might have grabbed a third in the second quarter. He forced Willie Richardson toward the sideline, played it safe, and draped himself all over his man instead of going for the ball.

Despite the interceptions, Randy could also have been a Super Bowl III goat because of the Baltimore flea-flicker just before halftime. For two weeks, Walt Michaels and Buddy Ryan had thrown the play at the Jets' defense in practice, but the guys never got the hang of how to stop it.

The play was directed at Beverly. Randy, at right corner, bit on the Colts' sweep to the left side of the Jets' defense and permitted his man, Orr, to run free down the sideline.

"Beverly [watched Matte start the sweep and] let Orr go and momentarily got caught in no-man's land," described Bill Baird. Happily for Beverly, all the little things that can go right or wrong on a play went the Jets' way. Three things had to occur for the play to work for Baltimore.

One, Morrall had to spot Orr inside the Jets' 10-yard line (which he didn't). Two, if Morrall saw Orr, the long throw–challenged QB was standing flat-footed on his own 48-yard line and had to wind up and fling a long, arcing, accurate 50-yard throw. Three, Morrall's heave had to arrive before Baird or Beverly, both pulled out of position by Matte's fake run, recovered and galloped to reached Orr downfield.

A Morrall throw would have hung in the air, perhaps high enough that the two speediest backs in the secondary, Baird and Beverly, could get to Orr before the ball arrived. Baird was racing from the center of the field, Beverly jetting down the sideline. Michaels maintained that Beverly would have been "able to scramble back into the play and break it up." As it turned out, Morrall threw the ball in another direction and was intercepted.

Weeb Ewbank, true to form, didn't open the Jets' bank account very wide for his conquering Jets players before the next season. "In camp the next summer," Mike D'Amato shared, "Randy told us that when he went in to negotiate his new deal and asked for a fifteen-hundred-dollar raise, Weeb shook his head and said, 'You're going to price yourself out of the league.'"

In 1969 exhibition action, Beverly excelled throughout the preseason schedule, then he pulled a groin muscle in the closing contest in Dallas. He was solid in the first two games of 1969, but in the very next game he pulled a groin muscle again. He played thirteen games that season but was never fully healthy. Beverly's injuries and Cornell Gordon's inconsistency at right corner created a defensive liability that was never fixed.

That off-season, on March 9, 1970, Randy Beverly was dealt to the San Diego Chargers for wide receiver Richard Trapp. Beverly was waived by San Diego and he returned to the new AFC East with the Boston Patriots in 1970 and 1971. In 1974, Randy accepted a tryout with the ill-fated New York Stars of the World Football League. He didn't make the roster, marking the end of his pro football career.

SPECIAL TEAMS
UNDERAPPRECIATED SUICIDE SQUADDERS

MARK SMOLINSKI	#30
BILL RADEMACHER	#23
PAUL CRANE	#56
EARL CHRISTY	#45
STEPHEN THOMPSON	#85
JIM RICHARDS	#26
MIKE D'AMATO	#47
KARL HENKE	#70
RAY HAYES	#73
JOHN NEIDERT	#63
JOHN DOCKERY	#43

MARK SMOLINSKI

SPECIAL TEAMS CAPTAIN #30   6'1"   215 LB.

The embodiment of the blue-collar player, he made Weeb Ewbank's first Jets squad and remained a vital contributor through the 1968 Super Bowl.

Mark Smolinski was one of four Baltimore Colts who were cut in 1963 training camp and made their way to the Jets. He performed with workmanlike production that first year in New York, playing fullback and special teams.

Not known for speed, Smolinski kept to himself the reality that his running ability was limited by a knee injury in the Colts' 1961 camp. The Colts had rehabbed it rather than have Mark undergo surgery—and it never completely healed. "I couldn't cut to my left because the knee would give way," he revealed. "It's something you don't tell anybody while you're playing, and I didn't."

Still, although light for the position at 215 pounds, Smolinski had a team-leading 561 yards and 3.7-yards-per-carry on the ground and grabbed 34 passes for 278 more yards. Mark became one of the faces of the new franchise; for instance, he appeared, football tucked under his right arm, in newspaper advertising for Gallagher's Steakhouse. But his major role at fullback was to block for weak-kneed QB Dick Wood, something he did very well.

Ewbank knew that Smolinski's skill set—size, speed, etc.—was limited, but Weeb saw reasons to retain Mark. After the 1965 Jets' (Mark's third) season, he put his thoughts about Smo's "tough-guy" contributions to the Jets on paper:

MARK SMOLINSKI / FB / 6'1" / 220 / 27 / 92%

A dependable "Got Man" player with very few outstanding plays and apparently never will have many. Valuable on [special] teams and good for squad morale as indicated by his election as captain of special teams. Limited speed for adequate running but good blocker and fine pass protector. Will play when hurt and could play TE and possibly LB.

In ensuing years, Smolinski saw less and less time in the backfield as young talented runners came on board. Blocking excellence for Jets quarterbacks was a requirement in Ewbank's offensive system, so Smo was occasionally thrown into the backfield to give Matt Snell a blow or to supplement pass protection.

Mark's Jets career predominantly involved special teams' "dirty work," which garnered minuscule acclaim and little financial reward. However, his leadership helped his special teams' troops (kickoffs, punts, kickoff and punt returns, field goal, and PATs) excel. Somehow in the crazy, unpredictable world of special teams, he stayed sufficiently fit to run onto the field each week. "I wasn't stupid enough to hit a guy with a seventy-number head-on. Maybe I was a little bit smarter than the normal cat," he chuckled. A broken thumb (it got stuck inside a Boston Patriot player's helmet) sidelined him for one game. Now approaching eighty years of age, he admits to a three-year-old neck problem, perhaps football related or a sign of arthritis.

In the 1960s, special teams players ran, hit, and were belted beyond twenty-first-century pro football norms. The Players Association had barely been born and didn't have the clout that decades later would make the case for special teams' rules changes to safeguard player safety.

Salaries were so low and there was no minimum salary in place, making players very replaceable. Injured "teamers," as they were known in football circles, were revived with smelling salts. To these warriors, being knocked senseless on the field wasn't sufficient cause for them to stay moored to the bench. They feared losing their roster spot. After a short respite on the sidelines, many returned to the field, subjecting themselves to possible further injury that could and did haunt them years later.

Special teams were, and remain to this day, primarily young, healthy players not good enough to start at an offensive or defensive position. A few top special team performers—those who rack up a disproportionate number of tackles—get noticed and can be promoted to one of those other starting roles. (That happened with Al Atkinson in 1965.)

Smolinski stood out for having earned a permanent special teams leadership role. Weeb Ewbank preferred to name captains for the Jets, but players voted to install Smolinski as captain of special teams in 1965 and annually reelected him. He was the only Jets player to win his captaincy multiple times between 1963 and 1968.

Mark played in the middle of the Jets' kickoff team—in the wedge where the most violent hitting took place. Smolinski said that the wildest special teams guy on the Jets was linebacker Jim O'Mahoney, who was there in 1964 and 1965. "Bill Rademacher, Paul Crane, and Jeff Richardson were real good, too," Smolinski said. On Jets punt returns, Mark was positioned where linebackers usually stood, guarding against a fake punt. After the kick was away, he peeled back to block for the return man. On the field goal and extra-point teams, taking advantage of his blocking, Smolinski was set off the left side of the line, next to the tight end.

Smolinski's leadership was vital because the five-man Jets coaching staff was so busy with their offensive and defensive assignments. Paying attention to special teams, which can be on the field for approximately 25 percent of plays in a typical game, was an afterthought. "We don't play much on special teams. We try to instill pride. We want prestige," Smolinski once remarked about his squad.

At one juncture, offensive line coach Chuck Knox "came over and paid attention to us," explained Smolinski. "He noticed we were on the field and could use a little direction and coaching; that was the first time anybody paid attention to us. He'd spend twenty minutes a week on some planning, instead of us running downfield with abandon."

Knox learned the momentum that a very good special teams play could provide a team. "On 'teams,' you've got to hit or be hit. You play with reckless abandon," Knox noted. "You turn your body loose. . . . And if you do it well—if you hit hard—the hitting becomes contagious and carries over to the offense and defense."

Before Super Bowl III, Smolinski led the film review of the Colts' special teams' formations and tendencies. Mark pointed out to his men that Colts blockers crisscrossed each other to get a preferred angle on opposition tacklers, a tactic used by Kansas City, San Diego, and Buffalo in the AFL. It could lead to devastating blind-side blocks and explosive returns.

Like Knox, a handful of Jets starters recognized the importance of special teams and jumped on board. It became a badge of honor for some of the team's most valuable offensive and defensive stars (for example, Gerry Philbin, Al Atkinson, Larry Grantham, John Elliott, Winston Hill, Matt Snell) to cover a kick or a punt in tight, important games. Expert tacklers all, they didn't want to leave anything to chance when a win was within the Jets' grasp.

Even as Smolinski was captaining special teams, he occasionally made cameo appearances at fullback and TE. In 1967, he got a temporary second life at fullback when Matt Snell (in the first game of the year) and Emerson Boozer (in game seven) left the lineup with severe knee injuries that decimated the rushing attack. Blocking to protect Joe Namath was prioritized. That year, the Jets pinned the only regular season loss, 27–14, on the Oakland Raiders, who represented the AFL in Super Bowl II. Mark's pass blocking for Namath was instrumental in the Jets' win. It deadened Oakland's blitz, and Joe Namath picked apart the Raiders' secondary.

Another gold-star year for Smolinski was 1968, where he made game-changing contributions in two separate contexts. In game two, after the Boston Patriots had closed to within 20–17, Mark picked up a punt blocked by Paul Crane and ran it in from the 3-yard line for a score. It kicked off a run of 24 unanswered Jets points.

Two weeks later, he filled in at TE for the hampered Pete Lammons. The Jets trailed San Diego 20–16 in the final quarter at Shea when Mark made a pair of key catches on the Jets' desperate final drive, including a reception that set them up inside the Chargers' 5-yard line. Emerson Boozer ran in the winning TD.

Special teams coverage was well done by both sides in the AFL Championship Game. In Super Bowl III, the Colts' Tim Brown nearly broke a punt return before Matt Snell blasted him out of bounds.

Smolinski made one unassisted tackle and was in on several assisted tackles on Jets kickoffs and punts.

The Super Bowl III locker room was filled with euphoria and expectations of a Jets return for Super Bowl IV, but reality can bite. "This was the championship of the world. None of us had been there. Many don't ever get there," remarked Smolinski. "Some people think they can get there the next year again. It doesn't work like that." It didn't for the Jets.

Smolinski said the Super Bowl convinced him to retire: "I'd been in pro ball for eight years, and I was on my way out. That game gave me the best way to make my bows," Mark said. His financial goals had been met from his combined $23,500 AFL and Super Bowl championship checks, and with that he walked away from football.

"I felt lucky to not have suffered physically the way some guys did. Serious injuries could have happened to any one of us. I was making about eighteen thousand dollars with the Jets. I had never negotiated for a higher contract. Heading into the '69 season, Weeb called and offered a higher salary, but I said it was kind of late to do that," he said.

BILL RADEMACHER

SPECIAL TEAMS #23   6'1"   190 LB.

Never given hope of being a Jets' starter, he was invited to camp and played a limited number of games from 1964 to 1967. His breakthrough year was 1968.

Bill Rademacher was like that very specialized implement in a mechanic's tool kit that is used so irregularly it is easily overlooked and forgotten—but when you need it, it does the job. From 1964 through 1967, Weeb Ewbank activated Rademacher for a handful of games to play safety, cornerback, wide receiver, and, most of all, special teams.

Rademacher was signed as a free agent out of Northern Michigan in 1964, but before he reported, Bill did some unusual preparation. "The Green Bay Packers had a defensive back, Jesse Whittenton, who owned a local bar and I went over there and he agreed to let me work out with him," Rademacher said. "So, I hitchhiked sixty miles to Green Bay and practiced with the Packers.

"I met Vince Lombardi a few times, and Phil Bengtson, one of the assistant coaches, told me that if I didn't make the Jets that the Packers would fly me to Green Bay to try out for their program. That was quite a boost to my morale. I never did tell Weeb Ewbank that. If it wasn't for the Packers, I don't think I would've ever made it because it gave me a lot of confidence. . . . I'm sure that was the number-one reason I made the Jets."

Weeb saw Bill's potential, which he dictated in evaluating Rademacher after the 1964 and 1965 seasons (where he got on the field for six and four games, respectively). The Jets' team was being built from the ground up and they were scouring the country for young football talent that could be coached up to become creditable professional performers. Bill had the chance to be one of those guys, but he never was starter material.

BILL RADEMACHER / Safety / 23 / 6'1" / 190

Started 1964 as a flanker. Spent most of training camp on offense. Moved to defense for 11th game of season. Aggressive play and better than average speed makes him worthy of full training season on defense.

Played the entire season in Jersey City as cornerback for them. Was performing well, but not outstandingly as he should in that league. Practiced entire season with defensive backs but I could not observe any noted improvement. Capable backup man but not particularly good on teams. Too erratic and nervous to be a good performer. Everyone felt he had natural ability, speed and hands but has not found a job in two years now and I don't believe he ever will.

Rademacher was persistent. In late September 1966, Bill was on the roster as a deep man on kickoff and punt return teams. In mid-October, he played wide receiver. In the summer of 1967, Bill was called up by the army, then rejoined the Jets in late November and was activated for a December 3 game versus Denver at Shea Stadium.

The 1968 season, however, was a much different story for Rademacher. He was still around when the final cuts were made in training camp, and he played all fourteen regular season games, plus the AFL Championship Game and Super Bowl III. Weeb had faulted his special teams' work in the past, but this time he made the roster on the strength of his good work on it.

When the Jets edged the Houston Oilers, 20–14, at the Astrodome, Rademacher covered the special teams fumble caused by a Gerry Philbin tackle that iced the win. In the AFL Championship Game, Bill got credit for downing a Curley Johnson punt before a Raider could pick it up and run—the only instance of a Jets or Raiders player receiving special teams credit on the official AFL score sheet. Bill flew his mom and dad to the Super Bowl, where he made two special teams tackles.

In the summer of 1969, Bill and John Dockery worked out together at the Hofstra training complex and, strangely enough, it came down to a choice between the two of them for a single roster spot. Dockery got the nod. "The Jets needed someone who could play both offense and defense, and they thought John played defense better than me," Bill shared.

He ended up accepting the invitation of his former position

coach on the Jets, Clive Rush, to join the Boston Patriots. Rademacher had caught 3 passes for 14 total yards in a Jets uniform in five years. At Boston in 1969, he grabbed 17 for 217 yards and 3 touchdowns. He experienced the highlight of his professional career on October 26 in his first professional start on offense when Bill grabbed 6 passes, including his first pro TD (a 22-yard reception, beating Dockery) against the Jets at Shea Stadium. He retired after the 1970 season.

Bill Rademacher made it a point in retirement to always wear his Super Bowl ring. He lost it in 1970 while skiing, but as good fortune would have it, a young man spoke aloud to people around him about the big ring he had just discovered on the slopes.

Late in life, Bill was beset with physically debilitating problems. He was yet another victim of CTE-related dementia. In February, 2017, he suffered a catastrophic fall at his assisted living facility, fracturing his neck, resulting in paralysis. To his dying day, April 2, 2018, he remained a hometown hero to the 8,600 people of Menominee, Michigan.

PAUL CRANE

LONG SNAPPER, LINEBACKER #56   6'3"   212 LB.

The quiet, devout Christian had the respect of every teammate for his integrity, modesty, outstanding long snapping, and occasional linebacker duties.

Perennial AFL all-star right linebacker Larry Grantham, who claimed to tip the scales at a ridiculous 195 pounds, was backed up by someone as light—the lanky, slender Paul Crane. Although listed in the game program at 200-plus pounds, Paul admits, "The first game I started, I was 185 pounds. Verlon Biggs, a big guy, was right next to me. He knocked everybody down and I made a tackle or two." Most of his time with the Jets, Crane tipped the scales at 205; by his seventh and final season, Crane had eaten enough (and maybe his metabolism had slowed sufficiently) to bump him up to 215 pounds.

Crane was a member of two Alabama national title teams, in 1964 (with Joe Namath) and 1965. His productivity at center (he was also a 'Bama linebacker) earned Paul all-SEC honors both years and all-American, SEC Lineman of the Year, and Birmingham Touchdown Club Alabama MVP honors in 1965.

The Jets signed Paul as the long snapper for punts, plus cover man or blocker on the other three special teams. "He had the best long snap in pro football at the time," assessed center John Schmitt, "consistently back on a clothesline in seven- or eight-tenths of a second."

As the long snapper, Crane had the unenviable task of delivering the football fifteen feet back to punter Curley Johnson, and then, a millisecond later, backtracking or stepping forward to deter a charging opposition player, regularly with a thirty-pound or greater advantage. Crane's job didn't end with the punt on its way; he fought his way upfield, evading and countering blocks by the return team.

Gerry Philbin, who roomed with Crane over a couple of years, was agog about his roomie's special teams responsibilities. Philbin, who played left tackle on the Jets' field goal and extra point special teams, pointed out that "Paul took a pounding! People don't realize the shots that people on special teams take from the defense. And Paul had to snap *and then* block and protect himself. He had to stand there and defensive players could unload on him."

When Crane was on defensive special teams, he put points on the board. He blocked punts in 1968 against Boston (resulting in a Jets touchdown) and Houston (a two-point safety). He also tried to have some fun hitting people.

In the Super Bowl, on the kickoff team, Paul lined up to the left of kicker Curley Johnson. "I noticed on the film that Baltimore had a big guy on the front line who probably weighed 260 or 270," described

Crane. "He watched the ball until it was kicked, then he would turn and start running down the field. I had decided that I was going to catch him when he turned.

"Anyway, I hit him right under his chin, and it almost knocked me out... and he was still up. And then I looked back, and it was like a bull who had just been shot. He started stumbling and in a few yards he was down. The official called me for being offside. I think he just flagged me for hitting the guy. I've looked at the film and I still don't think I was offside."

The native of Pascagoula, Mississippi, and full-time resident of Alabama conditioned himself to bear with the shocking late fall and early winter Northeast weather. Freezing temperatures and snow were not remotely what a southerner was accustomed to. The abysmal weather also wreaked havoc on field conditions. "The flat areas at Shea Stadium were just plain hard; then you got into some grass down there somewhere. One game we played there I remember vividly," he shared. "The dirt infield was exposed and it had rained, which turned to sleet and then the sleet turned to snow. Every time a player's foot hit the infield, you slid and created lumps of sleet or snow and dirt that froze. It was not fun at all if you got tackled or knocked down and you happened to land on one of those rough patches."

Paul was the perfect southern gentleman, a member of the Fellowship of Christian Athletes, leader of the Jets team prayer before and after games, and a deeply religious Southern Baptist. "He didn't drink, smoke, or swear," noted Paul Rochester, who did his share of each. Bill Baird said, "Paul lived what he believed, but didn't preach to you." Some observers found great irony in the genuine bond and esteem between two Alabama grads, the straight-laced Crane and the swinger Joe Namath.

Occasionally, Crane was employed at linebacker. Other teams and coaches might have licked their chops at the sight of the tall, rangy, 205-pound Crane at linebacker, hunched slightly behind the Jets' defensive line. It didn't faze Weeb Ewbank, who prized Paul's heart, determination, smarts, and football tools. "Paul is a fine linebacker on a team that already had three good linebackers," he wrote in one of his two books. "It was a good thing he was around during the [1969] season, with Atkinson, Baker, and Grantham having their injury troubles."

With Ralph Baker sidelined, Crane got his first start in game one of the 1969 season. It was O. J. Simpson's pro debut—the Jets' first official outing since Super Bowl III—and Paul proved his worth with 2 interceptions and a fumble recovery. He ran in his second pick 23 yards for the final score in the 33-19 victory. "I was watching on television back home," related Baker, "and I was afraid I wouldn't get my job back." When Buffalo met the Jets again later that season, Crane blocked a field goal on Buffalo's opening drive in a low-scoring Jets win at Shea.

Paul knew the Jets' defensive system cold, so when Al Atkinson injured his shoulder in the first half of Super Bowl III, Paul instantly strapped on his helmet and ran onto the field. In that definitive emergency, there was no dip in execution. The Colts went right after Crane, dumping a swing pass to fullback Jerry Hill, whom Crane took down after a 1-yard gain. He finished up the half and expected to continue, but Atkinson was determined and did play the second half.

It wasn't until the 1970s that Paul received a regular starting opportunity at linebacker. He basically bowed out of the pro game after Washington Redskins receiver Charlie Taylor's crack-back block wrecked his knee in 1972. In the next year's training camp, the Jets provided him little chance to prove his knee's stability to play linebacker. "I got to snap the ball to the punter twelve times," he recollected. "Every time I asked to play, they said, 'We know what you can do.'"

Crane wears his Super Bowl ring "fairly often. There's not many people in Mobile who have played in a Super Bowl, so you become a little bit of a celebrity," he said. "If I'm speaking somewhere, I'll pass it around. The ring and the Super Bowl give me entry to talk about something else, and I do a fair amount of speaking for drug education, principally because we lost our son to drugs."

Humility deters Paul from any boasts about his football career. He'd sooner stand before any group and monotonously proclaim: "That's very kind of you, but being in the right place and right time with the right coaches and right teammates is an experience few have. I often think about the players I was associated with. I thank God they were in my life."

EARL CHRISTY

KICK RETURNER, DEFENSIVE BACK #45   5'11"   195 LB.

Earl grew from free agent signee to the Jets' 1967–68 kickoff and punt return specialist.

Earl Christy insists he never fumbled a kickoff or punt in his three years as a New York Jet. The "truthiness" of that claim may rest in how one defines a fumble. It doesn't have to be caused by a defensive hit; for Christy, that's exactly what occurred in one of the most celebrated pro games of the 1960s. Christy's fumble was caused by a collision with a teammate.

In the *Heidi* Game, after the Oakland Raiders pulled ahead with forty-two seconds left, 36–32, Mike Eischeid squib-kicked to Christy. It bounced off Earl's chest and squirted out of his hands. Christy retreated to regain possession and began sprinting upfield. But Mark Smolinski, running back toward Christy to help make a block, inadvertently struck Christy's right arm and knocked the ball free.

"My own teammate knocked the ball out of my hand . . . no Raider touched me. But the NFL had to put it down as a fumble," explained Earl, who smiles about it today. Smolinski doesn't recall what happened on the play, but said with a laugh, "A fumble is a fumble." Regardless of the cause, it skipped toward the end zone, where the Raiders' Preston Ridlehuber covered it for a TD. Christy's saving grace, of course, was the Jets ousting the Raiders in the AFL Championship Game and following that up with their stupefying win in Super Bowl III.

Earl never registered a TD during his Jets career on a kickoff or punt; however, as he noted, "Al Davis paid me one of the greatest compliments: One of the good things about the Jets—they always get good field position from their kickoff returns." Earl had his "moments," particularly two in the Super Bowl season. First was his potency in game three in Buffalo, best known as Joe Namath's first of two 5-interception debacles. Three of Namath's turnovers became Buffalo TDs, so Earl had a busy day returning Buffalo kickoffs.

During that game, Earl established a Jets team mark with 169 yards on 4 returns (42.3 yards per return). He nearly broke one for a TD, thrown out of bounds 3 yards short of the goal line. Then, of his 3 kick returns in the AFL Championship Game, he saved his best for last, gaining an important 32 yards so that Joe Namath had very good field position after Oakland had taken its first and only lead in the game. Two plays later, Namath hit Don Maynard with a bomb that placed the football on the Raider 6, followed on the subsequent play with a TD to Maynard.

Although he was always an outstanding athlete, Earl's promotion to Jets return specialist (replacing Bake Turner and Maynard) in 1966 had been unexpected. In high school, he ran track and field, threw the shotput, and excelled at basketball and football. In 1965, the Jets scouted Emerson Boozer at Maryland Eastern Shore; on the same squad they made note of Earl, a running back and wide receiver. Boozer would become part of the Jets family in 1966. Christy's reputation was a tireless guy who gave everything he had on every play. "The game is won on the practice field" was his motto.

"They called me 'the Robot' in college," he related. "They called me 'Timex' on the Jets [because] I never wore out." (A famous 1960s Timex watch ad campaign showed torture tests on its waterproof wristwatches. In one spot, a cliff diver wore the watch and hit the water at 85 mph. In another spot, a Timex was run through a dishwasher. In both situations, the Timex watch "kept on ticking.")

Christy revealed that he had never returned a kickoff or punt until his final college game. He had hoped to attract the attention of his favorite team, the Baltimore Colts, but when that went by the board he signed as a free agent DB and return specialist with the Jets in 1965. He was cut but was offered a slot on the taxi squad. He spent weekends in Jersey City, learning how to employ his 4.4 speed.

"Walt Michaels came down to watch us play and I told him in the locker room that I was going to 'run one back tonight.' I did, for about eighty yards, and the Jets brought me up immediately," Earl said. He was activated for the Jets' final six 1966 regular season games. "Before my first game, at War Memorial Stadium in Buffalo in front of fifty thousand people, I was very nervous," he recalled, "and I remember Verlon Biggs coming over and saying, 'Just like being in college and everything. You just catch the ball and run.'"

Earl lined up alongside Boozer on kickoffs, giving the Jets a pair of speedy return men for games nine through fourteen. He was paired with Bake Turner for punts. By 1967, Earl was one of the kick return specialists (10 attempts), collaborating with Boozer (26) and Bake Turner (4). He shared punt return duties with the sure-handed Bill Baird (16 and 25, respectively). Earl had scary speed and never called for a fair catch; Baird was more focused on possession. The tandem tied an NFL record for fewest fair catches in a season (3), a mark that was eclipsed in the 1970s.

The pairings repeated themselves in 1968, when Christy, who

had originally signed for $11,500, then $14,000 in 1967, was rewarded a small raise, to $15,000. In 1968, Earl recorded 25 kickoffs, Bake Turner 14. On punt returns, Christy, again unwilling to call for a fair catch, registered 13, Turner 14, and Baird 18.

Speaking about his return philosophy, Christy said, "Nowadays, you hear about a punt return guy 'dancing,' meaning heading east or west. I tried to run hard north and south, to take the ball and run as fast as I could and get up to my blocker. I fought for every yard."

He owned up to a pregame faux-pas before the AFL Championship, a sign of the game's tension: "I had dressed and left the locker room," he recounted. "Randy Beverly looked down at me; I looked down. I didn't have football pants on—only my long johns. I told Beverly not to tell anyone. Of course he did, to Cornell [Gordon]."

The coin flip for Super Bowl III took place in private about one hour before kickoff. Weeb alerted Earl that the Jets would receive, which left Christy a bag of nerves. Thanks to the Jets' defense and Baltimore's need for a late-game onside kick, Christy's only Super Bowl return came on that opening kickoff, and there wasn't a single punt opportunity. He savored the fact that four other Maryland Eastern Shore graduates (Boozer, Johnny Sample, and the Colts' Charlie Stukes and Jim Duncan) played that day. In the post–Super Bowl giddiness that continued all the way back to the team hotel, the fun-loving Christy said he and George Sauer Jr. thought seriously about jumping "into the pool with our clothes on." (They didn't.)

Earl was the first of the Super Bowl Jets to be given a pink slip, a jolt to many of his teammates. Joe Namath, in particular, had become a close friend. Christy's release via waivers happened in late July, prior to the College All-Star Game. Weeb Ewbank had not let him defend his job, noting to beat reporters that two rookie return men offered more offensive and defensive potential in addition to special teams.

Winning Super Bowl III may well have had a more lasting effect on Earl's life and prospects than just about any other teammate, from becoming a member of the Harlem Wizards to working in local radio and television; undertaking missionary work in Africa, Europe, and South America; mentoring boys and girls to do something with their lives; giving numerous speeches as an ordained minister to youngsters, eclectic groups, and future generations of Jets in their locker room; down to untold new businesses and founder of the Athletes for Education Association.

STEPHEN THOMPSON

SPECIAL TEAMER, DEFENSIVE LINEMAN #85   6'5"   245 LB.

Few Jets played TWO games against the Baltimore Colts in the 1968–69 season. Steve did.

The Jets battled the Baltimore Colts *twice* in the 1968–69 season. January 12, 1969, is the celebrated date everyone remembers, but due to Weeb Ewbank's relationship with the Colts, five months earlier, on July 30, 1968, the same two teams had engaged in a rookie scrimmage at Memorial Stadium in Baltimore.

One of a very few New York Jets to have participated in both games was their 1968 second-round college draft pick, defensive end Stephen Thompson. The scrimmage turned out to be disastrous for the rookie lineman, who suffered cartilage damage that evening without being hit. "I had hurt my knee my senior year at University of Washington," revealed Thompson. "The trainer taped me up, said everything would be fine, and threw me back into the game. I went through the rest of the season and even played in a couple of all-star games. Then, in the scrimmage against the Colts, I made a move on a guy and my knee went out."

Weeb Ewbank was more upset than anyone (except for Thompson), lauding the rookie's superior QB pressures that night and calling Steve "our only pass rusher out there until he got hurt." It was a doubly bittersweet compliment. Thompson noted a few days later about the first weeks of his pro camp: "In college, [our defense] was 50–50 run or pass; here it's about 70–30 pass and I was better against the run [at Washington]." Thompson's recuperation through the first ten games of the regular season deprived Walt Michaels and Buddy Ryan of one more quality defensive lineman and turned Steve into a nearly full-time special teamer upon his return.

Thompson doesn't know if the Jets were aware of him before the East-West Shrine Game in San Francisco on December 30, 1967. "Only Dallas had talked with me. Weeb scouted me in that game," said Thompson, who recalled being "measured, weighed, and timed on short sprints." When the Jets called his name at the draft, he was shocked. "I knew who Joe Namath was, and that's all. I didn't really follow pro football," he admitted.

The Jets advised Thompson what they told most players: Joe Namath got most of the team's salary budget. But minimum salaries for high draft picks were going up in the pro game, and Steve signed a multiyear deal for $17,000 annual salary, plus a $15,000 signing bonus. "I thought I'd died and gone to heaven," he said. It got even better when he collected a portion of the AFL Championship and Super Bowl winnings.

Jets management told Steve they hoped that drafting him would push Verlon Biggs. Apparently, Biggs thought nothing about Steve's threat as a replacement; he extended a kindness to Thompson. "Verlon took me to Harlem," Steve shared, "and brought me to a guy who made me a custom pair of shoes. I stood on a piece of paper, he drew my foot and then made me shoes to fit—a multicolored zip boot. They were cool and the best-fitting shoes I've ever had."

The 1968 regular season dragged on as Steve dutifully went through rigorous exercises to rebuild his knee. He stood on the Jets' sideline and in game number ten watched the *Heidi* Game, his knee fully healed. When the Jets knew that Mike Stromberg wouldn't return that season and would undergo knee surgery, Thompson was activated. The week after the disappointing Oakland loss, Steve made his Jets debut in San Diego on special teams. On one punt, Thompson was clipped from behind across his surgically repaired knee, but was relieved that it had held up. Taking on Miami home-and-home, plus Cincinnati at Shea, Steve sprinted effortlessly up and down the field, with an occasional tap on the back to take Biggs' place at defensive end for a play or two.

He was part of the Jets' AFL Championship victory against the Raiders, participating on special teams, but was mostly noticed as one of three Jets (joining Mike D'Amato and Ray Hayes) to hoist Weeb on their shoulders and carry him in triumph off the field. Thompson said Ewbank never got comfortable, lost his balance, and began to slide backward and off the players' shoulders. "I grabbed and pulled his leg to hold on to him and prevent him from falling back," Thompson recalled of the infamous situation. "It's been reported that a fan yanked on his leg, injuring his hip. Maybe, but if you look at the picture of that moment I grabbed him, he's not smiling—it's a grimace, and he was in pain."

In Super Bowl III, Steve ran with the kickoff team, positioned to the right of kicker Curley Johnson for the Jets' five kickoffs. He did have one opportunity to play with the defensive line. "Midway in the third quarter, Buddy Ryan called me over and pointed out that the Colts' left tackle had a bad right knee," recounted Thompson. "'Look at him, he's favoring his right side,' Buddy said. 'I want you to give him a hard charge to the outside and then go inside, and you'll have a straight shot at Unitas.' He sent me in for Biggs with that instruction—a hard outside charge, grab the tackle by the shoulder, and go inside.

"So, I went in and *I totally forgot what Buddy just told me.* I made a big loop around the outside of the tackle to try to get Unitas. Buddy motioned me out of the game and sent Verlon back in. 'Why didn't you do what I asked you to do?' he asked me. I was so nervous and said, 'I don't know.' Meanwhile, Biggs did exactly what Buddy asked me to do, and didn't get a sack either, but he put a hit on Unitas."

For Thompson, his presence in Super Bowl III has received bigger and bigger impact over the fifty succeeding years. "I wear my ring every day; I can't go anywhere without somebody noticing it," he explained. "Nobody was interested in it twenty years ago. Today, I'm seventy years old, but people see my ring, ask if I played in a Super Bowl, and the older I get, the more interesting the reaction. In Dallas a few years ago, I was wearing a Jets jacket and the ring at a Jets-Cowboys game. A hundred people around me were chanting and offering to buy me a drink, like I was a rock star."

Steve became a Jets starting defensive lineman in 1969. He stepped into Paul Rochester's role as left defensive tackle before shifting to right defensive end when Biggs was felled by an injury. "I reported with a mustache and sideburns," Thompson recalled, "and Weeb looked at me and said, 'I don't like mustaches. If you play as well as I expect, I won't say anything.'" (He had his best year.)

A shoulder injury ended his 1970 season after twelve games. He publicly threatened retirement that off-season, was talked out of it by Ewbank, then changed his mind after a few weeks in 1971 and left training camp. Returning to the West Coast, he moved his family to a Christian community, then out of nowhere got the football "itch" and unretired during the 1972 season.

That return to New York, he is convinced, led to an encounter with God and a reckoning with his inner demons. He had his leg broken against Miami. "At that time, I was really living in two worlds—one with my wife, Starla, and, at the same time, I was trapped in a separate existence controlled by a sexual addiction," he shared. "None of my teammates knew it, but once in a while I was consorting with prostitutes behind my wife's back. I was a Christian in name, but not in conviction and behavior, and yet I couldn't find a way out.

"A voice spoke to me in my head. God said I was going down the wrong road and where I ended up was not going to be pretty. It was as if a knife had cut through my heart. I was instructed to confess my sins to my wife. I wrestled with telling her; God put graces on Starla for me.

"One night, it felt like I had an angel on one shoulder saying, 'Trust God,' and a devil on the other shoulder, saying, 'Don't tell her—she'll leave you.' I woke up in the morning, opened my heart, and confessed my sins to my wife and she forgave me. She spent the next two or three years helping me deal with my addictive thinking. We celebrated our fiftieth wedding anniversary on July 3, 2015. That encounter with God changed everything for me."

Steve went into private business after football and at age thirty-nine he was invited to become an assistant pastor in Everett, Washington. In 1991, Thompson became head pastor of the Marysville, Washington, Victory Foursquare Church, where for more than two decades the football player turned minister gleefully reminded his church staff every week that "Sunday is a game day."

His sermons regularly referenced football in general and aspects of his career. He was known to deliver a sermon wearing a Jets jersey, discussing what football offered in the way of life lessons. He retired from the ministry in 2015.

JIM RICHARDS

SPECIAL TEAMS, STRONG SAFETY #26   6'1"   180 LB.

Smart, resourceful, and a little lucky, he was one of two rookie DBs to play special teams and survive the suicide squad meat grinder in 1968.

The second of three eighth-round draft choices in 1968, Jim Richards was the youngest member of the Super Bowl Jets squad. Richards was a college defensive back and punt returner of some renown at Virginia Tech. "But I was surprised to be drafted," Jim said, even though Walt Michaels had personally scouted and asked Hokies' coaches about him. "One day, I came back to my dorm from an engineering or physics class and a teammate was holding the pay phone in the hallway. 'Somebody named Ewbank wants to talk with you,' he told me."

Jim's rookie training camp at Hofstra University came at a time of major societal upheaval in the United States. He had never competed against black players in high school or college, but his roommate, an African American draftee, helped him get to know everyone in camp. "On that Jets team, it didn't matter if you were black or white," he explained. "We all went to dinners and nightclubs, and never gave skin color a second thought."

As a rookie, Richards, in shock at the talent around him, kept mostly to himself. He was comfortable in the traditional rookie mode of being seen but not heard. Once Jim's roster spot was solidified, some Jets veterans warmed to him, notably punt/kickoff returner Earl Christy. Richards commented, "Johnny Sample stayed on the field to show us what we needed to know." Offensive lineman Jeff Richardson became one of Richards' fast friends. "I got cold-cocked in a preseason game and I remember Jeff asking, 'Jim, are you okay?' and then he literally picked me up and carried me off the field," Jim related.

Richards believed that his performance in Richmond, Virginia, against Boston during the preseason earned him a roster spot. "I got to play free safety, and I ran down on kickoffs and punts and made three or four tackles," he recalled. When near the end of the exhibition season the Jets took on the NFL's Detroit Lions, Richards learned a couple of important lessons.

"I was ready to make a tackle on the kickoff team and got hit on a cross-block by some guy wearing fifty-something," Richards said. "He had snuck up on me from the other side of the field and cold-cocked me. I never saw him, but I learned to vary my speed and scan everybody around me to avoid getting belted from a blind side."

What happened in his first professional game in Kansas City doesn't register in his memory bank as richly as the celebratory flight back home. "We got back pretty late at night and I was focused on picking up one of the stewardesses," Richards laughed. "I left my playbook on the plane. Big no-no. On Tuesday I had to turn it into Weeb. I walked in, and who's in Weeb's office but Joe. He was berating Namath and fined him two hundred dollars. I said to myself, 'Thank you, Lord.' I wasn't the only one; I paid my fine and you can bet I never lost my playbook again."

All through the 1968 schedule, Jim lined up on the far right end of the Jets' kickoff formation, hugging the sideline. The hitting on kickoffs and punts was ferocious. The greater the speed as he raced downfield, the greater the velocity of bodies colliding with each other.

He got a dose of Oakland's reputation as hard hitters, in addition to cheap-shot artistry, in the infamous *Heidi* Game. "After I was involved in tackles on the first couple of kickoffs and punts, George Atkinson of the Raiders knocked me down with a cheap shot after the whistle. On the next punt, I repaid the favor and took him out," recalled Richards. "As I was coming off the field, Buddy Ryan saw one of the Raiders coming up behind me and he yelled out, 'Jim, look out behind you.' When Buddy did, the guy stopped and ran off the field."

Richards felt lucky as he witnessed the season end for numerous other rookies on the suicide squad. USC's Gary Magner hadn't made it out of preseason, first-round pick Lee White had been cut down in the first game, and the veteran Billy Joe was chopped down in the *Heidi* Game. Once the Jets clinched the AFL East late in 1968, Ewbank began resting veterans. In games eleven through thirteen, Jim returned punts, including a personal-best 37-yard return. As the season marched toward early winter and the thermometer plummeted, Jim learned how important it was to stay warm, "particularly if you are running fast," he said. "I had to be careful not to pull a hamstring. I couldn't sit on a bench; I walked up and down the sideline."

The North Carolina–born Richards pined for halftime, when he could jump into the locker room sauna in full uniform. He made several tackles in the AFL Championship Game, but more than anything he remembers that "it was so cold that I had an icicle coming off my helmet."

On his way to Florida to play in Super Bowl III, Jim had to make a stop at his alma mater. "As a student, I had joined ROTC, so I had a two-year commitment to fulfill as a lieutenant after graduation," Richards explained. "They agreed to defer me for two years so I could sign with the Jets. I went back to Blacksburg to tell my teachers that I would be two weeks late to classes because of the Super Bowl. My electrical theory teacher said that now he had heard every excuse possible."

Jim had pulled a hamstring in the championship game, which it was speculated might cause him to miss the Super Bowl, but he was fully recovered by game time. Jim recalled the intensity of the Jets' film sessions in Fort Lauderdale, Florida. "Most of the offensive and defensive starters said, 'We can stop these guys; they aren't as good as teams we've played,'" Jim remembered. He saw frustration with a number of the Colts in the game itself. "In the second half, the Colts were throwing their helmets," he said.

The 1969 season presented more playing time for Richards because strong safety Jim Hudson was injured more than he was healthy. Jim had plenty of smarts and more speed than Hudson, but not the solid, muscular body to play the position. The consensus was that Richards performed admirably in his ten games in the role, with 3 interceptions and just about everything Ewbank and Walt Michaels expected. Jim was pleased by the playing time, but his lack of physical assets and shortage of experience were a hindrance.

Jim knew that after the 1969 season he would depart the Jets for his two-year army commitment. When he rejoined the Jets late in the 1971 season, he worked out at wide receiver and served as a spare coach, then came to training camp in 1972 but was released. Father Time had worn down his capabilities and natural speed.

Jim Richards' two-year Jets career and role on the Super Bowl III team is still heralded almost fifty years after the fact in his Virginia surroundings. "It gets a lot of publicity; even now, I speak to a lot of civic and youth groups. I talk about football and the *Heidi* Game and some of my Joe Namath stories," he said.

He occasionally weaves in one of the secrets of the Super Bowl Jets: unity, which "was crucial to our success. Even to this day," he said, his voice breaking during a Skype session, "I love every player on that team. We're like a bunch of brothers. We didn't have team chemistry *because* we were winning," Richards declared. "*We won because* of the intangibles that come from team chemistry." He sees God as the reason behind the Jets' cohesion and personal commitments from forty-five players.

MIKE D'AMATO

SPECIAL TEAMS, SAFETY #47   6'2"   205 LB.

How lucky can one guy be? A twenty-seven-year-old, tenth-round pick from Hofstra earned a spot on the Super Bowl champion Jets in his only season.

The Jets center, John Schmitt, who knew teammate Mike D'Amato during their one overlapping year at Hofstra, has kidded D'Amato over the years, calling him the "luckiest white guy who ever played pro football" for his single season with the Jets that ended with a Super Bowl win.

Many elements in Mike's personal story made him a fish out of water in pro football. He was a Brooklyn kid who never played high school football and later a twenty-seven-year-old Jets rookie. After high school, instead of heading to college, Mike went to work for a bank on Wall Street. He realized college was required for his future, but a potential Vietnam service commitment led him to serve in the Air and National Guard. By 1965, with that duty behind him, he was twenty-three, married, and he and his wife were expecting their first child. Hofstra beckoned with a football scholarship. He excelled in football but also was an all-American lacrosse player.

Thanks to friends in the right places at Hofstra, D'Amato was listed as two years younger in the official game program (born March 1943 versus the real date of March 3, 1941) than his actual age. In his senior season, the Dallas Cowboys seemed most interested in him, but D'Amato, who graduated with honors and a business degree, was claimed in the NFL draft by the Jets in the tenth round.

D'Amato was activated by the Jets after first-round pick Lee White's game-one injury and somehow he survived fifteen games on the so-called suicide squads. John Schmitt complimented him "for really, truly making his name on special teams." D'Amato volunteered, "It's not taking it too far to say that we played for the love of the game." Mike was a solid 205-pounder with 4.5 speed, "but more quick than fast," he admits. That made him a possible backup for Jim Hudson, but on occasion he could have been aligned alongside Bill Baird on punt returns. "I had been the punt return guy at Hofstra," Mike noted.

D'Amato was not much more than a barely noticed name on the roster until the *Heidi* Game in Oakland, where he had his first and only extended playing time at strong safety. Late in the fourth quarter, a national football audience watched Raiders running back Charlie Smith catch a Daryle Lamonica pass and, with a step on D'Amato, outrun Mike down the right sideline for the go-ahead touchdown.

To those old enough to have seen it on TV, D'Amato has always borne the brunt of criticism for Smith's late TD. According to teammates, those condemnations are completely undeserved. Mike has always accepted the blame, but says "except for that one play, I had a pretty good game. I broke up a few passes to the tight end and made some tackles. We were caught in the wrong defense on the TD. I had responsibility for the first running back coming out of the backfield, unless he came inside. That's exactly what happened; the fullback came out of the backfield, went inside, and I began to move in that direction, then here came Charlie Smith out of the backfield to the outside and he had that one step on me."

Weak-side safety Bill Baird, who called signals for the defensive backs, said the Smith TD "was not Mike's fault. Oakland came out in a formation which Walt Michaels had made an adjustment for in practice earlier in the week. Jim Hudson was in the room and Mike wasn't. Mike hadn't played much at safety and didn't know Walt's defensive modification. That put Mike in a tough spot."

D'Amato was in and around some of the most prominent off-field moments with the AFL Championship Game and Super Bowl. He had helped other Jets hoist Weeb Ewbank on their shoulders and cause the GM and coach's hip injury. In pre–Super Bowl Miami, on three occasions he was a passive witness to Joe Namath's Super Bowl bravado. "I was in the restaurant with six or eight of the guys when we heard Joe guarantee that we were going to win," he said, referencing Joe's fabled encounter with the Colts' Lou Michaels. "We kind of cringed," D'Amato said. "We didn't want to do anything to rile up the Colts."

D'Amato sat with Namath on the bus caravan that transported the Jets and others from the team hotel to the Orange Bowl. "Joe was cracking jokes, keeping everybody loose. Every time we passed the Colts at the toll booths, they all had their heads down," Mike remembers. "I think that was important," indicating the mental and emotional readiness of the two teams. After the game, in which D'Amato played special teams, if you look closely, Mike ran alongside his friend Jim Hudson and Namath as the QB made his number-one salute.

The world championship served him well in the short and long term. "Right afterward, a fellow who wanted to help get me some commercials told me about a game show with Bill Cullen called *Eye Guess*." (Cullen was one of America's favorite 1960s game show panelists and hosts, notably for *The Price Is Right*.) "I won a car, everything you could win—twenty thousand dollars' worth of stuff—and Bill [Cullen] said to me, 'You won the Super Bowl and now you come here and wipe us out.'"

Mike's pro career was very short. He was waived in 1969 training camp and retired later that season after some time in the Canadian Football League. D'Amato is one of the few Jets who have made it a point to always wear their Super Bowl ring. "I always felt that's what you should do with it," he said. For the decades he lived on Long Island, he was always identifiable by complete strangers as the local guy wearing the ring.

KARL HENKE

DEFENSIVE END, SPECIAL TEAMS #70   6'3½"   250 LB.

After playing special teams for eight games, Karl Henke's Super Bowl ring did more than glisten on his finger. It gave him inward confidence.

Professional football wasn't an unfamiliar, star-striking place for rookie lineman Karl Henke. His brother Ed, seventeen years his senior, played with some prominence in the All-American Football Conference in 1949, then much of the 1950s for the San Francisco 49ers and three seasons in the 1960s with the St. Louis Cardinals. "Whenever the 49ers played in Los Angeles, Ed would get our family five tickets," Karl said.

The Jets had three picks in the eighth round of the 1968 college draft. The last selection had been acquired from the Houston Oilers, who signed defensive lineman Richard "Bud" Marshall, after gaining his AFL rights held by the Jets. Weeb Ewbank negotiated a 1968 eighth-rounder from the Oilers, and Karl Henke, out of the University of Tulsa, became Jets' property with that twenty-second pick in the round, the 214th overall choice in the draft.

On most pro teams, Henke's size and weight would have translated into linebacker material. On the Jets, he became a defensive lineman in the mold of similarly built 245-pounders Gerry Philbin and John Elliott, which is to say undersized. Karl ran a 4.8 in the 40-yard dash and claimed he could outlift any player in the weight room except Verlon Biggs. "Our trainer, Dr. Nicholas, saw me working out one day and remarked that I was quite a physical specimen," Henke said.

In the regular season, Henke usually sat on the sidelines, except for special teams. Halfway through the year, the Jets needed a linebacker more than a lineman; Mike Stromberg was not recovering from an early season knee problem and John Neidert had been claimed on waivers from Cincinnati. Henke was deactivated to make roster room for Neidert and never got onto the field again. Once deactivated, he joined the taxi squad, but the minor-league Bridgeport Jets' season was mostly over at that point. Standing on the sidelines as a deactivated player but included in every locker room meeting, Henke was witness to a handful of the most memorable moments of the Super Bowl campaign.

The Jets wanted to play Oakland for the AFL Championship. Henke believed, "We would have had a tougher time with Kansas City." In Fort Lauderdale, before Super Bowl III, Karl came to understand the genius of Weeb Ewbank. "A very smart guy, he knew how to place his players in the right places at the right times," Henke said. "He was the main cog in the wheel for that Super Bowl win. We saw films and Weeb picked things apart with a fine-tooth comb."

Nearly five decades removed from that 1969 game, Karl still has vivid memories of his buddies on the defensive line. "In the Super Bowl, we didn't get in on the quarterback much, but we harassed the hell out of them all day," Karl said with obvious delight. "Gerry [Philbin] was in their face constantly; Verlon Biggs was beating the living hell out of Baltimore's left tackle. Verlon hurt him somehow, and was beating him so bad that he had him limping from the huddle to the line of scrimmage. He took the guy and threw him like a rag doll."

Henke was voted a half share of the AFL Championship and Super Bowl jackpots. His tenure with the Jets ended in August 1969, when he was traded to the Boston Patriots for a future draft choice. However, it was his Super Bowl ring that turned out to be life-changing.

In 1968, he had been labeled in training camp for how especially quiet he was. In his everyday life, he only wore the ring once in a while. "But over the years, that ring has been noticed. People would ask what it is," he commented. The ring pulled him out of his shell and boosted his communication with others. "I had something to say and talk about. I'd tell them and they'd say, 'My God. That's quite an accomplishment.'

"In my jobs over the years, I wore it quite a bit. Everybody knew I played for the Jets, and it was always a really big deal. The ring helped me communicate with people on the job. It would change anybody's life to be on a Super Bowl team. I became proud of having been part of it and I'm happy to talk about it."

RAY HAYES

DEFENSIVE TACKLE, SPECIAL TEAMS #73   6'5"   248 LB.

The Jets' twelfth-round choice in 1968 hung on with the organization by agreeing to play on the taxi squad for two seasons.

Ray Hayes never took anything for granted, not in high school, college, or as a professional with the New York Jets. The Jets made him their 1968 twelfth-round draft pick out of the University of Toledo, where he had earned Mid-American Conference All-Conference honors. Hayes assumed that his college coach, Frank Lauterbur, had been in touch with Jets assistant coach Clive Rush, who had jumped from Toledo to Weeb Ewbank's staff in 1963.

His final college season was one to remember—Toledo tied for the MAC championship, a first for the school in the conference. "It was good times," he said. "But I could not have foreseen what happened in 1968 with the Jets happening to me."

Ray shaped his body and built strength during his college summers by baling hay on his grandfather's farm, and he set out to make an immediate impression with the Jets. Upon signing a $12,000 contract, with a slim $1,500 signing bonus, Hayes embarked on an unorthodox approach for any player's first professional training camp. "Rookies arrive a week before the old pros come in," he said. "I committed myself to be the first person at every drill, which gave me as much time as everyone else, and I found the veterans appreciated someone volunteering to go first, to give one hundred percent until the whistle blew."

Hayes was accustomed to hearing the blunt truth about his performance. "My defensive line coach at Toledo, Jack Murphy, was similar to Buddy Ryan," Ray noted. "He told it like it is. If you did good, he said so. If you screwed up, he'd tell you that, too. No fluff." Players had their own way of letting Hayes know he was playing well, especially when he got the better of a veteran offensive lineman.

"I liked playing defensive tackle and I remember lining up opposite Dave Herman in practice. If a rookie beat him, on the next play he would drop back to pass protect and John Schmitt, the center, would drop down behind you. The ball was snapped, Dave rushed at me and, as soon as I took a step towards Dave, I tripped over Schmitt."

Because special teams were going to be his jobs in the regular season, Hayes' personal Super Bowl season highlight occurred during the exhibition schedule, off the field. Ray was congratulated by Jets coaches before the final preseason game in Cleveland that he had made the team. "I remember it so well," he said almost fifty years later. "I called my wife, who loaded up a U-Haul trailer and drove to Cleveland, where the Jets were playing the Lions. I was going to meet her after the game at the hotel to drive to New York. She had just delivered our first child a few days before, and the baby detected my wife's stress and began rejecting her nursing by projectile vomiting. They were taken to the hospital, where my wife received a shot for her nerves. The situation calmed down and the police brought them back to the hotel in a paddy wagon."

His alma mater connected him with Verlon Biggs in a running joke. "Verlon always said to me, 'Where did you go to school?' I'd tell him University of Toledo. He could never remember it. It seemed like every two days, we'd have the same silly conversation. At the twenty-fifth Super Bowl reunion, I thanked Larry Grantham for finally clearing things up with Verlon. The two of them had driven together somewhere, and Verlon asked Grantham where did that Hayes go to school? Larry told him 'Tiddle-Dee-Doo.'"

Winning Super Bowl III didn't teach Ray Hayes any life lessons, although the *Heidi* Game assuredly did. "That game taught me it's not over till the fat lady sings," said Hayes. "A lesson from that season was how you take the field—your job, whatever it is, every day—and come out a winner. You do what you are capable of doing, whatever that is. Give one hundred percent every time and you leave the field a winner no matter the score."

The *Heidi* Game was his last for the Jets that year before deactivation, and Ray said the team received a reminder of the loss to Oakland when they returned from the West Coast. "We got back to New

York after beating San Diego, and Mattel Toys had arranged to place a Heidi doll in all of our lockers," he shared.

Ray played nine regular-season games on special teams in 1968, so playing over half the schedule earned him a full Super Bowl share. Steve Thompson says Ray "helped Buddy out with special teams, always holding play sheets for Buddy and was just a real faithful 'do-whatever-he-was-asked' kind of guy. He wasn't as gifted, he wasn't as quick as other guys, but he had a great attitude." After Ray was deactivated, he said his new assignment was "to guard Weeb so that he didn't get mobbed. I was beside him for the AFL Championship and Super Bowl III," Hayes pointed out.

Ray Hayes, technically, remained a Jet in 1969 and 1970. He played in preseason games, hoping to climb his way back on to the playing roster. "I was on the taxi squad those two seasons, worked out with the scout teams early each week, and went to Bridgeport on weekends," he recalled. "Walt and Buddy watched the film" but he never was activated either year. His football career ended after 1970 and he returned to Michigan, where today he is a township supervisor.

He has no regrets about his Jets career. He wears his Super Bowl ring on special occasions. "People always want to see it. I've been stopped and asked about it," he said. "The dream is to be a champion in something. Great memories. I don't know that I would have done anything particularly different," he mused. "Part of the reason for that is because when you are trying to do your best every time— which is what I tried to do—what regret could you have?"

JOHN NEIDERT

SPECIAL TEAMS #63   6'2"   230 LB.

Paul Brown did John the biggest possible favor by trading him from the expansion Cincinnati Bengals to the Super Bowl–bound New York Jets.

"I was one lucky SOB," states John Neidert. "Not too many guys can come to a Super Bowl–bound team in the middle of the season." Neidert had opened the 1968 season with the expansion Cincinnati Bengals, the new AFL franchise owned, operated, and coached by the immortal Paul Brown. He "was a great coach, but he had no interest in building bonds or rapport with his players," according to Neidert. That would be apparent to John by the ninth game of that season.

University of Louisville linebacker Neidert, drafted by Cincinnati with its third of nine 1968 sixth-round draft choices, was the 145th overall pick by NFL/AFL teams. He signed for $15,000, then Cincinnati coaches told him his 225-pound frame "was too small, so I tried to gain weight," he remarked. He added twenty pounds, then kept piling on more, some of which he had to lose when he got to training camp.

He exclusively played special teams for the Bengals before Brown abruptly put him on waivers after the ninth game of the season, with the team struggling at 2-7. No one with the Bengals bothered to notify Neidert of Brown's decision; he found out that his services were no longer required from watching local Cincinnati TV.

Special teams are a proverbial player meat grinder, so the 6-2 Jets, who had lost linebacker Mike Stromberg in the second game of the season, put in a waiver claim for Neidert on November 6, 1968. John relished the change of scenery. "The Jets were in first place and had a 'we're going to win' mindset," he said.

That next Sunday, Neidert got a rude introduction to Shea Stadium in the most frigid home game of the 1968 season. On the kickoff squad, Neidert played R3 (the third player to the right of kicker Curley Johnson) and was assigned to the guard position on the punt defending team. The Jets vanquished the Houston Oilers in a driving, freezing rain, one of his few games in the Super Bowl campaign that Neidert remembered vividly forty-eight years later. "The field was terrible; the infield was so hard that you'd slip and slide with your cleats on. I cut my hand," he said, "but it was so cold that it wouldn't bleed until I got into the locker room."

The next week, the Jets visited the Raiders in the *Heidi* Game, where the viciousness of special teams reared its head and cut the legs out from under one of the Jets. After Jim Turner's field goal gave the Jets a 32–29 lead with 1:05 left in the fourth quarter, Curley Johnson kicked off to Oakland. Neidert recalled that just before Curley's boot, Buddy Ryan called John over and told him and Billy Joe, playing L3, to switch positions.

As Neidert thought back to his days on special teams, he was reminded of "a lot of weird sounds when you are running down the field and hitting the other guy hard to bust the wedge. You've got to be a little off-center to play special teams," he stated, "but that's how a rookie makes a pro team." Racing downfield, Joe, in Neidert's usual lane, was battered by the Raiders' Wayne Hawkins and tore up his knee so horrifically that it ended his season and, ultimately, his career. The possibility that it could have happened to Neidert, and not Billy Joe, was not lost on John.

John thought the *Heidi* Game, which left countless Jets dumbstruck after their last-minute loss, was transformative. Instead of licking their wounds, the practices for the upcoming San Diego game and group hangouts every night that week in Southern California restored team morale and purpose. They didn't lose another game that season.

Since John was one of the newest and least recognizable faces on the roster, his Super Bowl experiences were a world apart from those of his teammates'. One day was set aside for every player on both teams to meet with the press, although the media was within hailing distance of the players just about every day. John had a low-key personality and maintained a low profile. "I told Dave Anderson [of the *New York Times*] that the only way that I would be asked a question was if someone from the *Akron Beacon Journal* was there," said the Akron, Ohio, native. No one was.

"I could see how much our older players wanted this game, and you didn't want to let them down," he noted. In the game, John came close to making one big special teams play. "Preston Pearson had one nice return; I think I missed him at the three-yard line," he reflected. The locker room "was pretty wild [even though] Joe didn't want to let the media in because almost all of them didn't believe in us."

In some ways, the post–Super Bowl campaign was a more personally rewarding season for Neidert. In the Jets' mini Super Bowl—their 1969 preseason battle with the New York Giants—John helped escort Mike Battle to the end zone on Battle's 85-yard punt return. Middle linebacker Al Atkinson got injured in the final 1969 preseason game for the second year in a row, opening a starting role for Neidert.

In the opener in Buffalo, Paul Crane started for left linebacker Ralph Baker. Weeb didn't want the Bills to know ahead of time that Atkinson wouldn't be in the lineup, either, and he even played it coy with his own team. "The special teams lineups for the next week's game were always listed on the board on the previous Monday, and I didn't see my name on the list that week," John said. It didn't occur to him that he wasn't on the list because he would start at middle linebacker.

"Weeb came up to me on the bus to the 'Rockpile' [Buffalo's War Memorial Stadium] and said, 'John, you're going to start at middle linebacker, but we're going to introduce Al because they are going to honor us as the Super Bowl champions.'" That day, Neidert grabbed an O. J. Simpson fumble and Crane accounted for three turnovers. "The two linebackers held up," Weeb said afterward. "That's how you win a championship—with depth."

Neidert started several more games in 1969 as the Jets' linebackers came up with assorted physical problems. He was traded to the Chicago Bears in 1970, where torn muscles in his knee during the 1971 preseason led to the end of his professional career. Before his release, John appeared as an extra in the made-for-TV film *Brian's Song*, the tearful story of Chicago Bears running back Brian Piccolo's sudden, shocking, losing battle with cancer.

Endlessly proud of having been part of a world championship, Neidert said he has never flaunted his ring. Although a teacher in southwestern Florida, he rejected its ability to motivate young players. Still, he is regularly surprised by fans who ask if he's *the* John Neidert who was part of Super Bowl III. He loves confirming that. "They're big Jets fans," he said with some delight.

JOHN DOCKERY

SPECIAL TEAMS #43   6'0"   185 LB.

If John could hit a curveball—"heck if I could have hit any pitch," he says—he'd have been playing minor league baseball in 1968 and not for the Jets.

John Dockery spent half of the 1968–69 season on the Jets' taxi squad and became the only member of that group promoted to the team. He hit the field with the Jets for the last three games of the regular season and was part of the magical ride to the Jets' only AFL Championship and the startling Super Bowl III victory.

While a valued contributor, the word Dockery uses to describe his 1968 season is *lucky*, accompanied by a hearty laugh. John was surprised to be playing professional football that year and even more surprised that he played for a Super Bowl winner. But he was a top-flight athlete and, as his Harvard degree would attest, highly intelligent.

"Dock," as he was known, was a cornerback and skinny running back on the Harvard Crimson football team. After he graduated in 1966, he signed a $2,500 bonus with the Boston Red Sox and he beat the bushes as a minor-league utility player. After Single-A ball in

1967, Dockery went to spring training with the defending American League champion Boston Red Sox, rubbing shoulders with the likes of Tony Conigliaro, George Scott, and Sparky Lyle. In the summer of 1968, he was part of the Sox Double-A team, when the Red Sox organization determined that he was a capable outfielder and second baseman, but an instant out at the plate. "If I could hit the curveball, if I could hit any pitch—even a fastball—I would have probably been playing baseball all of 1968 and not football with the Jets," John admitted.

Following his release, Dockery faced an uncertain future and was in the dumps, but he had great friends in the right places. "George Paterno, the brother of Penn State football coach Joe Paterno, was my high school coach at Brooklyn Prep, a Jesuit high school. After graduation, he became a friend and mentor, and stayed in touch while I was at Harvard," elaborated Dockery.

He recalls, "After the Red Sox let me go, George talked with me about what I could do next. I'd played sports all my life, four sports in high school, three in college. Out of nowhere, George asked, 'Would you like a shot at football?' I'd never thought of that possibility. He asked a second question: 'If you had a shot to go to a pro camp, would you take it?' I said, 'I've got nothing better to do.'"

George Paterno and Joe Paterno called Weeb Ewbank, who agreed to give John a look. He attended the Jets' 1968 training camp and was cut August 14, but a few weeks later when Ewbank was formulating his taxi squad, Dockery got another tryout. The Jets were practicing at dilapidated Downing Stadium, on Randall's Island (situated beneath the Triboro Bridge—today the RFK Bridge). Constructed during President Franklin Roosevelt's 1930's Works Progress Administration, its claim to fame was its lightposts, salvaged from old Ebbets Field.

After the workout, Weeb offered Dockery a spot on the Jets' taxi squad. He practiced during the week with the Jets, then drove to play on Friday or Saturday night for the Bridgewater Jets. "It wasn't exactly 'the big time,'" he said, referring to the towns and the caliber of play, but not at all belittling the experience. John's expectations on this semipro level weren't exalted; the competition and the atmosphere around the ACFL reminded him of minor-league baseball.

"I was honest with myself. I went to Bridgeport with a positive attitude and the goals of playing cornerback and learning the finer points of the position," he stated. "I saw a few guys on all the teams who had played in the NFL, so I knew I belonged. I buckled up my helmet and tried to do everything better than everyone else. I figured that was my way to get a look from Weeb. I played reasonably well and, to add to my usefulness, volunteered to play special teams," Dockery remembered. "The ACFL season had ended when Speedy Duncan ran back a punt for a touchdown against the Jets in San Diego. Weeb decided to get a new special teams player—I was the guy who was lucky enough to get yanked up."

Ewbank's call up was a "complete surprise. He told me, if I did well, I'd have a chance to go to the championship game and make some money. Special teams are called 'the suicide squad.' Hey, after what I've been through, I'd run downfield and tackle the side of a building."

On New York Jets special teams, John's role was to run downfield and force the opponent's return specialist into the middle of the field, where a gang of bodies would surround him and take him down. Dock thought playing on the outside was a sign of his luck. "Out there," he said, "you don't have people coming at you from all sides. Guys come at you from one direction. There's a science to kickoffs and punts, and the further inside you are, the more chances you have to get whacked."

At his first AFL appearance at Shea Stadium, he said, "I felt like there was a very large aura around the field as I lined up to play." Jets practices opened John's eyes as well. "I watched in amazement how much time Joe Namath, George Sauer, and Don Maynard spent after practice perfecting Joe's throws and the receivers' routes," he noted. "The pursuit of perfection, particularly by Joe, was remarkable."

In those sessions, John played cornerback and was an emergency fill-in wide receiver when Joe Namath needed a warm body to throw to. "The ball came out of Joe's hand with zip," John distinctly recalled. "One of the first times that I was his pass target, I ran an in-route and his throw bent my middle finger so far back that it was pointing in the opposite direction. The trainers had to snap it back in. Painful."

Dockery made an important special teams tackle on speedy George Atkinson in the AFL Championship Game. That struck him before Super Bowl III. "It's what makes being here so much better," he stated. "The feeling that you've contributed something, that you're not just a body. It makes you feel that, in a way, you're earning all the money that's coming."

John hit it off with the intellectual George Sauer Jr. as well as Joe Namath. The latter relationship blossomed into a chummy and lucrative business affiliation between the superstar QB and the special teamer and defensive back. In 2017, John, Joe, and other teammates (until recently, Winston Hill, and now, Earl Christy) marked the forty-sixth summer of the Joe Namath Football Camp for 8- to 18-year-olds in Connecticut. It was slated to close in 2018.

Dockery followed up his Super Bowl year with a big 1969, playing in all fourteen games. He worked his way into a starting role at left corner, where he snatched five interceptions. Coach Ewbank's efficiency ratings put John at 88 for the season, barely beneath the 90 percent efficiency that earned a bonus. "Weeb gave me the $2,000 anyway," he revealed. "That from a man with short arms and deep pockets" (an inference to Weeb's tightness with the buck).

John played with the Jets through 1971–72, then moved on to the Pittsburgh Steelers for the 1972–73 and 1973–74 seasons, just missing being part of another Super Bowl winner when Pittsburgh won its first NFL championship in 1975.

Dockery had a lengthy career as a television and radio sports reporter. Aside from cohosting a Sunday night sports recap with Bill Mazer on Channel 5 in New York, John analyzed college football for ABC and later served the identical role for the NFL on CBS. He evolved into a sideline reporter for CBS college football coverage and, after that, on NBC's telecasts of Notre Dame home games. Radio also became part of Dockery's resume—he analyzed *Sunday Night Football* for Westwood One and, finally, did sideline work for broadcasts of *Monday Night Football.*

The native New Yorker returned to the city when his football playing was over and he opened Cambridge Corporate Services, an employee outsourcing business, in 1991. That business still benefits from Dockery's Super Bowl experience. "People still really like to talk about that Super Bowl game, what it was like to be there. It absolutely helps in business," he admits. "And the ring creates excitement."

ASSISTANT COACHES
THEY TURNED COLLEGIANS INTO ALL-PROS

CLIVE RUSH	OFFENSIVE ASSISTANT
WALT MICHAELS	DEFENSIVE ASSISTANT
BUDDY RYAN	DEFENSIVE LINE/SPECIAL TEAMS
JOE SPENCER	OFFENSIVE LINE
GEORGE SAUER SR.	PERSONNEL DIRECTOR

CLIVE RUSH

ASSISTANT HEAD COACH AND UNOFFICIAL OFFENSIVE COORDINATOR

Confidence in their Super Bowl game plan put smirks on the faces of Clive and Weeb.

The Super Bowl Jets' secret weapon was Clive Rush, a devoted, focused offensive coordinator with a preference for wide-open play whose importance to the Jets offense flew under the radar with fans and the media. He receives unanimous credit from his offensive unit for his Super Bowl III game plan, which, predicated on film of the Colts defense, added to the conviction of most Jets of their impending victory.

Rush graduated from Miami of Ohio, where he had played end and punter, in 1953. After one year with the Green Bay Packers, he turned to coaching. His Miami of Ohio connection (the so-called "cradle of coaches") led him to rub shoulders with a who's who of

1950s and '60s college football coaching luminaries. Most of them did not share Clive's preference for wide-open offense, but he coached under Hugh Devore at the University of Dayton in 1955, Woody Hayes at Ohio State from 1955 to 1957 and in 1959, and at Oklahoma as an assistant to Bud Wilkinson in 1958. (Ohio State won the national championship in 1957 while he was there.)

Clive also became friends with Ara Parseghian (who coached at Northwestern and Notre Dame), Johnny Pont (Yale, Northwestern, and Indiana), Carmen Cozza (Yale), and Bill Mallory (Colorado, Northern Illinois, and Indiana). In 1960, Clive got his first head-coaching job at Toledo University.

Short on personnel to execute his offense, Rush suffered three consecutive losing seasons. But his Miami of Ohio connections led Weeb Ewbank to Rush. Setting up his first New York Jets staff in 1963, Ewbank recruited Clive as assistant head coach and unofficial offensive coordinator.

Game planning was one of Rush's strengths. He also drew raves for his refinement of the performance of skill-position players. Bake Turner, one of those beneficiaries, explained, "He and I worked on my pass patterns. I was quick, but not fast straightaway. I could change direction quickly, and Clive taught me, Don [Maynard], George [Sauer Jr.], and Pete [Lammons] some really good pass pattern adjustments based on our individual proficiencies."

Demonstrating that Clive had a strong relationship with more than the Jets' prized receivers, Matt Snell noted that "back then, assistant coaches didn't get a lot of adulation. Without Clive, Weeb wouldn't have added to his reputation with the Jets. Clive knew offense—how to design a system, how to draw up plays, and play calling. Clive was the reason that our offense clicked; he put all of us in the best position to use our best skills. He was a thinking man's offensive coordinator, and he continually made adjustments." Curley Johnson added that Rush was a great listener when players offered ideas.

Paul Crane saw Rush as "somewhat of a perfectionist—and he needed to be." Emerson Boozer said Clive "didn't leave any stone unturned." Bake Turner remembers Clive "always looking for new teaching techniques, like receivers turning backwards, having the ball thrown to us and having us turn at the same time."

Super Bowl III was Namath's national showcase to display his ability to read defenses, the result of hours of personal instruction from Rush. Clive's son, Doug, recalled his dad understanding that turning Namath loose to throw when and where he wanted had its risks—and Clive was willing to accept those. "He felt, 'You win by the sword, you lose by the sword.' It was the price you paid with a talent like Joe," Doug said.

Rather than berate Joe for passes gone wrong, Clive rationalized that pass plays could go awry for many reasons. Receivers sometimes did not run their patterns correctly, defenders were very capable of making great plays, and the unusual depth of Joe's normal throws—15 to 20 yards—meant any of his missiles could be "off." Clive watched Namath's good and bad moments, always maintaining his cool on the sideline, upstairs in the booth, and during film sessions.

Weeb Ewbank's private typewritten personnel evaluations held nothing back about refinements that were necessary even for big talents like Don Maynard. Specific improvements in the speedy wide receiver's game fell to Rush. "Clive made Maynard a better player, made Bake a better player. Of course, Maynard made him a better coach, too," assessed Curley Johnson. Added Bake Turner: "He was always the first to congratulate me on a first-down catch, TD, or a great catch. He was more of friend than a hard-nosed coach." Complimented Maynard: "Clive was a real motivator and winner."

Doug Rush pointed out that "behaviorally, he was the opposite of Michaels and Ryan in film sessions." Michaels and Ryan were stern, even harsh with players about any defensive mistake. Michaels even needed to vent his frustration directly to Joe Namath after Joe's five-interception games. Clive's offensive philosophy did not criticize Joe. What made it all the more remarkable was Namath's "reported resistance to any coaching in his early years with the Jets. He developed a rapport with the patient Rush and respect flourished between them," reported the *New York Times*.

Clive and Weeb saw Super Bowl III as an opportunity for the Jets' smallish, quick, highly intelligent, and skilled offensive line to use its speed, athleticism, and youth to outflank Baltimore's older, slower defenders. "The Jets went into the game with a very confident game plan that would wear out the Colts with speed and deception, use every inch of the field, laterally and back," recalled Doug. "They simplified the playbook. My dad and Weeb were very humble men, but I recall that they felt so confident about their creative planning that they had smirks on their faces."

Few NFL loyalists publicly gave the Jets a chance in Super Bowl III. One exception was former Packers coach Vince Lombardi. Clive Rush's defensive counterpart on the Colts, Chuck Noll, was also quietly of the same mind. Noll had been a defensive assistant to Los Angeles/San Diego Chargers coach Sid Gillman from 1960 to 1965 before joining Don Shula in Baltimore. According to Michael Mac-Cambridge's 2016 book, *Chuck Noll: His Life's Work,* Noll had a better feel for the problems an AFL team could pose and he worried all week about defensing Namath. His wife, Marianne, remembered Noll being edgy in the days leading up to the game.

Before Super Bowl III, Rush and Noll were the Boston Patriots' two leading candidates for head coach. Unfortunately for Noll, the Jets and Namath lived up to his concerns and riddled the Colts' defense. Boston lost interest in Noll and turned its attention to Rush. (Some consolation prize: Noll became the Pittsburgh Steelers' head coach, where he started a twenty-three-year Hall of Fame coaching career.)

Doug Rush says that if his father ever had a regret, it was leaving the Jets for Boston after the Super Bowl. He had been promised to succeed Weeb as coach of the Jets, but Ewbank signed a new three-year contract to remain GM and coach following the game. Ewbank counseled Rush not to accept the Patriots job because he foresaw several inherent problems that would make the job untenable. Some of Clive's most loyal Jets players felt their nonpareil assistant coach was a great assistant, but simply not head-coaching material. Clive lasted twenty-one games in the bad Boston situation before he resigned for health reasons in 1970.

After joining George Allen in Washington for six weeks in 1971, Clive stepped away from football. He approached the Jets about returning as offensive coordinator in 1976 but was rebuffed by new head coach Lou Holtz, so he coached at the nearby Merchant Marine Academy on Long Island that year. He died August 22, 1980, after mowing the lawn one afternoon and suffering a heart attack in his sleep that night. A beloved, devoted father and husband, he was forty-nine years old and left behind three boys and a daughter. He was the first member of the Super Bowl Jets' organization to pass away.

WALT MICHAELS

UNOFFICIAL DEFENSIVE COORDINATOR

Jets who played on the defensive side of the ball all but pledged allegiance to Walt, a tough, critical, no-nonsense coordinator.

Every member of the Super Bowl Jets' defensive platoon immediately describes Walt Michaels, the team's unofficial defensive coordinator and designer of defensive game plans that slowed and stopped opposing offenses, as "tough and no-nonsense." That description was constructed during his eleven years of standout linebacker and special teams play for Paul Brown's Cleveland Browns championship teams of the 1950s. The *Cleveland Plain Dealer* named him the twenty-first best Cleveland Brown of all time. Michaels adopted Brown's philosophies, emphasizing teaching, creativity, and intelligence, as he transitioned from NFL All Pro (1957–61) to a coaching career in 1962.

He spent that season with the Oakland Raiders, but his stay lasted only that year and he joined Weeb Ewbank as the New York Jets' defensive line coach in 1963. Weeb and Michaels knew each other from Cleveland. Ewbank's five years as an assistant with the Browns had overlapped Walt's first two years with Cleveland.

Walt's full-time Jets coaching career was slightly delayed for one week. Not much was made of it in newspaper game accounts, but safety Bill Baird, between fits of laughter, told us how the thirty-four-year-old Michaels put uniform No. 34 (his longtime Browns number) back on one last time. Due to injuries, the Jets were short of linebackers for the first game of the season on September 8, 1963, when they faced the Patriots in Boston. Boston won easily 38–14. Patriots QB and future Super Bowl Jet Babe Parilli chuckled as he related to us "seeing that old guy running around in the Jets defense, and I went right at him."

Once Walt put his cleats away for good, AFL offenses had less and less to smile about. "Walt ran a standard four-three defense [four down linemen and three linebackers]—like most other teams—but with a lot of offsets, people in gaps, stacking linebackers," Ralph Baker explained. "Walt wanted to force offenses to rework their plays somewhat when they played us. Our defense might have been complex to opponents, but not to us. We were fairly heady; we had above-average football intelligence and each of us knew where our help was and we took advantage of that." Michaels had a basic defensive tenet: "If you hit people, you win. You take the guys out on the field and see who hits the hardest."

The three linebackers whom Walt molded into one of the AFL's magnificent defensive units could not have been more different, but he made that work. "If my guys can do something better than the other team—even if they know we can do it better—we're going to win," he noted. "I had three different types of linebackers, but we used them right."

Michaels inherited Larry Grantham, a holdover from the New York Titans. He was undersized (at 6'0" the same height as Walt) but also remarkably quick, a shrewd defensive signal caller, and a two-time AFL all-star. "We were all loyal to Walt," said Grantham. "He was down-to-earth, and we knew about his playing career. He helped me by permanently moving me from the weak side to right-side linebacker."

Ralph Baker, the Jets' 230-pound left-side linebacker, was in the physical mold of Michaels. "Ralph's academics were way up there," Michaels said. A tall 6'3", not particularly fleet of foot but exceptionally smart, Baker was hard on himself, vowing not to make the same mistake twice. Michaels scouted Baker at Penn State and signed him to a Jets contract in 1964. "I loved Walt," Baker said. "My high school coaches and Penn State linebacker coach Dan Radakovich had started making me into a good linebacker and Walt finished the job. Walt didn't believe in devising a defense and having his players fit into it; he drew up defenses that his personnel could flourish in."

Middle linebacker Al Atkinson, the most ferocious hitter of the trio, may have been the apple of Walt's eye. He, too, admired Michaels' Cleveland Browns' heritage. After Atkinson was waived by the Buffalo Bills in 1965 training camp, he hoped he'd be claimed by the Jets because of Michaels. "I was fortunate to go to New York," Atkinson said, "where Walt took me under his wing and good things gradually happened for me and my play from there."

Mike Stromberg, who filled in for Atkinson in the first two games of 1968 until lost for the season with a knee injury, called Michaels "the best coach I ever played for. He was real, no bulls--t, wouldn't pull any punches." John Dockery said, "Walt was a man of few words; he exemplified strength and discipline. He held you to a higher level."

Jim Richards remarked: "You didn't want to cross Walt. He was a mean dude, and you made sure you did what he wanted you to do. I recall an off-field example. There was a union strike at Hofstra and we were there for summer camp, and the union didn't want us to cross the picket line because we were in the players' union. But we did and the union guys put tacks on the ground in the parking lot, and several of our guys got a flat tire. Walt went out to the parking lot and asked who the head guy was. 'What can I do for you?' the guy said. Walt picked him up in the air and told him, 'If any more of our players have a flat tire, you are not going to want to see me.'"

When the Jets launched their five-year plan to build a championship team in 1963, Michaels, like every one of his peers around the league, doubled as a scout. "His players needed to be smart, as well as athletic," observed Paul Rochester. Never impressed solely by where guys played their college ball, Walt traveled in the Northeast each Saturday when the Jets weren't scheduled to play Saturday evening or Sunday on the road. He made recommendations, but still the final draft decision was always made by Weeb.

How history would have changed if Ewbank had followed Michaels' advice that the Jets grab a guard out of Texas A&M in the first round of the 1967 draft. Michaels urged the stud, Gene Upshaw. Weeb opted for Paul Seiler with the fourteenth pick in that first round. Upshaw went three selections later to Oakland, where he had a fifteen-year Hall of Fame career.

In 1968, it happened again. The Jets selected Texas A&M–Commerce tackle Sam Walton in the third round with the draft's seventy-second pick. Michaels had pressed Ewbank to draft Maryland–Eastern Shore tackle Art Shell. Oakland, again, grabbed Walt's favorite, this time with the eightieth pick in that same third round. Shell was a mainstay for fifteen years in Oakland and also entered the Hall of Fame.

In the high-scoring AFL, defense was not ignored but it tended not to be emphasized. Michaels wanted his defense to hound quarterbacks and ball carriers, but it wasn't entirely predicated on overwhelming physicality. Michaels made confusing opposition offenses the key. "Walt's defense wasn't complicated, it was just different," explained Ralph Baker. "It was also extremely basic. He thought that any pass completed over forty yards was probably the fault of the defensive line; the quarterback had been given too much time to get rid of the ball."

One of Michaels' goals was to limit AFL teams to 17 points or less a game. In the 1968 regular season, Jets opponents scored 280 points, but subtract nine opponent touchdowns directly scored off interceptions, fumbles, kickoff returns, and punt returns and the points against the Jets defense is reduced to 217, or 15.5 per game. Walt had no patience when the Jets' offense was sloppy in protecting the football. Two occasions during the Super Bowl season drew his ire.

The first came against Buffalo. Joe Namath wanted to light up the scoreboard against the two-touchdown-underdog Bills, and five of his passes were intercepted, three run back for touchdowns. On the flight back to New York after the 37–35 loss, Walt invited Namath to join him at the front of the plane, where he tore into him about foolishness of risky passes and how they turned around games. Michaels mentioned the advantage Joe had with the Jets' league-leading defense, and he suggested the defense would stymie opposing offenses—and Joe would benefit from a short field and greater scoring potential.

Walt hoped the conversation left an impression on Namath, but two weeks later the Denver Broncos came to Shea Stadium and intercepted Joe five more times. None were run back for scores, but it led to a second stunning Jets upset loss in three weeks. Michaels addressed the dispiriting situation by sending one of his guys, Namath's buddy and road roommate, strong safety Jim Hudson, to repeat Michaels' message. This time the communication stuck with Namath, whose head was bowed in the locker room in front of reporters after the loss.

For the next four games (all wins), Namath's gung-ho offensive style was reined in and the Jets defense and Jim Turner's reliable field goal kicking took over. Over the Jets' final nine regular season games, the defense held opponents to less than 17 points seven times—all victories. Michaels' point about the defense winning games was taking hold. The Jets' high-powered offense, under control, in concert with a productive kicking game and the league's top defense, was a hard combination to overcome.

In 1967, when J. D. Donaldson left the Jets for Paul Brown and the expansion Cincinnati Bengals, Michaels moved up to linebacker and defensive backfield coach (plus "unofficial" defensive coordinator, with game-planning duties). Showing his respect for Michaels, Namath made a point of saying in his post–Super Bowl III book, "I'm with Walt Michaels 110%. He bleeds every time our defense gives up a yard. He gets sick every time we get scored on. He gets high on victory.... I'm the same way."

The section devoted to the defense in Weeb Ewbank's playbook during his years with the Jets noted a "bend, don't break" philosophy. That was a nod to professional offenses, which Weeb and Michaels knew could never be completely throttled. It was expected they would move the ball, so allowances were made for the opposition's short- and medium-length drives. Emphasis was put on controlling the opposition to short distances per play. Larry Grantham revealed Walt's belief that drives of ten or so plays would often lead to a turnover because players were human and mistakes could be forced and, in any event, were inevitable with defensive pressure.

Walt proved his mettle from 1963 through 1967 by creating a superior defensive lineup even though the Jets were short of talent. The AFL was obsessed with signing flashy offensive players, who were far easier to locate than defensive stoppers. In the league's early years, top-notch players usually entered their first AFL camp in an offensive spot. If the team was stacked or just competent at the player's first position, the rookie would get a look at a different position—and increasingly his new destination was on defense. For instance, on the Jets, a superathletic wide receiver or collegiate QB ended up in the defensive backfield. That took place with Cornell Gordon, Bill Baird, and Jim Hudson. An offensive lineman might find a home at linebacker or the defensive line, like John Elliott. A would-be linebacker could be directed to tight end, which is what happened to Pete Lammons.

For AFL scouts and coaches, finding a capable cornerback or safety was especially difficult. It was not quite like looking for a needle in a haystack, but the lack of attention to a quality secondary particularly slowed the development of AFL defenses (especially with the tremendous league-wide concentration on the passing game). Walt Michaels' finest coaching achievement may have been in this area. Between 1964 and 1967, the Jets' drafts put just about zero emphasis on defensive backs. The five Super Bowl Jets defensive backs were four free agents and one draft pick. Aside from veteran Johnny Sample, Michaels tutored, trained, and crafted football unknowns with limited DB background into polished, solid defensive players—and created his reliable secondary.

No member of the Jets organization took Oakland's last-minute victory in the November 17, 1968, *Heidi* Game at the Oakland Alameda Coliseum harder than Michaels. One of his other defensive tenets was instilling great pride and poise in the Jets defenders. They were one of the AFL's least penalized units, but that day game officials called five face-mask penalties among a team record 13 infractions on the Jets. In addition, all-stars Jim Hudson and John Elliott were tossed from the game. In utter frustration after the agonizing, last-minute loss, Michaels and team orthopedist Dr. James Nicholas loudly banged the door to the officials' locker room. Walt and Weeb Ewbank were fined by the NFL for their vociferous public criticism of the officials, which included showing the New York press that week's game film of Oakland's dirty play.

The 1968 AFL Championship Game, played just five weeks after the *Heidi* Game, was a sharp test for Michaels' defense. The Jets blamed themselves for surrendering five touchdowns to Oakland's offense those few weeks earlier, and they had confidence having handed the Raiders their only 1967 regular season loss the year earlier in New York. Larry Grantham remembers Michaels preparing a game plan that accounted for late December New York weather; Shea's uncommon, tormenting, swirling winds; and Oakland QB Daryle Lamonica's windup throwing motion.

Lamonica completed 1 of his first 13 passes and finished 21 of 34 for 401 yards but with only 1 TD. The Jets' takeaway of Oakland's running game (19 carries for 50 yards, versus 146 for Oakland a month earlier) put extra pressure on Lamonica to move the ball through the air. Unbalanced offensive attacks are known to ultimately fail on the scoreboard; Oakland didn't meet the challenge that afternoon.

Oddsmakers didn't question the Jets-Colts Super Bowl matchup strictly on offense. They thought Baltimore would have little trouble scoring against the Jets' defense. Walt had much more confidence in his unit, especially after viewing three Colts' game films provided by the NFL, plus a fourth from Weeb Ewbank's son-in-law, Charlie Winner, the coach of the St. Louis Cardinals.

The opening sentences in Michaels' Super Bowl game plan stated, "The Colts are not supermen, particularly on offense. Oakland had better running backs and quarterback by far. San Diego had better wide receivers and Morrall, #15, is on a par with [John] Hadl. In other words, he cannot throw outs."

Under a section titled "Special Notes," Michaels warned about

John Mackey's unique capabilities at tight end. Walt termed him "the only superstar on their offensive team" and instructed strong safety Jim Hudson and free safety Billy Baird to always be aware of Mackey, to watch out for a reverse or a tight end screen to him. Tom Matte earned a special mention for an ability to pass from his halfback position.

Michaels told us, "I believed in keeping things at a real low-key level, not a lot of fanfare. I wasn't scared by the importance of the game. It was just another football game. The scores in Super Bowls I and II didn't matter; remember I played in that other league. Their guys and our guys came out of the same schools and were coached by the same guys, and we all put on our pants one leg at a time.

"People say we did things differently in the Super Bowl from other games that year, but we did the things on defense that we could do best," Michaels said. "Our guys told the offense before each game how many points we would hold the other team's offense to; before the Super Bowl, we told them we'd hold Baltimore under twenty points."

After the Super Bowl triumph, the Jets' defense didn't get a fraction of the credit it deserved. For all the hoopla about Baltimore's defense being a wrecking crew, Walt Michaels' unit actually surrendered fewer yards in a league known for its offense during the fourteen-game AFL regular season than had the Colts. To this day, Jets' detractors point to Baltimore's "bad luck" in the game.

The Jets' "bend, not break" defensive scheme performed precisely as designed that day. The Colts went up and down the field several times in the first half, but John Mackey never dominated. The Jets' front five (Biggs, Elliott, Rochester, McAdams, and Philbin) didn't register a sack, but continually harassed Morrall and Johnny Unitas. Four interceptions—from Beverly, Hudson, and Sample—resulted from QB pressure and the secondary's coverage ability. The Colts, for the only time that season, did not get on the scoreboard by halftime and scored just seven points in the game.

The charm, talent, and legend of Joe Namath will always domi-nate Super Bowl III conversation, but no Super Bowl defense ever made a bigger difference in as historic a game as Walt Michaels' group did on January 12, 1969. For a half century, his guys have known their contribution and loudly saluted their defensive archi-tect, and now all Jets fans have a reminder and an insight about the other half of the story of Super Bowl III.

BUDDY RYAN

DEFENSIVE LINE COACH
SPECIAL TEAMS COACH

Buddy began his professional coaching career with the Jets in 1968, and over the years began adapting how his defenses attacked offenses as he saw Weeb's success protecting Joe Namath.

On June 27, 2016, the NFL Network cut away from its planned pro-gramming to report the death of Buddy Ryan. The immediate reac-tion to anyone who drops the name "Buddy Ryan" is to think of the overwhelming "46" defense that Ryan invented and incorporated as the defensive coordinator of the 1985 Chicago Bears. Yeah, he had meritorious moments before then and Ryan made attacking the quarterback in the most unusual ways an art form.

It is not as commonly recognized, though, that Buddy's outspo-ken, bold, and brash professional coaching career began as defensive line coach for the Jets' 1968 Super Bowl III team, and even the NFL Network conveniently overlooked or forgot that he was also the Jets' special teams coach that year. Perhaps it was because back then, as Jets special teams' captain Mark Smolinski related, the special teams unit didn't pore over film every week like the offensive and defensive platoons did. Rookie special teams demon Jim Richards admitted, "Buddy was outspoken about none of us making mistakes;

however, he coached special teams only when you screwed up. If there was one thing about Buddy that stuck with me, it was discipline."

Buddy Ryan would not accept being a run-of-the-mill assistant coach. According to his son, Rex, he had been offered an AFL coaching position several times before accepting Weeb Ewbank's offer. Presumably, those were from the Buffalo Bills, but Rex believed that Buddy had financial security concerns about the AFL.

How Buddy landed his role with the Jets was anything but ordinary. With the departure of head defensive coach J. D. Donaldson to Cincinnati after the 1967 season, Weeb and the newly designated unofficial defensive coordinator, Walt Michaels, needed a defensive assistant. Ryan had coached defense at the University of Buffalo (where between 1962 and 1965, the defensive unit had recorded 12 shutouts), University of the Pacific, and, most recently, Vanderbilt. According to defensive end Gerry Philbin, he and WNBC radio sportscaster Bill Mazer both knew Buddy from Buffalo and gave the strongest possible recommendation to Ewbank.

"I would say that Bill was probably the biggest reason Buddy got hired," Philbin explained. "Bill Mazer knew football and would have recommended Buddy for any job. Bill had become a giant media guy in New York and Weeb listened to him." Gerry remembers how he touted Ryan: "Weeb asked me to come to New York, sat me down, and asked a bunch of questions about Buddy. I told him how good a coach he was."

Some of Ryan's defensive ideas were seen as out of step with traditional defenses. "At practice, we couldn't rush the quarterback and one time, Buddy told the defensive linemen to throw up their hands and make Joe throw out of the hole," recalled defensive tackle Paul Rochester. "Buddy said, 'It'll make it tougher for Joe to make a completion.' Paul responded, 'Maybe so, but you hear that sizzling noise when Joe's pass goes over your head? It'll break my fingers.' We didn't have to do it after that."

Buddy Ryan was a no-nonsense "disciplinarian," according to John Dockery. Added Smolinski, "He liked people who played football the old way. If you were a hitter, you were in Buddy Ryan's camp. If you didn't like to hit, Buddy would ask you to leave. I used to room with Jim Turner, and Buddy didn't have a warm spot for him because he thought of Jim as a kicker, although he was our backup tight end, fullback, and quarterback."

It was on special teams that Ryan might have shown most of his creativity with the Jets. "When we were returning a punt, Buddy had us going after the punter and chasing him off the field," Philbin remembered. "When we played Houston, George Blanda was the Oilers' quarterback, kicker, and punter, and I remember chasing him out of bounds after he got his kick away. He wanted no part of me and went to the sidelines so quickly."

Buddy's commitment to get the quarterback led to a money pool for the defensive lineman who got the most hits on the quarterback. Lineman Steve Thompson said, "Buddy wanted you to put a hurt on people. We were taught that if the QB threw an interception, he [the QB] was now on defense, [so we needed to] go get him. I remember a few seasons after the Super Bowl, we played the New York Giants and Fran Tarkenton threw an interception. By the time I got to him, I was the third defensive lineman to hit him. Fran grabbed my face mask and started swinging. He hit me with his hand on my helmet and I laughed. Buddy loved that stuff."

Ray Hayes, another rookie lineman in 1968, who primarily served on special teams that year, shared most players' appreciation for Ryan's steadfast honesty and forthrightness about each guy's effort and results. Hayes remembers, "If you screwed up, he told you that you screwed up. If you did a good job, he told you that, too. He just wanted things done right."

Grantham described as "highly critical" how Ryan and Walt Michaels conducted their weekly game film dissection. "Buddy and

Walt dished out a little praise," shared Larry, "but they spent most of the time pointing out where you lined up wrong, covered the wrong guy, didn't rush from the outside like you were supposed to do, or didn't contain."

Players of all stripes freely admitted they played their butts off for Buddy Ryan, much of it due to his motivational techniques. "He was more psychologist than coach," testified Philbin. "I think of how intense he was and how much he got out of me and other players. Buddy knew everybody was different and he tried to figure out how to get that mean streak out of each of them." Philbin added, "I've never seen anyone better at bringing the animal out of you."

Ryan formulated one-to-one, hopefully personally inspiring messages for players. Carl McAdams said, "I liked his sense of humor. He'd be cynical and would motivate guys with derogatory remarks—not childish; it was man talk. He wasn't a stand-up speech guy in front of the team. He'd find a way to get under your skin." John Neidert was reminded by Ryan that Cincinnati had waived him. That effort to get inside Neidert's head wasn't necessary, the player said. "Somebody trying to knock your head off should get you fired up, or something's wrong," he remarked.

Jets players who loved Ryan concede that he had no patience for mistakes, especially from rookies learning the ropes. Some Jets players earned Ryan's wrath and didn't enjoy his relentless panning of their play. Karl Henke, nearly five decades after the fact, still has a bone to pick with Ryan for jumping all over him after the rookie lined up offside. "I never got encouragement from him," Henke said. "The day the Jets traded me to Boston, I got called into the coach's office, and Buddy yelled loud enough for me to hear, 'Who's Henke?'"

Jim Richards conceded, "Buddy could be hard-core if you messed up and didn't do things you were supposed to do." Ryan admitted, "Most rookies thought I didn't like them because I was on them all the time to hurry their progress." Grantham didn't beat around the bush: "Buddy liked veterans." Former Jets coach Rex Ryan explained that his dad did all he could to minimize or eliminate mistakes, especially on special teams, and that made veterans a better fit.

Buddy learned an important "aha"—that he needed to adapt his defensive attack modes—when he saw how Ewbank obsessed on and protected Joe Namath. Ryan knew his already aggressive "hit the quarterback as hard and as often as you can" philosophy needed adjusting when he witnessed Ewbank's intricate pass-blocking schemes. With other offenses sure to copy Ewbank's cutting-edge quarterback blocking methods, Ryan knew he had to come up with ever more creative ways to overwhelm or bedevil pocket protection.

That thinking gave birth to the defensive concept that later became the "46" defense, which some Jets believe actually had its roots in Jets practice sessions. "We played around with a variation of the '46,' with three down linemen and five linebackers, but we never used it in a game," said Rochester. "I doubt Walt was crazy about the idea." Grantham said it might have been used late in a game as a functional "prevent defense," here or there, when the Jets were ahead. Larry didn't give it a positive review.

Through it all, the rough and gruff Buddy Ryan had a human, tender side. The daughter of Jets equipment manager Bill Hampton, Beth Wallace, says she was twelve years old in 1968 when one Saturday afternoon she and the children of Jets players, coaches, and team management entered Buddy's Shea Stadium office. They had been forewarned not to touch Ryan's blackboard, which was spilling over with defensive diagrams. So, of course, the kids erased all of it. Why leave an empty board? Beth drew flowers, lots of flowers.

Buddy and Bill Hampton commuted together from their apartments to and from Shea, and that day Beth said she sat nervously in the back seat as her dad took the wheel, with Buddy riding shotgun. Not long into the drive, Ryan turned around, smiled, and told the young girl, "Beth, those are the prettiest flowers I've ever seen."

After he left the Jets, Buddy had a stopover in Minnesota (1976–77), where as defensive coordinator and defensive line coach he coached the final years of the Vikings' renowned front four, known as the Purple People Eaters. Buddy got his big chance and a pretty free hand when he joined the Chicago Bears. He created so much player loyalty among Bears defenders (as Michaels had with his guys on the Jets) that four years later, when Chicago hired Mike Ditka in 1982 as head coach, Buddy's men successfully lobbied owner George Halas. Instead of Ditka naming his own defensive coordinator, Halas told his new coach that the decision had been made to retain Ryan.

In Chicago, Buddy for the first time had full freedom to experiment and unleash his defensive philosophies that Walt Michaels had considered too radical. Supreme athletic talent that perfectly fit the "46" defense brought it to life. The confusion it caused offenses, combined with the muscularity, savage aggressiveness, and efficiency of the Bears' personnel, created one of the NFL's best-ever defenses.

Most of the Super Bowl Jets say they were surprised by Buddy's success with the Bears and later as the Philadelphia Eagles' head coach. They had experienced Buddy fifteen years earlier, and his natural urge to dabble in and develop new attacking defenses wasn't welcome in New York. Rochester said, and Grantham agreed, that Walt Michaels tutored Ryan about all aspects of defensive line play. "Buddy took it and improved on it," said Rochester. Buddy's creativity was crimped as a Jets assistant. "Buddy knew he could push his new ideas on Walt only so much," Jim Richards said. Grantham added, "Buddy was creative with us; he just didn't have as many opportunities here as he had later."

JOE SPENCER

OFFENSIVE LINE COACH

He wasn't one of the hot-head coaching candidates on the Jets staff, but that doesn't tarnish his Super Bowl Jets coaching achievements.

Weeb Ewbank built a reputation for selecting the finest assistant coaches, guys who were not household names in the football fraternity, but could they coach! His first assistants in 1963—Chuck Knox, Clive Rush, Walt Michaels—all would become NFL coaches. Knox built and coached up the Jets' young offensive line until he left after the 1966 season. Ernie Zwahlen had a one-year stay after Knox. "Big, strong, rugged" Joe Spencer, two years removed from offensive line responsibilities with the Houston Oilers, came down from the CFL's Edmonton Eskimos and stepped into the Jets' offensive line situation on March 7, 1968. He didn't disappoint.

The relationship between Weeb and Spencer dated back to Spencer's years playing tackle for the Cleveland Browns in the 1940s at the same time that Ewbank was the defensive line coach. Joe and Buddy Ryan had a connection as graduates of Oklahoma A&M (now known as Oklahoma State), Spencer in the 1940s and Ryan in the early 1950s.

As tales of the coaching contingent that oversaw the Super Bowl Jets grew over decades, Spencer's work was consistently underplayed. Joe was quoted in the newspapers but he never received the publicity or the recognition that Rush, Michaels, and Buddy Ryan did. Being a little older than the rest, he was offended by Ewbank's lowball salary scale. "When I played pro ball, it seemed like the coaches made all the money. Then, when I became a coach, it seemed like the players made it all," Spencer explained later.

Weeb was tighter with his assistants than his players. A February 1968 payroll data sheet about pay for the assistants (prior to the hiring of Spencer and Ryan) showed a low of $15,500 for Zwahlen,

$17,000 for Michaels, $17,500 for Personnel Director George Sauer Sr., and $19,000 for Rush. (There was not a second defensive coach at the time.) Showing how poorly Weeb's assistant coaches were compensated, Spencer and Ryan roomed together at the YMCA in Flushing, one subway stop and a healthy walk from Shea Stadium.

Spencer's pay was likely equal to Zwahlen's, and he coached for Weeb until 1970. He didn't take crap from anybody. His son, Jeff, said one day a mugger in New York City confronted Buddy and Joe and demanded their wallets. "Dad swung at the guy and missed; Buddy hit him flush, knocked him onto the street and under a bus."

New York Post columnist Paul Zimmerman, in a review of the Jets' success in 1968, wrote: "A pair of Oklahomans, Joe Spencer (offensive line) and Buddy Ryan (defensive line), arrived on the scene and got increased performance out of their charges." In the case of the normally reserved Spencer, the progress took place without any hoopla. He made the Jets' offensive line—always geared to protect the passer—more effective.

The horses up front—Winston Hill, Bob Talamini, John Schmitt, Randy Rasmussen, and Dave Herman—had always understood that their primary job was to ward off any pressure on Joe Namath. Spencer focused them on improved run blocking. He coached his guys that any block that makes a defender move a half-step out of position and miss a tackle is an effective block. He was also a strong proponent of offensive linemen attacking their defensive counterparts on pass plays. "By playing more aggressively on the line of scrimmage," he said, "you tie in your pass-blocking with blocking for your running plays and draws."

John Schmitt called Spencer "an old-school lineman; there was a Big Bertha blocking dummy—a three-hundred-pound bag—that he had us block over and over." The big bag was emblematic of his coaching style and the instrument of the trade that he personally related to. His son was reminded of a picture hung on the wall at home with Spencer standing alongside one of those oversize blocking bags.

"My dad was a strict, traditional coach," said Jeff Spencer, seventy years of age when we spoke in 2017. He explained his dad's old-school nature with an anecdote about Joe Namath. "I loved watching Joe when dad was coaching with the Oilers. I told my dad how exciting Namath was; he told me that Joe was just one of those 'long-hairs.' But, once he got to work with Joe and saw the physical beating that Namath constantly took, he couldn't say enough about Joe's toughness."

The 6'4" 260-pound ex-lineman was pleasant, yet demanding, ran the O-line by the book, and was very detail oriented. "He won the confidence of players," Bob Talamini said, "because he never beat up on any of his guys emotionally." Spencer himself explained, "What sense is there in yelling at a player in practice and embarrassing him in front of the group? That just makes him feel uptight, and that's when a player really starts making mistakes. I try to talk to him man-to-man, tell him what he did wrong and advise him how to correct it."

One afternoon prior to the Super Bowl, to maintain conditioning, Spencer inflicted a "grass drill" on the Jets' offensive and defensive linemen under the Florida sun. The exercise had the team's largest, burliest players hurtling to the ground, falling on their chest and rolling to one side. Then Spencer yelled and they quickly rose to their feet and awaited the order to repeat the process, this time rolling to the opposite side. Coach Spencer had them do it thirty-five times, gave them a brief respite, and then pushed them to complete the strenuous activity thirty additional times. Talk about conditioning. (Several players asked for more.)

Clive Rush designed the Jets' offensive game plan, but Joe Spencer guided and drove the horses that opened the holes for runners and bolted shut any openings to reach Joe Namath. The Jets scored a team record 419 points and 29.9 points-per-game in 1968—and they did it while throwing 10 fewer interceptions than in 1967, 7 fewer touchdown passes, scoring 5 more rushing TDs, allowing the fewest sacks of any team in the AFL with the league's most immobile QB, and maintaining a 3.4-yard-per-carry average. The secret: playing it safe near the red zone and allowing kicker Jim Turner to set two NFL kicking records.

Spencer's offensive line philosophies meshed beautifully with Weeb Ewbank. The Jets staff had always sought outstanding collegiate football talent *with* brains to handle the Jets' sophisticated offense and defense. "There's no place for dumb people on the line," Spencer remarked. "I've seen guys who could block a house away, but they only had muscle between their ears." Spencer, described as a "bear of a man," noted that 95 percent of the blocking calls took place at the line of scrimmage.

Joe Spencer also played a critical recruitment role for the Super Bowl Jets. He had been the Houston Oilers' offensive line coach from 1961 to 1965 and picked up an AFL championship ring when they repeated as league champs in a double-overtime win over Dallas in 1962. Spencer advised Ewbank about the availability and advisability of prying guard Bob Talamini, whom Spencer had developed into an all-AFL guard, away from the Oilers. Bob was quitting football in 1967 after making All-Pro for an umpteenth time, asking—and being rebuffed by Houston—for a $3,000 raise.

For a future third-round draft pick, the Jets got Talamini, a mauler who added talent, depth, and versatility to the blockers in front of Namath. Paul Zimmerman called Talamini's acquisition for a draft pick "a steal . . . Talamini gave the Jets a tough lineman who could battle the best tackles in the league on even terms."

Jeff Spencer said that his dad was confident, but not predicting victory to the family prior to Super Bowl III. Still, he noted that Spencer played a larger role than historically stated in the game. From the press box, Spencer called many of the effective running plays directed at the right side of the Baltimore defense in Super Bowl III. "It was one of the happiest days in my life," said Spencer, and his son Jeff noted that his dad had told him that it was his proudest achievement in a thirty-year coaching career.

It seems as if Clive, Walt, Buddy, and Joe, the Jets' assistant coaches, collected the full $25,000 winners' share—$10,000 for the AFL Championship and $15,000 for the Super Bowl. It's noteworthy because Weeb Ewbank deducted more than $1,000 from the players' AFL winnings to cover added Shea Stadium expenses for the AFL Championship Game.

After Spencer left the Jets in 1970, he coached for the St. Louis Football Cardinals, the University of Kansas, the WFL's Chicago Fire in 1974, the Kansas City Chiefs, and the New Orleans Saints. During a Saints' practice in 1983, Spencer, standing on the sideline, was run over by one of the team's linebackers. It permanently damaged his spinal column and relegated Joe to a wheelchair. He left football in 1985.

Spencer, a survivor of the Battle of the Bulge—Hitler's last major World War II offensive—died on October 24, 1996, at age seventy-three. In addition to his name, birth date, and date of his passing, his tombstone has one simple word: "Coach."

GEORGE SAUER SR.

DIRECTOR OF PLAYER PERSONNEL

George's tremendous eye for college talent was indispensable to Weeb Ewbank in drafting the core of Super Bowl Jets starters during the franchise's formative years.

His legend is basically forgotten in the twenty-first century, but for three decades beginning in the 1930s George H. Sauer was one of football's most identifiable names. Sauer was a member of three Nebraska high school championship football teams, before starring at the University of Nebraska. A gentle giant, the 6'2", 190-pound fullback and defensive end was "a smashing fullback, tremendous left-footed punter," and adept passer on the Huskers' offense, then a standout defensive end when the opposition had possession of the ball. Ed Schwartzkopf, who was part of the wave of Nebraska football players that followed Sauer, gushed, "Everybody wanted to be George Sauer."

George played in the East-West Shrine All Star Game in 1933; his two-touchdown performance in a 12–0 win by the West earned him a slot on the all-time Shrine team. Sauer is one of only six Nebraska Cornhusker football players whose names are on display in the bronze tunnel-walk gates at the University of Nebraska's Memorial Stadium.

After college he played for the Green Bay Packers for three seasons before retiring after the Packers' 1936 NFL championship. He got a 1937 coaching job with the University of New Hampshire, then served in the navy (reaching the rank of lieutenant commander on the USS *Enterprise* in the Pacific) during World War II. After the conflict, he coached at the University of Kansas (1946–47), capturing consecutive Big Seven conference co-championships. Sauer moved to coach Navy in 1948.

His first Navy football squad went winless, playing the toughest schedule of any team in the nation. Yet Sauer's team made its mark and he won "Coach of the Week" honors from United Press for engineering "one of the biggest upsets of the year—an astounding 21–21 tie with Army's all-conquering cadets." Wrote UP's Carl Lundquist, "In the dressing room after the game, tears streamed from his eyes and he wasn't the least bit ashamed of them."

It left a lasting impression on Coach Sauer's kin. "It was the most incredible upset, to me, in football," George Jr. told the *Houston Chronicle* in 2004. "I have a picture of the team captains and my dad sitting between them and they are holding a banner saying 'It Can Be Done.'"

From 1950 to 1955, Sauer ran the football program at Baylor. Dr. Jerry Marcontell, who played end his sophomore season for Coach Sauer (along with future NFL stars Del Shofner and Bill Glass), says he ran a no-nonsense program. Sauer was "a big guy; always wore a T-shirt with 'Baylor Athletic Department' on it and shorts, even when it sometimes got cold in November. He had huge arms and a chest that filled it out. Players respected and played hard for him. Nobody would have thought of crossing him; he was all business."

Back then, as George would emphasize as the Jets' top talent scout a decade later, Sauer prized players with character. "We got beat at Texas A&M in a close game," recollected Dr. Marcontell, "and the next day, three starters—our center, two guards, and the reserve quarterback—were kicked off the team because someone reported them being at a nightclub in Waco drinking the night before the game."

Marcontell described Coach Sauer as an "offensive genius for that time." Sauer taught his quarterbacks how to exquisitely hide the ball on handoffs. "I remember watching Baylor play when I was in high school," the doctor said. "There was a fake handoff to the fullback, who ran into the line so convincingly that no one saw the halfback circle out of the backfield and catch a pass for a touchdown. It was called back because the officials had blown the play dead— even they thought the fullback had the ball and was stopped at the line." Dr. Marcontell also noted Coach Sauer stood out in the 1950s as someone who "liked to throw the ball 'long,'" 30 to 40 yards.

Early in 1962, the New York Titans hired Sauer to be general manager and assistant coach on Bulldog Turner's staff. Later that year, Sauer proved his mettle in the Titans' last college draft. Prior to Sauer, the Titans' draft choices had been selected based on college football magazines. In 1963, Sauer recommended and helped draft LSU cornerback Jerry Stovall, Jackson State flanker Willie Richardson, and Syracuse TE John Mackey. None signed with the Titans—all went on to big-time NFL careers. There were also two late-round, "futures" selections (juniors with remaining college eligibility), guard Dave Herman and QB Mike Taliaferro.

Sauer, with an unexpired Titans contract for $17,500, was the single member of Titans' management retained by Jets general manager and coach Ewbank. Frank Ramos, the Jets' longtime PR director, waved off any thought that the money owed to Sauer induced Weeb to keep George around. There was no argument about Sauer's long-standing football reputation, instincts, and acumen.

Sauer was pictured with Weeb and Ewbank's four assistant coaches, all attired in shorts, at the first Jets training camp in Peekskill. "George was a tough, old-fashioned coach. He always stood his ground," said Walt Michaels, who shared that coaching philosophy, perhaps with even more vehemence. With his two years of exposure to Titans players, George had the best handle on their talent level. Seventeen dotted the roster on opening day, a number that gradually was whittled down during the season.

By 1964, Sauer had become a central cog in the Jets' plans to enlist collegiate talent. Gerry Philbin recalled Sauer approaching him after scouting Gerry's University of Buffalo squad and the University of Delaware. "George put in a good word about me," Philbin said. Ralph Baker, also a member of the Jets' 1964 college haul, complimented Sauer, saying, "The one person I think has not gotten the credit he deserves is George Sauer Sr. Very seldom do you hear him mentioned. He had a skeleton scouting staff and he did an amazing job bringing in so many of the guys in the first three years who made up our Super Bowl team."

With only eight teams in the AFL, each one was in good position to draft many of the players they had scouted and preferred. Gil Brandt, who famously spent thirty years in the Dallas Cowboys' personnel department, told ProFootballTalk Live in April 2017 that teams drafted players on scouts' gut feelings in the 1960s. When you consider that draft selections today are based on character, quickness, agility and balance, strength and explosion, competitiveness and mental alertness, that makes successful player selection in George Sauer Sr.'s time with the Jets that much more remarkable, if not downright lucky.

In 1965, Sauer's contacts and personal connection with the

University of Texas paid big dividends. The Jets' top brass—Werblin, Ewbank, and Sauer—were at the 1965 Orange Bowl game where Texas upset the top-ranked Alabama Crimson Tide. Joe Namath signed the following morning, followed soon by free agents Longhorn QB/safety Jim Hudson and George's son, split end George Sauer Jr. They developed into AFL all-stars. A third future AFL All-Pro, Jackson State DE Verlon Biggs, and Cornell Gordon completed the best draft in Jets history.

In 1966, the Jets dipped back into Texas for TE Pete Lammons, but Sauer's big find and catch was Maryland Eastern Shore halfback Emerson Boozer. Carl McAdams, the Jets' prized third-round choice, a linebacker, said Sauer joined Sonny Werblin in signing him.

In 1967, with an agreed-upon merger between the NFL and AFL scheduled for 1970, George's job of beating the bushes for talent got a lot harder. He and Weeb had to deal with a combined NFL-AFL "common draft." With sixteen NFL and ten AFL teams making selections in each round, the Jets and every other AFL team had to wait sixteen picks longer before it was their turn to make another selection. That made draft picks more important and every player evaluation much more critical. That year's draft was solid: starting guard Randy Rasmussen, lineman John Elliott, backup offensive lineman Jeff Richardson, and linebacker Mike Stromberg.

In 1968, Sauer got a raise after making the case to Ewbank that "the New York Jets have become a great power and one of the strongest franchises in professional football." That year's Jets college draft didn't bring in any athletes who made a lasting contribution, but Ewbank and Sauer fingered a handful of rookies who made important Super Bowl campaign impacts. Third-rounder Sam Walton held down right tackle for ten games and highly athletic rookies Jim Richards and Mike D'Amato, plus Karl Henke, Ray Hayes, and Steve Thompson strengthened special teams. Two top picks, Lee White (first round) and Gary Magner (fourth round), never had a chance to shine due to season-ending injuries.

Sauer was typically low-key before Super Bowl III. "I heard that the team had confidence about winning but were deliberately being quiet about it," admitted Sauer's daughter, Dana Keifer. In the wake of Super Bowl III, Clive Rush became the head coach of the Boston Patriots and George Sauer Sr. accepted the Patriots' general manager position two weeks after Rush. He held down the role for two years, left over a difference of opinion, and returned to Waco, Texas, to help a junior college expand its athletic program.

Dana Keifer described her father as "having the greatest sense of humor, [being] very outgoing and serious, but someone who always found something good in everything." George was stricken with Alzheimer's disease and suffered its worsening debilitating effects for a decade. He died on February 5, 1994.

PART THREE

18

HOW SUPER BOWL III CHANGED EVERYTHING

The stunning result of Super Bowl III was best captured by sports columnist Jim Murray in the January 13, 1969, *Los Angeles Times*: "On Sunday afternoon, the canary ate the cat. The mailman bit the police dog. The minnow chased the shark out of its waters. The missionaries swallowed the cannibals. The rowboat rammed the battleship. The mouse roared, and the lion jumped up on a chair and began to scream for help. . . . It was like the turkey having the farmer for dinner, the rabbit shooting the hunter, the dove pulling the feathers out of the eagle."

But the Jets' victory did not shake the NFL hierarchy's belief in the superiority of its league. Perhaps the most public exhibition of that came from NFL Films. Steve Sabol, the son of the unit's founder, Ed Sabol, was tasked with preparing the official Super Bowl III film. Steve had grown up a fan of the Baltimore Colts and admitted he "just couldn't bring himself to make the Jets look like heroes after winning the big game." He decided to use the film to pay "homage" to

Johnny Unitas rather than focus on the Jets. "As a sports documentary it was a disaster," he fessed up.

Sabol wasn't alone. The *New York Times*'s football writer William N. Wallace felt Super Bowl III was a victory of mediocrity over quality. He wrote on January 14: "Namath proved a single athlete can take a mediocre cast of characters a long way. There is nothing special about the Jets in the office or on the field. . . . If you took 35 of the 40 Jets and put Denver Bronco uniforms on them who could tell the difference?" (Denver had won three games that season.)

Despite the NFL's outward denials, it was impossible for business-as-usual exchanges between the team owners of the merging leagues. Many Super Bowl Jets players say they understood the unspoken implications of their win, that made it more than a Jets' victory. Commented defensive end Gerry Philbin, "There was more to the game than the fifteen thousand dollars for the winner. It meant even more to the owners; it saved the American Football League. It solidified the merger coming in 1970 and all the AFL franchises that weren't doing well—Buffalo, Boston, Denver. It was a colossal win. One hundred percent of the future of some AFL franchises was at stake [in the outcome of the game].

"The AFL was called second-rate and no one likes to be called that," Gerry continued. "After the game, we could raise our heads as high as anybody and carry ourselves with dignity. It solidified the fan base and raised the image of our league with all the NFL fans."

Super Bowl III's most immediate effect was the continuation of the game itself. A 2009 NFL Films presentation stated that after Green Bay's one-sided wins in the first two Super Bowls, NFL commissioner Pete Rozelle was considering unspecified ways of bypassing the AFL as a future Super Bowl combatant. His attitude completely changed after Super Bowl III. While NFL owners were licking their wounds over the Jets victory, Rozelle, who had fought the idea of a merger for much of the 1960s, saw the sunny business side of real competition between the merging leagues.

In June 1966, the original merger announcement had left AFL teams delirious about the prospect of becoming part of the National Football League. For some teams, it was perceived as relief after seven years of unalterable financial pain. In March 1969, the restructuring of the merged leagues was slated to be resolved—and Super Bowl III's result put AFL team owners in a much stronger position from which to bargain. Yet, early on, Super Bowl III's outcome had dashed AFL owners' hopes for a friendly, cooperative merger. NFL owners still did not see the AFL as the NFL's equal and they seemed unwilling to confer any respect for the upstart league even after the Jets' win.

NFL owners threw their weight behind the idea of maintaining the two leagues in their current state with a schedule that mixed in a few interleague games. That didn't suit AFL teams; all ten wanted NFL teams to visit and pack their stadiums. The only constant every owner agreed on was the $18 million indemnity to be paid to the New York Giants ($12 million) and San Francisco 49ers ($6 million) over twenty years for the Jets' and Raiders' encroachment into those two NFL teams' territories.

An agreeable number of interleague games could not be configured with sixteen NFL teams and ten AFL teams. Oakland owner Al Davis suggested that three NFL teams be incentivized to move their franchises to the newly christened American Football Conference, home to all the former AFL teams. The dual thirteen-team conferences seemed plausible, but could NFL teams be talked into accepting it, and which NFL franchises would make the switch?

A $3 million pot of gold was created for each shifting team ($19.6 million in 2018 dollars). After much debate and cajoling, the Cleveland Browns were the first to give their approval. There was a natural rivalry with the AFC Cincinnati Bengals and their owner-coach Paul Brown. Moving the Browns was ironic because it was the second time that the Browns had changed leagues; it had been one of three All-America Football Conference (AAFC) teams absorbed into the NFL in a 1950 merger.

The second NFL club to shift to the AFC also had AAFC roots. An AAFC team called the Baltimore Colts had been absorbed into the NFL in 1950. It moved south and became the Dallas Texans, then was sold to a group led by Carroll Rosenbloom in 1953 and moved back to Baltimore. Seeing a great new rivalry, Colts owner Rosenbloom agreed to join the AFC if his team was in the same division as the Jets. Regrettably for Rosenbloom, the change in regular season opponents from NFL West teams (the Rams, 49ers, etc.) to the AFC East did not sit well with Baltimore fans. Almost twenty years after buying the franchise and relocating it to Baltimore, Rosenbloom had to find a graceful exit from the city. In July 1972, Robert Irsay bought the Los Angeles Rams and traded the franchise to Rosenbloom for the Colts.

The third team to make the move, the Pittsburgh Steelers, took the transfer money but were driven more than anything else by their interest in continuing a geographic rivalry with the Browns. The formerly moribund Steelers made out the best of the three relocated franchises. Pittsburgh became a dominant team from their new position within the AFC, winning the Super Bowl in 1975, 1976, 1979, and 1980.

The owners' merger plan looked to maximize TV revenues. Completion of the 1966 merger could not be finalized until 1970 because of existing network television contracts, thus final planning had been set aside until 1969. After Super Bowl III, CBS and NBC were intent on maintaining their pro football broadcast rights. The long-time voice of NBC Sports, Curt Gowdy, thought the Jets' upset was "the most financially important game" in American sports history. "That [game]," he said, "changed the whole thinking of the sportsman's mind [about the competitiveness of the AFL versus NFL]."

In 1966, CBS and the NFL had agreed to a two-year contract, with the option for a third year at $18.8 million, cutting in each NFL team for a $1.2-million slice of the pie. NBC's 1964, five-year, $36-million deal with the AFL provided $900,000 for each of the eight AFL teams.

Beginning in 1970, CBS and NBC, combined, agreed to pay the NFL a total of $156 million over four years; plus ABC entered into a three-year deal, at $8 million per season, for the new *Monday Night Football* series. That meant the twenty-six professional teams saw their aggregate annual payments jump from $26 million to $47 million, or $1.8 million per team.

In his 1971 critique of NFL politics and economics, *They Call It a Game,* former Cleveland Brown Bernie Parrish noted how "Namath and his teammates' performance secured the two leagues, at the very least, $100 million in future television revenues." The succeeding four-year TV network contracts in the mid-1970s produced revenues of $218 million, nearly $2.1 million per team per annum. These escalating TV revenues made pro football the lone sports league with shared revenues by its teams.

Parrish's number in 1970 was a vast underestimation of the importance of Super Bowl III to long-term financial impact. It was reported in March 2017 by *Forbes* staff writer Kurt Badenhausen that the NFL collects $5 billion annually from American TV networks, plus $2 billion for overseas viewing. If that was split evenly between thirty-two teams, each would collect $218 million annually.

On the heels of the twenty-six teams' financial windfall in 1969, professional football players in both leagues were also big winners. Weeb Ewbank's notes from his tenure as general manager and coach show the salary of every member of the Jets in 1967: for instance, center John Schmitt ($20,000), Matt Snell ($32,000), Gerry Philbin ($24,000), and Larry Grantham ($22,000). The season after Super Bowl III (before the new TV revenues kicked in), leveraging their championship status, Schmitt was making $30,500, Snell $38,000, Philbin $45,000 (after refusing to report to camp), and Grantham $30,000.

How the AFL's nine other teams felt about the Jets' Super Bowl III win was exemplified in several different ways. Star AFL players, including Kansas City's Buck Buchanan, Bobby Bell, and Willie Lanier, joined the celebration in the Jets' Orange Bowl locker room. The eleven Jets who played in the AFL All-Star Game in Jacksonville the week after the Super Bowl received a wildly enthusiastic reception from their peers for the legitimacy that Super Bowl III had bestowed on the entire league. As mentioned by Pete Lammons, some of the AFL old-timers still say "thank you" to him. And, as documented in some of this book's profiles, a ring from the Super Bowl has very special meaning.

Super Bowl III even changed local fan loyalty for part of a day. In perhaps the best example of how much fans from AFL cities treasured the Jets' accomplishment, look at opening day of the 1969–70 AFL season. In their first game since Super Bowl III, the Jets traveled to Buffalo, where for probably the only time in football history, (1) the opponent's fans welcomed the visiting team at the airport with resounding cheers of "Thank you, Jets," (2) the Jets ran out on the Bills' home field on Sunday afternoon to a standing ovation, and (3) Buffalo cheerleaders saluted the Jets by unfurling a green-and-white sign that said CHAMPS.

For most of the 1960s, the NFL had thought of the AFL as the "Mickey Mouse League." One of the lesser-remembered changes leading into the 1970 merger was pushed through by Buffalo Bills president of public relations Jack Horrigan. He convinced NFL brass to recognize AFL player and team accomplishments by including them in the NFL record book; for instance, Don Maynard eclipsing Raymond Berry's pass reception marks, and the Jets' Steve O'Neal's 98-yard punt against the Denver Broncos during the final AFL season. (It remains the record for the longest punt without a touchback.) A team record that still stands is 17 consecutive games without surrendering a rushing TD, established by the Buffalo Bills between 1964 and 1965.

Super Bowl III had lasting effects on both of the combatant teams. The upset threw the Baltimore Colts' organization into a tizzy. Ernie Accorsi, who years later would become the GM of the Colts, Browns, and New York Giants, joined Baltimore in the spring of 1970, in a public relations capacity. "When I got there, most of the people who coached, played, and worked for the Colts were still in disbelief, in denial," he wrote.

Accorsi recalled the first regular season Colts-Jets meeting, at Shea Stadium in October 1970. "I sat in the first row of the press box," he described, "with [Colts] GM Don Klosterman, [owner Carroll] Rosenbloom, and Rosenbloom's son Steve. I can still feel the electricity and tension and especially the mood of Carroll."

The Colts dominated early, grabbing a 22–0 lead, but if Baltimore truly believed that Super Bowl III had been a fluke, they got a dose of reality. Joe Namath began throwing and throwing, all but pulling the Jets even. Although the Colts won that afternoon, Accorsi said, "I can still hear the groans and sounds coming from Rosenbloom. I remember thinking, 'We have to play this team again in two weeks and twice a year from here on? How is he going to endure these games?'"

Rosenbloom told his wife, Georgia, several times that he had made a mistake replacing Weeb with Shula in 1963. Georgia Rosenbloom mentioned it to Weeb and his wife, Lucy, in 1972. The loss in Super Bowl III led to an irreparable falling-out for Shula with the Baltimore owner. After the Colts suffered through a disappointing 1969–70 post–Super Bowl season, Shula bolted from the Colts to join the Miami Dolphins. The Colts won the Super Bowl the next season, but Rosenbloom erred again in this coaching decision. Shula would win two Super Bowls in Miami and become the NFL's all-time winningest coach (347).

Thanks to Super Bowl III, the value of the Jets' franchise more than doubled overnight. Tad Dowd, a PR whiz and good friend of Namath, said the $6 million evaluation of Sonny Werblin's financial people at the time he sold his portion of the Jets in early 1968, mushroomed to $16 million after they upended the Colts. Today, Statista estimates the Jets are the NFL's ninth most valuable franchise ($2.75 billion).

Jets fans had to dig deeper into their wallets for tickets. "Hundreds of telephone protests" hit the team's office from season ticket holders, complaining that the cost of a Jets box seat had become among the highest in pro football: $8, for 20,500 Shea Stadium seats. The highest price for a reserved seat, $6.50, was established for 39,000 Shea locations. (Box seats had peaked at $7.50 in Baltimore and Detroit in 1968.)

The Jets went into a tailspin in the 1970s, showing only sporadic signs of the franchise's former glory in the decades that followed. Walt Michaels, overseer of the Super Bowl III defense, was the first to resurrect memories of the Super Bowl team, when he became head coach in 1977. Walt had a couple of losing seasons, two .500 campaigns, a 10-5-1 record in 1981, and a 6-3 record in a strike-shortened 1982 season. The Jets reached the AFC Championship Game that year but were shut out by the Miami Dolphins on a rain-drenched field that the Dolphins had deliberately left uncovered to slow down the Jets' speedy roster. After that fiasco, the NFL took control of all playoff game fields.

Future Hall of Fame coach Bill Parcells took over the Jets in 1997, and one year later had them in the AFC Championship Game, where Denver overcame a Jets halftime lead and triumphed 23–10. Parcells had the Jets' best coaching record, 29-19, and winning percentage of any Jets coach (60.4 percent) in his three years.

The most successful postseason coach was Rex Ryan, the only man to take the Jets more than once to the AFC title game. The two seasons that Ryan's Jets had winning regular season records (2009 and 2010), he guided them to within one game of a Super Bowl appearance. They lost to Indianapolis and Pittsburgh, respectively.

Yet the esteem that Jets fans hold for the 1968 team is remarkable. The Kansas City Chiefs won their only Super Bowl one year after the Jets and have not made a return trip to the big game in forty-nine years. Their fans do not have a similar reverence for their sole Super Bowl–winning team.

The Jets have many long-suffering fans. There have been only 15 winning seasons out of 50 (23 losing seasons) since 1968. The franchise's all-time record, 397-478 entering 2018, gives them the worst winning percentage (.454) and fewer victories than any original AFL team.

Celebrating the fiftieth anniversary of the 1968–69 championship team in 2018 has extraordinary meaning, complemented by the fact that the thirty-plus surviving members of that team are all over seventy years old. Unless a fountain of youth is discovered, this is their last hurrah. Similarly, it is probably the last best opportunity to engage Pro Football Hall of Fame voters in a call to action to induct two exceptionally worthy candidates from the Jets' Super Bowl team, Winston Hill and Larry Grantham. Both are deceased.

When the Titans became the Jets, Sonny Werblin commissioned a military-like fight song for his new team that was used from 1964 to 1967. "Go Go Go Go Jets" has a 1960s feel to it, but the words ring as true today for a Jets fan as it did back then:

Go, go, go, go Jets
Let's go, go, go Jets
Let's show them how to move that ball
Let's go, go, go Jets
The mighty green will beat them all
You are New York's best
The pride of north, south, east, and west
You're the greatest yet
C'mon and let's go, go, go, go Jets

Enjoy it with video at: https://www.youtube.com/watch?v=Mm59rWhFqzs.

On the fiftieth anniversary of Super Bowl III, I still savor the euphoria, the rush, the pride in having been a Jets fan. The fight song takes me back to my youth, but it's time to regain that feeling again. Go, go, go, go Jets!

SUPER BOWL III PLAY-BY-PLAY

JANUARY 12, 1969

SUPER BOWL III AT MIAMI'S ORANGE BOWL.

WEATHER CONDITIONS:
73°F (23°C), OVERCAST, WINDY, 20 PERCENT CHANCE OF RAIN.

ATTENDANCE: 75,389

This official play-by-play of Super Bowl III contains "**enhanced**" notations with **additional bolded information** that highlights the contributions of the thirty-nine other Super Bowl Jets.

Tackles for each play and/or coverages (for incomplete passes) are shown in parenthesis.

New York won the coin toss and elected to receive.

FIRST QUARTER

New York possession (15:00)

	Michaels kick 2 yards into end zone, Christy 25-yard return (Hawkins tackle).
NY 23 1–10	Snell 3 run left tackle [**Jets open with a shift, Boozer blocks Shinnick**] (Shinnick tackle).
NY 26 2–7	Snell 9 run between LG & LT [**Blocks by Boozer, Talamini and Hill**] (Volk tackle).
NY 35 1–10	Boozer run toward right end, tackled in backfield; loss of 4 (Shinnick tackle).
NY 31 2–14	Namath 9 pass to Snell in right flat [**Herman ties up Bubba Smith**] (Boyd tackle).
NY 40 3–5	Snell draw middle, loss of 2 (Miller tackle).
NY 38 4–7	Johnson 44 punt to B 18. Play nullified and Baltimore penalized 5 yards for offsides.
NY 43 4–2	Johnson 39 punt, Brown 9 return (**McAdams tackle**).

Baltimore possession (10:55)

B 27	1–10	Morrall 19 pass to Mackey (**Elliott, double-teamed by Colts offensive line, tackle, turns up field to make the tackle**).
B 46	1–10	Matte 10 sweep right (Baker tackle).
NY 44	1–10	J. Hill 7 sweep left (**Biggs misses tackle behind line of scrimmage, but Hudson cleans up**).
NY 37	2–3	Matte 1 run left (**Elliott hit by Colts LG, then Colts RG, then by fullback Jerry Hill, still makes the tackle**).
NY 36	3–2	J. Hill 5 run right tackle (**Rochester arm tackle throws Hill off balance, Baird completes tackle**).
NY 31	1–10	J. Hill run right, loss of 3 (**Philbin tackle using one arm**).
NY 34	2–13	Morrall pass to Orr underthrown, incomplete (**Elliott outstretched arm forces Morrall to throw over him**).
NY 34	3–13	Morrall 15 pass to Mitchell (Baird).
NY 19	1–10	Morrall pass to Richardson short and dropped [**after Morrall sees Richardson covered in the right flat, is rushed, turns and throws short to the right sideline**]
NY 19	2–10	Morrall pass to Mitchell overthrown, incomplete [Grantham pressures from weak side; **Philbin gets hands on Morrall but fails to sack him**].
NY 19	3–10	Morrall run evading rush [**Philbin runs by Morrall in backfield, Morrall ducks under Biggs sack attempt, Grantham misses tackle at the line of scrimmage**], no gain (Atkinson tackle).
NY 19	4–10	Michaels' 27-yard field-goal attempt was wide right, no good

New York possession (5:33)

NY 20	1–10	Namath pass to Snell dropped.
NY 20	2–10	Namath 2 pass to Lammons (B. R. Smith, Lyles tackle).
NY 22	3–8	Namath 13 pass to Mathis (Gaubatz tackle).
NY 35	1–10	Namath pass to Maynard overthrown, incomplete. (**Maynard beats Colts' deep zone—2 strides past Logan deep right sideline**)
NY 35	2–10	Namath 6 pass to Sauer (Lyles tackle).
NY 41	3–4	Namath pass to Sauer overthrown, incomplete.
NY 41	4–4	Johnson 38 punt, Brown 21 return (Snell tackle).

Baltimore possession (3:05)

B 42   1–10   Morrall pass to Mackey dropped, incomplete.

B 42   2–10   J. Hill 3 run middle (**Elliott drags him down from behind**).

B 45   3–7   Morrall long right sideline pass to Richardson broken up (Sample).

B 45   4–7   Lee 51 punt downed at NY 4.

New York possession (1:58)

NY 4   1–10   Snell 4 run over right side [**Rasmussen clears the way**] (Shinnick tackle).

NY 8   2–6   Snell 5 draw right [**Behind Boozer block**] (Curtis tackle).

NY 13   3–1   Namath 3 pass to Sauer left (Lyles tackle), fumbled, Porter recovers for Baltimore at NY 14

Baltimore possession (:14)

NY14   1–10   J. Hill run left tackle, gain of 1 (**Hudson closes down left side, Hill slowed down by Grantham, finished off by Philbin**).

END OF FIRST QUARTER: Baltimore 0, New York 0

SECOND QUARTER

B 13   2–9   Matte 7 sweep left (Beverly, Hudson tackle).

B 6   3–4   Morrall pass to Mitchell off his shoulder pad and intercepted in end zone, Beverly no return, touchback [**Atkinson barely tips pass at line of scrimmage, altering its course and turning spiral into a floater**]

New York possession (14:09)

NY 20   1–10   Snell 1 run left tackle (Braase tackle).

NY 21   2–9   Snell 7 run left tackle [**Blocks by Hill and Talamini**] (Shinnick tackle).

NY 28   3–2   Snell 6 run left end [**Boozer block on Shinnick, Snell breaks Shinnick tackle**] (Lyles tackle).

NY 34   1–10   Snell 12 draw around left end [**Boozer block on LB Shinnick allow Snell to turn the corner**] (Lyles tackle).

NY 46   1–10   Namath pass to Sauer broken up (Shinnick), incomplete.

NY 46   2–10   Namath [**beats Curtis blitz**] dumps swing pass to Mathis for six yards (Bubba Smith tackle).

B 48   3–4   Namath [**perfect pass protection by OL**] 14 pass to Sauer (Lyles tackle).

B 34   1–10   Namath 11 pass to Sauer (Volk tackle).

B 23   1–10   Boozer 2-yard spin run right [**lead block by Snell, hole opened by Schmitt**] (Shinnick tackle).

B 21   2–8   Namath (**facing heavy blitz**] 12-yard swing pass to Snell [**Rasmussen double teams Bubba Smith; Snell runs through tackle for extra 5 yards**] (Gaubatz tackle).

B 9   1–G   Snell 5 run right tackle [**Rasmussen fires out straight ahead, Herman blocks Bubba Smith out of the way**] (B. R. Smith tackle).

B 4   2–G   Snell 4 run over left tackle, touchdown [**Hill seals left side, Boozer slows Volk; Snell breaks Volk attempted tackle at 5, scores**] (9:03).

J. Turner kicked extra point.

New York scoring drive: 80 yards, 12 plays, 5:06

New York 7, Baltimore 0

Baltimore possession (9:03)

Johnson kick to B 2, Pearson 26 return (Richards slows Pearson, Smolinski finishes).

B 28   1–10   Morrall pass to Richardson overthrown, incomplete. [**Beverly angle coverage forces Richardson route out of bounds**]

B 28   2–10   Morrall 30 pass play to Matte [**Pass thrown in left flat, Baird misses tackle**] (Hudson knocks him out of bounds).

NY 42   1–10   J. Hill 4 run right tackle (Atkinson tackle).

NY 38   2–6   Matte run right, no gain [**Rochester undercuts Matte**] (Biggs, Atkinson on tackle).

NY 38   3–6   Morrall pass to Mackey broken up (Sample), incomplete.

NY 38   4–6   Michaels' 46–yard field–goal attempt wide right, no good.

New York possession (6:37)

NY 20   1–10   Boozer 1 run right (Logan tackle).

NY 21   2–9   Namath backpedals [**against blitz by all 3 Colts linebackers, plus Volk**], completes 35-yard pass to Sauer (Lyles tackle).

B 44	1–10	Snell 9 yard run outside LT [**Boozer lead block takes out Shinnick**] (Gaubatz tackle).
B 35	2–1	Snell 3 yard dive up the middle [**Schmitt, Talamini open hole**] (Shinnick tackle).
B 32	1–10	Namath pass to Maynard [**again beats Colts' deep zone**] overthrown deep right side, incomplete.
B 32	2–10	Namath pass to B. Turner underthrown, incomplete.
B 32	3–10	Namath sacked, loss of 2 (Gaubatz tackle).
B 34	4–12	J. Turner's 41-yard field-goal attempt straight up the middle, no good.

Baltimore possession (4:13)

B 20	1–10	Morrall 6 pass to Richardson on right sideline (Sample knocks out of bounds).
B 26	2–4	Matte 58 run around right end [**Baker misses tackle in Colts' backfield**] (Baird makes tackle, saves touchdown)
NY 16	1–10	J. Hill 1 run left tackle [**Biggs and Elliott stuff their side of the line**] (Atkinson, Hudson tackle).
NY 15	2–9	Morrall pass to Richardson intercepted at NY 2 by Sample; no return.

Two-Minute Warning.

New York (2:00)

NY 2	1–10	Snell 2 yard run up the gut (Shinnick tackle).
NY 4	2–8	Snell 3 yard run over left guard (B. R. Smith tackle).
NY 7	3–5	Snell draw left, no gain (Bubba Smith tackle).
NY 7	4–5	Johnson barely gets 32 punt off under pressure from Alex Hawkins, Brown fair catch. Play nullified by offsetting penalties: illegal procedure against New York and roughing the kicker against Baltimore.
NY 7	4–5	Johnson 39 punt, Brown 4 return (Neidert and Crane tackle).

Baltimore possession (0:43)

| NY 42 | 1–10 | Morrall 1 pass to the left to J. Hill (Beverly tackle). |
| NY 41 | 2–9 | Matte takes handoff [**eludes ankle tackle from McAdams on sweep**], Matte sweeps right, laterals back to Morrall, Morrall pass to J. Hill middle intercepted at NY 12, Hudson 9-yard return to NY 21 as time expires |

HALFTIME: New York 7, Baltimore 0

THIRD QUARTER

Baltimore possession (15:00)

Johnson kickoff to goal line, Brown 25 return [**Dockery slows Tim Brown at 18**] (Rademacher and Smolinski tackle).

B 25	1–10	Matte 8 run, [**Biggs wraps arms around Matte, knocks ball loose**, fumble recovered by Baker for New York at B 33.

New York possession (14:25)

B 33	1–10	Boozer on draw, 8 run left [**Hill takes Braase wide, Talamini seals off B. R. Smith, Snell blocks Shinnick**] (Volk tackle).
B 25	2–2	Snell 4 run up middle [**Schmitt and Rasmussen open hole**] (Bubba Smith tackle).
B 21	1–10	Boozer crossbuck 2-yard run left [**Rasmussen blocks Shinnick**] (Curtis tackle).
B 19	2–8	Namath 5 pass to Snell (Boyd, then Curtis **needed to make tackle**).
B 14	3–3	Snell 3 run over right guard [**Rasmussen opens hole**] (Gaubatz tackle).
B 11	1–10	Boozer run left end, loss of 5 (Lyles tackle).
B 16	2–15	Namath sacked, loss of 9 (Bubba Smith tackle).
B 25	3–24	Namath pass to Lammons broken up (Logan), incomplete.
B 25	4–24	J. Turner, 32-yard field goal from left hash mark (10:08).

New York scoring drive: 8 yards, 9 plays, 4:17.

New York 10, Baltimore 0

Baltimore possession (10:08)

Johnson kick to B 5, Brown 21 return (Rademacher and D'Amato tackle).

B 26	1–10	Morrall pass to Mackey, deep down middle, overthrown, incomplete. (Hudson)
B 26	2–10	Morrall pass to J. Hill, no gain (**Grantham solo tackle in left flat**).
B 26	3–10	Morrall run evading rush [**by Biggs**], loss of 2 (McAdams tackle).
B 24	4–12	Lee 44 punt, Baird no return (S. Williams tackle).

New York possession (8:04)

NY 32	1–10	Namath 1-yard swing pass to Mathis (Curtis tackle).
NY 33	2–9	Namath 14 pass to Sauer [**perfect pass protection by OL**] (Volk tackle).
NY 47	1–10	Namath pass to Maynard overthrown, incomplete.
NY 47	2–10	Boozer 4 run left [**Mathis lead block on Porter**] (B. R. Smith tackle).
B 49	3–6	Namath R to L crossing pattern 11-yard pass to Lammons (Logan tackle).
B 38	1–10	Namath pass to Maynard on right sideline, incomplete.
B 38	2–10	Namath 14 pass over the middle to Snell (Curtis tackle).
B 24	1–10	Mathis draw up the middle, 1 yard [**Boozer blocks Shinnick**] (Shinnick tackle).
B 23	2–9	Namath pass to Maynard incomplete, catch beyond end line. Namath apparently hurt, shaking his right hand.
B 23	3–9	Parilli pass to Sauer underthrown, incomplete.
B 23	4–9	J. Turner, 30-yard field goal from left hash mark (3:58).

New York scoring drive: 45 yards, 11 plays, 4:06

New York 13, Baltimore 0

Baltimore possession (3:58)

Johnson kick hit goal post, touchback.

B 20	1–10	Matte 5 sweep right (**Baker shakes off blow, makes tackle**).
B 25	2–5	Unitas pass to Matte, no gain (Grantham tackle).
B 25	3–5	Unitas pass to Orr high, dropped, incomplete (Beverly).
B 25	4–5	Lee 38 punt, Baird fair catch.

New York possession (2:24)

NY 37	1–10	Snell 3 run straight up the middle (B. R. Smith tackle).
NY 40	2–7	Namath pass to Sauer, deep left sideline, overthrown, incomplete.
NY 40	3–7	Namath 11-yard slant-in pass to Sauer (Lyles tackle).
B 49	1–10	Namath 39-yard post pattern pass to Sauer (Lyles tackle).
B 10	1–G	Snell 4 run right tackle [**Schmitt takes out B. R. Smith, Rasmussen and Herman double team Bubba Smith, force him inside**] (Gaubatz tackle).

END OF THIRD QUARTER: New York 13, Baltimore 0

FOURTH QUARTER

B 6   2–G   Snell 3 run left tackle. Play nullified; Baltimore penalized 3 yards (half the distance) for offsides.

B 3   2–G   Snell sweeps left, no gain (Volk tackle).

B 3   3–G   Mathis 1 run off left guard [**Talamini pulls Miller left, Schmitt seals off Roy Hilton, Snell lead blocks Gaubatz up middle**] (Gaubatz tackle).

B 2   4–G   J. Turner, 9-yard field goal from left hash mark [**extreme wide angle**] (13:26).

New York scoring drive: 61 yards, 8 plays, 3:58.

New York 16, Baltimore 0

Baltimore possession (13:26) Johnson kick 6 yards into end zone, Pearson drops, picks up, 33-yard return (D'Amato).

B 27   1–10   Unitas 5 yard pass to Mackey (Grantham leg tackle)

B 32   2–5   Matte 7-yard sweep right (Baker and Atkinson).

B 39   1–10   Unitas 5 pass, right sideline, to Richardson, pushed out of bounds (Sample).

B 44   2–5   Matte 19 run off left tackle (Hudson).

NY 37   1–10   J. Hill 12 run right tackle [**Baker misses ankle tackle**] (Baird)

NY 25   1–10   Unitas pass to Richardson, wide and high of the mark, incomplete (Sample).

NY 25   2–10   Unitas deep pass to Orr intercepted in end zone, [**Elliott hand in air in front of throw**] Beverly tight coverage, no return, touchback.

New York possession (11:06)

NY 20   1–10   Boozer 2 yard draw up middle [**Schmitt pushes up middle, Snell block on Porter, clears way for Boozer**] (Miller).

NY 22   2–8   Snell 2 run over left guard [**Schmitt and Talamini blocks**] (Porter).

NY 24   3–6   Boozer 7 sweep left [**Sauer blocks Shinnick**] (Gaubatz).

NY 31   1–10   Snell 10 run left, sweeps around left edge [**Talamini and Boozer seal off left side, block on Porter frees Snell, Hill leads Snell around left corner, Snell bounces off two tacklers, knocked out of bounds**] (Curtis).

Baltimore penalized 15 for personal foul.

B 44 1–10 Snell 7 yard run straight up the middle [**Sauer, Rasmussen, Talamini blocks**] (Bubba Smith).

B 37 2–3 Boozer 2 yard run over right guard [**Rasmussen opens hole**] (B. R. Smith).

B 35 3–1 Mathis run over left guard, no gain (Michaels).

B 35 4–1 Jim Turner's 42-yard field–goal attempt from inside left hash mark, no good wide left.

Baltimore possession (6:34)

B 20 1–10 Unitas pass to Mackey broken up (Hudson)

B 20 2–10 Unitas pass to Richardson overthrown, incomplete.

B 20 3–10 Unitas pass to Mackey wide, incomplete.

B 20 4–10 Unitas 17-yard pass to Mackey (Beverly).

B 37 1–10 Unitas pass to Richardson high and overthrown, incomplete.

B 37 2–10 Unitas swing pass to J. Hill [**crowd, including Baker, Atkinson**], incomplete.

B 37 3–10 Unitas 11 pass to Mackey (Baird). New York penalized 15 for personal foul—late hit by Elliott.

NY 37 1–10 Matte 1 run left (Biggs).

NY 36 2–9 Unitas 21 pass to Richardson (Sample).

NY 15 1–10 Unitas pass to Matte overthrown, incomplete. (Baird)

NY 15 2–10 Unitas 11 pass to Orr on NY 4 (Beverly). NY penalized 2 yards (half the distance) for personal foul, late Atkinson hit on Orr. Ball placed on NY 2

NY 2 1–G Matte run up middle, no gain. Play nullified and New York penalized (half the distance) for offsides. Ball placed on NY 1.

NY 1 1–G Unitas QB sneak up the middle, no gain [Elliott, Atkinson stuff the middle] (Biggs).

NY 1 2–G Matte tries to go over the top, stopped, no gain (Atkinson).

NY 1 3–G Hill 1 run over left tackle, touchdown (3:19). Michaels kicked extra point.

Baltimore scoring drive: 80 yards, 14 plays, 3:15

New York 16, Baltimore 7

New York (3:19)

Michaels onside kick, Mitchell recovered for Baltimore at NY 44.

Baltimore possession (3:14)

NY 44 1–10   Unitas 6 pass to Richardson (Sample).

NY 38 2–4   Unitas 14 pass to Orr (Beverly).

NY 24 1–10   Unitas 5 yard pass to Richardson (out of bounds).

NY 19 2–5   Unitas pass to Richardson broken up (Sample), incomplete.

NY 19 3–5   Unitas pass to Orr underthrown, incomplete [**pressured and dumped as he throws by Rochester and Philbin**]

NY 19 4–5   Unitas pass to Orr incomplete. [**tipped away by Grantham.**]

New York possession (2:21)

NY 20 1–10   Snell 1 run over right guard (Bubba Smith). Baltimore–first time out.

NY 21 2–9   Snell 6 run right [**Rasmussen, Boozer and Herman blocks**] (Logan).

Two–Minute Warning.

NY 27 3–3   Snell 4 run off right tackle (Gaubatz). Baltimore–second time out (1:54).

NY 31 1–10   Snell 2 run right tackle (Boyd).

NY 33 2–8   New York penalized 5 yards for delay of game.

NY 28 2–13   Snell 1 run up the gut (B. R. Smith).

NY 29 3–12   New York penalized 5 yards for delay of game.

NY 24 3–17   Snell 3 power sweep left [**behind Rasmussen**] (Austin).

Baltimore–third time out (:15)

NY 27 4–14   Johnson 39 punt, Brown no return, out of bounds.

Baltimore possession (:08)

B 34   1–10   Unitas pass to Richardson, overthrown, incomplete (Sample).

B 34   2–10   Unitas 15 yard pass to Richardson (Sample).

FINAL SCORE: NEW YORK 16, BALTIMORE 7

Source: Play-By-Play provided by Pro-Football-Reference.com; Additional data in bold based on NBC Super Bowl III, video, NFL Films, and official Super Bowl III game film.

ACKNOWLEDGMENTS

It took me almost fifty years to work up the gumption to write this book. I was sixteen years old the day in January 1969 that my favorite New York sports team—the Jets—took the field to play the "unbeatable" Baltimore Colts. I remember sitting in a recliner in my parents' living room when sometime in the second quarter I jumped up, fists clenched, as Gerry Philbin and Verlon Biggs both had a shot at sacking Colts' QB Earl Morrall. "Get him . . . get him," I yelled. My father—not at all familiar with football and sitting on the couch at the back of the room—was stunned and spit out, "Bobby, what's wrong with you?"

My uncle Charlie, a big sports fan, came immediately to my defense. "Leave Bobby alone," he told my dad. "He's experiencing something he's going to remember for the rest of his life." As it turned out, Uncle Charlie could not have been more correct. Over four subsequent decades, I waited for the Jets to make a return trip to the Super Bowl—which they almost did on three occasions—but I quickly shrugged off those losses. It was easy because there has always been Super Bowl III to feel good about.

So, although my dad died in 2012 and my uncle in 1980, my deep thanks go to them for being there on January 12, 1969, sharing the moment with me and establishing a memory that remains vivid to this day. My late mom was very patient with my sports TV viewing that day and on many other afternoons.

None of Super Bowl III's previous anniversaries—the tenth, the twenty-fifth, etc.—meant anything to me, but the fiftieth in 2018 does. I've been a business writer for better than forty years, and a huge baseball, football, basketball, and hockey fan for a decade beyond that. I always wanted to write about sports, but I never did.

At Super Bowl time in 2015, I was standing around in our family room while my sons, Charlie and Michael, sat on the couch and the NFL Network showed NBC's original Super Bowl III broadcast. My wife, Linda, walked in, asked what we were watching, and remarked, "When are you going to write your book about that team? You've always talked about doing that." I defensively responded, "I would, but I need to find a unique angle. There's no need for another book about Namath." Within minutes, I had that elusive angle.

Charlie told me "that eighty-one on the Jets looks like a good defensive end." I told him, "That's Gerry Philbin. He was an All-Pro several times and one of my favorite players." Michael asked me about "that number seventy-five. He looks pretty good, too." I explained that No. 75 was Winston Hill, an All-Pro tackle more times than I could remember. At that moment, I turned to Linda and said, "I've got the angle. I'll do a book about the 'rest of the team.'"

So, deepest thanks go to my beautiful, wonderful, patient wife, who encouraged my project from the start and tossed out numerous good questions along the way for me to consider. She listened as I retold my conversations with Jets players (told me I was having too much fun!), and she was more thrilled and prouder than I think I was when HarperCollins said they wanted to publish my book. On top of everything else, she's my biggest booster. She has wasted few opportunities to mention the upcoming availability of this book to friends, acquaintances, and most everyone else.

My sons deserve utmost credit for crystallizing the focus of this book, and my daughter, Lani, and son-in-law Josh, who live overseas, were unwavering in their support. And I can't wait for my grandchildren to be old enough to see what their grandpa did before they knew how to read and write.

On to the players. It's one thing to say "I'm going to speak to the 'rest of the Jets,'" and quite another to speak with them. I never thought about the impracticality of first finding them and then convincing them to speak with me. Enter Chris Clow, the associate editor for my small publishing company. I found a few players on my own, then ran into a "search" roadblock. Chris, seeing my frustration, told me he had a way to use the Web to locate the phone numbers and addresses of any player. It is the book's deepest, darkest secret.

Sometimes we couldn't locate a particular player, so Chris dug up some newspaper stories or blogs that mentioned the player's wife and children, which helped locate our subjects. Chris had another website that helped us find some players who had done a nice job of blending in with their communities. It also was vital in tracking down families of the six deceased players and four coaches and owners, plus others who today play a vital role in the lives of a handful of Super Bowl Jets no longer equipped to handle all their affairs. I've told Chris to his face how great a part he played, and I'm glad to put it out there for the world to know.

Chris and my other associate editor, Jo Anne Nathan, served another absolutely essential role. Neither knew much about football, so they were perfect subjects to tell me whether each profile I wrote of a Jets player or coach was personally interesting and compelling. With Chris and Jo Anne, I got incredible, real-world, male and female perspectives. Jo Anne also happens to be about as good a copy editor as exists.

Naturally, the stars of this book and my heroes—the forty-five Super Bowl Jets players, five coaches, personnel director, and the team's five owners from 1963 to 1968—earn my most personal thank-you. I was warned that certain players would want to be paid—and not one ever raised the issue. Some said it straight out, others inferred how incredibly pleased they felt after forty-eight years to finally tell their personal stories. I told them what I remembered about their formative Jets careers and, to a man, they opened up with funny and poignant anecdotes and personal feelings. I thought I knew a lot about the 1968 Super Bowl team, and I'm proud to share the ton of information that was news to me.

One thing I never anticipated was the relationships that blossomed from my player conversations. Matt Snell, who had famously not spoken to New York newspapers for decades, agreed to speak with me. My thanks to Gary DeFilippo, who helped make that possible. Matt and I don't talk often, but we've developed a great mutual respect. Until he died, Larry Grantham took my call just about every week—even when he was not feeling well—and never tired in teaching me what pro football defense is really all about. Since his death in 2017, I've felt a palpable void in my life. Pete Lammons' precise memories of Super Bowl III were complemented by a great, ever-present sense of humor. The first time I called and asked to speak with "the greatest tight end in Jets history," he said, "Hold on. Let me see if he's here."

Gerry Philbin was there to help me fill information voids about what was happening inside the clubhouse and gain a better grasp of football situations. Bill Baird was extraordinarily generous with his time and most helpful because he was the only constant in the Jets' secondary from 1963 to 1969. Because two of the starters who played alongside him had died, Bill's insights about the late Johnny Sample and Jim Hudson were indispensable. Bill, you were a far better player than the fans and I knew in the 1960s. John Schmitt knew as much about Joe Namath on the field as Joe. He shared that as part of his remembrances, with no strings attached and in a tremendously entertaining way. Billy Joe was hesitant at the start, then became one of my most enjoyable new friends. He became my go-to source for details concerning racial discrimination in pro football during the 1960s and about recovery from serious knee injuries during the 1960s, a time filled with experimental surgeries.

With only a few exceptions, the Super Bowl Jets are not Internet savvy. So, important elements would be missing from this book without the technical assistance from Mrs. Paul (Nancy) Rochester; Mrs. Curley (Janet) Johnson and Curley's son, Curley Jr.; Mrs. Bill (Louise) Baird; Mrs. Mark (Janice) Smolinski; Mrs. Jim (Mary Kay) Turner; Mrs. John (Joanne) Schmitt; Verlon Biggs' brothers, Dennis and Robert; Mrs. Emerson (Enez) Boozer; Mrs. Dave (Roma) Herman; Mrs. Carl (Marg) McAdams; Mrs. Cornell (Alfreda) Gordon; John Elliott's wife, Nancy Catledge; Jim Hudson's wives, Wendy Hudson and Lise Hudson; Mrs. Paul (Heiki) Crane; Mrs. Don (Anna) Maynard and Don's son, Scot; Bill Rademacher's guardian, Tom Bengtson; Sonny Werblin's sons, Thomas and Robert; Joe Spencer's son, Jeff; Dana Keifer, the daughter of George Sauer Sr. and sister of George Sauer Jr.; Mrs. Karl (Yolanda) Henke; Mrs. John (Lindy) Neidert; Mrs. Bill (Burnsie) Mathis and Bill's son, Billy Mathis Jr.; Mrs. Al (Peg) Atkinson; Mrs. Larry (Peg) Grantham and Larry's son, Jamie; Winston Hill's daughters, Heather Hill and Hovlyn Hill May (and grandson Grant Winston Staffer); Walt Michaels' daughter MaryAnn; Gerry Philbin's son, Doug; Clive Rush's son, Doug; Weeb Ewbank's daughters, Jan Hudson and Nancy Winner, plus his son-in-law, Charlie Winner; Phil Iselin's son and daughter, Jim Iselin and Kay Iselin Gilman; RemembertheAFL website curator Ange Coniglio; Bill Hampton's daughter, Beth Wallace; Dr. Jerry Marcontell; the Walter Havighurst Special Collections & University Archives at Miami of Ohio University; Pete Fierle at the Pro Football Hall of Fame; Bryan Yeatter; Michael MacCambridge; Bill Gutman; Dave Anderson; Ed Bleier; Jeremy Schaap; Sal Marciano; and Cass Jackson.

Former Jets AFL opponents (a veritable all-star roster)—Lance Alworth, Billy Shaw, Fred Biletnikoff, Len Dawson, Bobby Bell, Ed Budde, Ed Rutkowski, Booker Edgerson, Butch Byrd, Rich Jackson, Ron McDole, Jim Otto, Mike Stratton, John Hadl, Pete Banaszak, and Preston Ridlehuber—shared their recollections. A few Baltimore Colts—Jerry Hill, Bobby Boyd, and Sam Ball—to their credit, did, too. I am indebted to ex-Jets' QBs Mike Taliaferro, John Huarte, and Bob Schweickert; Bill Mathis' buddy and former New York

Giant Tucker Frederickson; quarterback Jerry Rhome; and Hall of Fame defensive end Claude Humphrey.

I am particularly grateful to Jay Pomerantz, a great Jets fan and, in terms of Super Bowl Jets' memorabilia, "the man." My introduction to Jay was fortuitous for every Jets fan; the time I spent with him was a delight, and the doors he opened for me had incalculable value. Jay had purchased the Weeb Ewbank estate; he opened his Jets Cave to me, pulled out several eye-opening documents, and told me to have fun examining everything Weeb's files had to offer. Aside from a closet full of game-worn Jets jerseys, imagine having exclusive access to Super Bowl Jets' general manager and coach Weeb Ewbank's playbooks, personal player evaluations, and player ratings. For the first time, everyone gets an inside look at the evolution of the team that was lucky to win five games in 1963 and, six years later, was blessed with the talent to win the Super Bowl. Thank you, Jay!

I had written half of this book before a local acquaintance, David Silverman, advised me to get an agent. Why? How? "Trust me," he said. "Just do it." With Google's help, I found a website listing every literary agency in the country; then I narrowed the overwhelming list down to agencies working with sports books. Two hundred emails later, I had conversations with a half dozen agents, and in a few days it was down to two. One of them would be in Chicago in a few days and invited me to meet her: Dawn Michelle Hardy of the Serendipity Literary Agency.

What a stroke of luck! It had never occurred to me that my book wouldn't get published. I'd just call every sports publisher I could find. When I met Dawn, that all changed. With a laugh, she asked how had I convinced thirty-five Jets players to speak with me. She was a football fan—actually, like her dad, a Jets fan—but she asked what was special about this book, why would it sell, and who would purchase it. "What—you have the book half written?" she said in disbelief. Within two weeks, Dawn told me her dad loved the idea and Serendipity wanted to represent me—and we were off and running.

Dawn told me that one of the reasons for her interest was that I had such passion, having written so much of a book without a publisher. She kept me in the loop about progress, a few offers, and then on my birthday in 2017 an email informed me that HarperCollins wanted the book. After entering into a contract, Dawn displayed ungodly patience throughout a few of my freak-outs. Thank you, Dawn, for your thoroughness, professionalism, kindness, and sincerity!

Special thanks are also due Tad Dowd, probably the top Jets historian for the 1960s; former Jets PR director Frank Ramos; Bill Ryczek, author of *Crash of the Titans*, the exhaustive history of the Jets' New York AFL predecessor; James Flamberg, who shared his script for a Super Bowl Jets motion picture; Doug Miller for hard-to-get pictures; my editor at HarperCollins, Matthew Daddona; longtime friend Joel Lipsky for his legal advice; and the enthusiastic content advisors: Bob Swedlow, Denise Freedman, and Jonathon Heiliczer.

And a final, special thanks to Kevin Lonnie, the friend who suggested *Beyond Broadway Joe* for the title of this book. Good call, Kevin.

NOTES

CHAPTER 1: BEFORE THERE WAS A SUPER BOWL

3 Founded in the 1920s: *NFL.com.*

4 Between 1921 and 1939: *NFL.com.*

4 If they drew 15,000: Marty Glickman with Stan Isaacs, *The Fastest Kid on the Block* (Syracuse, NY: Syracuse University Press, 1996) p. 120.

4 After four expensive and hard-fought years: Craig R. Coenen, *From Sandlots to the Super Bowl: The National Football League* (Knoxville: University of Tennessee Press, 2005), p. 135.

4 The NFL decided: Coenen, *From Sandots to the Super Bowl,* p. 136.

5 Two such individuals were oilmen: Larry Felser, *The Birth of the New NFL: How the 1966 AFL/NFL Merger Transformed Pro Football* (Guilford, CT: Lyons Press, 2008), p. viii.

5 Lamar Hunt's effort to: William J. Ryczek, *Crash of the Titans: The Early Years of the New York Jets and the AFL* (Jefferson, NC: McFarland, 2009), p. 15.

5 Wismer had some financial means: Ibid., p. 155.

6 In 1960, $200,000 was split: Ibid., p. 34.

6 the Titans were impaired by their home field: Ibid., pp. 11, 111.

6 "was like playing in a vacant lot": Ibid., p. 112.

6 Wismer lost $500,000 in 1960: Ibid., p. 155.

6 his economic fate was tied to a fifteen-year contract: Ibid., p. 159.

7 His dreams of success: Ibid., pp. 159–60.

7 Won-lost records document: *NFL.com.*

7 A look at the Titans' drafts: *Pro-Football-Reference.com,* New York Jets Draft History.

8 By 1962, as the AFL: Ryczek, *Clash of the Titans,* p. 254.

8 The Titans' final campaign: Ibid., p. 268.

8 The AFL stepped in: Ibid., p. 251.

8 At the end of 1962,: Ibid., p. 257.

8 The AFL revoked: Ibid., p. 270.

8 Aside from a mostly underwhelming roster: Ibid., p. 133.

CHAPTER 2: THE FIVE-YEAR PLAN

12 Weeb even came with a recommendation: Paul Zimmerman, *The Last Season of Weeb Ewbank* (New York: Farrar, Straus & Giroux, 1974), p. 260.

12 At the April 16, 1963, press conference: *New York Times*, April 16, 1963.

12 Titans returnees who reported to Peekskill: Ryczek, *Clash of the Titans* pp. 271–72.

12 "In 1963, we had three teams": Dave Anderson, *Countdown to Super Bowl* (New York: Random House, 1969), p. 18.

12 In 1964, 1965 and 1966, the Jets drafted: *Pro-Football-Reference.com*, New York Jets Draft History.

CHAPTER 3: WINNING THE AFL CHAMPIONSHIP GAME

15 The official game temperature was 37degrees: Pro Football Hall of Fame.

15 The Jets' offensive game plan: *Weeb Ewbank Personal Notes* (Jay Pomerantz), *New York Jets' 1968 AFL Championship Game Plan*.

15 The Jets' wide receivers would aggressively attack: Ibid.

15 The Jets rushed 34 times for 144 yards: Pro Football Hall of Fame.

15 As the joyous: *New York Times,* December 30, 1968.

CHAPTER 4: REACTIONS TO JOE'S "GUARANTEE"

19 He thanked his parents: Anderson, *Countdown to the Super Bowl*, pp. 163, 165.

20 Well, even Namath almost: *NFL Films: Football's Greatest Games: Super Bowl III*.

20 "If we can't pass on these guys": *St. Petersburg Times Online Sports*, December 9, 1999.

20 Ralph Baker suggested: Dave Anderson, *Countdown to the Super Bowl*, p. 170.

20 Earl Christy grabbed Jets' broadcaster: *MusicRadio77.com/Harmon SuperBowl.html*.

20 Bill Rademacher told newspaper columnist: *Newark Star-Ledger*, January 26, 2009.

20 Gerry Philbin saw only the guarantee's: Anderson, *Countdown to the Super Bowl*, p. 170.

CHAPTER 5: SUPER BOWL III: JETS 16, COLTS 7

25 Propelled by Joe Namath's celebrity: Nielsen TV ratings.

25 At the Jets' team breakfast: Johnny Sample, Fred J. Hamilton, and Sonny Schwartz, *Confessions of a Dirty Ballplayer* (New York: Dial Press, 1970), p. 187.

26 The Jets received the opening kickoff: *Razulu.com.*

28 "I guarantee we won't embarrass": *New York Times*, December 30, 1968.

29 Invited to a Colts' practice: *Golden Football, NFL Championship: 1968 Super Bowl III—New York Jets vs Baltimore Colts.*

29 The Los Angeles Rams had upset Baltimore: *Golden Football, NFL Championship: 1968 Super Bowl III.*

30 *New York Post* football writer: *New York Post*, January 2, 1969.

30 Minnesota Vikings' All-Pro Offensive tackle: *New York Post*, January 3, 1969.

30 "Almost certainly, no other quarterback": *Sporting News*, January 25, 1969.

30 "He beat our blitz more than we beat him": *New York Post*, January 13, 1969.

30 "One time, I came at him": *Sporting News*, January 25, 1969.

30 "Namath psyched two teams": *New York Times*, January 14, 1969.

30 An NFL documentary captured: NFL Films, 2016, Super Bowl III.

CHAPTER 6: DAVID A. "SONNY" WERBLIN

37 The five-man syndicate: *New York Times*, November 23, 1991.

38 Werblin thought any: *Sports Illustrated*, July 19, 1965.

38 "We're going first class": *New York Times*, September 20, 1963.

38 He invited Matt's family: Sean Deveney, *Fun City: John Lindsay, Joe Namath and How Sports Saved New York in the 1960s* (New York: Sports Publishing, 2015), p. 32.

38 After his historic career in: *New York Times,* November 23, 1991.

38 He told confidants: *Sports Illustrated*, July 19, 1965.

39 When he retired from MCA: Ibid.

40 After selling 3,800 season tickets: *New York Times*, March 20, 1964.

40 Total Jets home attendance: Ibid.

40 After doling out $140,000: *PopHistoryDig.com/topics/joenamath.*

41 "We went down to Birmingham to meet Joe": Lawrence Linderman, *Playboy*, December 1969.

42 Though it might have been hyperbole: *New York Times*, October 24, 1966.

45 "He told me to get to know New": Zimmerman, *Last Season of Weeb*, p. 265.

45 Ewbank was lenient about Joe's: Ibid.

45 Werblin gave Namath even more room: *New York Times*, August 15, 1966.

45 Werblin offered to buy out: Deveney, *Fun City*, p. 194.

45 "At least I had the fun": *New York Times*, December 6, 1968.

CHAPTER 7: WILBUR "WEEB" EWBANK

47 (after trying to replace): *New York Times*, May 23, 1968.

47 he became the first coach: *New York Times*, April 9, 1963.

47 130-129-7: *Pro-Football-Reference.com*

48 "It's very difficult": Zimmerman, *The Last Season*, p. 99

48 "I'm a teacher": Ibid, p. 102.

49 "Weeb Ewbank is the one man": Ibid., p. 260.

49 "Weeb had impressed": Linderman, *Playboy,* December 1969.

50 However, New England Patriots coach: NFL Network, *A Football Life: Bill Belichick—Cleveland '95*, October 3, 2012.

50 A sampling of Weeb's profiles: *Weeb Ewbank Personal Notes.*

52 (A sample, Dave Herman's 1968 analysis): Ibid.

55 uncomfortable coaching soccer-style kickers: Zimmerman, *The Last Season*, p. 245.

55 improved under Ewbank: *Pro-Football-Reference.com.*

56 (Jets linemen extended their arms): Mark Krieger, *Namath* (New York: Penguin Books, 2004), p.181.

56 Jets 1967 Offensive Line Blocking Grades: *Weeb Ewbank Personal Notes.*

56 "Weeb taught me all the basics": *Utica Times*, November 25, 2015.

56 Ewbank's private records show that sacks: *Weeb Ewbank Personal Notes.*

57 estimates show Joe Namath went down: Stuart Chase, *Pro-Football -Perspective.com.*

59 Namath's best-paid bodyguard: *Weeb Ewbank Personal Notes.*

59 he did, in fact, know what every: Ibid.

59 His three-year Jets contract in 1963: Ibid.

59 Joe Namath, the most important: *New York Times*, November 18, 1994.

CHAPTER 8: JOE NAMATH

63 Joe was the youngest quarterback (25): Stuart Chase, "Joe Namath Has Become Football's Most Misunderstood Quarterback," *Pro-Football -Perspective.com.*

64 NFL Hall of Famer: Titans' Owner 'Bud' Adams' National Conference Call, *TitansOnline.com.*

65 "I thought that even with an operation": Deveney, *Fun City*, p. 14.

65 Namath deferred much of the money: Barry Warner, *JustVibeHouston .com*, October 12, 2015.

65 As Namath lay on his back: Ibid.

66 Ewbank entered an evaluation of his prized QB: *Weeb Ewbank Personal Notes.*

67 Even ten years later: Associated Press, July 31, 1975.

68 "He has what we call fast feet": Bill Gutman, *Miracle Year 1969: Amazing Mets and Super Jets* (Champaign, IL: Sports Publishing, 2004), p. 90.

68 "I'd say I save at least": Linderman, *Playboy,* December 1969.

68 Weeb Ewbank saw something distinctive: Zimmerman, *The Last Season*, p. 19.
69 "If I were to get hit": Linderman, *Playboy,* December 1969.
70 "A ballplayer has to be relaxed": Ibid.
70 Asked if he made "a point of doing that": Ibid.
70 "We should have won": NFL Films, *America's Game: The 1968 Jets.*
71 "Joe thinks he was elected": Ibid.
73 In the opening quarter: *New York Daily News,* January 22, 2011.
73 Namath described the Raiders' pounding: Linderman, *Playboy.*
73 Ewbank was advised: Deveney, *Fun City,* p. 225.
73 Namath considered sitting it out: Paul Zimmerman, *New York Post*, December 31, 1968.
74 "The only thing that scared me": Deveney, *Fun City,* p. 227.
74 "Lots of times, just before the snap": Joe Willie Namath and Dick Schaap, *I Can't Wait Until Tomorrow: Cause I Get Better Looking Every Day* (New York, Random House, 1968), p. 54.
75 The locker room was beset with: HBO, *Namath: From Beaver Falls to Broadway,* January 28, 2012.
75 at Alabama he couldn't understand: Ibid.
75 he stunned Ewbank in requesting: Deveney, *Fun City,* p. 100.
75 Paul Zimmerman, the *New York Post*'s: Zimmerman, *The Last Season,* p. 63.
75 unsightly 220 career interceptions: *Pro-Football-Reference.com.*
75 In the recesses of the locker room: HBO, *Namath: From Beaver Falls.*

CHAPTER 9: "O" LINE: IT PROTECTED NAMATH AT ALL COSTS

78 Hill rode his man: Bent Double, *The Jets Blog Hall of Fame: Winston Hill,* June 25, 2009.
78 "Winston Hill was probably": Eulalia Hill-Allen, *Another Hill to Climb.*
79 Hill was also an ironman: Bent Double, *The Jets Blog Hall of Fame: Winston Hill.*
79 saluted Winston as a forerunner: *Sports Illustrated,* September 5, 1994.
79 "Winston Hill was our best offensive lineman": Weeb Ewbank, as told to Neil Roiter, *Goal to Go: The Greatest Football Games I Have Coached* (New York: Hawthorn Books, 1972), p. 118.
80 The Colts saw his potential but: Anderson, *Countdown to Super Bowl,* p. 51.
82 Clark Judge, who has covered: Clark Judge, *TalkofFameNetwork.com,* December 2014.
82 Herman played "guard": Zimmerman, *The Last Season,* p. 5.
85 "Bubba managed to run over him": Ewbank as told to Roiter, *Goal to Go,* p. 141.
85 the best of the NFL's 1970s defensive tackles: Zimmerman, *The Last Season,* p. 242.

97   Paul Zimmerman wrote in: Paul Zimmerman, *New York Post,* January 13, 1969.

97   Walt Michaels, who coached: *Pro-Football-Reference.com.*

100   He plied his craft: Paul Zimmerman, *New York Post*, January 10, 1969.

100   Bob once told the *Post* columnist: Larry Merchant, *New York Post*, December 26, 1968.

101   Talamini displayed: Zimmerman, *New York Post*, January 10, 1969.

102   Weeb Ewbank's compliments flowed: Dave Anderson, *New York Times,* July 21, 1968.

102   Walton was the lone rookie: *New York Times*, August 4, 1968.

102   In his pro debut: Anderson, *Countdown to Super Bowl*, p. 99.

102   Five more interceptions that day: Dave Anderson, *New York Times,* October 14, 1968.

CHAPTER 10: RECEIVERS: SUNSHINE, THE FAST RAY BERRY, BAKE, AND BIG BOY

107   He was coming off one of: *Pro-Football-Reference.com.*

108   He had skipped game fourteen: Anderson, *Countdown to Super Bowl,* p. 122.

108   According to Namath, Don apologized: Namath, *I Can't Wait Until Tomorrow*, pp. 63–64.

109   "Some writer later said": Bob McGinn, *The Ultimate Super Bowl Book* (Minneapolis, MVP Books, 2012), p. 31.

110   Sherman also told him to shave: Don Maynard and Matthew Shepatin, *You Can't Catch Sunshine* (Chicago: Triumph Books, 2010), p. 94.

110   "I could run faster backwards": Ira Berkow, *New York Times*, January 29, 1987.

110   In 1960 *and* 1962: *Wikipedia.org,* Don Maynard.

110   In Weeb's personnel evaluation: *Weeb Ewbank Personal Notes.*

111   That season, Namath's 14 TDs to Maynard: *Pro-Football-Reference.com.*

111   Maynard claimed that he taught Namath something: Michael Jackson, *The Game Before the Money: Voices of the Men Who Built the NFL* (self-published, 2014), p. 111.

112   "Every time Don's broken": Namath and Schaap, *I Can't Wait Until Tomorrow,* p. 131.

112   Case in point: Anderson, *Countdown to Super Bowl*, p. 58.

112   Maynard performed best against: Dave Anderson, *New York Times,* September 16, 1968.

112   In the *Heidi* Game at Oakland: Dave Anderson, *New York Times*, November 18, 1968.

113   Namath admitted that: Maynard and Shepatin, *You Can't Catch Sunshine,* p. 234.

113   Wrote Jets beat writer Paul: Paul Zimmerman: *A Thinking Man's Guide to Pro Football* (New York: Dutton, 1970), p. 90.

114 Respected by Weeb Ewbank: *Weeb Ewbank Personal Notes.*

114 a "dress code" that brandished: Maynard and Shepatin, *Can't Catch Sunshine*, p. 164.

114 retrofitting a 1955 Ford coupe: Ibid., pp. 147, 131.

114 Maynard's unconventional football approaches: Ibid., p.76.

114 on a sloppy field: Ibid., p. 72.

115 His game-day white Puma: Ibid., p. 163.

115 he ordered football's first V-neck: Ibid., p. 165.

115 Don had equipment manager Bill Hampton: Ibid.

115 a custom molded helmet: Ibid., p. 186.

115 plus two long cleats: Ibid., p. 227.

115 "I don't remember slipping one time": Ibid., p. 231.

115 Maynard told Jets beat: Zimmerman, *A Thinking Man's Guide*, p. 90.

115 But he has never forgotten: Zimmerman, *The Last Season*, p. 209.

116 when NFL Commissioner: Dave Brady, *Washington Post,* January 13, 1969.

116 averaging 4.1 yards: *Sports-Reference.com*, Bake Turner.

116 Bake made a sensational debut: John Hogrogian, *The Coffin Corner: The Jets' First Training Camp* (Volume XVII, No. 3, 1995) pp. 10–16.

117 "He ain't gonna to beat me out": Maynard and Shepatin, *Can't Catch Sunshine*, p. 148.

117 His 71 catches: *Pro Football Reference.com*, Bake Turner.

117 Bake hooked up with Wood: Ibid.

117 Weeb's assessment of Bake: *Weeb Ewbank Personal Notes.*

119 Turner grabbed 8 passes for 145 yards: *New York Times*, August 2, 1969.

119 AFL's leading punter: *New York Times*, November 11, 1969.

119 In 1970, Bake was in Boston: *Pro-Football-Reference.com*, Bake Turner.

122 and "train [the boy] to be a grid star": Carl Lundquist, *United Press*, December 3, 1948.

122 twice he was a first team: *Pro-Football-Reference.com*, George Sauer Jr.

122 "I would describe George as": Ewbank, *Goal to Go*, p. 115–116.

122 Ray Berry retired in 1967: *Pro-Football-Reference.com*, Raymond Berry.

124 Coach Ewbank dictated a glowing: *Weeb Ewbank Personal Notes.*

125 a contact lens: Anderson, *Countdown to Super Bowl*, p. 83.

125 grabbed 63 passes: *Pro-Football-Reference.com*, George Sauer Jr.

125 ended one game story: Dave Anderson, *New York Times*, November 11, 1968.

126 He filled his playbook: Anderson, *Countdown to Super Bowl*, p. 81.

126 His concentration was so: Andy Barall, *New York Times*, May 17, 2013.

126 My problem this week: Anderson, *Countdown to Super Bowl*, p. 81.

126 My problem this week: Ibid.

126 George Jr. remembered how: David Barron, *Chron.com*, January 29, 2004.

127 Winston Hill told his teammate: Anderson, *Countdown to Super Bowl*, p. 221.

127 In the locker room after Super Bowl III: *NFL Network*, George Sauer's Sudden Retirement, November 6, 2012.

128 statistical grade: *Weeb Ewbank Personal Notes*.

128 It turned out that Ewbank's: *Pro-Football-Reference.com*, George Sauer, Jr. and Raymond Berry.

128 in walking away: Frank Litsky, *New York Times*, May 11, 2013.

128 Dane Knutson, who stocked shelves: Jack Williams, *New York Times*, July 23, 2013.

128 In addition to solid blocking: *Pro-Football-Reference.com*, Pete Lammons.

128 Dr. Jim Nicholas, who knew: Anderson, *Countdown to Super Bowl*, p. 96.

CHAPTER 11: RUNNING BACKS: POWER, SPEED, AND A LOT OF BLOCKING

136 the 49ers' backfield had: Ryczek, *Crash of the Titans*, p. 50.

137 the team's leading rusher: *Pro-Football-Reference.com*, Bill Mathis.

137 with two years of Mathis' work: *Weeb Ewbank Personal Notes*.

137 After 1965, Ewbank dictated: *Weeb Ewbank's Personal Notes*.

138 Bill's 22 in 1966: *Pro-Football-Reference.com*, Bill Mathis.

138 the Jets pounded the ball: *Pro-Football-Reference.com*.

139 Bill's final year with the Jets: *Pro-Football-Reference.com*, Bill Mathis.

140 The fourth-leading rusher: *Pro-Football-Reference.com*, Matt Snell.

143 Matt's 941 rushing yards: Ibid.

146 "I knew how good Matte was": Anderson, *Countdown to Super Bowl*, p. 184.

146 Snell had one more: *Pro-Football-Reference.com*.

149 his rookie year with 455 yards: *Pro-Football-Reference.com*, Emerson Boozer.

151 Boozer regained "his old flash": Dave Anderson, *New York Times*, January 8, 1969.

152 Emerson attended both: William C. Rhoden, *New York Times*, January 26, 2010.

152 Weeb Ewbank called Boozer: Ewbank, *Goal to Go*, p. 116.

153 Emerson also retired as the Jets': *Pro-Football-Reference.com*, Emerson Boozer.

154 1961 Sun Bowl: *SunBowl.org*, 1961 Sun Bowl.

155 (only 377 yards: *Pro-Football-Reference.com*, Billy Joe.

155 His rushing numbers slipped: Ibid.

155 He ran the ball 37: Ibid.

156 "It worries you to death": Bill Surface, *New York Times*, December 14, 1969.

156 In his rehab: Ibid.

158 *Deseret News* sportswriter: Dan Pattison, *Deseret News*, October 29, 2000.

158 "Many pro scouts prefer": Dave Anderson, *New York Times*, December 28, 1967.

158 In training camp: Dave Anderson, *New York Times*, July 20, 1968.

158 After White returned: Sam Goldaper, *New York Times*, August 6, 1998.

158 White saw significant: *New York Jets 1968 Yearbook*.

128 he sent Weeb Ewbank: *Weeb Ewbank Personal Notes*.

128 He ran the ball 63 times: *Pro-Football-Reference.com*, Lee White.

CHAPTER 12: THE KICKERS: "KING OF THE 43-YARD PUNT" TANK, AND "GOLDFINGER"

161 Eight times, he was one of: *Pro-Football-Reference.com*.

161 Only two other punters: *Jets.com*.

162 He commented that "Curley: Ewbank, *Goal to Go*, pp. 117–18.

163 Weeb's private notes: *Weeb Ewbank Personal Notes*.

164 Curley told William J. Ryczek: Ryczek, unused notes for *Crash of the Titans*.

165 Joe Namath noted in his first: Namath and Schapp, *I Can't Wait Until Tomorrow*, p. 162.

165 Namath wrote, "'She' talked": Ibid., p. 41.

165 Don Maynard became: Ibid, p. 165.

168 In fourteen games: *Pro-Football-Reference.com*, Jim Turner.

169 Eleven kickers went on to surpass: *Pro-Football-Reference.com*, NFL Points Scored Single-Season Leaders.

169 [31.8 points per game]: *Sports Reference.com*, 1963 Utah Aggies Stats.

170 Jim looked good enough: *Weeb Ewbank Personal Notes*.

170 "I'm not concerned with Turner": Dave Anderson, *New York Times*, August 28, 1967.

171 including 11 out of 16: *Pro-Football-Reference.com*, Jim Turner.

171 During Turner's eight-year: Ibid.

174 Eight would have set: *BleacherReport.com*, New York Jets 12 franchise records that will never be broken.

174 "There will never be": McGinn, *The Ultimate Super Bowl Book*, p. 28.

174 "We saw panic": Harvey Frommer, *Celebrating Broadway Joe Namath—Part II*, January 12, 2000.

175 born in Rochester, Pennsylvania: Dick Burdette, *Kentucky Babe* (Self-published by Burdette, 2011), p. 3.

175 he was the star QB for: *University of Kentucky Sports Information*, July 15, 2017.

175 As a Boston Patriot: *Pro-Football-Reference.com*, Babe Parilli.

176 Turner's 73.9 percent field goal accuracy: *Pro-Football-Reference.com*, Jim Turner.

177 the only placeholder in the 1960s: *Pro-Football-Reference.com*, NFL Total Field Goals Made Single Game Leaders.

CHAPTER 13: DEFENSIVE LINE: DOMINATING AGILITY, QUICKNESS, AND SMARTS

180 After one game: Dave Anderson, *New York Times*, October 28, 1968.

180 At the conclusion of: *Weeb Ewbank Personal Notes.*

181 After the 1965 season: Ibid.

191 Weeb Ewbank wrote in his: Ibid.

192 Ewbank graded Biggs' effectiveness: Ibid.

193 Four days before the Super Bowl: Anderson, *Countdown to Super Bowl*, pp. 132–33.

194 On June 7, 1994: Associated Press, June 8, 1994.

195 *New York Times'* football: William Wallace, *New York Times*, December 7, 1965.

197 Diagnosed by Dr. Nicholas: Anderson, *Countdown to Super Bowl*, p. 138.

197 "That kid is in tears": Ibid.

198 McAdams wasn't there, either: Dave Anderson, *New York Times*, December 4, 1978.

201 Ewbank told the: Gutman, *Miracle Year 1969*, p. 26.

201 "John Elliott's meteoric": Paul Zimmerman, *New York Post*, January 2, 1969.

201 Three-quarters into: Paul Zimmerman, *New York Post*, November 16, 1968.

201 "The offense didn't know": Gutman, *Miracle Year 1969*, p. 33.

201 He protested, unsuccessfully: Ibid, p. 79.

CHAPTER 14: LINEBACKERS: THREE DIFFERENT STYLES CAME TOGETHER

207 He was a first team: *Pro-Football-Reference.com*, Larry Grantham.

208 Writing about the Jets': Dave Anderson, *New York Times*, October 25, 2008.

208 The 1959 University of: *Wikipedia.org*, 1959 Ole Miss Rebels Football Team.

208 "I played linebacker": Rick Cleveland, *Mississippi Today*, June 20, 2017.

215 Ralph recovered only: *Pro-Football-Reference.com*, Ralph Baker.

218 After the 1964 season: *Weeb Ewbank Personal Notes.*

218 After Baker's sophomore: Ibid.

221 In one game, he: Anderson, *Countdown to Super Bowl*, p. 75.

221 "We all resent Al": Zimmerman, *The Last Season*, p. 298.

221 "large, rough rookie": *New York Times*, December 19, 1965.

222 In Coach Ewbank's 1965 postseason: *Weeb Ewbank Personal Notes.*

223 Walt Michaels stressed: Anderson, *Countdown to Super Bowl*, p. 75–76.

226 "Let's space the ends": Ibid., p. 226.

227 "In college, I": Don Laible, *Utica Observer Dispatch*, September 19, 2014.

228 Joe Namath complimented: Art Shamsky and Barry Zeman, *The Magnificent Seasons: How the Jets, Mets and Knicks Made Sports History and*

Uplifted a City and the Country (New York: Thomas Dunne Books, 2004), p. 30.

228 Walt Michaels observed: Ibid.

229 The Jets' internal tackling data: *Weeb Ewbank Personal Notes.*

229 but took an awkward step: Dave Anderson, *New York Times*, August 9, 1969.

229 was waived from the squad: Gerald Eskenazi, *New York Times*, September 4, 1969.

229 he fought for a Jets roster spot: *New York Times*, August 28, 1970.

CHAPTER 15: DEFENSIVE SECONDARY: IT THRIVED WITH FREE AGENTS & FORMER QBS

233 Weeb wrote about Baird: *Weeb Ewbank Personal Notes.*

233 Of Baird's cornerback: Ibid.

241 Weeb Ewbank evaluated: *Weeb Ewbank's Personal Notes.*

244 the pair of red shorts: Anderson, *Countdown to Super Bowl*, p. 126.

245 Somehow, he impressed: *Weeb Ewbank Personal Notes.*

248 Ewbank described Hudson: Anderson, *Countdown to Super Bowl*, p. 115.

248 Michaels told reporters: Ibid., p. 126.

248 "Best way to handle him": Dick Young, *New York Daily News*, January 5, 1969.

248 "That's one reason why": Ibid.

248 One of Namath's lasting: Namath and Schaap, *I Can't Wait Until Tomorrow*, p. 68.

252 Perhaps, that's why Joe Namath's comment: Namath and Schaap, *I Can't Wait Until*, p. 9–10

253 saw him as vicious: Dave Klein, *The Game of Their Lives: The 1958 NFL Championship* (Boulder, CO, Taylor Trade, 2008), pp. 91–94.

253 Johnny called for a fair catch: Jere Longman, *New York Times*, January 21, 2001.

254 caught stealing: Klein, *Game of Their Lives*, p.100.

254 consider the American Football: Sample, Hamilton, and Schwartz, *Confessions of a Dirty*, p. 129.

255 "He'll end up suing": Dave Klein, *The Game of Their Lives*, p. 93.

255 "You can help us": Sample, Hamilton, and Schwartz, *Confessions of a Dirty*, p. 136.

255 he approached Eagles coach: *Washington Times*, April 28, 2005.

257 led the penurious Ewbank: Ewbank, told to Roiter, *Goal to Go*, p. 117.

257 Team defensive data show: *Pro-Football-Reference.com.*

257 the *New York Post* disagreed: Sample, Hamilton & Schwartz, *Confessions*, p. 86.

258 "I don't think I've ever seen you": Anderson, *Countdown to Super Bowl*, p. 65.

258 "Grade school, high school": Ibid, p. 194.

258 made it a point to tell Johnny: Larry Fox, *New York Daily News*, January 4, 1969.

259 "I hate guys who steal": Sample, Hamilton, and Schwartz, *Confessions*, p. 194.

259 Looking back about a half: Tony McLean, *Los Angeles Sentinel*, May 13, 2010.

260 In 1962, at Wildwood: *ShoreNewsToday.com*, The Leader of the Wildwoods, November 4, 2013.

260 *New York Post*'s columnist: Milton Gross, *New York Post*, January 15, 1969.

261 "Randy runs the 40": Anderson, *Countdown to Super Bowl*, p. 116.

261 An exasperated Weeb Ewbank: *http://njsportsheroes.com*/randybeverly fb.html, Randy Beverly.

261 In an intrasquad game: Frank Litsky, *New York Times*, August 6, 1967.

261 a suddenly revived: Frank Litsky, *New York Times*, November 13, 1967.

261 On October 1: Frank Litsky, *New York Times*, October 2, 1967.

261 On November 13: Frank Litsky, *New York Times*, November 14, 1967.

261 "Beverly broke up passes": Ibid.

262 It limited KC to only 83: Ibid.

263 "I was kind of careless": Dave Anderson, *New York Times*, October 6, 1968.

263 with Beverly snatching: Dave Anderson, *New York Times*, November 25, 1968.

263 Warren Wells, caught 3: Dave Anderson, *New York Times*, December 30, 1968.

263 The Jets' pass defense: *Pro-Football-Reference.com*, 1968 New York Jets Statistics, 1968 Baltimore Colts Statistics.

263 "From our one look": Robert Markus, *Chicago Tribune*, December 31, 1968.

264 "He's tricky": Markus, *Chicago Tribune*, December 31, 1968.

264 "Will it be all right": Ibid.

264 The two thefts made: Eric Thompson, *SportsBettingDime.com*, October 7, 2015.

264 "Beverly just might have": Randy Lange, *NewYorkJets.com*, January 30, 2014.

265 Randy said in 1996: Gerald Eskenazi, *New York Times*, August 15, 1996.

265 "We were the forgotten": Lange, *NewYorkJets.com*, January 30, 2014.

265 In a 1976 retrospective: Tony Kornheiser, *New York Times*, December 5, 1976.

266 Beverly would have been: McGinn, *The Ultimate Super Bowl Book*, p. 33.

266 He was solid in the first: Dave Anderson, *New York Times*, September 26, 1969.

266 on March 9, 1970: *New York Times*, March 10, 1970.

266 Randy accepted a tryout: *Wikipedia.org/wiki/Randy_Beverly*.

CHAPTER 16: SPECIAL TEAMS: UNDERAPPRECIATED SUICIDE SQUADDERS

268 Smolinski had a team-leading: *Pro-Football-Reference.com*, New York Jets 1963 Roster.

268 he appeared, football tucked: *New York Times*, November 9, 1964.

268 After the 1965 Jets': *Weeb Ewbank Personal Notes*.

270 "We try to instill pride": Frank Litsky, *New York Times*, October 20, 1966.

270 Knox learned the momentum: Ibid.

271 a tactic used by Kansas City: Anderson, *Countdown to Super Bowl*, p. 172.

271 It deadened Oakland's blitz: : *New York Jets 1968 Yearbook*.

273 Weeb saw Bill's potential: *Weeb Ewbank Personal Notes*.

274 Rademacher covered: Anderson, *New York Times*, August 27, 1968.

274 In the AFL Championship: *Official 1968 AFL Championship Game scoresheet*.

274 single roster spot: Anderson, *New York Times*, September 6 1969.

274 "they thought John played": Murray Chass, *New York Times*, October 27, 1969.

275 At Boston in 1969: *Pro-Football-Reference.com*, Bill Rademacher.

278 "Paul is a fine linebacker": Ewbank, as told to Roiter, *Goal to Go*, p. 163.

278 Paul proved his worth: Dave Anderson, *New York Times*, September 15, 1969.

280 "But the NFL": Toni L. Sandys, *SPTimes.com*, February 1, 2003.

280 team mark with 169 yards: *NewYorkJets.com*.

280 gaining an important 32 yards: *Official 1968 AFL Championship Game scoresheet*.

281 By 1967, Earl was one: *NFL.com/history/randf/records/team/punt returns*.

281 The tandem tied an NFL record: *NFL.com, Jets.com*.

284 calling Steve "our only": Dave Anderson, *New York Times*, July 31, 1968.

294 His brother Ed: Dave Anderson, *New York Times*, August 4, 1968.

295 negotiated a 1968 eighth-rounder from the Oilers: *revolvy.com*.

295 became Jets' property: *prosportstransactions.com/football/draft Trades/Years/1968.htm*.

295 Joined the taxi squad: William Wallace, *New York Times*, November 1, 1968.

296 traded to the Boston: Gerald Eskenazi, *New York Times*, September 4, 1969.

300 drafted by Cincinnati: *Pro Football Reference.com/teams/cin/draft.htm*.

300 put in a waiver claim: Associated Press, November 7, 1968.

302 John helped escort: Norm Miller, *New York Daily News*, August 18, 1969.

302 "That's how you win": Dave Anderson, *New York Times*, September 15, 1969.

305 "Hey, after what I've been": Paul Zimmerman, *New York Post*, January 7, 1969.

306 special teams tackle on: Ibid.

CHAPTER 17: ASSISTANT COACHES: THEY TURNED COLLEGIANS INTO ALL-PROS

318 The section devoted to: *Weeb Ewbank's Personal Notes.*

320 Michaels' Super Bowl game plan: Ibid.

328 "Big, strong, rugged": Bob Broeg, *St. Louis Post-Dispatch*, July 26, 1971.

328 on March 7, 1968: *New York Times*, March 8, 1968.

328 "When I played pro ball": Kevin Carroll, *Houston Oilers: The Early Years* (Austin, TX: Eakin Press, 2001) p. 170.

328 February 1968 payroll: *Weeb Ewbank's Personal Notes.*

329 in a review of the Jets': Paul Zimmerman, *New York Post*, December 31, 1968.

329 "By playing more aggressively": Leo Zainea, *Chicago Tribune*, August 18, 1974.

330 "What sense is there": Ibid.

330 inflicted a "grass drill": Anderson, *Countdown to Super Bowl*, pp. 48–49.

330 Jets scored a team record: *Pro-Football-Reference.com*, 1968 New York Jets Results.

331 "There's no place for dumb": Zainea, *Chicago Tribune*, August 18, 1974.

331 for a draft pick "a steal": Zimmerman, *New York Post*, December 31, 1968.

332 During a Saints' practice: Bob Collins, *South Oklahoma City Leader*, April 20, 1994.

332 "a smashing fullback": Carl Lundquist, *United Press*, December 3, 1948.

333 George played in the: *The Omaha World-Herald*, December 2005.

333 Sauer is one of only six: Ibid.

333 His first Navy football squad: Lundquist, *United Press*, December 3, 1948.

333 "In the dressing room": Ibid.

336 after making the case to Ewbank: *Weeb Ewbank's Personal Notes.*

CHAPTER 18: HOW SUPER BOWL III CHANGED EVERYTHING

341 was best captured: Jim Murray, *Los Angeles Times*, January 13, 1969.

341 most public exhibition: Rocco Constantino, *BleacherReport.com*, September 18, 2012.

342 football writer William N. Wallace, wrote: William N. Wallace, *New York Times,* January 14, 1969.

342 NFL Commissioner Pete: NFL Films, *Full Color Football: The History of the American Football League* (Episode 4, 2009).

343 A $3 million pot of gold: Larry Felser, *The Birth of the New NFL,* p. 192.

344 Rosenbloom had to find: Ibid., p. ix.

344 In 1966, CBS and the NFL: Ken Fang, *AwfulAnnouncing.com,* January 25, 2013.

344 agreed to pay the NFL a total: Fang, *AwfulAnnouncing.com,* January 25, 2013.

345 In his 1971 critique: Bernie Parrish, *They Call It a Game* (New York: Dial Press, 1971).

345 The succeeding four-year: Ken Fang, *AwfulAnnouncing.com,* January 25, 2013.

345 the salary of every member: *Weeb Ewbank's Personal Notes.*

345 The season after Super Bowl III: Ibid.

346 Super Bowl III even changed: Ange Coniglio, *RemembertheAFL.com.*

346 For most of the 1960s: *Wikipedia.org/wiki/Jack_Horrigan.*

346 "When I got there": Felser, *The Birth of the New NFL,* p. ix.

347 "I remember thinking": Ibid.

347 Rosenbloom told his wife: Zimmerman, *Last Season of Weeb Ewbank,* p. 149.

347 Jets fans had to dig deeper: Dave Anderson, *New York Times,* February 20, 1969.

INDEX

ABOUT THE AUTHOR

Bob Lederer is a writer and the founder of RFL Communications. A former resident of Flushing, New York, and current Jets fan from the team's inception in 1963, he scrupulously followed the New York Jets through its early ups and downs—and its transformation into a championship contender. The Jets' victory on January 12, 1969, when Bob was sixteen years old, was the most exciting sports day in his life. He lives in Illinois.